HOLIDAYS IN THE DANGER ZONF

Critical War Studies
Tarak Barkawi and Shane Brighton, Editors

Holidays in the Danger Zone: Entanglements of War and Tourism
DEBBIE LISLE

HOLIDAYS IN THE DANGER ZONE

Entanglements of War and Tourism

Debbie Lisle

CRITICAL WAR STUDIES

UNIVERSITY OF MINNESOTA PRESS
Minneapolis · London

Frontispiece: Members of the Fourth Marine Regiment, Sixth Marine Division bathing in a bomb crater on Naha Airfield, June 1945. National Archives photo 127-GW-128899. Courtesy of the Still Picture Branch, National Archives and Records Administration.

Copyright 2016 by the Regents of the University of Minnesota

All rights reserved. No part of this publication may be reproduced, stored in a retrieval system, or transmitted, in any form or by any means, electronic, mechanical, photocopying, recording, or otherwise, without the prior written permission of the publisher.

Published by the University of Minnesota Press
111 Third Avenue South, Suite 290
Minneapolis, MN 55401-2520
http://www.upress.umn.edu

Printed in the United States of America on acid-free paper

The University of Minnesota is an equal-opportunity educator and employer.

22 21 20 19 18 17 16   10 9 8 7 6 5 4 3 2 1

Library of Congress Cataloging-in-Publication Data
Names: Lisle, Debbie, author.
Title: Holidays in the danger zone : entanglements of war and tourism / Debbie Lisle.
Description: Minneapolis : University of Minnesota Press, 2016. | Series: Critical war studies | Includes bibliographical references and index.
Identifiers: LCCN 2016002832| ISBN 978-0-8166-9855-4 (hc) |
ISBN 978-0-8166-9856-1 (pb)
Subjects: LCSH: Tourism—Political aspects. | War and society. | Geopolitics. | Dark tourism.
Classification: LCC G156 .L47 2016 | DDC 338.4/791—dc23
LC record available at http://lccn.loc.gov/201600283

Contents

Introduction: Entanglements of War and Tourism............ 1

1. The Double Vision of Empire: The Gordon Relief
   Campaign, 1884–85 29

2. Tours of Duty, Tours of Pleasure: Battlefield Journeys and
   the Rise of Militourism, 1914–45 69

3. Bipolar Travels: Tourism and Conflict at the Edges of
   the Cold War 124

4. Global Interventions: Contested History and the Rise of
   Dark Tourism 181

5. Connecting Tourism and Terrorism: Milblogs, Soft Targets,
   and the Securitization of Travel....................... 239

   Conclusion. Touring Otherwise: The Ethical Possibilities
   of Entanglement................................... 281

   Acknowledgments 297

   Notes 303

   Bibliography 313

   Index 375

INTRODUCTION

Entanglements of War and Tourism

In March 2009, Tourism Australia launched a multi-million-dollar advertising campaign titled "No Leave, No Life" that aimed to unlock nearly 130 million days of annual stockpiled leave—the equivalent of 350,000 years of holidays—to increase efficiency, productivity, and morale (Tourism Australia 2009a; 2009b). Tourism Australia provided companies with a range of training tools, resources, and advice on logistics that would encourage workers to take their annual leave *within* Australia. As the then minister of tourism explained, "by using their leave to take a holiday at home, Australians are helping their mates who depend on tourism for their livelihoods and achieving a better balance between their work and personal lives" (Australasian Leisure Management 2009; Australian Associated Press and Gallo 2011). "No Leave, No Life" warned companies of the risks involved when workers did not take their annual leave, including poor performance, decreased motivation, low morale, and reduced productivity, and offered guidance on how to positively transform the "no leave culture" in the workplace (Tourism Australia 2009c). This seemingly innocuous advertising campaign tells us much about the increasingly blurred lines between the public arena of work and the private pursuits of leisure—especially how employers and state authorities are intervening in and seeking to manage the nonwork time of citizens. Indeed, the "No Leave, No Life" campaign is an expression of the increasing governance of modern life—how our entire lives (including our pursuits of leisure and travel) are subject to various political interventions aimed at reorienting our dispositions, incentivizing our behaviors, and harnessing our aspirations in ways that ultimately make us more governable (Burchell, Gordon, and Miller 1991; Foucault 2010a; 2010b; 2011; Walters 2012). These interventions by a mixture of state, public, private, and commercial forces are sometimes enthusiastically welcomed as helpful strategies to enhance our well-being, happiness, and productivity and are sometimes fiercely resisted as oppressive mechanisms of order, control, and surveillance. What particularly interests me about the "No Leave, No Life" campaign is the manner in which it stages such an intervention through the well-established military practice of structured leave, also known as rest and relaxation (R&R). As military leaders have always known, a well-rested workforce/fighting force is also more productive, more efficient, and less likely to make mistakes. This militarized message was articulated most clearly in the branding and promotional imagery of the "No Leave, No Life" campaign: employees are like soldiers, and as such, they require periodical vacations from battle to recharge their batteries and return to the front line more rested, revitalized, and rejuvenated. Here the front line is the "work–life battle," where employees have to fight constantly against the pressures of a career that threatens to swallow up their whole lives. The message is simple: the only way to have a life worth living—and to win the work–life battle—is to spend any stockpiled annual leave taking regular vacations within Australia.

In direct mimicry of Joe Rosenthal's Pulitzer Prize–winning image of American soldiers raising the flag on Iwo Jima in 1945, the main "No Leave, No Life" advertisement (see Figure 1) replaces U.S. Marines with a white nuclear family enjoying a beach holiday (Hariman and Lucaites 2007, 93–136). Here, the detritus of Mount Suribachi, the unfurling of the American flag, and the stark black-and-white palate of Rosenthal's image are replaced by a warm beach with gentle waves, a colorful sun umbrella, and a lush summertime palate overlaid with a calming sunset. This juxtaposition is effective in its simplicity: the familiarity and instant recognition of the Iwo Jima icon makes audiences comfortable and therefore willing to uncritically accept the attached significations of leisure, relaxation, and travel. It suggests that the feelings of togetherness, victory, and patriotism unleashed by Rosenthal's image can also be achieved by ordinary men and women if they win the work–life battle by taking their regular vacations in Australia. The reward for success in this battle is that workers—like soldiers on leave from battle—rediscover their "real" selves,

INTRODUCTION 3

FIGURE 1. "Win the Work Life Battle," Tourism Australia, 2009.

reconnect with family and friends, recharge their batteries, and improve their overall well-being. This image works like all successful advertisements in that the clear central message is understood immediately by a mass audience. However, to suggest that such instantaneity makes this image easy to understand is to miss the multiple registers through which it signifies. Indeed, there are much richer and more complex meanings suggested by the juxtaposition of militarization and tourism so neatly expressed by this advertisement.

Using the "No Leave, No Life" campaign as a starting point, this book teases out the multiple and deeply entrenched connections between war and tourism that are either ignored altogether or dismissed as a superficial oddity. It asks how the serious activities of war and the frivolous activities of tourism intersect and explores how both practices constitute themselves by similar productions of difference. Though the purposes of war and tourism seem unrelated and even antithetical (one oriented toward political violence, the other toward leisure), they both produce foreignness within a global order that must be either conquered through military combat (i.e., vanquishing the enemy) or consumed through tourism (i.e., commodifying the Other). To put it simply, although the goals of war and tourism are entirely different, both practices are structured in advance by shared productions of difference. Certainly the book addresses the familiar geopolitical structures that produce and enable difference in the global realm (e.g., states, civilizations, communities, cultures), but it is also concerned with the gendered, racial, class, sexual, emotive, and affective differences that underscore and constitute these wider geopolitical structures. Central to this book is the claim that the productions of difference shared between war and tourism are politically important because they are also shared productions of asymmetry, domination, and violence. With that in mind, this book is best understood as a critical exploration of the multiple asymmetrical logics that privilege the position of the colonizer—in this case, occupying soldiers and/or visiting tourists—at the expense of local subjects whose rich, multiple, and varied lives are preemptively reduced to either enemies or exotic Others. By understanding war and tourism as constituting themselves through *shared* productions of difference and domination (rather than through an instinctive opposition between violent conquest and leisured consumption), surprising connections start to appear. These include, for example, how soldiers become tourists while on leave from war, how sites of battle become future tourist destinations, and how tourists often function as cultural diplomats. As both war and tourism are, and have always been, thoroughly global mobilities, it is no surprise that military adventures overseas are constantly becoming entwined with long-established tourist itineraries. But what is at stake in that encounter? Do these two oppositional practices actually see the world in similar ways? Do they coproduce familiar geopolitical cleavages or expose new ones? This book is a sustained effort to render the war-tourism connection *un*-surprising: to critically examine the relations between these different global mobilities and to reveal how they jointly sustain, transform, and sometimes dismantle dominant geopolitical orders.

Focusing on the productions of difference and domination shared between war and tourism is a necessary starting point, but it remains both insufficient and unsatisfying. Limiting the approach this way produces a reductive account of the power relations under scrutiny and suggests that global encounters (e.g., between soldiers, tourists, locals, and enemy combatants) only operate through overdetermined, unidirectional, and monolithic modes of authority. Certainly the intersections of war and tourism are characterized by moments of oppression, exploitation, and violence, but the manner in which military infrastructures and tourism populations encounter foreign landscapes and foreign Others—and indeed, the manner in which they encounter each other in foreign landscapes—is heterogeneous, emergent, provisional, multiple, complex, and ambivalent. As Mary Louise Pratt (1992) so memorably argued, sites of global encounter are never static landscapes of power; rather, they are rich and varied contact zones with multiple mobilities, identities, pasts, and futures. To avoid the reductive analytical horizons that often flourish amid structuring binaries such as here-there, us-them, domestic-international, and even war-tourism, this book understands productions of difference and domination as fundamentally contingent and thus examines the manner in which structuring binaries are secured but also negotiated, troubled, fractured, disassembled, multiplied, reworked, and rearticulated. Rather than reduce the entanglements between war and tourism to simple productions of difference and domination, this book is an effort to open up the complexity, contrariness, and heterogeneity of these encounters. To be sure, occupying militaries and tourist populations often engage with Otherness through deeply offensive modes of domination, but they also deploy alternative dispositions, such as curiosity, desire, aversion, paternalism, indifference, solidarity, and resentment. My insistence on the multiplicity and contingency of war-tourism encounters is an effort to show how these entanglements are always much more than domination: they are important moments of ambiguity in which alternative voices, critical dispositions, and more open futures can be articulated. That is the modest aim of this book: to open up the space of encounter a little further so that the voices usually silenced by dominant arrangements of war and tourism can be heard in all their cacophony, harmony, and dissonance.

This book is primarily interested in the global nature of the structures shaping war-tourism encounters—the powerful and historically specific world orders that constitute the geopolitical relations between state, nonstate, and transnational actors; direct the everyday encounters between citizens and foreigners; and determine the mobility and immobility of various global populations. Certainly scholars in tourism studies have engaged directly with questions of global war and conflict and have given us insight into how the tourism industry responds to the outbreak and cessation of violence (Andrews 2014; Butler and Suntikul 2013; Endy 2004; Fyall, Prideaux, and Dallen 2006; Pizam and Mansfield 1996; Pizam and Smith 2000; Smith 1998; Sönmez 1998). Likewise, scholars in international relations (IR) have examined how different arrangements of peace, war, and stability affect global tourism, especially how the current neoliberal order entrenches unequal relations between hosts and guests (Chin 2008; Clancey 2008; 2009; Hazbun 2008; Lisle 2000; Vrasti 2012). While much of this work provides insight into how tourism operates in times of war, too often it assumes a problematic hierarchy between the practices of war and tourism. By separating the frivolous concerns of tourism from the serious concerns of war, the pursuits of leisure and travel are understood to be entirely subordinated to geopolitics, subject to the whims of foreign policy, and made irrelevant as the realpolitik of war takes over. This commonsense separation and hierarchization of war and tourism operates through a much wider consensus about the capacity for tourism to create peace. The easiest way to understand this consensus is through what I call the tourism-peace model—the idea that tourism

International Order	Peace	War	Peace
Time	→	→	→
Travel	Tourism	No Tourism	Tourism Again

FIGURE 2. Tourism–peace model.

prospers during times of peace and suffers during times of war (Lisle 2006b, 340–43; Weaver 2000).

As Figure 2 suggests, the cycles of peace and war that punctuate world order are mapped onto the cycles of growth and stagnation that punctuate the tourism industry. Therefore, when peace reigns in the world, tourism prospers, visitor numbers go up, and revenue increases—but when war erupts, tourism stagnates, visitor numbers and revenue plummet, and eventually leisure travel stops altogether. The consensus expressed by this model is widely adopted by tourism industry professionals and reproduced by tourism studies scholars who argue that "safety, tranquillity and peace are a necessary condition for prosperous tourism" (Pizam and Mansfield 1996, 1; see also Fyall, Prideaux, and Dallen 2006, 153). Within this understanding, tourism studies scholars uncritically accept the temporal demarcation of war and peace and structure the epistemic foundations of their inquiry accordingly; that is, they examine and compare tourism through the three primary categories of before, during, and after war (Butler and Suntikul 2013; Smith 1998). Unsurprisingly, industry and policy approaches reproduce the same epistemic arrangement when they draw on academic literature to claim that tourism increases global harmony, reduces conflict, and generates revenue—a claim that is extremely powerful in postconflict situations where tourism is used to kick-start development and anchor wider reconstruction efforts.

The simplicity—and thus attraction—of this model is actually a profound depoliticization that rests on a number of highly problematic assumptions. Primarily, the temporal demarcation between times of war and times of peace is unambiguous and fixed and therefore assumes that tourism is a temporary and dependent form of mobility and that war is the causal factor determining the rise and fall of visitor numbers and revenue. This reductive account of temporality and causality ignores that modern mass tourism is a *constant* form of global mobility that flourishes all over the world despite (and sometimes because of) war, conflict, and atrocity. It also effaces the important transitional periods between war and peace in which antagonism, enmity, and hostility continue to develop (e.g., fragile postconflict transitions). Second, by failing to engage with the critical literature on globalization, the tourism–peace model is ahistorical in that it assumes that there have always been, and will always be, clear cycles of war and peace. Those of us working against the supposedly universal claim that war is inevitable seek to demonstrate that particular world orders—bipolar, multipolar, unipolar—arise in specific historical moments because they serve the interests of "great powers" at the expense of the many populations and subjectivities that exist outside of such an elite agenda. Assuming an ahistorical account of world order makes it impossible to ask which *particular* arrangement of global power arises at a specific historical juncture; who that arrangement serves; and how it orders the practices of, and encounters between, war and tourism. Third, this model assumes that tourism is a wholly benign form of mobility because it creates global harmony (largely by generating increased revenue) and therefore exists in opposition to war's more obvious features of violence, enmity, and destruction. This ignores not only the manner in which tourism is complicit in many forms of exploitation, inequality, and animosity between privileged guests and subordinate hosts but also the unseen and often undocumented practices of leisure and travel that soldiers pursue when they are not engaged in direct combat (e.g., R&R excursions). Finally, the tourism–peace model assumes that the preferred way to understand war's ability to determine the patterns of tourism is through an economic lens. Because tourism is a profit-making industry central to the flourishing of the global economy, it helps to generate the connectivity, collectivity, and harmony necessary for global economic growth. In short, tourism is the world's "peace industry" (D'Amore 1988a; see also Askjellerud 2003; Blanchard and Higgens-Desbiolles 2013; D'Amore 1988b; Haessly 2010; Litvin 1988; Tomljenović 2010). Such an approach ignores the multiple registers of difference silently at work within and between the economic processes of the tourist industry (e.g., culture, race, gender, class, religion, ethnicity) and effaces how these registers of difference—coupled with entrenched economic inequalities—are often the seeds for political struggle and violence.[1] What emerges from these assumptions is a powerful normative claim that posits an end goal (peace) and a prescriptive idea about how tourism should operate to achieve that goal (by, for example, fostering cross-cultural understanding) (Khamouna and Zeiger 1995, 81). In other words, by creating "an understanding between peoples and tolerance of each other's ways," tourism will miraculously increase economic growth for everyone, generate global reconciliation, reduce the chances of war, and, ultimately, lead to peace (Brown 1989, 270; see also Kim and Crompton 1990; Kim and Prideaux 2003; Kim, Prideaux, and Prideaux 2007; Var, Brayley, and Korsay 1989; Var, Brayley, and Korsay 1989).

This book is an extended effort to deconstruct the normative claims underscoring this consensus and offer a more critical, reflexive, and heterogeneous account of the relations between war and tourism. In this sense, *Holidays in the Danger Zone* offers a genealogy of the relationships between war and tourism: it is an effort to uncover the dominant power-knowledge relations that structure these practices in particular historical circumstances and to show how asymmetrical arrangements of power and knowledge produce and shape the way subjects relate to themselves, to each other, to dominant institutions, and to their material surroundings (Foucault 1997, 41–81; Rabinow 1984, 76–100; Shiner 1982). But *Holidays in the Danger Zone* also examines how far dominant arrangements of power and knowledge have penetrated—how numerous techniques of governance actively shape our everyday lives, aspirations, behaviors, sensations, imaginations, and interactions. In this sense, *Holidays in the Danger Zone* is contributing to a wider project of opening up registers that were previously unacknowledged or assumed to lie outside of the political—registers that include the everyday practices of leisure and tourism. This more expansive account of the political is what Foucault was referring to when he inverted Clausewitz's claim to read that "politics is the continuation of war by other means" (Foucault 2003a, 15; 2007). If war is the "grid of intelligibility" through which social power operates, then politicizing everyday life, leisure, and tourism requires an analysis of their martial framing, warlike behavior, and agonistic structure. Unsurprisingly, such an inversion also requires an analysis of how the practices of war and combat—especially on "foreign" battlefields—are infused with moments of leisure and punctuated by experiences of travel.

Commenting on the new formulations of methodology that arise from such a starting place, Michael Shapiro (2013, xv) outlines the kind of critical thinking required for unexpected juxtapositions to be taken seriously (see also Bleiker 2009):

> To *think* (rather than to seek to explain) in this sense is to invent and apply conceptual frames and create juxtapositions that disrupt and/or render historically contingent accepted knowledge practices. It is to compose the discourse of investigation with critical juxtapositions that unbind what are presumed to belong together and thereby to challenge institutionalized ways of reproducing and understanding phenomena.

With that idea of *thinking* in mind, this book takes apart the assumed coupling of tourism = peace and explores the political work that is produced by such an equation. It positions tourism and war alongside and within one another to refute the unidirectional and singular causality inherent in such an equation. In that sense, it follows William Connolly's (2005, 870) account of resonance by examining how "heretofore unconnected or loosely associated elements *fold, bend, blend, emulsify, and dissolve into each other,* forging a qualitative assemblage resistant to classical modes of explanation." Such a critical methodology enables me to demonstrate through many historically embedded examples how even the most benign and well-meaning tourist experience is structured by antagonistic geopolitical forces and how even the most violent military campaign contains moments of leisure, pleasure, and travel. More generally, it allows me to uncover the widespread productions of difference that underscore such seemingly unconnected phenomena—to show that war and tourism do not just coincidentally intersect but are rather co-constituted on a much more foundational ethico-political level. Establishing this profound entanglement is about contesting the dominant and uncritical approaches that posit an entirely reductive and unidirectional relationship between war and tourism and finding ways to let the rich, complex, and plural connections between these two practices emerge.

Architectures of Enmity: Framing War–Tourism Entanglements

Claiming that practices of war and tourism reproduce difference and domination against the backdrop of established world orders alerts us to the presence of geopolitical imaginaries—the dominant arrangements of global power that prevail in given historical moments and order the behaviors, orientations, and practices of subjects (e.g., policy makers, soldiers, tourists, refugees), spaces (e.g., states, borders, landscapes), and temporalities (e.g., histories, memories, futures). Because these imaginaries are constructed by relations of power that stretch around the world, they are riven with constitutive asymmetries that are central to understanding war and tourism's shared productions of difference and domination. These asymmetries are best understood as "architectures of enmity" that shape our understandings of the world through antagonistic framings of identity and difference (Shapiro 1997; 2007; 2009; see also Gregory 2004, 17-29; Gregory and Pred 2007). For Michael Shapiro (1997, ix-xi), these architectures of enmity are formed when collectivities try to "reproduce their unity and coherence" by manifesting themselves territorially (e.g., claiming a homeland) and consequently generate "the meanings of self and Other" that any bounded geography requires. Much of Shapiro's work explores the geopolitical productions of domestic, interior homelands as contrasted with distant, foreign outsides, the virtue of which is to demonstrate how *all* geopolitical imaginaries rely on the reproduction of fundamental logics of enmity expressed by differential identities (e.g., civilized–barbarian), spatial boundaries (e.g., East–West), and discrete temporalities (e.g., modern–premodern). Using architectures of enmity as a framing device allows us to see that our ability to conceive of the world in its entirety—what Heidegger (1977) called the "world-as-picture"—is not a neutral image: it is saturated with all manner of *particular* imaginings that privilege some subjects, spaces, histories, and futures over others (Shapiro 2009, 18-19; see also Chow 2006, 12-13, 29-31; Mitchell 2005b, xiv-xv).

This book explores the evolution of dominant geopolitical imaginaries from the late nineteenth century to the present. It looks at the entanglements of war and tourism within these imaginaries and explores how these connections sometimes reify the central architectures of enmity, and how they sometimes refract, redirect, and disrupt them. Specifically, it analyzes the movements, practices, and interactions of Western military forces and tourist populations primarily from the United Kingdom and America (but also from Europe, Canada, and Australia) as they produce, encounter, and negotiate "foreign-ness" in North Africa, the Middle East, Southeast Asia, the Pacific, the Caribbean, and East Africa. As this trajectory makes clear, *Holidays in the Danger Zone* is framed by a sustained engagement with the experiences, practices, and consequences of colonial encounters. I begin in the late nineteenth century not because this is the first time war and tourism intersected (indeed, Seaton 1999 shows how tourists have always been spectators of combat) but because this is when empire's force and reach were augmented by the emergence of modern mass tourism—when the occupying functionaries of various colonial powers stationed around the world were joined by middle-class tourists who were taking advantage of the group adventures offered by companies such as Thomas Cook & Son. Here, the structuring architecture of enmity through which occupying forces operated was a colonial order that reproduced—often violently—distinctions between civilized subjects and uncivilized barbarians. However, the presence of tourists in colonial outposts at this time forced a recalibration of that binary: certainly some foreigners were considered inhuman and worthy of extinction, but others were considered intriguing, curious, exotic, and worth encountering. As Ali Behdad (1994) rightly argues, the multiple engagements with difference introduced by tourists in the late nineteenth century were part of a larger fracturing of empire that helped to intensify the pace of decolonization in the early twentieth century.

By the time the First World War had extinguished itself in 1918, a number of important war-tourism entanglements had developed, not least the widespread use of personal cameras by military officers at the front. As part of the wider practice of Great War commemoration that began immediately after the war, battlefield tourism—including the collecting of war souvenirs from the trenches—became another way for modern subjects to express mourning, sacrifice, and loss. These commemorations reflected the geopolitics of the Great War in that they were focused mainly on European battlefields (e.g., the Western Front) but also extended to the Eastern frontiers of the war (e.g., Gallipoli). By the time of the Second World War, that geopolitical containment of enmity had stretched around the globe from Europe into North Africa, the Indian subcontinent, and the Pacific Rim. There is, of course, an important antecedent for this global sensibility: the dramatic rise of mass tourism between the wars meant that millions of Western subjects were *already familiar* with the world outside of their national borders because they had experienced it personally on cruise ships, airplanes, trains, or cars or aspirationally through travel posters, travel magazines, postcards, newspapers, and newsreels. What makes this period particularly interesting is how the touristic framing of global destinations that developed between 1900 and 1914 and again in the 1920s and 1930s shaped how militaries encountered foreign battlefields. To make political sense of those encounters, it is necessary to examine how that global sensibility continued to be saturated with the experience of colonialism despite the fact that decolonization was already under way. For example, the dominant global sensibility at work during the Second World War—that an absolute evil exemplified by the camps at Auschwitz must be resisted by *all* civilized peoples—often effaced the many colonial asymmetries still at work in the global system (e.g., the reliance on Commonwealth soldiers to fight European battles or the exploitation of labor and resources from the Global South in support of the war effort) (Barkawi 2005; 2013; Barkawi and Stanski 2012). What I explore further in the book is the extent to which the global practices of tourism within and between both world wars facilitated the structural conditions bequeathed by colonialism.

By the end of the Second World War, the imbrications of the global and the colonial were quickly rearranged into the bipolar architecture of enmity that constituted the Cold War: one was contained within either an American or Soviet sphere of influence. This rearrangement of world order meant that the dominant geopolitical opposition of America versus the USSR assimilated multiple global populations (mainly residing in the Global South) into one or another sphere of influence. This process of assimilation was aided by the unprecedented growth in global travel and the construction of the tourism industry's modern infrastructure (e.g., airports, hotel chains, large-scale tourist attractions) in the early decades of the Cold War. So, for example, although Western travelers could not visit the USSR or travel behind the Iron Curtain, they could certainly go everywhere else, and they did so with enthusiasm. At the same time as millions of Western tourists were venturing out into the world, of course, modern militaries were being redistributed to the edges of the bipolar order in places like Korea, Hungary, Vietnam, Angola, Czechoslovakia, and Afghanistan. This book explores how the intense growth of postwar travel could not help but entangle itself in these new outposts of geopolitical tension.

With the fall of the Berlin Wall in 1989, the emerging global order was marked by an intensification of globalization such that more conflicts began to erupt and intensify (e.g., the Gulf War, Chechnya, Bosnia, Somalia, Rwanda) at the same time as people were visiting new destinations and discovering new ways to travel (e.g., backpacking, gap years, food tourism, voluntourism). But armed militaries and tourists were not the only people on the move during the 1990s: ethnic conflicts produced millions of displaced persons, refugees, and economic migrants and, consequently, an increasing concern with state borders, immigration, and access to citizenship. Here, the architecture of enmity transposed the bipolarity of the Cold War into a more horizontal arrangement with clear echoes of empire: there were civilized people living in peace, traveling in peace, and enforcing peace, and there were barbarians descending into war, retreating into homogenous cultural communities, and claiming that humanitarian interventions were another form of imperialism. However, at the same time as the geopolitical border between civilization and anarchy was hardening, tourists—often called "dark tourists"—were enthusiastically exploring destinations widely considered off limits. This juxtaposition was especially evident in places like Sri Lanka and the Dalmatian Coast, where an extensive and established tourism infrastructure continued to host visitors despite ongoing hostilities. One of the most significant developments in the 1990s was the intensification and rapid growth of postwar tourism and commemoration in areas emerging from conflict. In places like Northern Ireland, Cyprus, and South Africa, tourism was seen as central to revenue generation and reconstruction, but it required a unified national narrative to develop. Here, public debates around tourism and reconciliation reveal important fissures, erasures, and exclusions in the way national narratives invoked (or failed to invoke) the norms of civilization against a constantly threatening anarchy.

The disparate, multiple, and wide-ranging collection of dangers that constituted the "Coming Anarchy" (Kaplan 1994; 1997) in the 1990s coalesced into a singular threat on September 11, 2001. Anarchy was no longer an amorphous and disorganized horde of barbarians at the gate; rather, it now had a face and an intention to do harm. Particularizing the enemy as radical Muslim terrorists—and more specifically as al-Qaeda—and claiming they were exceptional in their violence, extremism, and ideology enabled Western governments to pursue more invasive, pernicious, and violent actions in the name of fighting such an unprecedented threat. Within this context, one of the clearest entanglements between war and tourism emerged: the entire tourism industry has been securitized by, and thus made subordinate to, counterterror measures aimed at fighting an exceptional terrorist threat. This wholesale governance of the tourism industry in the name of security can be seen in developments such as the biometric security technologies used at airports to delineate between safe and risky travelers; the government warnings about where it is safe to travel; and the increasingly enclave-like resorts in the Global South that protect privileged travelers from the precarious conditions of local life around them. Again, the echo of colonialism is undeniable: a clear distinction is emerging between those elite bodies who are deemed safe to travel and enjoy tourist experiences and those subjugated bodies who either do not have the resources to travel (and thus become hosts serving the needs of elite bodies) or whose mobility is labeled as risky (e.g., refugees, displaced persons, economic migrants) and therefore subject to invasive practices of surveillance, control, and incarceration. What needs to be interrogated here is how the extensive reach of counterterrorist measures (e.g., biometric passports, dataveillance, risk registers) are able to mobilize the everyday practices of leisure, travel, and tourism in their efforts to identify new enemies, manage risky populations, and counter lurking threats. How are these measures of surveillance, ordering, and control distributed? Which bodies are produced as more risky than others, and what are the consequences of those decisions?

Setting the story of war-tourism entanglements in chronological order is not meant to imply a clear origin point with a linear and progressive trajectory. These juxtapositions did not suddenly begin in the late nineteenth century, nor have they progressed into a mutually beneficial or fully acknowledged collaboration. There are similarities across time, for sure, but there are also vast differences in between the late nineteenth century and now, as well as odd intensifications, circulations, fractures, and reverberations. This book explores particular entanglements of war and tourism within historically bounded architectures of enmity and shows how those entanglements were, and continue to be, shaped by the long reach of colonialism. This is not a monolithic understanding of colonial experience in which homogenous occupying forces are forever pitched against a singular primitive world; rather, I understand colonialism as a more mobile, plural, and fractured set of mobilities and encounters that are often overdetermined by asymmetries that favor the occupying power. As Wendy Brown (2006, 6) helpfully explains, dominant architectures of enmity change over time, but they are fueled by continual reproductions of difference and domination:

> In the mid-nineteenth through mid-twentieth centuries, the West imagined itself as standing for civilization against primitivism, and in the cold war years for freedom against tyranny; now these two recent histories are merged in the warring figures of the free, the tolerant and the civilized on one side, and the fundamentalist, the intolerant, and the barbaric on the other.

Brown's approach helps to reveal how the tourism-peace model is unable to acknowledge, let alone address, how historically grounded manifestations of colonialism have shaped the practices of, and relations between, war and tourism. In effect, the consensus surrounding the tourism-peace model is a powerful expression of unacknowledged privilege and authority. Neither the practices of war nor the practices of tourism strive for peace in random ways—they strive for it by advocating *particular* norms and values and spreading those around the globe (Shapiro 1997, 15). This book traces how *particular* norms and values were disseminated through the practices of war and tourism during successive global orders: British values of civilization during empire; Anglo-American notions of freedom and liberty during the two world wars; American ideas of consumerism during the Cold War; and Western norms of tolerance and diversity during globalization and the War on Terror. To expose the particularities of such norms and values—especially when they masquerade as universally applicable—is to contest the structuring hierarchies of the tourism-peace model that separate geopolitics from everyday life, privilege those who will further benefit from tourism's growth, efface the constitutive (and continuing) reach of colonial experience, and entrench a world in which the frivolous practices of leisure are forever subordinated to the serious world of international affairs. However, to think effectively against such a consensus, and to develop an epistemological framework within which the juxtaposition of tourism and war can be critically explored, it is necessary to ask much larger questions about how war-tourism entanglements can be seen in the first place, let alone critically examined.

Ways of Seeing: Visuality, Materiality, Practice

Reflecting on the amateur photographs of American soldiers in the Pacific theater during the Second World War, Carolyn O'Dwyer (2004, 33, emphasis added) argues that "the ease with which tourist pleasure is incorporated into military culture and the inextricable merging of projects of benign exploration with those of armed invasion may be attributed to their fundamentally similar politics of looking: *a parallel structure of gazing.*" O'Dwyer's claim offers a useful opening into the epistemological terrain sustaining this book by suggesting that a shared way of seeing orders the practices of both war and tourism. Bringing the diverse practices of fighting wars and taking holidays together through a "parallel structure of gazing" can reveal how truth claims are generated, how subjectivities are arranged into privileged-excluded binaries, how a singular past and future are arranged, how a homogeneous territory is delineated, and how a collective "we" is able to operate as the empowered agent of history. What is important about O'Dwyer's ocular metaphor is that claims about "ways of seeing" are much more fundamental and ontological than simply seeing; that is, what we see doesn't simply reflect reality but actually brings it into being. Mike Crang (1997, 362; see also Jay 1994, 362–328) describes this deeper understanding of visuality as a process of envisioning:

> envisioning is a way of being-towards the world. It is not a case of pictures showing what is "out there," nor indeed what is "in here," but rather how objects are made to appear for us. It is a way in which the world is apprehended as picturable, it is "enworlded" by being enframed. In this sense images are not so much counterposed to reality as a route through which worlds are created.

Crang suggests that our *ways of seeing* are always already *ways of being*: what is seen and unseen tells us a great deal about what is and what is not, what exists and what is pushed out of reality, and what is deemed possible or banished to the realm of the impossible. Going back to O'Dwyer, this account of visuality suggests that the Second World War images she was analyzing were much more than simply inert photographs because they revealed something important about how American soldiers actually behaved, moved, and explored in their foreign surroundings. By this I certainly do not mean that pictures "tell the truth" about "what actually happened"—far from it. What I mean to say is two things: first, that visual representations like photographs must be understood within a wider context of production (i.e., who is the photographer and who or what is the subject? Who or what is in the frame and who or what is outside it? What are the power relations generated by this field of vision?), and second, that visual representations are never inert, nor do they deliver monolithic and unidirectional messages. What I am articulating here is a much more political understanding of visuality that affords agency to the visual record and seeks to understand the multiple forces that bring an image, a gaze, or a dominant "way of seeing" into being. When the Second World War photographs that O'Dwyer examines are approached through this deeper and more politicized understanding of visuality, a whole new field of practice becomes available for interrogation. What this means is that the soldiers' understanding of the Pacific as simultaneously a theater of war and a holiday paradise—an understanding expressed through hundreds of amateur photographs—is saturated with multiple meanings that tap us into adjacent trajectories of colonial conquest, nation building, and tourist consumption.

Certainly scholars in visual culture have explored what is political about our dominant ways of seeing (Crandall 2005, 20; see also Elkins 2008; Jay 1994; Silverman 1996; Mitchell 1994; 2005; Rose 2001; Levi Strauss 2005), but this study takes its lead more explicitly from those who address the ontological grounding of embedded power relations and the visualities these produce. Judith Butler, for example, argues that dominant ways of seeing mobilize existing power relations through practices of "framing"—that delimiting norms at the ontological level "are enacted precisely through specific frames, visual and narrative, that presuppose decisions about what will be unframed, and what will be left outside the frame" (Butler 2007, 954; see also Butler 2005; 2009). In other words, prior acts of classification and prioritization operate at the ontological level by arranging what is allowed to be perceived in the first place, which means that framing is about deciding—or delimiting—what will be present in the visual field itself. Here Butler's work resonates with Jacques Rancière's (2004; 2009) claims about the distribution of the sensible, or how dominant modes of perception produce and secure the norms, conventions, and roles of the dominant social order. While these insights tell us much about the relationship between seeing and being (and, indeed, the production of dominant ways of seeing), some have argued that they don't elaborate enough on the spatial, political, and everyday outworkings of visuality (Elden 2005; Nelson 1999). In this sense, I agree with David Campbell's (2007) argument that more work needs to be done showing how the power-knowledge-subject constellations that emerge in dominant ways of seeing are reproduced and circulated within *already familiar* geopolitical imaginaries (e.g., deepest, darkest Africa; the exotic Pacific paradise; an inscrutable Middle East).

These critical efforts to politicize our ways of seeing are helpful in foregrounding the ontological and geopolitical character of O'Dwyer's claim that war and tourism have a "parallel structure of gazing." However, while the trope of visuality is enormously useful for unpacking these shared orientations, it is also limited in terms of what it can tell us about the everyday life, practices, and encounters between those in charge of the visual frame, those being visualized, those outside of the frame, and those in the viewing audience. To expand the analysis beyond the ocularcentric register of the visual, this book argues that envisioning is a deeply embodied and profoundly material mode of encounter. With that in mind, I explore the practices, behaviors, and encounters that are entailed in the "parallel structure of gazing" supposedly shared by military forces and tourist populations; in other words, I take account of the multiple relations not only between these populations and the Others they confront but also between these mobile bodies and the territories they move through, the objects they carry with them, and the material infrastructures that shape their circulations. My own navigation through this intellectual terrain starts from an important critical shift in Foucault's work when the rather overdetermined account of disciplinary power evident in his earlier work gives way to a more nuanced account of productive power mobilized by governmentality, techniques of the self, and biopower. For me, that shift produces a much wider, richer, and textured field of analysis because it positions subjects within multiple and sometimes contradictory forces, it disrupts the foundational subject–object distinction that privileges embodied subjects (especially "seeing" subjects), and it shows how increasingly invasive techniques of governance proliferate not through coercion but because subjects willingly and enthusiastically embrace them. This expanded field of analysis opens up most clearly when Foucault shifts from using discourse (which privileges linguistic and grammatical orderings) to the idea of a *dispositif* that begins to take account of the multiple and extralinguistic forces shaping the order of things. A *dispositif,* then, is a

> thoroughly heterogeneous ensemble consisting of discourses, institutions, architectural forms, regulatory decisions, laws, administrative measures, scientific statements, philosophical, moral and philanthropic positions—in short the said as much as the unsaid. Such are the elements of the apparatus. The apparatus itself is the system of relations that can be established between these elements. (Foucault 1980, 194)

Importantly, this shift from a disciplinary account of power to a more diffuse apparatus of forces is evident in Foucault's account of visuality. Certainly his early work is useful for showing how particular and historically specific ways of seeing (e.g., the panopticon, total surveillance, the medical gaze) privilege certain viewing subjects (e.g., the prison warden, the doctor) while subordinating others to that authoritative gaze (e.g., criminals, patients) (Foucault 1991; 2001; 2003b). However, as many critics have argued, this account often neglects the productive capacities of seeing: how dominant ways of seeing are seductive because they show us things we have never seen before, they bring us into a world of other like-minded subjects, they mobilize our feelings and passions, and they encourage us to *do* things (Bal 1993; Flynn 1993; Jay 1986; Melville 1996; Mitchell 1994, 58–84; Rajchman 1988; Shapiro 2003). That link between vision and action can only be theorized when the mode of perception is understood as embodied; that is, seeing is only one part of a wider sensorium that includes touching, hearing, and smelling and that taps us into the affective register by foregrounding the physical sensations that are mobilized during acts of perception (Crary 1992; 1999; Massumi 2002; Mitchell 2005). Critically interrogating the affective register is politically important: this is where the subject's physical and biological matter is *always already attached* to the material world around it, and therefore where modernity's powerful subject-object distinction can be most effectively collapsed and reordered (Anderson 2014).

These shifts—from disciplinary to productive power and from ocularcentrism to multisensory seeing-being—are enormously helpful in trying to excavate what is important about the relationships between war and tourism. They allow us to acknowledge the thoroughly embodied nature of these practices (i.e., that war and tourism are not just about a "parallel structure of gazing" but also about the enrollment of millions of sensing bodies); the techniques used to shape the behavior and movement of those bodies; the management of relations within and between those bodies; the new and more innovative strategies aimed at making those bodies more governable; and the preparation of those bodies for numerous interventions in the future. Some good examples of how macro structures such as states, economies, and cultures work to order these bodies are the recruitment strategies deployed by modern militaries that use the promise of global travel to entice young men and women to enlist. Thus, in 1914, the U.S. Marine Corps produced recruitment posters with the following headline: "Action? You said it! Right Now! Travel? Sure! China, Japan, Hawaii, Philippines, Guam, West Indies. Adventure? Oh Man!"

(Diller + Scofidio 1994, 19). And lest we think such interpellations have become more subtle, just after the first Gulf War the U.S. Navy used the same tactic in a 1993 television advertisement: "The Navy, it's a chance to travel around the world and see places most people only read about" (Diller + Scofidio 1994, 20; see also Bickford 2003; Lair 2011, 190–91). Although these structural forms of power are important, they provide only a partial and rather elite view of the ways in which war and tourism intersect. To get at the more embodied, affective, and everyday registers of war-tourism encounters, this book supplements O'Dwyer's claim about a "parallel structure of gazing" with a broader empirical grammar about the embodied *practices* of soldiers, tourists, and Others and the *materiality* of the social field they move through.[2]

I want to argue that the principal architectures of enmity under scrutiny in this book gain traction most powerfully in what Margaret Werry (2011, xxxiii) calls the "tactical domain of everyday life: the myriad ways of knowing and being, of seizing pleasure, of dwelling or moving, and of contesting or exerting authority" (see also Barkawi and Brighton 2011; Barkawi and Stanski 2012; Minca 2009; Sylvester 2010; 2012). Within that "tactical domain of everyday life," architectures of enmity do not simply enroll and exclude particular bodies and populations, they also make themselves felt—and indeed achieve their power—by enrolling and excluding objects, landscapes, infrastructures, atmospheres, and materials; in other words, militarized and touristic subjects relate to themselves, to each other, and to preconstituted "foreign Others" through the objects that constitute their agency (e.g., cameras, guidebooks, postcards, guns, helmets, rations, jeeps, uniforms), the territorial markers that position them (e.g., front lines, border crossings, areas of operation, war zones, destinations), and the material infrastructures through which they move (e.g., occupied cities, hotels, airports). For example, the movement of U.S. Marines across the Pacific during the Second World War cannot be understood without exploring their relations with the steel landscape of their aircraft carriers—a landscape that was carefully maintained, intimately explored, and often artfully decorated. Likewise, the movement of present-day tourists through major airports cannot be understood without exploring their intimate encounters with elaborate security checkpoints, scanning machines, cameras, and specially designed software used to distinguish between safe and dangerous travelers. Paying attention to the detailed and intricate material lifeworlds of these mobile populations (and, of course, the many ways these lifeworlds intersect) is the start of a larger process of unpacking. Certainly it helps us to see how modes of domination endure across time and space, but more importantly, it helps us to identify the fissures and gaps within which alternative and resistant voices are always articulating themselves.

Itineraries of Entanglement: Text, Image, Object

Holidays in the Danger Zone is not the first effort to critically explore the entanglements of war and tourism. Artists and architects Diller + Scofidio's (1994) book *Back to the Front: Tourisms of War* combines artwork, commissioned essays, film stills, maps, and photographs in an effort to trace the visual, aesthetic, and cinematic connections between the practices of warfare and the experiences of travel. The idea germinated in their installation *Suitcase Studies: The Production of a National Past,* which placed images, maps, and postcards of two key tourist sites in American culture—the beds of past presidents and national battlefields—in fifty open Samsonite suitcases (Diller + Scofidio 1994, 32-106). That initial idea was pushed into more intellectual realms by the collected essays in their book that necessarily draw from a number of traditions—architecture, photography, history, philosophy, cinema, art history, and literature.[3] While these essays offer useful historical and philosophical insights, for me, the strength of *Back to the Front* lies in the minute and precise details of how, exactly, the two everyday practices of warfare and tourism are sutured together. For example, Diller + Scofidio provide a detailed taxonomy of the contents of a soldier's rucksack and compare that with the same taxonomy of a traveler's carry-on bag (Diller + Scofidio 1994, 22-27; see also Stinson 2014). The juxtapositions are at once obvious and jarring: the combat helmet and the sun visor, the ammunition belt and the money belt, the sight of the rifle and the zoom lens of the video camera. Indeed, the book contains hundreds of images in which these two practices intersect: soldiers posing for souvenir snapshots, famous tourist landmarks being bombed, soldiers storming sandy tourist beaches, guidebooks to famous battlefields, and tourists arming themselves with hi-tech protective gear. The strength of Diller + Scofidio's project is that it demonstrates how the practices of war and tourism align most clearly in the domains of visuality, art, and aesthetics and in this sense corroborate O'Dwyer's claim about a "parallel structure of gazing." But I am also inspired by the way Diller + Scofidio attend to objects within the field of perception as a way to deepen their account of visuality and aesthetics (indeed, as installation artists, they are acutely aware of the constitutive relations between bodies, objects, materialities, infrastructures, and atmospheres).

I want to suggest that Diller + Scofidio's combination of visuality, aesthetics, objects, and materiality is a *political* orientation that offers a creative and critical opening through which to explore the juxtaposition of war and tourism. Of course, I am not the only scholar to be struck by the war-tourism connections expressed so eloquently by Diller + Scofidio; indeed, I am also energized by more recent scholarship on specific war-tourism juxtapositions in France, the Philippines, Hawaii, and Vietnam (Endy 2004; Laderman 2009; Lair 2011; Vicuña Gonzalez 2013). Building on this emerging literature, *Holidays in the Danger Zone* mobilizes a wide range of textual, visual, and historical data from the late nineteenth century to the present to explore the multiple entanglements of war and tourism. It examines official government and military sources (e.g., military policies, government press releases, political speeches), media accounts (e.g., broadsheet and tabloid journalism, news reports, newspaper sketches, blogs), commercial sources from the tourism industry (e.g., travel guidebooks, travel company archives, pamphlets, promotional material, travel magazines, tourism advertisements), and wider cultural resources (e.g., films, television programs, travelogues, personal photographs, social media, novels, artistic installations, memoirs, diaries, personal souvenirs, museum collections and exhibits). It identifies and analyzes the reproduction of distinct geopolitical imaginaries—in this case, historically bounded architectures of enmity—and illustrates how such orders are both secured and unworked by the combined practices of tourism and war. Like the voracious travelers it follows, *Holidays in the Danger Zone* enthusiastically traverses many disciplinary terrains, including IR, sociology, anthropology, geography, architecture, history, visual culture, design, politics, and literature, in its effort to interrogate how dominant world orders are produced, resisted, and negotiated. Though the book is up front about its genealogical approach and critical orientation, it pursues a tricky and sometimes fraught path between postcolonial, poststructural, and feminist positions. Although I understand the logics of asymmetry reproduced by colonialism, Western metaphysics, and patriarchy to be overwhelming and mutually reinforcing, they are never totalizing enough to preclude challenge, disruption, and resistance. Indeed, part of the purpose of this book is to demonstrate how unruly moments that question and disrupt dominant geopolitical imaginaries often occur when and where we least expect them. My aim is not to speak for those moments of irruption but rather to help create more space in which the richness, complexity, and diversity of those moments can flourish.

While *Holidays in the Danger Zone* addresses the more fundamental entanglements of war and tourism in terms of their mutual productions of difference and domination, it pays particular attention to the two primary crossover practices entailed in the juxtaposition: when soldiers become tourists, and when tourists enter war zones. As the "No Leave, No Life" campaign suggests, one of the most familiar and long-standing intersections of war and tourism is the experience of soldiers on leave. Some form of leisure and recreation has always been built into military deployment, and it is within this framework that soldiers most commonly experience tourism in foreign lands. No war is ever a succession of constant battles 24/7: we know that combat is always interspersed with the concerns of "normal civilian life"—eating, sleeping, washing, relaxing, keeping fit. And we know that soldiers pursue moments of leisure and respite every day when deployed in a combat zone, especially when stationed in, or rotating through, temporary army bases. While those moments of leisure-in-battle are themselves intriguing, I am more interested in scheduled rotations of R&R, when soldiers have the opportunity to become tourists in a foreign land. Official R&R rotations are the military's recognition that it is necessary to refresh troops at regular periods, and therefore leave is built into military scheduling and infrastructure and managed under the more comprehensive area of military logistics—the science of moving and maintaining large militaries during war (Cowan 2010; 2014; Van Crevald 1979; Pagonis and Cruikshank 1992). Because R&R must take place behind the front lines of battle, it operates through a clear spatial boundary—the battle zone versus the safe zone—through which a number of attending differentiations are produced. Allied territories in proximity to foreign combat zones are particularly important here: they are near enough so that soldiers with minimal leave can access them; they are safe behind the front line; and they provide the soldier with the opportunity to relax amid exotic places and people. But these proximal R&R sites must offer a careful calibration of similarity and difference: its exotic character must be different from home (and thus appropriate for leisure, tourism, and relaxation), but it must be an *even more exotic* culture than the one soldiers have just spent their time killing and destroying. This is not to suggest that R&R sites operate as hermetically sealed enclaves of pleasure and security; indeed, even in gated tourist resorts the dominant regimes of governance are constantly disrupted, transgressed, and reordered by hosts and guests alike (Edensor 1998; 2000; 2001; Freitag 1994; Jaakson 2004; Judd 1999; 2003; Minca 2009). With this in mind, R&R sites must be understood as complex spaces of encounter where off-duty soldiers and local populations negotiate two overlapping regimes of order: a militarized order of war that justifies the presence of a soldier overseas in the first place and a touristic order that preemptively positions privileged guests and servicing hosts.

Of particular interest here are the transitions between soldiering and leisure in which a militarized order of war—a hypermasculine, aggressive, and violent mode of surveillance and control—is supposed to retreat in the face of a tourist order that provides uncomplicated experiences of leisure, pleasure, and cross-cultural encounter. Far from retreating, however, the logics of differentiation that justify violence in the war zone are carried over into the R&R site in a less extreme form. Whereas killing others is not legally permitted outside of the battlefield, the exploitation of others in the pursuit of pleasure, leisure, and relaxation certainly is. This is why the experience of R&R is so central to my argument about how war and tourism reinforce each other's modes of domination: the power relations, antagonisms, and differentiations that are taken to their extremes during acts of war (i.e., demonizing, dehumanizing, and killing enemy Others) also shape the operation of tourism (i.e., encountering, commodifying, and exploiting exotic Others). It is no surprise, then, that this book examines militarized prostitution as the ultimate example of how the military desire to conquer and the tourist desire to consume intersect on the bodies of local women, girls, and boys. What makes the operation of prostitution during wartime significant for me is the way it is brought into the orbit of military logistics and morale—the same orbit in which other forms of military leisure and tourism are also situated. Indeed, Cynthia Enloe (1990; 2000) shows us that prostitution is always part of the rational calculation of providing soldiers with experiences of leisure to maintain morale and productivity—as if the lives of millions of women and children can be disregarded and reduced to the equivalent of material goods necessary for boosting the well-being and efficiency of soldiers.

The soldier's age-old pursuit of leisure, recreation, and tourism outside the battlefield has always been mirrored by the traveler's desire to look upon the spectacle of war—to observe the buildup of animosity (in some cases witnessing actual combat) and, most importantly, to visit famous historical battlefields as a form of commemoration. This desire is by no means new; indeed, Seaton illustrates how this mode of tourism developed through the Middle Ages and the romantic era and cites the battlefield of Waterloo as the "paradigm instance of the symbiosis of warfare and sightseeing"—what he calls "thanatourism" (Seaton 1999, 132; see also Lloyd 1998, 19–23). Rather contrary to the tourism–peace model, tourists are not deterred by war and often seek it out as a form of extreme spectacle. Recently, scholars from tourism studies and related fields have labeled these practices "dark tourism" to describe how visitors are inexorably drawn to macabre sites of death in the form of live war zones but also to the memorabilia of warfare contained in battlefields, cemeteries, and war memorials, which, according to Valene Smith (1998, 131), now constitute "the largest single category of tourist attractions in the world" (see also Lennon and Foley 2000; Seaton 1996; Sharpley and Stone 2009; Stone and Sharpley 2008; White and Frew 2013). At various points in this book, but especially in relation to post-1989 developments, I take issue with the way the dark tourism literature is unable to address the global power relations inherent in these practices, how it dismisses this phenomenon too easily as an offensive form of voyeurism, and how it reproduces the linear and progressive trajectory of the tourism–peace model. By starting from a position that sees war and tourism as always already entangled, I want to think more critically about why tourists engage with sites, exhibits, and objects of war. What formations of power, knowledge, truth, and authority are mobilized in these sites, and to what extent do tourists accept this constellation? Of particular interest here is how the often unruly and disorienting encounters with "real" sites, exhibits, and objects of war are recuperated through powerful discourses of commemoration and reconciliation. In a variety of locations from Auschwitz to Ground Zero, tourists piously perform the rituals of solemnity and respect required at sites of mass death. But when modern tourism infrastructures are imposed upon sacred ground where vast numbers of people were killed, there are always excessive moments where visitors do not obey the expected norms of reverence and piety. Whereas the dark tourism literature judges these unruly moments as distasteful and moralizes them as voyeuristic, I want to think more carefully about these encounters by positioning them as important moments of resistance to dominant forms of commemoration.

The loosely chronological arc of the book is not intended to provide a comprehensive history of these two crossover experiences. Instead, its genealogical method draws out historically specific snapshots, episodes, and moments in the multiple entanglements of war and tourism from the late nineteenth century to the present. The pages that follow traverse the most serious of political events, including war, atrocity, holocaust, forced migration, and genocide. But I am interested in how these obvious instances of political violence are translated, refracted, and reimagined in less obvious registers—how, for example, they find expression in cultural practices like advertising and marketing (e.g., the "No Leave, No Life" campaign) and how they reverberate so powerfully through the industries of leisure and tourism. This is not a unidirectional force outward from warfare to leisure; indeed, one of the ways to deconstruct the powerful hold that warfare has over the social order is to explore its hidden moments of pleasure, leisure, relaxation, and play. In that sense, the book can be understood as an elongated practice of drawing out the geopolitical assumptions and parameters hidden in practices of tourism and the touristic and leisured frames of reference that are smuggled into military deployments.

1

The Double Vision of Empire

The Gordon Relief Campaign, 1884-85

In late summer 1884, the British travel company Thomas Cook & Son entered into an unprecedented contract with the British government. They agreed to organize all the transport, fuel, and food for the planned military expedition up the Nile into northern Sudan to rescue General Gordon, who was under siege in Khartoum. The story of Gordon's fate in Sudan is a famous one; as Winston Churchill argued, the British people "watched with breathless interest" as the rescue mission wore on and eventually failed (Churchill 1949, 60, also 35-68; Valiunas 2002, 3-44). The tale has been popularized and mythologized in many cultural translations, including A. E. W. Mason's 1902 novel *Four Feathers* and its successive film adaptations (Korda 1939; Kapur 2002) as well as the infamous film *Khartoum* starring Charlton Heston as General Gordon and Laurence Olivier as the Mahdi (Deardon and Elisofon 1966). Because these literary and cinematic accounts of Gordon's adventure are epic in scope and style, they do not linger on the logistical, practical, embodied, and interpersonal mobilizations that were required to get a colonial army hundreds of miles up the Nile and into the African desert. Nor do they question the underlying structure of colonial occupation which saw multiple forms of British governance (e.g., military, institutional, moral, educational, civil) imposed on the spaces and subjects of Egypt. This chapter focuses specifically on the role Thomas Cook & Son played in the Gordon Relief Campaign in 1884 and explores how interactions between occupying military personnel, European tourists, local Egyptians, Sudanese subjects, migrant workers, and Others were shaped by the prevailing geopolitical imaginary of empire—more specifically, the British Empire of the late nineteenth century. It examines the production of a particularly Orientalist version of Egypt across the networked horizon of colonial governance that mobilized not only the official lifeworlds of occupation forces (e.g., military personnel, diplomats, administrators) and the burgeoning tourism industry (e.g., European tourists, directors and owners of tourism companies, tour guides, middlemen, local tourist workers) but also the lifeworlds of a variety of populations both living in and moving through Egypt in the late nineteenth century (e.g., migrant laborers from across North Africa, the families of occupying forces, prostitutes, journalists, spies, and other displaced persons). The chapter asks three related questions: (1) which subjects, objects, spaces, and moments were produced and secured within this Orientalist account of Egypt and which were effaced, marginalized, and rendered invisible; (2) to what extent was this dominant account of Egypt challenged, unworked, and deconstructed; and (3) how was this struggle revealed in a variety of official and cultural sources (e.g., diplomatic communications, commercial contracts, newspaper sketches, lithographs, posters, and photographs)?

Although Edward Said (1978, 31–37) examined how European culture consistently positioned Egypt as inferior, Timothy Mitchell (1988) provides a more comprehensive account of how Europe "enframed" the material reality of Egypt—how Egypt's military authority, educational system, governing structures, and urban plans were completely transformed in accordance with European, rather than Egyptian, visions. Following a number of postcolonial scholars who have reimagined Said's arguments with respect to travel and tourism, this chapter troubles Orientalism's reductive categories of colonizer–colonized; explores how manifestations of empire were always incomplete, contradictory, and riven with failure; and calls attention to the alternative orderings that were always already present in late-nineteenth-century Egypt (Behdad 1994; Gregory 1999; 2001; 2003; 2005; Kaplan 1996; Pratt 1992; Spurr 1993). Focusing specifically on the intermingling of tourism and military occupation during the Gordon Relief Campaign of 1884–85, this chapter examines how the complex, multilayered, and ubiquitous geopolitical imaginary of empire made itself felt through one particular colonial adventure. The contractual arrangement between Thomas Cook & Son and the British military is important because it secured a complementary network of power relations that shaped the way British soldiers, European tourists, and a variety of local and migrant Others related to themselves, each other, and their material surroundings during a discrete episode in Egypt's colonial occupation. Did the various encounters between soldiers, tourists, locals, migrants, and Others always harmoniously fulfill the strategic dictates of empire? Or did these subjects encounter each other in unforeseen ways and, in doing so, produce alternative ways of seeing themselves and each other? Did they order, inhabit, and traverse their material surroundings piously, or did they creatively reimagine the landscapes and infrastructures they found themselves in? I want to argue that the diversity of subjects present in Egypt in 1884–85 were constantly jostling for position both within and outside of the wider geopolitical imaginary of empire. For example, sometimes practices of sightseeing were comprehensively disciplined by military strategy so that both tourists and soldiers were aligned to a similar purpose; indeed, one of the questions I will ask in this chapter is how tourist practices that had long been established in Egypt throughout the eighteenth and nineteenth centuries suddenly became beholden to British military rule that was only established in 1882. But that joint enterprise was never as stable as it appeared and was often disrupted by all kinds of unruly, ambiguous, and provocative counterconducts. As Ali Behdad (1994) rightly argues, examining the manifestations of empire in the late nineteenth century through the lens of travel reveals its discursive fissures and helps produce an alternative trajectory toward the eventual dissolution of colonial rule.

Thomas Cook & Son and the Gordon Relief Campaign of 1884

Egypt had been a desirable destination for Europeans since the late eighteenth century, especially for travelers who had "exhausted the Grand Tour of Italy and were hungry for a new frontier" (Alsayyed 2001, 20). The burgeoning field of Egyptology—the study of ancient Egypt and its antiquities—drew many travelers to North Africa in search of ancient ruins, temples, and artifacts. However, such adventures were enjoyed primarily by wealthy European elites until Thomas Cook organized his first tour to Palestine and Egypt in 1869 (Fagan 1994, 193; Gregory 2001, 124). Very quickly, a popular tourism industry was established with a basic itinerary: from Alexandria to Cairo, then up the Nile by boat to Assiut, then on to Luxor and the Valley of the Kings. More adventurous tourists continued farther up the Nile over two treacherous cataracts (rapids) to the temples at Abu Simbel on the border of northern Sudan. During the 1880s, this itinerary was popularized and managed by Thomas Cook's son John Mason Cook, as Thomas himself was busy developing his "Round the World" journeys. The younger Cook had much more of a business mind than his father and saw the potential financial rewards that would accrue from building up the tourism industry in Egypt; indeed, the firm soon increased its existing resorts, hotels, restaurants, and other businesses along the Nile so that the whole river was soon referred to as Cook's Canal (Smith 2007; see also Hunter 2004, 37; Kark 2001, 158). Only a year after the first Thomas Cook & Son tour to Egypt, the firm was in charge of all passenger traffic on the Nile and had an exclusive contract from the British government to transport all mail and all military troops along the river. To consolidate its privileged position, the firm established a monopoly on all Nile tourist traffic by leasing two types of boats from the Egyptian government: first, the traditional Egyptian *dahabeah*—a small sailing vessel that came with a captain *(reis)*, tour guide *(dragoman)*, cook, and some rowers—which attracted small groups of wealthy tourists who had the means and the time to make the leisured nine-week journey up the Nile and back (Fagan 1994, 206–7; Gregory 2001, 116–17); and second, newer steam boats that cut the time of the river journey in half and carried far more passengers to the famous sites at Luxor and beyond. It was primarily the monopoly on steamer traffic up and down the Nile that allowed Thomas Cook & Son to manage the mass tourism that engulfed Egypt throughout the 1870s and 1880s and reap its financial rewards (Fagan 1994, 193; Gregory 2001, 123–27; Hazbun 2007, 5; Hunter 2004, 34–35; Reid 2002, 64–92).

By the time the British officially established colonial occupation in 1882, Thomas Cook & Son was already in charge of Egypt's by now well-established tourism industry. One of the most immediate concerns for British military forces was confronting the long-standing "problem" of rebellion in Sudan, where an indigenous movement had arisen under a powerful Islamic leader (the Mahdi). Their concerns were justified when the Mahdi's forces famously defeated the Anglo-Egyptian army at the Battle of El Obeid in November 1883, at which point the British government recalled General Gordon, whose experience as governor of the region in the 1870s outweighed his difficult reputation as a man who, in Winston Churchill's (1949, 39) words, "had always been identified with unrest, improvisation, and disturbance." Gordon was dispatched to Khartoum to arrange the immediate evacuation of all European citizens and coordinate the orderly exit of all Egyptian forces from Sudan. Like everyone else, the British military was dependent on Thomas Cook & Son for transport along the Nile; it is at this point that the firm became directly involved in the fate of General Gordon. In January 1884, John Mason Cook arranged for a steamer to take Gordon and Lieutenant Colonel Stuart as far as Korosko, from where they traveled by camel to Khartoum. On the completion of his river journey (February 1, 1884), Gordon wrote the following letter to Thomas Cook & Son:

> Gentlemen—before leaving for Berber I would wish to express to you my own and Lieut. Colonel Stuart's thanks for the admirable manner in which we have been treated while on your steamers. Your agents have also on every occasion shown themselves kind and obliging, and have in every way assisted us to the best of their ability. Hoping that I may perhaps again have the pleasure of placing myself under your guidance, I remain, ever yours truly, [signed] C. E. Gordon, Major-General and Governor General. (Gordon 1928, 1)

Gordon remained in Khartoum and was soon placed under siege by the Mahdi and his forces. The British government under Gladstone prevaricated over whether to send an expedition to rescue Gordon: the public was largely in favor, but the government was reluctant to commit further troops and resources to an area they were intent on evacuating.

From the very beginning of official discussions over Gordon's fate in Khartoum, John Mason Cook was involved in the logistics and strategy of any proposed operation. His presence at many high-level meetings at the War Office throughout the first half of 1884 reveals an important constitutive entanglement between Cook's tourism enterprise in Egypt and British military forces in the region (Thomas Cook & Son 1885). The government finally agreed to send a relief mission to rescue Gordon on September 2, 1884, and it was at this point that John Mason Cook received the official contract from the British government to organize all the logistics of transporting fuel and food from Britain and conveying troops and stores up the Nile to the foot of the second cataract—the British camp at Wadi Halfa in northern Sudan (Figure 3). Such a contract was unprecedented; indeed, it was the first time the logistics of a British military operation had been "entrusted to a private firm or individual" (Cook 1885, 7; Thomas Cook & Son 1885). Given Thomas Cook & Son's long-standing presence in Egypt and its monopoly on Nile river transport, John Mason Cook was in an advantageous position; as he argued, "the Government must either buy me out or they must give me the work" (Cook 1885, 8). Once the contract was signed, all of Cook's steamers were immediately taken out of use for tourist traffic going up the Nile so that British and Egyptian soldiers could be conveyed to the second cataract on their way to Sudan. This meant that tourists already present along the Nile at the end of summer 1884 were only able to use unoccupied steamers or the much slower *dahabeahs* for their return journeys back to Cairo. John Mason Cook traveled back out to Egypt to oversee the firm's involvement in the military operation, and by the end of November 1884, Thomas Cook & Son had successfully fulfilled the terms of its contract:

> Final records reveal that the firm moved about 11,000 British and 7,000 Egyptian troops, 130,000 tons of stores and war material, and 800 whale boats. To convey 40,000 tons of coal, 28 steamers operated between Alexandria and the Tyne and something like 6,000 railway trucks were used to convey fuel between Alexandria and Assiout while 7,000 others conveyed military stores. On the Nile, 27 steamers were kept moving night and day together with 650 sailing vessels of from 70–200 tons capacity. To man this convoy, about 5,000 men and boys, the fellaheen of Lower Egypt, were employed. (Thomas Cook & Son 1885)

The difficulty of any river travel up the Nile was conveying people and resources over the first and second cataracts south of Aswan. Thomas Cook & Son had ample experience surmounting this challenge:

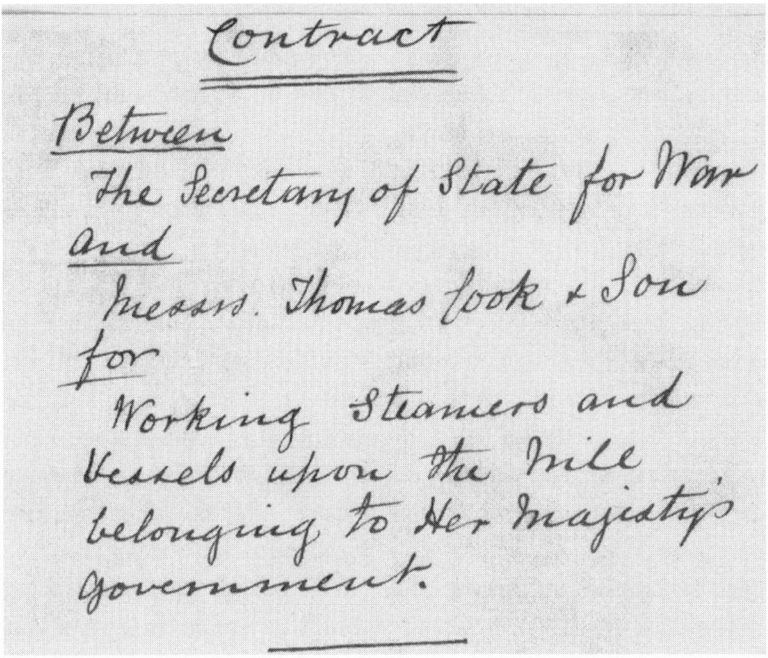

> Contract
>
> Between
> The Secretary of State for War
> and
> Messrs. Thomas Cook & Son
> for
> Working Steamers and
> Vessels upon the Nile
> belonging to Her Majesty's
> Government.

FIGURE 3. Contract between Thomas Cook & Son and the British government, 1884. Courtesy of the Thomas Cook Archive.

tourists disembarked before the rapids and made their way overland along the shore, while local laborers physically hauled the steamers, *dahabeahs,* and other boats through the cataracts and over the rapids. If the river levels were too low and the rocks too prominent, the boats would be moored, luggage would be carried along the shore, and passengers would settle onto new boats waiting on the other side of the cataract. Though Thomas Cook & Son had the logistical experience, technical knowledge, and extensive network of local labor to convey travelers, luggage, and boats over both cataracts, the British government wanted to increase the capacity of this existing tourism infrastructure so it could fully manage the troop numbers traveling up the Nile. To this end, the British government constructed an additional eight hundred Royal Navy whale boats for use on the Nile and imported several experienced whalers—or voyageurs—from Canada to work the cataracts and convey British troops closer to Khartoum. One of the biggest problems for the expedition was that beyond the second cataract, the Nile was largely unexplored and unmapped. All travelers left the river at Wadi Halfa (rechristened as "bloody halfway" by British troops, as it was halfway between Cairo and Khartoum), traveled overland, and joined the Nile farther upstream to avoid the four-hundred-mile bend in the river. Unsatisfied with this disruption to river travel, John Mason Cook traveled with the Gordon expedition to Wadi Halfa, whereupon he and his seventeen-year-old son Albert hired a *dahabeah* and small crew and spent much of December making their way up the Nile as far as Dongola to see whether it was possible to extend river travel and therefore alleviate the overland travel necessitated by the difficult second cataract. Cook met with local leaders in Dongola, and on his return voyage back down the Nile to Cairo, he enjoyed being conveyed by the Canadian voyageurs: "I was as easy as if I had been in my arm-chair at home: and I shot the whole of those cataracts, in the whaler, in a little over 11 hours, without touching a single rock; going through many of the same channels as occupied me 13 days on the upward voyage" (Cook 1885, 22).

As Cook was seeking to extend his company's influence beyond Wadi Halfa, British troops amassed in Korosko (between the first and second cataracts) during December 1884 and awaited news from Gordon about the continuing siege of Khartoum. The famous "camel corps" planned to cross the desert into Khartoum, while the rest of the troops were organized into a river column that would follow John Mason Cook's route farther up the Nile bend and into Dongola. While the river column was hindered by low water levels and difficult cataracts, the camel corps were more successful and defeated the Mahdi's forces at the battle of Abu Klea. None of this mattered, of course, as Khartoum fell only a few days before the camel corps arrived: Gordon was killed on January 26, 1885, and with him went the raison d'être of the entire expedition. The British immediately pulled out of Sudan, and the debacle was widely understood to be instrumental in the downfall of Prime Minister Gladstone. Unsurprisingly, the fallout from the Gordon Relief Campaign also affected the relationship between Thomas Cook & Son and the British government. Despite communication from the secretary of state for war commending the firm on its satisfactory fulfillment of its contract, disputes soon arose as to whose responsibility it was to pay for all the damages that the steamers had accrued on the military expedition (Campbell-Bannerman 1928, 6). The acrimony was never satisfactorily resolved, and the firm's relations with the British military "ended on a sour note"—indeed, the dispute likely cost John Mason Cook his knighthood (Peter Smith, pers. comm., November 5–6, 2007; see also Hunter 2004, 40).

Adventures in Orientalism?

Although the Gordon Relief Campaign has become the subject of many famous histories, it has only been recently that the role of Thomas Cook & Son in the expedition has been critically analyzed. Following the Orientalist framework developed by Said and Mitchell, Thomas Cook & Son was simply another Imperial agency that, like the British military, reproduced a colonizer–colonized framework that consistently favored European interests. The firm's involvement with the Gordon Relief Campaign was simply one more example of its avid support for British territorial expansion in Egypt—support that eventually allowed John Mason Cook "to establish a tourist empire from Cairo to Khartoum" (Hunter 2004, 39, also 28–54; Hamilton 2005; Withey 1995):

> Cook was now seen as a symbol not only of British presence but of British power in and even British sovereignty over Egypt.... The services that Cook had provided for the Anglo-Egyptian campaigns helped to identify the company with the stability and security—the civil order—that had been achieved through the exercise of political and military power. (Gregory 2001, 128, 132)

What we can draw from these insights is that the relationship between the British military and Thomas Cook & Son was forged, justified, and managed within the prevailing geopolitical imaginary of empire in circulation at the time. Although Thomas Cook & Son and the British military managed different and quite oppositional practices (i.e., leisure travel and national security, respectively), they were both committed to fulfilling the desires and objectives of empire.

Reading the events of 1884–85 through the lens of Orientalism reveals how both the tourism industry and the British military colluded in the reproduction of colonial asymmetries, chief among them a prevailing notion of "civilization." Europeans were in possession of civilization and were in the process of bringing it to the rest of the world through military occupation and cultural practices such as tourism. For example, the *Times* (1895) reported that Cook's fleet of steamers along the Nile during 1884 was one of the principal means of "keeping up some show of civilization in the Equatorial Provinces." Similarly, military commentators hoped that the security provided by British troops in boats operated by a British firm would "have a very salutary effect on the mind of the people in the riverain villages, which will gradually filter into the interior of the country" (*Naval and Military Gazette* 1884, 477). This account of civilization came with an attending account of barbarity that was to be countered and conquered by whatever means possible. In reproducing this logic, colonial rulers objectified the landscapes, cultures, and peoples of Egypt and made them available for a variety of interventions and mobilizations. Thus, when barbarity was located *within* the boundaries of occupied Egypt and threatened occupational powers and/or tourist enjoyment (e.g., in nascent nationalist forces or dissenting groups), it was subject to colonial authority and violence. However, when such barbarity was located outside Egypt's boundaries (e.g., in Sudan), Egyptian resources, labor, and energies were mobilized in the service of Britain's colonial enterprise by helping to extend the boundaries of civilization more comprehensively into Africa. By "civilizing" Egypt and battling barbarous forces both within and outside its borders, British colonial forces secured the people, places, and cultures of the region and made them more fully available for the enjoyment of European tourists. One site at which tourist and military forces came together in the reproduction of civilization–barbarity during the Gordon Relief Campaign was at the second Nile cataract near the border with northern Sudan. This landscape was understood to be so formidable that it threatened to prevent not just the progress of the military relief mission to Khartoum but also the progress of tourists farther up the Nile into the much-desired wilderness of Nubia. The cataract was constructed, visualized, and represented as insurmountable: this was barbaric space that symbolized everything the British were fighting against. To conquer such formidable and dangerous rapids, British forces relied on their own scientific and logistical experts as well as imported modern technology (e.g., Cook's steamers and the Royal Navy whalers) and appropriated any local knowledge that enhanced their technoscientific approach. For example, in a number of newspaper sketches of the Gordon Relief Campaign in the *London Illustrated News* and the *Graphic,* the threatening, dangerous, and intimidating landscape of the second cataract was consistently juxtaposed with the superior scientific and technical knowledge of Imperial forces sent to tame it (i.e., the British military and Thomas Cook & Son).

This territorialization of barbaric landscapes by "civilized" European knowledge and technology was mirrored by the securing of Imperial subjectivities against a variety of Others. Within the geopolitical imaginary of empire, Europeans occupied what Pratt (1992, 201–27) has called the "monarch-of-all-I-survey" position—the embodiment of authority that holds the power of representation. As John Mason Cook (1885, 9) himself explained, it was the European's job to "cast the eyes of the master over all." This privileged viewpoint did not secure itself by rendering others invisible; rather, it garnered its power by producing, managing, and policing a number of complex differentiations of Otherness. Whereas the civilized (and civilizing) European masters were primarily marked out by their authority, superiority, and privileged viewpoint, Egyptian, Sudanese, and other migrant bodies were produced through many different gradations of Otherness and arranged through many different levels of subordination. The point, of course, is that the power to produce, arrange, and manage difference in Egypt in the 1880s always emanated from the privileged "monarch-of-all-I-survey" positions inhabited by a colonial elite (e.g., John Mason Cook, British military officers). Just as the foreign spaces of Egypt and northern Sudan were produced as dangerous in order to be conquered and tamed by superior European knowledge and expertise, a complex taxonomy of Others was produced to confirm which ones were more or less threatening to the Imperial project. Indeed, some Others were deemed suitable and, indeed, useful for the purposes of British colonial rule and thus included and given a position within an Imperial taxonomy (e.g., laborers, the army, middlemen), but many subjects were deemed too threatening, too destabilizing, or too unproductive and thus were actively excluded. John Mason Cook, for example, expressed the variety of ways in which European subjects understood the Others they encountered: on the one hand, they were able, loyal, gentle, pretty, intelligent, distinguished, powerful, sincere, and clever, and on the other hand, they were frightful, submissive, scared, superstitious, like cows "chewing their cud," and "particularly fiendish and gorilla-like" (Cook 1885, 11–12, 17, 21–24). British military leaders expressed similar contradictions about the Egyptian soldiers who were either brave, hardworking, and patriotic or, as Winston Churchill (1949, 12) argued, "distinguished for nothing but their public incapacity and private misbehavior":

> It was perhaps the worst army that has ever marched to war.... They had no spirit, no discipline, hardly any training, and in a force of over eight thousand men there were scarcely a dozen capable officers.... Everybody at that time distrusted the capacities of the Egyptians, and it was thought the evacuation might be accomplished if it were entrusted to stronger and more honest men than were bred by the banks of the Nile. (31–32, 38)

Whether working for Thomas Cook & Son or the British military, the colonial occupation ensured that the variety of Egyptian, Sudanese, and Other subjects were overwhelmingly produced by the imperial eyes of European occupiers.

While difference and subordination were always secured by Europeans, their productions were not always negative; to be sure, locals could be romanticized, deified, and desired just as they could be demonized, exploited, and killed. The multiplicity of those differentiations was nowhere more apparent than in the encounters between Thomas Cook & Son and the variety of local subjects the firm employed, including boat captains, guides, translators, hosts, porters, cooks, cleaners, and souvenir sellers. Certainly the presence of the firm in Egypt from 1869 onward transformed the country's economic landscape and labor demographics, but the treatment of these workers as they were brought into a labor market controlled by an Imperial power was a delicate balancing act. While the superiority of the master could never be in doubt, that hierarchy was secured most effectively by portraying laborers as grateful for the economic growth being generated by tourism because it supposedly made them wealthier. As an article from the *Cook's Excursionist* explained, "the natives [were] never more desirous of seeing the British and American travellers, and deriving benefit from the amounts of money they invariably circulate"

(Cook 1885b, 3). More importantly, the British values of civility ensured that unlike Egyptian employers, Thomas Cook & Son would pay their workers "fairly." As John Mason Cook explained in 1885,

> to work these [steamers] we had a little army of our own of about 5,000 men and boys, consisting of the fellaheen of Lower Egypt, and I want to take this opportunity of confirming what I said at the War Office before this expedition started—that I know of no men who could and would work to the same extent and as willingly as the native fellaheen are, constantly working from sunrise to sunset. All they ask for is fair pay and fair treatment [applause] and not to have every piastre they earned, and every ounce of blood in their bodies taken from them by the rapacious Sheikhs and those in power. (9)

The last sentence reveals much about the racial and civilizational taxonomy at work in colonial Egypt: Cook positions his company as part of a *benevolent* governing force whose values of civility and fairness make it infinitely superior to the more corrupt indigenous possibilities and therefore actively welcomed by the Egyptian people.

The Gordon Relief Campaign exemplifies the multiple registers through which difference and hierarchy were secured within the architecture of empire. Certainly the British Imperial gaze can be understood as exclusive and racist: it embodied clear norms and values of civilization, stipulated which subjects could climb the progressive ladder of civilization (i.e., only white Europeans could reach the top), and secured that hierarchy by punishing internal dissent and defending itself against dangerous external threats such as the Mahdi in Sudan. But even when its project of bringing civilization, progress, and enlightenment to the barbarians was framed in more inclusive and progressive terms (e.g., trying to stop the slave trade, increasing national revenue from tourism), the British Imperial gaze constantly positioned local subjects in subordinate positions (e.g., "abject" and in need of help or "grateful" for employment and remuneration). What the Gordon Relief Campaign reveals is the extent to which Thomas Cook & Son and British military forces worked jointly to secure the geopolitical imaginary of empire through a progressive hierarchy of difference that rendered subjects in various states of subordination and secured that inequality by producing an exceptional external threat that had to be collectively opposed. Thus loyal, hardworking, and submissive local subjects were permitted to climb the ladder of civilization and occupy a number of endorsed positions within that hierarchy (e.g., servants, employees, lovers, guides), whereas the Sudanese barbarians threatening Egypt's borders were dismissed as simply a "debased and cruel breed" (Churchill 1949, 12, 8).[1]

Heterogeneous Productions of Empire

Reading the events of the Gordon Relief Campaign in 1884–85 in terms of civilization and barbarity is important because it foregrounds how European colonial rulers secured their superior position over local spaces, subjects, and populations. Despite acknowledging the many different ways that Otherness was produced to secure such colonial privilege, there is no sense in which that privilege was ever troubled, disrupted, or unmoored from its hierarchical foundations. In short, it suggests that the Imperial project was both overdetermined and monolithic even though relationships between Egypt and its colonial rulers in the latter part of the nineteenth century "were not the result of any transcendent logic or design" (Gregory 2001, 115). Instead, encounters between subjects in colonial space are better understood as unstable performances: at times they bolster the grids of power and knowledge underscoring empire, but the assumed subjects and spaces of those encounters are never completely captured or controlled. As Gregory (2001, 115–16) suggests, even within the most overdetermined colonial spaces, subjects always operate within *heterogeneous networks* and are therefore best understood through "a complex, foliated space of agency" rather than a strict colonizer–colonized dichotomy (see also Pratt 1992). While never losing sight of the very real and entrenched asymmetries that colonial rule produced, Gregory (2001; see also Gregory 1999; 2003) foregrounds the complex, multifaceted, and mobile aspects of empire through which visitors on Cook's tours envisioned Egypt. He acknowledges that European visitors may have "seen" Egypt within a well-established and familiar tourist gaze and goes on to argue that their encounters within that gaze always exceeded, disrupted, and subverted a reductive colonizer–colonized framework (115–16). To this end, Gregory demonstrates how locals and European travelers were consistently negotiating the spaces within which they encountered one another—especially aboard *dahabeahs* and steamers—and how those negotiations shaped the way that Europeans saw and framed Egypt.[2]

Gregory's intervention creates a productive space from which to critique Orientalist readings of tourism in colonial Egypt. It shows that positioning subjects in the role of either colonizer or colonized cannot account for the multifaceted encounters that took place between Thomas Cook & Son, tourists, and locals at this time. Starting within this critical space offered by Gregory, I want to push the argument in two directions. First, the concepts of "foliated agency" and "heterogeneous network" must also be applied to the military occupation of Egypt as well as the tourist economy to acknowledge that military personnel constituted a significant proportion of those subjects engaged in manifold encounters during the Gordon Relief Campaign (Ek 2000, 865). Indeed, the complex and multifaceted encounters that took place between European tourists and locals—the encounters described so well by Gregory and Hazbun—were also taking place between British soldiers, British officers, local Egyptians, Sudanese, and other migrant populations. Second, the material and nonhuman registers within the concepts of "foliated agency" and "heterogeneous network" must be foregrounded more clearly and forcefully.

Figure 4 is a sketch by *London Illustrated News* artist Melton Prior that represents one of Cook's requisitioned tourist vessels (a *dahabeah*) transporting camels up the Nile for the camel corps's departure to rescue Gordon. It is difficult to see how this scene could be read through an Orientalist framework in which the colonizer's superiority is always assured over those who are colonized. Indeed, it is unclear who, if anyone, is in charge of the operation—certainly not the small military figure under the camel's head, pointing ineffectually in the direction he wants the camel to go. The scene is constructed through an opposition between action and spectatorship: on the one hand, British soldiers and Egyptian laborers struggling in vain to move the camels onto dry land and, on the other hand, a series of spectators to this folly—the villagers watching from the hilltop, the camels and soldiers who have already alighted and are watching the efforts of their struggling colleagues, and crucially, the languid turbaned figure at the front and center of the image, resting on his waiting camel and watching the mayhem unfolding. The power relations here are inverted and confused: the authority of the Imperial power is undermined not just by the recalcitrant camels but also by the two figures on the right—a British soldier and an Egyptian or Sudanese laborer—who are working together. Indeed, the British soldier seems to have realized that the laborer's habit of bare feet and legs works rather better than military-issue leather boots. This is not an example of how an imperial power's superior scientific and technical knowledge is able to pacify foreign terrain or discipline uncivilized natives—quite the opposite. Power does not rest with those pursuing a course of action here (the British soldiers struggling with the camel)—it rests with the spectators looking on, including newspaper audiences looking at the image in January 1885. I want to argue that Prior's sketch visualizes a heterogeneous network in which different human subjects (British and Egyptian soldiers, Egyptian and Sudanese laborers, villagers, newspaper readers) negotiate with each other in an effort to harness and manage nonhuman forms (camels, boats, the Nile, the shoreline). Here the foliated space of agency is extended to material objects (the boat), natural obstacles (the river, the shore), nonhuman creatures (camels), and a surrounding atmosphere of frustration and impatience. Rather than visualizing how colonial rule is executed through institutional hierarchies and clear expertise, this sketch—perhaps inadvertently—reveals the contingent, complex, and heterogeneous nature of the colonial enterprise and its reliance on a series of constitutive human–nonhuman relations. For example, the figures with the most agency in this sketch—those able to determine and shape action by their stubborn recalcitrance—are the camels. Paying close attention to the material and nonhuman forces that shape colonial experience is an important effort to subvert the "master-of-all-I-survey" subject position usually assumed by imperial powers (in this case, British soldiers on the Gordon Relief Campaign). Indeed, including material and nonhuman forms in the "foliated space of agency" extends the scope of heterogeneity outside of anthropocentric coordinates and therefore generates multiple sites of possible reordering and resistance.

 Pursuing the concept of heterogeneity in the postcolonial field means paying attention to the complex entanglements between colonial forces—

FIGURE 4. Melton Prior, *Sending Camels across the Nile at Dongala*, London Illustrated News, January 3, 1885.

in this case tourist and military populations—that sometimes align in their reproduction of empire, but sometimes inadvertently recalibrate it through less hierarchical registers. Reimagining the events of 1884–85 as an experience of profound heterogeneity dislodges the hierarchical institutional framing that consistently positioned Thomas Cook & Son within the prior and more pressing concerns of the British military. Indeed, it is usually assumed that Thomas Cook & Son was entirely beholden to the British military—that the firm "could not have realized its goal of implanting a tourist structure on the banks of the Nile" (Hunter 2004, 33) without the guarantee of the British "envelope of security within which they were accustomed to moving" (Gregory 2001, 119).

However, when we look closely at the activities of British soldiers on the Gordon Relief Campaign, we notice a number of key reorderings in which they relinquished their security duties and engaged in multiple practices of tourism. Likewise, when we look closely at the operations of Thomas Cook & Son during the same campaign, we see that their commercial ethos often trumped the supposedly overriding strategic concerns of the British military. Indeed, the firm encouraged tourism throughout the winter season of the Gordon expedition, and John Mason Cook's own journey to Dongala in December 1884 was an effort to prove that he knew the region better than the British military officers. If we understand colonial Egypt through a heterogeneous network in which foliated agency includes both human and nonhuman actors, we are able to think more carefully about the detailed micropolitical registers through which the geopolitical imaginary of empire manifests itself. More specifically, such an approach allows us to trace the extent to which the practices of tourism and warfare are governed by that imaginary and the extent to which they reordered and subverted it. I am particularly interested in the everyday, mundane, and routine practices engaged in by multiple populations, for example, the serendipitous itineraries of tourists, the institutional decisions of military officers, the drills and routines of soldiers, the entrepreneurial bartering of locals, the rhythms and routes of laborers, and the navigations of migrant workers. How did these practices relate to one another? What new asymmetries did they produce, and how were subjugated bodies enrolled into the service of privileged orbits of action? More to the point, how did the practices of tourism and soldiering relate to one another and jointly to the "foreign" environment they moved through, in a condition where the British Empire was riven with fractures and slowly disintegrating?

Soldier-Tourists: Leisure Practices in the Gordon Relief Campaign

By the time the Gordon Relief Campaign began in September 1884, Thomas Cook & Son had been established in Egypt for fifteen years. As more and more middle-class people were making the journey out to Egypt themselves, those remaining in Britain were exposed to numerous sketches, paintings, photographs, newspaper stories, novels, guidebooks, postcards, and travelers' accounts about Egypt. This familiarity meant that the British officers and soldiers who traveled south for the Gordon Relief Campaign in 1884 were accustomed to the dominant British construction of Egypt and called upon it to make sense of the foreign surroundings in which they found themselves stationed. Thomas Cook & Son were, of course, central to Egypt's currency within British public culture at the time and were the primary institution producing and maintaining Egypt as a desirable place to visit. Both Thomas Cook and his son John Mason understood that the soldiers and officers serving throughout the British Empire—including in Egypt—were also a captive tourist market who would want to see the sights while off duty:

> After the opening of the Suez Canal (1869) Thomas Cook added army personnel serving in the Middle East and Asia to his growing list of clients. In his "Excursionist" magazine he advertises himself as an Army Agency and notes that he has "a register of Forward bookings and groups gentlemen and members of the Military and Civil Service together in new and improved second-class cabins on the P&O Company's vessels." The ordinary soldier as well as officers took advantage of Cook's excursion arrangements in the Holy Land and Egypt on their way to their posts east of Suez. From India, too, there were trips to Malaysia, Australia and New Zealand for soldiers on leave. The Cook's banking services, which include current accounts as well as travellers Cheques and Foreign Exchange was also much used by those in the service of Empire. (Thomas Cook & Son 1884)

The Gordon Relief Campaign was characterized by longer than usual delays and holdups both before and after the actual fighting. British troops already stationed in Egypt in 1884 waited day after day as Gordon's pleading from Khartoum fell on deaf ears in Gladstone's cabinet. As the British government deliberated from January until September 1884 over whether they would actually send a rescue expedition, resident and arriving troops took advantage of Thomas Cook & Son's already well-established tourist infrastructure as they waited for their instructions to travel up the Nile and rescue Gordon. As journalists reported at the time, many British officers were seen "lounging about Shepherd's Hotel in Cairo awaiting orders and incurring bills which run as high as $300 a week," as regular soldiers went on official tourist excursions: "The soldiers of the Guard regiments and the members of the camel corps before they started south were taken to see the pyramids and the Sphynx. It was a gigantic pleasure trip and no doubt the cost to England will be as pyramidical as was the picnic" (*New York Times* 1884, 7).[3] Figure 5 depicts British soldiers on one such organized tour.

These sightseeing escapades ordered the soldiers and officers within an extant tourist itinerary that brought British military personnel into direct

FIGURE 5. Troops on the Sphinx, circa 1882. Photograph by Otto Herschan.

contact with a variety of local subjects oriented to servicing the tourist economy (e.g., cooks, cleaners, porters, barmen, vendors, magicians, entertainers, tour guides, translators, horse and buggy drivers, souvenir sellers). Indeed, Figure 5 shows a number of Egyptian subjects—likely guides, middlemen, and Sherpas—within a half-staged group portrait (Osman 1997, 72–73). These encounters varied depending on military rank; for example, officers were stationed at the famous Shepheard's Hotel and thus situated at the heart of the British tourist experience (which included the Gezira Sporting Club and the ice cream parlor at Gropies), whereas regular soldiers were stationed outside of this circuit and therefore had very different tourist experiences (Dumper and Stanley 2006, 112). Shepheard's Hotel is absolutely central to the intersecting practices of tourists and soldiers during the Gordon Relief Campaign. Well before the British took official control of Egypt in 1882, it was established as the social, cultural, and political hub of British presence in the region; indeed, as Annabel Jane Wharton (2001, 44) argues, for more than a century, "Shepheard's was perhaps the most consistent site of elite Western patronage in Cairo."

FIGURE 6. Front terrace of Shepheard's Hotel, circa 1885. Photograph by Gabriel Lekegian. Courtesy of the Middle East Department, The University of Chicago Library.

Situated at the heart of Cairo's European quarter, Shepheard's Hotel overlooked the famous Azbakiyyah Gardens, which "filled nightly with Egyptians of every rank and race" and provided guests—including British officers—with "an 'Arabian Nights Entertainment': improvised for them always without care and without cost" (Edwin de Leon, as quoted in Wharton 2001, 44–45). Figure 6, by Turkish photographer Gabriel Lekegian, was taken in approximately 1885 and depicts the famous front terrace of Shepheard's Hotel, where privileged guests sitting in their wicker chairs had the perfect vantage point to indulge their "monarch-of-all-I-survey" position and from where "the Other was readily available, close enough to hear, smell and touch, as well as see" (Wharton 2001, 45).

Of course the front terrace of Shepheard's was also a place to be *seen*—not just by Egyptians but, more importantly, by other Europeans. Thus, while Egyptian life passed before the seated subjects like a theater scene (and while Egyptians served them food and drink as they watched the exotic spectacle unfold), European tourists and British military officers were on display for themselves, for each other, and for the surrounding milieu. While the asymmetries of position and privilege seem stark on the terrace of Shepheard's Hotel, this was no colonial panopticon of surveillance; rather, it was a more complex ordering of visuality, spatiality, and materiality. The famous terrace produced multiple intersecting gazes, a number of identity performances, varying displays of status, diverse trajectories of movement (e.g., those passing by on the street) and passivity (e.g., those seated on the terrace), and many crossover moments in which the lifeworlds of the street came into the hotel, and vice versa. What the rather gentle visual displays of Shepheard's terrace obscure, of course, are the many other encounters that took place backstage and out of sight, where the asymmetries of colonial rule were more extreme and less ambiguous. To be sure, those asymmetries permeated the internal organization of the hotel itself as the deployment of Shepheard's staff in front or back of house was marked by a clear racial hierarchy. However, it was in the red-light district directly behind Shepheard's Hotel, in the cafés, dance halls, taverns, and brothels, that lured European tourists and British military personnel into the "dangerous Orient," that the more violent intersections of tourism and armed occupation made themselves felt. Even though this area of Cairo was undoubtedly an urban heterotopia marked by various orderings and disorderings, it was nonetheless framed by the racial hierarchy of empire: the Wagh-al Birkah district housed European and foreign prostitutes (and was thus frequented by European tourists and British officers), whereas the adjacent Harat el Wasser district housed Egyptian, Nubian, and Sudanese prostitutes (and was thus frequented by regular British infantry and Egyptian soldiers) (Biancani 2012, 92–93; Fahmy 2002; Kuhnkhe 1990). It is here, in the urban spaces behind the sanitized facade of Shepheard's Hotel, that an important mode of governmentality was established that ordered and managed the everyday micropolitical and intimate encounters between tourists, soldiers, prostitutes, and locals.

As British military personnel waited in Cairo throughout 1884 for the Gordon Relief Campaign to be organized, their bodies—along with those of tourists, prostitutes, pimps, brothel owners, police officers, doctors, and nurses—become enrolled in, and governed by, a biopolitical apparatus of public health and social hygiene. Two years previously—just fifteen days after the British took over Egypt in 1882—a law was passed that regulated prostitution in Cairo (Biancani 2012, 163). Modeled on the French system of legalized prostitution, this law was about protecting the bodies of troops from venereal disease (VD) so they could remain productive soldiers in the service of empire: it was certainly *not* about protecting the bodies of local and migrant prostitutes.[4] Indeed, the colonial administration in Egypt held prostitutes responsible for sexually transmitted diseases (STDs) and their transmission, and thus it was *their* bodies—and not the bodies of British soldiers—that were subject to routine genital examinations, forced treatment for STDs, and weekly sanitary inspections to be issued with a health certificate so they could continue providing sexual services. This is a classic example of what Michael Brown has called "venereal biopower": the multiple techniques of government that operate through public and sexual health programs that render bodies (specifically the sexual desires and behaviors of bodies) and populations more knowable, more targetable, more governable, and thus more available for intervention (Brown 2009; Brown and Knopp 2010). Because this manifestation of venereal biopower was operative in a colonial context, it did not disaggregate or intervene in all bodies or populations equally (Walther 2013). Rather, the distinctions between normal and deviant bodies unleashed by efforts to control VD in Cairo during the Gordon Relief Campaign reproduced the prevailing understandings of gender, class, race, and sexuality that permeated the Imperial project. The bodies of the most disempowered (i.e., the Egyptian, Nubian, and Sudanese prostitutes servicing regular infantry in the Harat el Wasser district) were subject to more violence, more interventions, and more surveillance than the bodies of privileged subjects (i.e., European tourists and British military personnel). The regulation of prostitution in late-nineteenth-century Egypt was not just about systematic, state-sanctioned and institutionally organized interventions in the bodies of women for the purposes of maintaining healthy troops; it also changed the fabric of the city and the architecture of its governance. For example, colonial anxieties about sexual disease led to the construction of new hospitals and centers capable of administering

STD checks and to the development of a professional class (e.g., doctors, nurses, lawyers, police officers) able to manage the micropolitical interventions into the intimate lives of its inhabitants and visitors. The city itself became more spatially segregated as the red-light districts behind Shepheard's Hotel were further delimited from other, more salubrious parts of the city where "proper" tourists circulated (e.g., the promenades around Azbakiyyah Gardens). By framing the red-light districts behind Shepheard's Hotel as delimited areas of "vice," officials were able to justify increased surveillance and legal, medical, and police interventions as protecting "Cairo proper" from the "dangerous" characters made famous in tales of the "Dark Orient" (e.g., pimps, criminals, mercenaries, drug dealers, madams). By the time the Gordon Relief Campaign was under way in 1884, British soldiers and officers had already been interpellated into a city that regulated, spatialized, and contained their movements within an existing tourist infrastructure. Their off-duty time away from military training and preparation was structured by a well-established tourist economy that contained their explorations of Cairo and its famous surrounding landmarks within a well-trodden beaten path that offered now familiar performances of colonial encounter. Because the sexual escapades of military personnel behind the Shepheard's Hotel represented the most potential to deviate from those pre-scripted encounters, they became the subject of intense regulation, surveillance, and control.

The touristic framing of military life continued as soldiers and officers finally departed from Cairo and traveled up the Nile on Thomas Cook & Son steamers. Army diaries of the time exemplify the genre of colonial travelogues; for example, Lieutenant Colonel F. C. Denison records his arrival in Luxor and his visit to the home of the British Consul on the evening of October 16, 1884:

> On the way up, he showed me by the light of two lanterns the temple of Luxor. It is a magnificent pile of massive stones that have stood for 4000 years covered in many places with Hieroglyphics looking as perfect as ever. We saw a needle about 70 feet high erected by one of the Pharaohs, it is in a perfect state of preservation. I called on the Consul a Capt: and he kindly gave me a necklace taken from a mummy and asked me to put my name in his visitor's book. (Denison 1959a, 101–2)

THE DOUBLE VISION OF EMPIRE 53

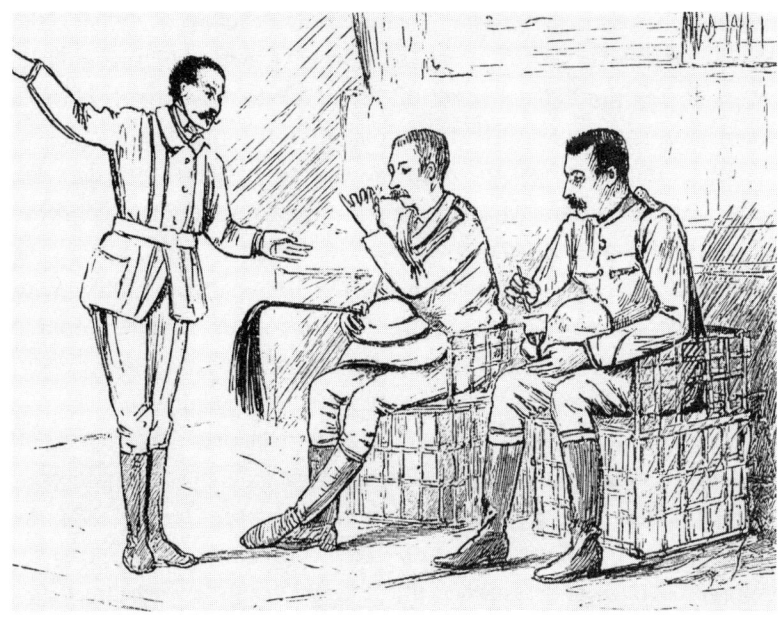

FIGURE 7. Frederic Villiers, *Cigarettes and Lemonade at the Temple of Cleopatra*, *Graphic*, November 15, 1884.

Similarly, Colonel Percival Marling, who led the camel corps at the battle of Abu Klea, wrote of a "lovely night under the palms with a full moon" and even engaged in a spot of recreational hunting (Marling 1936, 151). Because the colonial tourist infrastructure was already well entrenched along the Nile, the soldiers and officers traveling to rescue General Gordon slipped in and out of military and touristic dispositions—one moment actively strategizing the best way to conquer this foreign territory, the next moment passively observing the exotic landscapes, cultures, and antiquities on display. Touristic interludes on the journey up the Nile were frequent and often extended; for example, a sketch from the *Graphic* from November 1884 (Figure 7) shows British officers taking *Cigarettes and Lemonade in the Temple of Cleopatra* as a tour guide explains the relevant antiquities on display.

The slippage between military and touristic dispositions created multiple and sometimes contradictory ways of seeing Egypt: it was simultaneously a threatening colonial battleground *and* a coveted tourist destination, and Egyptians were simultaneously fellow soldiers on the Relief Campaign *as well as* exotic Others either facilitating tourist activities or "on display" for a colonizing tourist gaze. What the experience of these soldier-tourists suggests is that their raison d'être for being in Egypt—to rescue Gordon and fight the Mahdi—was constantly disrupted by the seductions of tourism. More to the point, such vacillations of purpose created important moments in which the heterogeneity of Egyptian space (especially the urban landscape of Cairo) could be articulated with greater force, and the subjects encountering each other upon that diverse terrain were able to express a more "foliated space of agency" that disaggregated, fractured, and dispersed a strict colonizer–colonized logic.

The polyvocal account of empire called forth by the soldier-tourists on the Gordon Relief Campaign was especially prominent in the experiences of a particular group of men who arrived in Egypt in October 1884: the 386 Canadian voyageurs in charge of conveying British and Egyptian soldiers across the cataracts in specially designed Royal Navy whaling boats. General Wolseley, who was in charge of the Nile expedition, remembered the expertise of the voyageurs from his previous assignment suppressing the Red River Rebellion in Manitoba in 1870 and hired them to help navigate the Nile cataracts. The voyageurs were gathered from Manitoba, Ontario, and Quebec; set sail from Halifax in mid-September 1884; landed in Alexandria in early October; and started work on the cataracts as soon as they reached Wadi Halfa on October 26, 1884 (Stacey 1959, 1–54; see also Boileau 2004; MacLachlan 1983; MacLaren 1978). These men were hired first and foremost as laborers with particular skills and expertise: they were not hired as soldiers and therefore did not wear uniforms and did not engage in battle. The voyageurs were not equivalent to the Egyptian and Sudanese laborers who facilitated the Relief Campaign—they were, it seems, in a different category altogether. Although they were hired for their river navigation skills, they were also valued for their loyalty to the British Empire that had been demonstrated in their earlier willingness to transport the British military across eastern Canada to quash Louis Riel's Métis rebellion. This rather in-between position meant that relations between the voyageurs and the British military were not always straightforward. As English lieutenant colonel Coleridge Grove remarked, "their manner was rough, and they were not disposed to take orders from anyone whose position they did not know. But when they understood that the officer—whoever he might be—had the right to give orders, they obeyed very willingly" (Grove 1959). As highly skilled laborers hired to assist in a military campaign, the voyageurs had to negotiate a number of competing forces—sometimes working in tandem with British soldiers to facilitate the strategic goals of the Gordon Relief Campaign, sometimes asserting their expertise to reorient those goals (e.g., when the cataracts impeded progress), and sometimes using their nonmilitary position as valued laborers to distance themselves from the campaign altogether.

Throughout these negotiations, the voyageurs confronted the complex racial taxonomy that underscored the British Imperial project. The majority of the voyageurs were white English and French Canadians, and it is not difficult to see how these subjects may have reproduced prevailing racial categories during their encounters with locals in Egypt and Sudan. Certainly terms like *nuggers* and *fuzzy-wuzzies* are commonplace in all accounts of the campaign, but there are also more subtle differentiations at work when the "superior" skills of the voyageurs are distanced from the "unskilled" work of the local Egyptians (Stacey 1959, 116). What is interesting here is that the overtly racist taxonomies underscoring empire were troubled by the presence of seventy-seven Canadian "Indians" in the voyageur party. This group had its own chosen foreman—Chief William Prince from Manitoba—and it included members of the Iroquois, Saultaux, Caughnawaga, Oka, and Métis tribes. While these seventy-seven individuals certainly would have been framed by the racial categories central to both the founding of Canada in 1867 and the maintenance of the British Empire, their presence on the Gordon Relief Campaign points to the constant disruption and excess of such categories and the transnational and heterogeneous networks that constituted the British Empire in the late nineteenth century (Blackhouse 1999; Henry and Tator 1999). Although all the voyageurs negotiated competing forces and authorities, these seventy-seven "Indians" had to confront the racialized nature of the colonial project more directly. Did their superior expertise at river navigation and boat handling make them equal to their fellow English and French Canadian countrymen? Or were they subject to further racial differentiation that aligned them more clearly with subordinated Egyptian soldiers and Sudanese laborers? How did these seventy-seven "Indians" make sense of their own position amid this odd assemblage of Imperial subjects, transport infrastructure, transnational labor relations, and occupied space, and how were they seen by fellow voyageurs, Canadian superiors, British military personnel, Egyptian soldiers, and Sudanese laborers?

When the Canadian voyageurs arrived back in Cairo in January 1885, a specially organized tourist expedition to the pyramids and the Sphinx was organized for them (Denison 1959b). General Stephenson, British commander in Lower Egypt, presided over the voyageurs' tour and brought with him fifty "English Ladies" on horseback to make up the party. Adding gender into this already heady mix of race, power, and empire, one account of the tour explains, "The Pyramids looked down on a meeting of two worlds that afternoon; and no doubt the English officers' wives and the rough boatmen from Caughnawaga and Three Rivers regarded one another with interest" (Stacey 1959, 31). This afternoon event is telling because it demonstrates how the voyageurs—especially the seventy-seven "Indians"—were situated within, and thus had to negotiate, complex and competing modes of governance. Primarily, they were produced and secured within a colonial military apparatus; after all, the reason they were treated to such an expedition in the first place was because they had successfully served a military campaign at the behest of the British Empire. But the voyageurs were also produced and secured within a prevailing tourism infrastructure that positioned the Sphinx and pyramids as desirable attractions and provided them with a cultural experience more common to middle-class holiday makers from Europe and America. As the voyageurs negotiated these crisscrossed frames of reference, they became the subject of another gaze altogether—that of the fifty "English Ladies" on horseback. The articulations of gender, race, and class in this encounter are dizzying: the "English Ladies" may have been able to express their own racial and class superiority upon their mounts, but too often that was at the expense of their own gendered and sexual freedom. As for the voyageurs, their ambivalent status as expert laborers imported from another colonial scene, and their immediate status as soldier-tourists, was now objectified by a feminine gaze that complicated power relations even further. The women and the voyageurs shared the status of being foreigners in Egypt, but the women's elevated socioeconomic status (secured by their position on horseback) would have simultaneously foregrounded the voyageurs' status as laborers but also challenged their usually privileged masculinity. For me, this afternoon interlude in January 1885 in which fifty "English Ladies on horseback" gazed down upon the voyageurs during an organized tour to the Sphinx exemplifies the impossibility of understanding empire through a simple logic of colonizer-colonized. The scene—the blending of soldiering and sightseeing—doesn't allow the binary to hold as the voyageurs and the English ladies continually circulate between both positions.

The tourist experiences enjoyed by the voyageurs in Cairo continued as they were conveyed home to Canada. Lieutenant Colonel Denison's diary reports that the group stopped at Marseilles for a spot of tourism, during which they visited the Palais Longchamp art gallery and purchased a number of souvenirs.[5] In London awaiting his own return to Toronto, Denison himself embodied the late-nineteenth-century urban tourist: he attended a service at Westminster Abbey, saw the Trooping of the Colors, dined out and attended the theater several times, went shopping for souvenirs, visited the Royal Academy to see some art, and took in some horse racing (Stacey 1959, 140–44). These continuations suggest that the strange collision between tourism and military strategy along the Nile in 1884–85 was not unique to the space of colonial Egypt. I want to suggest that the multiple, variegated, and ineffable experiences of soldier-tourists along the Nile in 1884–85 brought with them new relations, desires, and possibilities. Though the slippage between soldiering and tourism may have reinforced the asymmetrical coordinates of empire, it also contained within it a number of countervailing and puzzling encounters that revealed the heterogeneous circuits of agency and materiality that constituted occupied Egypt.

Tourist-Soldiers: The Militarization of Colonial Travel

It would be easy to think that mass tourism to Egypt stopped completely during the Gordon Relief Campaign, especially as Cook's steamers were now out of action for tourist purposes. Such a claim would confirm the prevailing understanding that tourist desires and practices were automatically subordinated to the strategic agenda of the British military, but this was not the case. By late summer 1884, the exotic appeal of Nile antiquities was too powerful for travelers to resist: there was no way European tourists were going to stop their journeys just to make way for a military skirmish in an adjacent country. This enduring touristic desire forced Thomas Cook & Son into a rather contradictory position during the long buildup and eventual fallout of the Gordon Relief Campaign. On the one hand, the firm facilitated a military campaign that would necessarily reduce the amount of tourism on the Nile (and thus reduce company revenue); but on the other hand, the firm continued to promote tourism along the Nile to maintain its customers' desire to see Egyptian antiquities. October to March was the most popular season for British travelers in Egypt and the Holy Lands, and every September, Thomas Cook & Son produced a dedicated advertising campaign for this purpose. The relevant sections on Egypt and the Nile in *Cook's Excursionist* magazine from September 1884 to December 1885 make for bizarre reading as they show how the firm itself—despite its official and well-publicized actions in aid of the British government—was unwilling to subordinate its popular tours to the dictates of military strategy.

Thomas Cook & Son took every opportunity to remind readers of the firm's patriotic role in the Gordon Relief Campaign. *Cook's Excursionist* magazine went to great lengths to reassure potential passengers that Nile tourism was still possible despite actions in neighboring Sudan (Cook 1884c, 3). Thus, as the firm was busy fulfilling its military contract, and as Wolesley's soldiers were traveling to northern Sudan on Cook's steamers, the November 1884 edition of *Cook's Excursionist* offered the following reassurance to potential travelers:

> From the inquiries we are having we are convinced that a number of intending passengers are simply waiting for the usual travelling resources to be placed at their disposal, to make tours of short or long description into Upper Egypt.... For the information of eastern travellers we may say that *Egypt was never more open for tourist traffic than at the present moment. All parts may be visited without the slightest difficulty or danger,* and as soon as the steamers commence running, we expect a considerable traffic. (Cook 1884b, 4, emphasis added)

The magazine continually repeated these reassurances, claiming that "there is not anything in the present state of the country to interfere with or prevent travellers from visiting all the chief points of interest between Cairo and the First or Second Cataracts" and that, despite the military use of the steamers, it was still possible to arrange a tourist voyage on "the best Dahabeahs on the Nile, which can be hired at moderate rates" (Cook 1885c, 3; 1884a, 3). Amid this complex maneuvering, John Mason Cook began to lay the groundwork for the Sudanese battlefields to become an important stop on future Cook's Nile Tours. He realized very quickly that Egypt was "rendered more than ever attractive to Englishmen by the military operations in the interior" (Cook 1884a, 3). Trying to put a positive spin on the continuing presence of the military in such a popular (and lucrative) holiday destination, *Cook's Excursionist* magazine confirmed that the tourist trade was actually thriving as a result of the military's presence in Egypt:

> The retention of British troops at Cairo and at various points on the Nile, has naturally had a stimulating effect upon passenger traffic between Great Britain and Egypt. Not only have the officers of those troops numerous friends desirous of paying a visit during the winter months, but the present state of Egypt, combined with the security always imparted by the presence of English soldiers, conduces to the conviction that the country is once more open to tourist travel. At the present moment, there is not anything in the position of political or military affairs in Egypt to interfere in the slightest degree with travellers between the Mediterranean and the First and Second Cataracts of the Nile. (Cook 1885a, 3)

While John Mason Cook was privately engaging in serious contractual disputes with the British government over who would pay for the damaged steamers, he was publicly welcoming his new customer base, which consisted of arriving British soldiers as well as their visiting friends and family.

It might appear that the "extraordinary self-confidence and assertiveness of most travellers" (Gregory 2001, 119) visiting Egypt throughout the Gordon Relief Campaign, and Thomas Cook & Son's efforts to encourage such custom, reveals a disregard for the seriousness of the conflict. This was certainly true of John Mason Cook himself, whose decision to keep traveling up the Nile in December 1884 required much more than just "self-confidence and assertiveness." Rather, his adventure was an extended effort to "play soldier" with his son Albert and to prove to the British military that he was better at organizing transport logistics than they were. Cook's desire for some kind of military legitimacy can be discerned in his Victorian portrait, painted circa 1890 (Figure 8). At first glance, this is Cook as a quintessential Victorian explorer: he is conquering exotic landscapes strategically (through the map that lies open on his lap) and visually (through his binoculars). In short, these are the "eyes of the master" surveying the empire he has helped to create and control. But what is most interesting about this portrait of Cook is its military framing: his safari suit is very similar to the khaki uniforms many soldiers in the British army wore during the Gordon Relief Campaign, and the relaxed but formal pose is not unlike many military portraits of the era.[6] Cook's sartorial choice and comportment express a desire for military legitimacy, but his account of the journey he took to Dongala in December 1884 as the troops amassed in Wadi Halfa suggests a more complex set of relations with the British military apparatus. On the one hand, he had to appear patriotic to his public so they would continue to use his firm's services, but on the other hand, he was intent on critiquing the British military's logistical and organizational decisions on the Gordon Relief Campaign. By positioning himself—rather than a military man—as the most competent person to navigate the Nile in northern Sudan, John Mason Cook simultaneously justified the British military's decision to hire his private company to do its work and revealed the military's inability to order, manage, and control the far reaches of its empire.

John Mason Cook comes across as a rather paternal figure in his 1885 travelogue, keen to indulge his seventeen-year-old son, who "was fired by the idea that if any Englishmen went to Khartoum, he would go also," while also reminding his audience (who dutifully applaud his sentiment) that he would have made the trip earlier himself had he not had so many important obligations to his existing and potential customers (Cook 1885, 9–10). This paternalism is artfully constructed, and there are many moments of benevolence and generosity demonstrated to those who help him on his way (e.g., his dragoman, the crew, the British soldiers of the Staffordshire Regiment) (11–14, 17–20, 29). But Cook's narrative also

FIGURE 8. Portrait of John Mason Cook, circa 1890. Courtesy of Charles Temple-Richards and the family of John Mason Cook.

legitimates his critique of the British military: his fifteen years' experience in the country meant that he knew Egypt and the Egyptians better than any military man did, and such knowledge meant that he was the only man capable of organizing the logistics of the Gordon Relief Campaign. Cook's confidence as a businessman facilitating a military expedition on foreign soil turned him, effectively, into a tourist-soldier who navigated, mapped, and opened the Upper Nile for the British military *and* for his firm's future expansion into Sudan. For example, he was adamant that the two navy men previously sent to map the region failed in their task because they ignored the changing seasonal water levels of the Nile—a mistake Cook would never make (8). His decision to continue on beyond Wadi Halfa in December 1884 in advance of the British troops, and to provide the British military with accurate maps of this previously uncharted section of the Nile, enabled Cook to demonstrate that his geopolitical knowledge was actually better than anything the military could offer themselves.

Cook's confidence—and indeed his arrogance—in presuming that he knew better than the British military permeated his entire voyage along the Nile. At the Dal cataract, Cook *knew* that they must take advantage of the available wind to traverse the rapids and thus disobeyed direct military orders from the presiding commandant to wait until the wind died down (17–18). By the time he arrived in Dongala, his superiority over military decision making was once again expressed when the Mudir offered to send him on to Khartoum with an escort:

> I have met with a great many singular circumstances, but this seemed the most astonishing I had ever met with. If I would rest there a fortnight he would send me to Khartoum! Here was England spending a few millions to rescue Gordon from Khartoum, and here was a gentleman who offered to send me there in a fortnight. (25)

Never mind that Thomas Cook & Son was the recipient of a large chunk of those millions being spent by England; John Mason Cook implies here that the military would be more successful—and more efficient—by following his lead. Emboldened by his success at navigating up the Nile farther than any military man had been able to do, Cook took it upon himself to engage in diplomacy on behalf of the government. Predicting the immanent evacuation of Gordon from Khartoum, Cook turned to his interpreter: "Ask his Excellency whether he does not think he is the proper man to govern Khartoum, because I have no objection to say the Khedive thinks he is, and desires to see him in that position" (26). It is unclear whether Cook was asking this question in an official or unofficial capacity, but either way, it took him one step further in his transformation: from a businessman into a soldier and from a soldier into a diplomat. This trajectory seems to justify the military framing of Cook's portrait, for as he took every opportunity to explain, it was his own tourist jaunt to Dongala in December 1884—and *not* a military expedition—that provided the British army with crucial navigational intelligence and geopolitical knowledge about the Upper Nile region. Indeed, Cook's belief that he was better at logistics than the military was, and his ability to secure the first private military contract, suggests that with respect to the events of 1884-85, tourism was never subordinated to the strategic plans of the military but rather actively shaped, directed, and produced them.

Double Nostalgia: Gordon's Endless Return

The complex interweaving of tourist practices, military adventures, and local encounters within the geopolitical imaginary of empire was not confined to the events along the Nile in 1884-85. Despite the acrimonious relationship that ensued between Thomas Cook & Son and the British government after their contract disputes in 1885, the company was once again tasked with transporting troops up the Nile for the second Sudan campaign in 1896-98, led by Lord Kitchener. The difference in this arrangement was that Thomas Cook & Son now owned its steamers outright and was therefore better able to dictate the terms of the contract.[7] Indeed, by the time Winston Churchill arrived in Egypt and encountered the "versatile and ubiquitous Cook," the firm was at its peak and had a "virtual monopoly" on all European tourism (Churchill 1991; see also Hazbun 2007, 26; Hunter 2004, 41-50). Throughout this period, the British military presence in Egypt had been further consolidated: the Egyptian ranks had been reorganized and strengthened, Sudanese regiments were added, the Arabic-speaking Kitchener was put in charge, the railways had been improved and extended, and the number of intelligence officers and spies had dramatically increased (Churchill 1949, 89-106). It is no wonder, then, that soldiers and tourists collided even more intensely in the late 1890s than they had done in 1884-85. Indeed, as the famous battles of Atbara and Omdurman were being waged in 1898, more than fifty thousand foreign tourists were visiting Egypt and traveling up the Nile on Cook's steamers (Steevens 1991, 111). And just as they had done in

1884–85, soldiers and officers took advantage of their time off to visit popular tourist destinations in and around Cairo and along the lower regions of the Nile. Indeed, during his "flying visit" to the temples at Luxor, Churchill himself observed some European tourists being gleefully photographed amid the temples and, in his familiar snobbish tone, dismissed them as "Philistines" (Churchill 1991, 199; see also Gregory 2001, 125–26). Thomas Cook & Son's participation in the second Sudan campaign proved to be a sound business decision: once victory was assured, the firm quickly established an office in one of the new hotels in Khartoum. Coming full circle back to 1884, the firm began to run tours to the battlefields it had played such a crucial part in opening up just fifteen years before, which meant that immediately after the second Sudan campaign, tourists could visit the sites they had read about during the failed rescue of General Gordon and "view the bones of the Mahdi's soldiers bleaching in the desert sands" (Hunter 2004, 44).

What makes these strange encounters between soldiers, tourists, and locals at the end of the nineteenth century different from those in 1884–85 was that they were taking place within a much more developed media culture that intensified the discursive and visual representations of this conflict. Throughout the 1890s, the invention and proliferation of the hand-held camera transformed the manner in which tourists saw and "captured" Egypt (Gregory 2003, 209–23; see also Hackforth-Jones and Roberts 2005; Ryan 1997). So while tourists continued to collect mass-produced stereocards, *carte-de-visites,* and the newly developed postcards, some of them were now able to produce their own individual photographs of Egypt (Osman 1997, 110). The increasing photographic presence of Egypt did not make itself felt in the press, however, because although the technology did exist to reproduce photographs in newspapers, artist sketches still dominated press reports of the region, just as they did in 1884. What was different now was that the British press had many more war artists and war correspondents stationed at the front—including, of course, the young Winston Churchill (Cecil 1998). By the time Kitchener's second Sudan campaign was under way, the presence of both Egypt and Sudan in British public culture had intensified: there were more press reports, war diaries, artist's sketches, and a few photographs of the battle itself in the British media, just as there were more personal experiences—and amateur photographs—of Egypt, because Thomas Cook & Son had made it even easier for the masses to travel up the Nile with their notebooks, typewriters, sketchbooks, and cameras (Harrington 1998; Sharf and Harrington 1998).

As Egypt's presence within Western circuits of popular media and culture intensified and multiplied throughout the twentieth century, the events of 1884–85 kept returning in paintings, stories, and especially films. For Gregory, this return constitutes a form of colonial nostalgia: a contemporary longing for the uncomplicated experience of colonial travel symbolized by those Victorian adventurers drifting languorously up the Nile on Cook's *dahabeahs* and steamers (Gregory 2001, 112–14, 140–41). I want to argue that the persistent return of the events of 1884–85 is also a form of nostalgia for colonial warfare in which the expansion of empire through military means was simply a natural extension of both might and right. Indeed, suppressing colonial insurrections in the nineteenth century did not require military leaders to address, let alone protect, the human rights of colonized Others, nor did they have to contend with so much questioning, criticism, and resistance to the "simple" and "natural" extension of Imperial power. Gregory is right, of course, to claim that any form of colonial nostalgia is dangerous because it allows us to efface the violence, repression, and exclusion that went into securing the reaches of empire. In this sense, any nostalgic production is more revealing about the present time in which it is produced than about the past time it longs for—and so it is with the cinematic re-visioning of Gordon's adventures in Sudan. These films are explicitly about the adventures of 1884–85, but implicitly they speak to a range of anxieties about empire, geopolitics, travel, and war in circulation at the time in which they were produced. Thus Korda's 1939 film *Four Feathers* speaks to the dissolution of the British Empire and anxiety at the rise of a new German one; the 1966 film *Khartoum* dispels anxiety about race relations, civil rights, and decolonization by recasting Britain's role in Sudan as a humanitarian one (Jones 2008); and the recent 2002 version of *Four Feathers* tries to pacify our anxieties about failed humanitarian interventions in the 1990s (e.g., Somalia, Rwanda) by recalling a more heroic rescue operation in Africa

(Weber 2005, 55–90). Although *Four Feathers* doesn't address the presence of tourism in Egypt at the time, *Khartoum* does include a number of scenes in which troops—and European tourists—travel up the Nile in Cook's steamers.

Unsurprisingly, perhaps, the travel company Thomas Cook & Son capitalized on these nostalgic cinematic images—especially *Khartoum*—in its marketing strategies in the mid-1980s. Figure 9 depicts its advertising campaign for a "Gordon Centenary Nile Cruise" in 1984, which took tourists up the Nile on Cook's steamers, into the battlefields of the northern Sudan, and on to Khartoum, where Gordon had his last stand. From a marketing perspective, this particular tourist experience can be seen as part of an emerging niche market of battlefield tourism that was, by 1984, well established in places such as Normandy and Pearl Harbor. But what most interests me about this advertisement is how it combines two different forms of nostalgia. On the one hand, the Gordon Centenary Nile Cruise in 1984 is nostalgic for privileged forms of colonial travel that have been lost with the onset of cheap mass tourism; but on the other hand, it is also nostalgic for conventional colonial battles—complete with camels and spears—that have been lost with modern forms of technological warfare. With that in mind, Cook's centenary tour to Khartoum requires a double critical interrogation: (1) what kind of violence, exclusion, and inequality actually underscored these sepia-tinted colonial pasts in which we are now seeking solace, and (2) what new formations of violence, exclusion, and inequality are we currently running away *from*?

For me, of course, the Gordon Centenary Nile Cruise in 1984 is simply more proof that the heterogeneous networks, scripted encounters, material infrastructures, and intersected visions of war and tourism have always been—and continue to be—implicated in one another. The events of 1884–85 in Egypt cannot be read as simply an assimilation of tourism into the strategic orbit of the British military—on the contrary. The visual and narrative documents of the Gordon Relief Campaign reveal that tourist practices and military adventures were in constant competition with one another. Because neither soldiers nor tourists could be entirely disciplined by either apparatus, their movements created slippages and fractures in the prevailing order of empire. This is not to ignore the

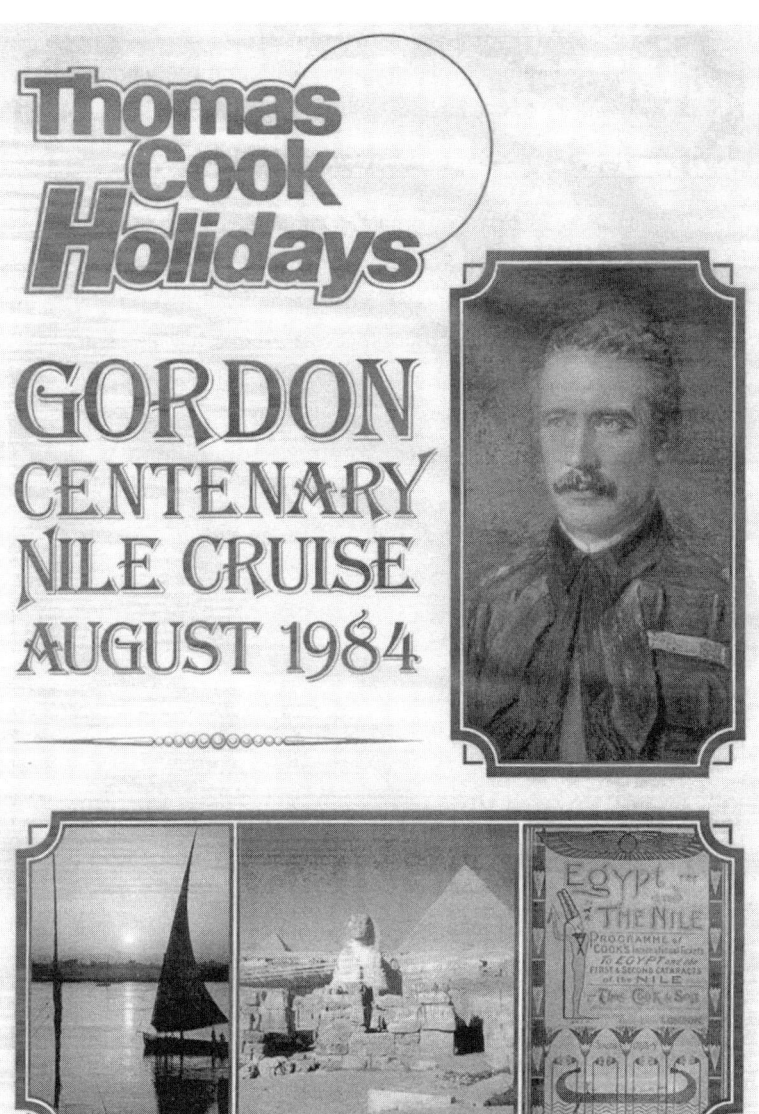

FIGURE 9. Advertisement for the Gordon Centenary Cruise, 1984. Courtesy of the Thomas Cook Archive.

overwhelming asymmetries that existed between privileged European colonizers and local subjects; rather, it is to suggest that colonial Egypt cannot be understood by a simple colonizer–colonized framework that flattens the heterogeneous practices of tourism, warfare, and colonial encounter. This chapter has focused on the specific events of the Gordon Relief Campaign of 1884–85 to draw out the heterogeneity, multiplicity, and contradictions that saturated both tourism and warfare; call attention to the productive slippages that developed as soldiers became tourists, and vice versa; and help create a critical space in which the foliated agency of local subjects can break out of the reductive colonizer–colonized logic. This is, of course, only the first step in highlighting the alternative orderings that were present in colonial Egypt; indeed, much more work needs to be done excavating how these slippages between tourism and soldiering enabled local populations, vernacular lives, and subaltern spaces to maneuver through the interstices of empire.

2

Tours of Duty, Tours of Pleasure

Battlefield Journeys and the Rise of Militourism, 1914–45

This chapter explores how the entanglements of war and tourism during the First and Second World Wars helped to extend the asymmetries and complexities of colonialism into a global context and, in so doing, mobilize the lifeworlds of many different populations. This is not to suggest that there was no global consciousness before 1914 or that globalization had not begun; rather, it is to suggest that new technological developments in communication (e.g., telegraph, photography, telephone) and transportation (e.g., automobiles, airplanes, luxury ocean liners) enabled more populations to travel the world themselves or to receive information and images about faraway places. Moreover, the new culture of consumption that emerged out of Western industrialization and mass production meant that foreign destinations could be commodified and packaged for the enjoyment of multiple Western demographics, social classes, and markets. These developments also had a profound effect on the conduct of warfare, not just in how armies were able to see, record, and target their enemies but also in how troops were recruited and trained; transported to and from combat zones; given medical treatment; and fed, clothed, and housed during battle (Brown 1998; Duffett 2012; Virilio 1989). Although it is conventional to understand the First World War as a Manichean battle between the Great Powers of Europe, its demographics were much more cosmopolitan and its reach much more global. For example, we know that soldiers fighting for the British Empire from 1914 to 1918 came from Canada, Australia, New Zealand, and South Africa, but less well known are the colonial troops, such as the Indian regiments and the Chinese Labor Corps, that populated the European theater of war. As Barkawi (2006a, 77) argues, these subaltern populations foreground the "cosmopolitan, culture-mixing aspects of the western front, often overlooked in accounts of clashing national armies" (see also Bailey 2011; Barkawi 2004; Fawcett 2000; Klein 2009; Koller 2011; Porter 2009). Because the First World War is usually understood as a clash between European nations, the military geographies of empires (e.g., numerous battles across the Middle East, North Africa, and Southeast Asia) are usually framed as a simple extension of European confrontation. Certainly these non-European battlefields must be understood within a colonial framing, but this chapter suggests that they gave rise to quite different encounters between military forces, local populations, and other traveling subjects. Looking more closely at the entanglements of tourism and war both within and outside of European battlefields, this chapter explores the moments of possibility created when tourist sensibilities emerged in war zones and when the horrors of combat continued to haunt postwar tourist practices.

This mapping of colonial asymmetries onto a global terrain intensified in the interwar years through the rapid growth of mass tourism—one of the many "frivolous" pursuits of leisure that characterized collective responses to the Great War. As mandated holidays became commonplace in Western labor forces, and air travel became commercially viable in the 1930s, more and more people were taking holidays to "exotic" destinations (Inglis 2000, 101–10; Urry 1990, 26–27). This sense of the international was also being articulated in diplomatic circles as the League of Nations tried (and failed) to construct a peaceful world order after the Treaty of Versailles. In effect, a global consciousness developed in the interwar years through both the "low" politics of tourism and the "high" politics of diplomacy: "the war had broken down international barriers, and it had resulted in the fostering of an ideal, an optimistic, peaceful internationalism—just the climate in which tourism was most likely to flourish" (Likorish and Kershaw 1958, 42; Page 2009, 47). By the time the Second World War began, that global consciousness translated into even more diverse troops confronting each other in multiple locations both within and outside Europe. For example, soldiers contributing to the Allied cause came from

American protectorates (e.g., Puerto Rico, Panama), the British Empire (e.g., Jamaica, British Honduras, Cyprus, India), and French dependencies (e.g., Cameroon, Indochina, Polynesia). Although Allied and Axis forces certainly confronted each other in familiar European battlegrounds (e.g., France, Belgium, Italy), they also clashed in "faraway" places like Morocco, Ethiopia, Lebanon, Madagascar, Manila, Singapore, Mandalay, Greenland, and Argentina. This diversity of participants and battlefields secured a global consciousness not just for the soldiers, officers, diplomats, spies, government leaders, and civilians directly engaged in warfare but also for the millions of people on various home fronts consuming information about the war and responding to its progress. What is significant about the intensification of this global consciousness in the Second World War is the extent to which the asymmetrical logics of colonialism continued to be mapped onto new worldwide architectures of enmity that had been forged, in part, through the practices, infrastructures, and imaginaries of both pre-1914 tourism and tourism during the interwar years. This chapter traces the emergence of a global consciousness as it was produced by both war and tourism from 1914 to 1945 and pays particular attention to the articulation, reification, and reordering of colonial asymmetries within that consciousness.

While the concept of "total war" explains how the war effort mobilized all of society's resources and citizens (Black 2010; Marwick 2001), it doesn't say enough about the governing rationalities operative at the register of everyday life, and in that sense, it cannot fully illuminate how practices of war and tourism intersect. Drawing from scholars of governmentality who have critically examined the two world wars (Farish 2005; Murdoch and Ward 1997; Rose 2010; Sparrow 2011), I want to explore how prewar dispositions of leisure and travel periodically reorient fighting forces toward foreign battlefields and enemy territory. Think, for example, of how officers brought personal cameras to the front for the first time during the First World War and framed their off-duty experiences through a familiar prewar tourist gaze. Subsequently, that same touristic sensibility intensified as multiple battlefield tours to the western front developed in the years immediately following armistice. Structured through an overarching ethos of commemoration and mourning, these tours inaugurated the modern form of war tourism we recognize today: the ability of mass crowds from all over the world to visit famous battlefields and sites of mass war death and the various strategies encouraging visitors to pay their respects to heroes and victims. Given the inexorable rise of mass tourism in the 1920s and 1930s, the everyday lives of soldiers during the Second World War were even more profoundly shaped by a touristic sensibility that troubled the militarized production and targeting of enemy territory. By this time, structures of official leave had been fully rebranded as R&R, integrated into military institutions and managed through troop logistics to produce what Teaiwa (1994) has called "militourism." For O'Dwyer (2004, 5), militourism is best understand as "the ways that tourism is enabled by a military presence and the degree to which military power may be de-politicized and elided by the projected fantasies of the tourist culture" (see also De Burlo 1989). During the Second World War, militourism was especially pronounced in places like the Pacific theater, where a long history of colonialism was intensified by wartime practices of racism, dehumanization, and violence. To fully elaborate on Teaiwa's and O'Dwyer's initial efforts to make sense of tourism, militarism, colonialism, and war in the Pacific theater of the Second World War, this chapter explores its direct antecedents: the tourist sensibilities that shaped the First World War and the lingering memories of war that shaped the interwar rise of tourism.

Holidays on the Front Line: Tourist Sensibilities during the Great War

Although various forms of leisure, entertainment, and organized leave have always been incorporated into army life, the dramatic modernization, industrialization, and technological developments of the First World War institutionalized these practices. The slow-moving nature of trench warfare on the western front meant that centers for relaxation, leisure, and entertainment were established directly behind the front lines and catered to soldiers circulating out of trenches and recuperating for their return to battle. These centers were organized primarily by volunteer and religious groups—most prominently the YMCA, which ran up to 90 percent of support and leisure services (Blanchard 1997; Lancaster 1986;

Thompson 2006; Wright 1917).[1] The YMCA canteens ranged from improvised dugouts to more permanent buildings and provided mail services, money order arrangements, a social space for troops to gather, and personal goods for purchase (e.g., food, toiletries, tobacco). The postcards that soldiers sent home from the front exemplify the latent tourist sensibility permeating the trenches of the Great War: these included the already scripted military-issue field postcards providing basic information for loved ones (e.g., "I am quite well" or "I have been admitted into hospital") as well as postcards with traditional images of cities, towns, monuments and buildings, holiday scenes, images of "life in the trenches," cartoons, portraits of famous people, poems, and photographs of famous landmarks (Booth 1997; Doyle 2010; Roberts 2008; Tomczyszyn 2004). As long as they didn't reveal any secure information, soldier postcards—like their tourist cousins—offered basic itineraries (e.g., "arrived in Dunkirk"), observations about the weather ("it is raining and cold"), and commentary on the everyday life of soldiering (e.g., "billeted in a large farmhouse"). In documenting the long stretches of army life away from battle, these postcards give some sense of how soldiers inhabited a familiar tourist disposition when translating foreign surroundings to their families and friends back home.

Although soldiers experienced leisure and entertainment in the form of organized musicals, bands, theatrical productions, and even horse shows arranged by the military (Australian Official Photographer 1918; Brooks 1917; Crawshay 1918), their primary encounter with leisure and travel was on official stretches of leave. Where feasible, most Allied soldiers were granted ten days leave after approximately one year of service—sometimes leave was granted earlier, but sometimes soldiers had to wait up to eighteen months (Clements 2012). These longer stretches were often interspersed with shorter periods of leave up to three days, but because leave included the time taken to journey back home, many Allied soldiers on European battlefields spent their shorter R&R allocations in London or Paris. The leisure industries of both cities—tourist organizations, hotels, restaurants, bars, nightclubs, theaters, cinemas, taxi companies, casinos, brothels, and so on—reoriented themselves so as to provide the leisure and entertainment required by soldiers circulating in and out of the front lines on short-term leave. For example, a poster emblazoned throughout Paris during the war enticed Allied soldiers into the famous Gaumont Palace cinema at Place de Clichy near Montmartre. Beside the image of a British soldier smoking a pipe and an American soldier smoking a cigar, the poster—in English—read,

> Hello!!! This is for you American and British soldiers on leave: Gaumont Palace: the largest moving picture show in the world—6000 seats, orchestra of 50 musicians, boys! There you will find on the screen Your own Artists in their Latest Productions, News from the whole world, Scenes of the war day by day, Films projected with French and English titles, various attractions, foyer, American bar, reading room, etc. Special prices for soldiers in uniform: if you want to spend a fine evening while in Paris go to the Gaumont-Palace. (Société des Établissements Gaumont, n.d.)

Allied soldiers lucky enough to survive the intense trench warfare on the western front and acquire official leave faced an instant transition: they had to disengage from dispositions of aggression, strategy, and violence and activate dispositions of leisure, pleasure, and tourism. This transition differed in speed and intensity depending on whether a soldier was returning home for his leave (e.g., an Englishman returning to London) or if he was spending his leave in a foreign location (e.g., an Englishman or Australian in Paris; an American in London). For example, W. G. Meudell, an Australian gunner who served on the western front from 1916 to 1918, wrote home contrasting the "joys of leave in England with the hard work of leave in Paris.... In Paris one must be sightseeing all the time, although very interesting, it is far more enjoyable to be shown around by someone whom you know" (Meudell 1918). The London–Paris circuit of leave provided various permutations of familiarity and difference for Allied soldiers; for example, for soldiers of the British Empire, London provided a cultural, linguistic, and sometimes physical home, whereas Paris provided enough cultural, linguistic, and physical difference to constitute a holiday away from the front line *and* away from home.

The diaries of many First World War soldiers—especially those Allied soldiers who were deployed to battlefields away from home—reveal how a tourist sensibility framed their encounters with foreign landscapes and people. To be sure, their primary reason for being abroad was to fight the enemy, and a majority of these diaries speak movingly of the patriotism that sustained the soldiers, their fears and anxieties during combat preparation, the horrors of battle, the friendships created and lost, and their individual confrontations with death. But outside of that purposive framing, soldiers commented in great detail about the foreign landscapes they were traveling through (often for the first time) and the local people they encountered. It is in this sense that First World War diaries can be read as travelogues: they document a soldier's journey away from the comforts of home, the adventures he has in foreign lands, and the triumphant return he hopefully makes (Lisle 2006a, 27–67). F. W. Hopps, for example, served as a motorcycle dispatch rider for the Royal Field Artillery and kept a detailed diary of his travels throughout France from 1915 to 1918 (Hopps, n.d.). Exemplifying a unique combination of the best romantic and dyspeptic travel writers, Hopps made detailed notes on every village he drove through. Amid constant complaints about the weather and his traveling companions, he declared most villages to be "rotten little places," awful and ugly towns with "nothing to see." However, some villages (e.g., Sarton, Morbecque) are described as "lovely" with "very nice people"; indeed, he rides through Ypres in between its many battles and declares it to be "a quiet little place ... very fine scenery. Very quiet front."[2] At Château de la Haie toward the end of the war (May 1918), he appears to be tiring of his tourist escapades through France and longs for the battle action that characterized his earlier entries: "Nice Chateau, weather fine. Have good time, plenty of cricket, etc., nice change but begins to 'drag' after 3 months.... Wish we were moving away to more exciting front" (Hopps, n.d.). For Hopps, a certain amount of leisure, tourism, and relaxation was permitted as a counterweight to the horrors of battle, but not *too* much, or the noble purpose of one's position abroad—to fight the enemy—was diluted.

Outside of the western front, it was impossible for Allied troops to get home for their allocated leave, which meant that R&R granted to soldiers on the southern front and in Mesopotamia was usually spent in occupied cities like Cairo. In these cases, soldiers had to transpose their Orientalist demonization of the Ottoman enemy into a less violent production of the nonthreatening "exotic East." For example, when wireless operator

Edgar Wooley was granted his ten days' leave, he became a typical British tourist in Egypt: he visited the Great Pyramids, went on a camel journey, and "walked all over the Sphynx" (Clements 2012, 13:10–14:05). Like their colonial predecessors, many officers on leave continued to enjoy the hospitality of the Shepheard's Hotel terrace (now requisitioned as British Army Headquarters), and thousands of soldiers and enlisted men on leave continued to frequent Cairo's brothels. Certainly the Orientalist hierarchy is evident in the way soldiers contrasted their superior civilization with that of the racially and culturally inferior people they were fighting against and living among, but that logic becomes much more complex when read through the lens of tourism. As they traveled to foreign battlefields beyond the European sphere, soldiers had to engage in a complex taxonomy of difference: certain forms of Otherness were to be vanquished on the battlefield, but some forms of Otherness (i.e., foreign populations in host cities like Cairo) had to be preserved for exotic tourist encounters. This difficult taxonomy is expressed in the diary of Second Lieutenant P. Bailey of the Seventh Cheshire Regiment, who recounts his sea journey from England to the Battle of Gallipoli in September 1915. Though the diary does address the specifics of military life (e.g., living aboard a crowded naval ship), most of it reads like a colonial travelogue through the exotic Mediterranean. For example, when his ship stops in Malta, Bailey comments on the "Maltese jabbering away like monkeys trying to sell fruits, cigarettes" as he goes ashore for some sightseeing, lunch, and shopping (Bailey, n.d., 15). While he is momentarily beguiled by a "naughty little girl" behind a shop counter who keeps giving him "bewitching side glances," Bailey is mostly irritated by the local entrepreneurs: "the absolute cheek of the Maltese guides who pester you to death and follow you along the street till you feel like kicking the beggars to blazes" (16). Over lunch at the Royal Hotel, Bailey reflects on the superiority of his own Imperial culture:

> Everywhere one sees signs of the Ruling Power. Policemen in white helmets at frequent intervals, the Union Jack flapping lazily down the Main Street and occasionally a pretty English girl to gladden the eye after the sight of so much native squalor. Poverty seems fairly general and the fellows coaling our boat eagerly snatched at old lumps of bread thrown down to them by our Tommies. (17)

The abject Maltese are not subjects to be conquered but rather creatures to be observed, pitied, and, because they are within the orbit of the British Empire, ultimately helped to climb the ladder of civilization. Whether commenting on foreign landscapes from the deck of his naval ship (e.g., "a more desolate, forbidding sight I have never seen") or the intimate streets of Malta or Alexandria, Bailey employs a field of vision popularized by colonial travel writers such as Gustave Flaubert, Robert Louis Stevenson, and Isabella Bird. However, while Bailey's "monarch-of-all-I-survey" position certainly objectifies difference, orders it into a hierarchical taxonomy, and secures colonial privilege, it does not display the confidence or robustness so characteristic of travel writing during empire. Instead of depicting a seamless journey from the familiar to the exotic and back again, Bailey's trip through the Mediterranean is continually destabilized by the impending battle at Gallipoli. The narrative is haunted by the "ominous sign" of the Allied hospital ships returning from the Dardanelles, his inability to feel brave in the face of his likely death, and a solitary and often melancholy disposition that puts him at odds with his more excitable and debauched shipmates. While Bailey's constant shifts between the dispositions of soldier and tourist often align to reproduce an Orientalist mode of domination, they also misalign in ways that trouble Britain's effort to expand its empire into the Middle East and Mesopotamia—an expansion whose folly was revealed most tragically in the Battle of Gallipoli in 1915.

In addition to these diaries, amateur photographs taken by officers at the front line provide key insights into the tourist framing of the First World War. Personal cameras such as the Kodak Brownie had been available to the public since 1900, and by dramatically reducing the cumbersome technology of nineteenth-century photography, these mini cameras (e.g., Brownie Model B Box; Vest Pocket Kodak) expanded the practice of taking pictures to a much wider demographic (Baker 2014). By the time the war started, amateur photography was a well-established middle-brow hobby with popular photographic clubs, societies, salons, journals, and magazines (Griffin 1995; 1999; Maddocks 2014). Given that a majority of Allied officers came from the upper and middle classes who had enthusiastically embraced amateur photography, and that one of the most popular photographic subjects within this visual culture was the "exotica" of foreign travel, it is no surprise that the officers who brought their Brownies to the front line also brought with them a prewar tourist sensibility. Although these amateur photographers occasionally tried to mimic the nineteenth-century conventions of professional war photography established by the likes of Roger Fenton and Matthew Brady, more often than not their images drew from the middle-brow forms of family photography, informal portraiture, and holiday snapshots that were prevalent in the prewar period.[3] However, instead of photographing the famous statues or landmarks of a holiday destination, officers photographed the iconic technology of war (e.g., tanks, airplanes, naval ships); instead of constructing family portraits, they took group shots of their battalions and regiments as well as individual portraits of their brothers in arms; and instead of pastoral landscapes and rural idylls, they photographed trenches, battlefields, detritus, and ruin (Taylor 1991, 24–25; see also Beurier 2004; Carmichael 1989, 120–39; Remus 2008). For me, the amateur photography of the First World War is important not just because it tells us what officers saw (e.g., tanks, trenches, ruins) but also because it reveals how they framed those objects through the prewar conventions of tourist photography and holiday snapshots.

This tourist sensibility led to an important division between those photographers who pursued a documentary ethos by hiding their role as active creators of the photograph and never appearing in front of the camera (e.g., "this is a visual document of what it is like over here") and those who pursued an evidentiary ethos by explicitly positioning themselves as subjects of their own photographic archive to prove the authenticity of their adventures (e.g., "this is me in an exotic location"). Like much photography before the 1920s, these documentary and evidentiary frames were foregrounded at the expense of the aesthetic primarily because photography was still considered a science rather than an art (Lisle 2011, 875–76). However, the further soldiers traveled away from central Europe and entered into the "exotic East," where the nineteenth-century Orientalist tradition of photography held sway, the tendency toward an evidentiary ethos increased. Indeed, Joanna Struk (2011, 53) argues that a "prevailing and essentially colonialist viewpoint was regarded as neutral" in the amateur photographs of the Great War and that "when soldiers took pictures they adopted and imitated this way of seeing and by doing so assumed the authority integral to the success of imperialism" (see also 54–56). This was particularly the case in photographs of Allied troops on periods of leave in fortified capital cities like Cairo, established staging posts such as the Greek island of Lemnos, or major cities in southern and southeastern Europe (e.g., Caucasus, Sinai, Mesopotamia) captured after successful military campaigns. For example, Captain Conrad T. Price (Second Battalion, Norfolk Regiment) fought in the Mesopotamian campaign to protect and extend British interests against the Ottoman forces. Once Baghdad was captured in March 1917, Price and his regiment took leave in the city: they stayed at the Maud Hotel on the shores of the River Tigris, enjoyed the services of the local YMCA, and engaged in some amateur tourist photography (Figure 10).

Of particular interest here is the substitutability of primary signifiers that supposedly anchor the protagonist to his exotic surroundings; in this case, we "know" Price is in an exotic location because of the surrounding palm trees, the desert landscape, and his standard-issue desert uniform. Compare this image with those of Lieutenant Colonel Osmund Fooks (Fourteenth Hussars), who had many photographs taken of his distinguished military career throughout the Middle East, Mesopotamia, and India, including a number of tourist interludes in Kashmir (e.g., hunting parties, cricket and polo matches, golf games) (Fooks 1914; 1917). The hunting images in particular speak to the mode of domination exercised by British colonial officers: the skulls and stretched animal skins he poses alongside not only signify his presence in an exotic land but also illustrate how leisure practices were complicit in the plunder of colonial resources and the acquisition of valuable souvenirs. The substitutability of exotic objects becomes clearest after the capture of Baghdad, when Fooks took a series of photographs with locals in the village of Kifri. As Figure 11 shows, a "real" Arab sheikh is meant to signify in the same way as the palm trees of Price's Baghdad photograph and the animal skulls of Fooks's Kashmir images. Humans, animals, things, and buildings were objectified and used as evidentiary markers of authenticity to prove that the protagonists—in

FIGURE 10. Captain Conrad Price on leave in Baghdad, 1918. Cat. No. HU 100119. Courtesy of the Imperial War Museum Archive, London. Copyright IWM.

this case, Price and Fooks—were actually present in the dangerous lands of the Oriental East. Choosing to include themselves within the image does not produce equivalence between the British officers and the exotic objects they pose beside; rather, it reinforces the Orientalist logic underscoring the conventions of tourist photography in the early twentieth century. The muted agency of these exotic signifiers is not amplified in the encounter; instead, it is forced to resonate through a range of asymmetries that privilege the bravery, adventuring spirit, and curiosity of the occupying soldier at the center of the picture.

The postcards sent, diaries written, and photographs taken by Allied soldiers during the First World War illustrate how battles were interspersed with moments of leisure and travel and how a soldier's journey through a foreign country was framed in advance by an established prewar tourist sensibility. More importantly, these documents reveal how the crossovers between practices of soldiering and tourism—especially in the battlefields outside of mainland Europe—mobilized prevailing colonial asymmetries. Foreign landscapes, objects, and people do not signify independently; rather, they appear in order to authenticate exotic surroundings, lend credence to the idea that war is a great adventure (e.g., "Join the army: see the world!"), and prove that Western empires civilize foreign populations through force *and* through leisure activities such as sport and tourism. Despite the disciplining context of empire, however, the alignment between war and tourism during the First World War was neither stable nor secure. We know that productions of Otherness during warfare slip very quickly between, on the one hand, enemy, adversary, and threat and, on the other hand, host, facilitator, civilian, guide, and translator. Those slippages and interstices create the potential for colonial asymmetries to be reordered: they produce unforeseen spaces in which the foliated agency of predetermined Others can be articulated, and they blur the confident field of vision deployed by authors, narrators, and photographers. When Fooks's First World War photographs are viewed with these interstices in mind, the sheikhs who indulge his photographic narcissism, the laborers who facilitate his hunt, and the caddies who accompany his golf games tap us into alternative assemblages of travel, encounter, and geopolitics. These return gazes cannot be understood as entirely passive, muted, or

FIGURE 11. Major Fooks with Kurdish sheikh in Kifri. Cat. No. HU 104019. Courtesy of the Imperial War Museum Archive, London. Copyright IWM.

abject but must instead be interpreted as indicators of agency, vibrancy, and life. This reassembling of visualized subjects and objects suggests that reading travel and tourism into the practice of warfare is troubling but also productive: it has the capacity to displace the preferred mode of domination and open up a more heterogeneous space in which the rich and varied lifeworlds of local populations can be glimpsed.

Tourist Commemorations of the Great War: Horror, Spectacle, and Escape

The immediate aftermath of the First World War was marked by two oppositional forces—both of which were enabled by the rapid growth of mass tourism in the 1920s. The first, and clearest, was the need to commemorate the unprecedented horrors of the war that led to the construction of numerous war memorials, the establishment of memorial rituals such as Remembrance Day, the birth of the Imperial War Museum, and—importantly—an extraordinary growth in battlefield tourism (Cornish 2004; Edkins 2003, 20–45, 57–72; Gregory 1994; Imperial War Museum, n.d.; King 1998; Saunders and Cornish 2009). Although there are many reasons why people wanted to visit the remnants of the Great War in person, one of the most compelling was the opportunity to experience a direct and unmediated encounter with the site of mass death—especially if one had lost a family member, friend, or lover. The second force at work in the aftermath of the Great War moved away from the horrors of the trenches and into the nostalgia of an uncomplicated past, the purity of nature, the frivolities of a growing consumer culture, and the exotic destinations of rapidly crumbling empires. Mass tourism, of course, facilitated these desires by ferrying millions of European holiday makers to the seaside, the beach, the fairground, newly constructed national parks, mountain ranges, famous European cities, and farther afield to "romantic" exotic cities such as Shanghai, Buenos Aires, and Havana. Unsurprisingly, this desire to travel also spawned a number of related consumer enterprises such as commercial airlines, travel companies, travel magazines, and advertising agencies. What most interests me about this tension between commemoration and escape that emerged in the 1920s is its mutual and inescapable entanglement: battlefield tourism was constantly trying to downplay the superficial aspects of the mass tourism infrastructure through which it operated, and the multiple forms of leisure and travel that emerged after armistice were unable to leave the memory of the trenches behind.

Certainly the label "Lost Generation" resonates, at least in part, from this irreconcilable tension between wanting to access the "real" remnants of war as a way to commemorate it and wanting to escape all traces of war as a way to forget it. In the immediate aftermath of the First World War, mass tourism facilitated both of these opposing forces: it catered to large numbers of visitors who craved unmediated and individuated access to the "real" remnants of war, and it offered pleasures and delights to divert survivors away from the lingering trauma of war. Drawing from insights about the complicated and contradictory cultural landscape of the Great War's aftermath (e.g., the rise of modernism, the break with tradition, new technologies of expression) (Fussell 1975; Saunders 2004; Winter 1995), I am interested in how tourism, commemoration, and escape folded into one another in the initial years following armistice.

What interests me about the battlefield tours that took place just after the First World War is how they foreground the multiple, contradictory, and often unruly experiences of tourists confronting sites of war, especially in the immediate aftermath of conflict. Indeed, the desire to confront the "real" remnants of war was not always disciplined by the prevailing mode of commemoration, and the burgeoning infrastructure of mass tourism through which visitors accessed the battlefields often produced rather impious and irreverent modes of encounter. For example, when the American Legion made its annual pilgrimage to the cemeteries and battlefields of France and Belgium in 1927, the ex-servicemen were seduced by the availability of alcohol and the relative strength of the U.S. dollar in France, which meant that their solemn tour of remembrance turned into "an epic escapade of whiskey-soaked good times" (Endy 2004, 16; Levenstein 1998, 271–75).

Focusing specifically on war tourism between 1919 and 1939, David W. Lloyd (1998, 40–44) argues that visitors should be categorized as either sacred pilgrims who traveled to the battlefields for the "higher moral purpose" of commemorating and honoring the dead or profane tourists who traipsed across this hallowed ground seeking some kind of morbid sensation while collecting ghoulish souvenirs such as bullet casings, shrapnel, and discarded helmets (see also Dunkley, Morgan, and Westwood 2011; Eksteins 2000; Iles 2008; Scates 2006; Seaton 2000; Winter 2010). Lloyd illustrates how newspaper stories, poems, and literature at the time consistently reproduced this sacred-profane dichotomy by valorizing those who had a right to visit battlefields (i.e., ex-servicemen and the bereaved who had lost relatives) and castigating those others—those *tourists*—whose very presence trivialized the entire experience. Although Lloyd is right to suggest that the sacred and the profane provide contrasting ways to imagine the battlefield tours of the 1920s and 1930s, this binary logic is too reductive to capture the complex, contradictory, and multiple reasons for the intensification of battlefield tourism in the aftermath of the Great War. Lloyd is working within a dominant frame that denigrates tourism as trivial, superficial, inauthentic, and morally offensive—precisely the characteristics that contrast with the gravitas, depth, authenticity, and moral truths of war (Buzard 1993). But there were many moments of boredom, leisure, and pleasure that characterized "sacred" visits to the battlefields and many moments of insight, empathy, and compassion that characterized "profane" encounters with the Great War. There is much more at stake in the tourist's desire to witness the detritus of war than the sacred-profane framework allows; indeed, physically encountering the debris, bomb craters, trenches, remnants, and ruins of such a cataclysmic event had the capacity to destabilize *all* visitors, from the most "sacred" to the most "profane." As Rudy Koshar (2000, 70) suggests, the Great War was "a moment of sublimity in all its enticing terror."

The difficulties of imposing an infrastructure of mass tourism on the widespread desire to encounter the detritus of the Great War in person, and the accusations of voyeurism that such an imposition produced, were experienced firsthand by companies who operated battlefield tours throughout France and Belgium in the 1920s.[4] Certainly tour companies understood the commercial potential of people's desire to encounter the authentic remnants of the war, but they also recognized a need to be careful about their marketing strategies to avoid accusations of being disrespectful or unpatriotic. To achieve this balance, tour companies such as Thomas Cook & Son directed their marketing to "everyone who is desirous of paying due homage to the memory of the Glorious Dead" rather than to increasingly reviled tourists (Thomas Cook & Son 1920d, 10). In the introduction to their first extended guidebook to the Great War battlefields (July 1920), Thomas Cook & Son framed these journeys as *everyone's* duty:

> We do not know—and we cannot know—*what war really means* until we have visited the Battlefields and the ruined towns and devastated miles upon miles in the North of France and Belgium. And it is our duty to visit them; it is a duty we owe to our manhood and womanhood and the common brotherhood which the best of us hope will now reign in the world. (Thomas Cook & Son 1920a, 2–3; see also Michelin, 1920)

The company's framing of its battlefield tours as a duty was repeated in Cook's monthly *Traveller's Gazette* throughout the 1920s. The company went to great efforts to establish that their excursions were absolutely not a form of ghoulish pleasure but rather a genuine opportunity to express one's patriotism, respect, and appreciation:

> Many thousands will this year avail themselves of the arrangements we have made for visiting the battlefields, not because of a morbid desire to view the wilderness of devastation, but in token of their heartfelt gratitude for the blessings of peace, which were only made possible by the sublime heroism and self-sacrifice of those who fought the good fight for freedom's sake. (Thomas Cook & Son 1920e, 8)

Thomas Cook & Son enacted an important transformation in the early 1920s: it turned sites of mass death and suffering into a viable tourist product that could be marketed as an opportunity for duty, commemoration, and patriotism. The firm's battlefield tours made it OK to visit these sites of death because the whole process was driven by a spirit of honor, reverence, and gratitude rather than morbid fascination. In this sense, Lloyd is right to suggest that the battlefield tours were lifted out of the common circuit of European mass tourism and imbued with greater authenticity: visits to the mass graves of Ypres and the Somme were considered to be special—more important, more meaningful, more real—and certainly more authentic than the commonplace visits to already iconic sites such as the Eiffel Tower and the Palace of Versailles. What made battlefield tours even more seductive, of course, was their worthy purpose of commemorating fallen heroes that allowed participants to indulge in the age-old denigration of tourists. Casting oneself as a reverent visitor *properly* commemorating the Great War was achieved by naming and shaming those other tourists—the vulgar kind who "go[ ] to gape at a battlefield (from a charabanc) as he would gape at a Cathedral or a criminal, his soul being packed in behind with the luggage" (Ewart 1920, 734; also Lloyd 1998, 43).

The problem for Thomas Cook & Son was that to sell its battlefield tours, the firm had to highlight the very things that made these visits seem ghoulish and morbid—the "real" objects, signs, and spaces that would bring visitors as close as possible to the experience of battle. In August 1919, less than a year after peace was declared, and only a few months after the Treaty of Versailles had been signed, Cook's *Traveller's Gazette* announced the following:

> Many objects meet the eye which appeal to the sensibility of the traveller, such as roadside graves and their crosses; aeroplanes that have been brought down and lie where they fell; empty trenches and dug-outs; derelict tanks battered by enemy shell; transports and debris of every kind. (Thomas Cook & Son 1919, 12–13)[5]

The material remnants of the Great War—the objects that remained on the battlefield—were a source of constant anxiety and fascination for both the tour guides and the visitors themselves. Guidebooks offered strict warnings about touching the objects: "Visitors to the battlefields are particularly warned against touching grenades, shells, loose wire, and suchlike objects lying in the war area" (Thomas Cook & Son 1920a). And yet, tourists were encouraged to carefully inspect the "mine craters and shell holes [and] ruined redoubts and dug-outs where bitter hand-to-hand fighting took place"; have a "thorough visit" through the "trenches, dugouts, big guns and all the debris of the Battlefield"; and, most importantly, collect souvenirs of the battle such as shell casings, helmets, and gun parts (Thomas Cook & Son 1920b, 11; 1920c, 9; 1926, 19). Focusing specifically on the shells of the First World War,

Nicholas J. Saunders (2002, 22) offers a useful account of the potency of material remnants of war:

> Shells devastated landscape as well as people, transformed economies, altered gender relations through an industrialized military complex, became art and icon, and possessed symbolic resonances which ambiguously combined Modernism and pre-war realities.... Rich in symbolism and irony, shells were mediators between men and women, soldiers and civilians, individuals and industrialized society, the nations which fought the war, and, perhaps most of all, the living and the dead.

The weight of such meanings produced a great deal of anxiety over these material objects—the desire to own such powerful souvenirs was about finding resolution to the tensions of modern life, but the act of acquiring these objects felt dubious and disrespectful. To alleviate such anxiety, the battlefield tours interspersed destabilizing encounters with material objects with opportunities for proper reverence and commemoration. For example, Thomas Cook & Son's most popular automobile tour of the Somme let tourists wander through devastated battlefields and collect souvenirs of the war, but it also made sure they stopped at existing memorials (Thomas Cook & Son 1924). The juxtaposition of acquiring the material debris of war and commemorating the dead was made explicit in the obligatory postlunch stop at Newfoundland Memorial Park: "an immense tract of Battleground that is being preserved in the condition that it was at the close of the war. Here can be seen trenches, dugouts, big guns and all the debris of the Battlefield, the whole atmosphere being that of five years ago" (Thomas Cook & Son 1924, 18). Upon entrance to the park, visitors were directed to perform displays of reverence, piety, and solemnity at the sight of such destruction but were then overtaken by tourism's economy of consumption as they were encouraged to wander into the park and touch, identify, and collect the objects they were supposed to be revering. These competing desires illustrate that tourist encounters with the Great War battlefields were framed not by the solitary positions of the "preferred" sacred and the "distasteful" profane but by a constant negotiation between these two irreconcilable positions.

This complex interplay between commemoration and tourist consumption is exemplified in the experience of Mrs. L. K. Briggs from Harrogate, North Yorkshire, who visited Ypres and the battlefields every year from 1919 to 1939. Usually accompanied by her daughters, Mrs. Briggs began her annual journeys to visit the grave of her son, Private Claude Briggs, who was buried in Bedford House Cemetery just south of Ypres.[6] One of her daughters brought a Kodak personal camera on these trips, and later a Cine camera, and the resulting photographs provide an invaluable visual record of the changing battlefield landscape over the course of the interwar period. Given the initial reason for the Briggses' journeys, the first photograph album detailing their visits to the Ypres Salient in 1919–20 includes many images of the landscape and cemeteries around the battlefields where her son fought and was eventually buried, including Shrewsbury Wood, D'Houthulst Forest, Hooge, and Sanctuary Wood. However, these personal photographs are outnumbered by those documenting the ruins, remains, and detritus of war—from the rusted and half-submerged German ships in Zebrugge to the carcasses of airplanes, decomposing tanks, shell craters, bombed churches, and burned forests surrounding Ypres. Because the photographs pursue a documentary ethos, Mrs. Briggs and her daughters rarely appear in the frame: they are subjects and producers of the archive but rarely its objects. Occasionally one of them poses beside a rusted tank or an airplane carcass, but overwhelmingly the photographs depict the ruined landscapes, objects, and infrastructure of war. As if to distance herself from the destruction depicted in the photographs, Mrs. Briggs arranges her album and the accompanying narrative index through an objective mode of representation: information is documented, delivered impartially, arranged sequentially, and only occasionally interrupted by Mrs. Briggs's evaluative claims.

This rather dispassionate documentary ethos comes apart in a curious moment on the Briggses' first journey to Ypres in summer 1919, when Mrs. Briggs and her daughters encounter a "Chinaman" near the Hooge battlefield. In the narrative index, Mrs. Briggs prefaces this moment with an account of the Chinese Labor Corps and her own opinions that the Chinese are not a "smiling and bland" race but are actually lazy, ungrateful, and dangerous. Explaining how the Chinese revere their ancestors, Mrs. Briggs states,

> His contemporaries however are very cheap. If he got annoyed with a friend on the battlefields of Belgium, he could just wait until his friend (or enemy) was a safe distance away, then stoop down and pick up a bomb or grenade—anything explosive that was lying about—and throw it at him. If the man happened to be chatting with half a dozen others, that did not worry John Chinaman at all—he just blew them all up. As the ground at war time was literally strewn with explosives, and one could hardly walk without stepping on them, he was rather a dangerous person. (Briggs, n.d., notes filed under "C")

Having explained the Chinese race as threatening and reckless, Briggs then describes how "one of them followed us for some distance in the battlefields, and I noticed that our soldier-guide was not pleased. I suppose we have reason to congratulate ourselves, that he did not take a dislike to us" (Briggs, n.d.). In this curious encounter amid the wreckage of war, Miss Briggs decided to take a picture of their pursuer (Figure 12). The off-center framing, blurred edges, and washed-out color of the image suggest that it was perhaps a surreptitious photograph furtively captured as the Briggses' party hurried away from the strange interloper. What is curious is how the "Chinaman" comes to function as a photographable object akin to the ruined structures and battle detritus that populate the rest of the Briggs photographic archive. Certainly the visual and narrative objectifications of the "Chinaman" were enabled by tourism's growing ability to commodify any object or experience and turn it into something worth consuming, but they were also enabled by the context of empire. Unlike the "Frenchmen" and "Belgians" whom the Briggses regularly meet on their travels, the "Chinaman" is singled out: his racial inferiority equates him with the other objects deemed worthy of being photographed by Miss Briggs and methodically described by Mrs. Briggs (e.g., the derelict tank that the "Chinaman" stands beside). Not even his labor in aid of Allied forces during the war is enough to lift him out of his position as an objectified Other: he is worthy enough as an object to be photographed but not worthy enough to be admitted into a cross-cultural encounter with the Briggses and their tour guide.

Though this photograph certainly recalls the familiar colonial asym-

FIGURE 12. A "Chinaman" by a derelict tank at the top of Observatory Ridge, Hooge, 1919. Cat. No. Documents 21795. Courtesy of the Imperial War Museum Archive, London.

metries that framed the photographs of Price and Fooks, the figure of the "Chinaman" is more explicitly ambivalent. His out-of-place condition renders him a curious oddity that is easily consumed by the prevailing tourist gaze, but Mrs. Briggs describes him as threatening and violent— traits that suggest active agency, capacity, vibrancy, and mobility. In this sense, the "Chinaman" cannot be equated to the derelict tank he stands beside because his agency continually exceeds this positioning. His pose in the photograph reinforces this ambivalence: he appears content to be photographed (i.e., he has stopped for the moment and is resting on his back foot), and yet he also appears to be on the verge of movement— possibly pursuing the Briggses' party, but possibly on a wholly different trajectory. Nothing more is said of this strange encounter, but it is one of the main points of animation in the Briggses' initial visit to Ypres.

For me, this brief interruption is important because it destabilizes the "monarch-of-all-I-survey" subjectivity so carefully constructed by the Briggses' party during their battlefield tours. Present in their very first postwar journey is a strange and spectral presence—an out-of-place figure that cannot be easily slotted back into a landscape of now-pacified European nations. The "Chinaman's" agency, no matter how constrained by the Briggses' visual and narrative accounts, cannot help but resonate outside of the dominant coordinates that seek to position him. He forces viewers—both then and now—to acknowledge that Europe cannot constitute itself without its Others.

Creating Destinations: Tourist Sensibilities and the Second World War

The battlefield tours of the First World War were only a small part of the much larger growth in global tourism during the interwar years. Developments such as the institutionalization of paid holidays; the rise of commercial airlines (e.g., Imperial Airways, Pan American); dramatic expansions in rail, sea, and road travel (e.g., transatlantic cruise liners); and the birth of the modern seaside resort (e.g., the Riviera, Blackpool) facilitated the rapid growth of mass tourism throughout the 1920s, rising again in the late 1930s after the Great Depression (Löfgren 1999, 166–70; Middleton 2007, 1–16; Page 2009, 45–49). As John Urry (1990, 27) argues, "by the Second World War there was widespread acceptance of the view that going on holiday was good for one, that it was the basis of personal replenishment. Holidays had become almost a marker of citizenship, a right to pleasure." The interwar years are often considered the golden age of travel because the period struck a careful balance: mass tourism was now available for more and more people, but its particular combination of leisure and consumerism managed to retain an aura of luxury (Gregory 1991; Hadaway 2013). Unsurprisingly, this democratization of travel was constituted by significant productions of difference, as mass tourism in the 1920s–1930s was largely a Western phenomenon.

As the interwar tourism market continued to mobilize more and more industrialized populations, an oppositional voice began to materialize in those individuals who eschewed the emergence of mass culture, harkened back to a nineteenth-century sense of colonial adventure, and did everything in their power to label themselves "travelers" rather than "tourists." For Paul Fussell (1980), these figures were exemplified by British literary travelers of the 1930s, such as W. H. Auden, Christopher Isherwood, and Evelyn Waugh, who escaped a stale and constrictive England (with its now legal and increasingly formulaic holiday structure) to embrace warmer, more exotic, more "natural" climes. It is not difficult, of course, to discern the structures of empire that enabled this dissenting form of travel. Following Ali Behdad's (1994) formulation, they were "belated" travelers in the sense that they longed to experience the racial and class privilege of the great colonial adventurers, scientists, civil servants, administrators, and military officers who had journeyed to exotic lands before them. For Fred Inglis (2000), these "Imperial Travelers" were an essential part of the deeply pessimistic tone of early modernism that was born in the aftermath of the First World War—a combination of revulsion for the modern, urban, alienating life that produced industrial death in the trenches and a longing for "somewhere more remote, more exotic but also more elemental in its way of life; more natural, naturally, because simpler, less industrial, freer, more dignified, permitting one to lose one's ghastly conventionality and other people's even ghastlier pretensions and inauthenticity" (81).[7] While the growth of mass tourism in the interwar years helped to normalize the values of accumulation, commodification, and consumption so fundamental to modern consumer culture, these disgruntled "independent travelers" sought to escape such vulgar consumerism by finding solace in "exotic" places where the racial and class privilege of empire gained them entry, but where "convention" had not wrecked authenticity, nobility, and purity. Of course, by the 1930s, movements for decolonization across the Global South were already well under way—movements that compromised the colonial privilege of these Imperial Travelers and imbued their work with feelings of loss, melancholy, and self-pity. When the Second World War broke out in 1939, it did so in the midst of an emerging cultural distinction between the increasing popularity of mass tourism that had taken hold throughout the 1920s and the latter part of the 1930s and its scornful doppelganger: the independent Imperial Traveler. Both sensibilities—the tourist and the traveler—would shape the practices of officers, soldiers, sailors, marines, pilots, and other military subjects throughout the war as well as their encounters with a number of "foreign" populations throughout the world.

The powerful tourism culture of the interwar years directly shaped military strategy during Hitler's "Baedeker raids" on England in 1942 (Rothnie 1992; Whiting 1987). In retaliation for an Allied bombing of Lübeck that had destroyed its Old Town, Hitler began a campaign targeting culturally important British buildings rather than the traditional military targets of airstrips, army barracks, and munitions factories. After the first attack on Exeter on April 23, 1942, Nazi leader Baron Gustav Braun von Sturm declared, "We shall go out and bomb every building in Britain marked with three stars in the Baedeker Guide" (BBC 2005b). Famous destinations such as Bath, York, and Canterbury were already known and visible within an established European tourist circuit and were home to many famous churches, cathedrals, and buildings. Although more than sixteen hundred people were killed during these raids, it is widely believed that the raids failed to reach their objective because the valued historic buildings so central to the three-star Baedeker rating remained undamaged. Both the British decision to target the Old Town of Lübeck and Hitler's decision to target historic buildings in Britain exemplify the way that tourist attractions—in this case, sites of cultural heritage—have strategic value during war. Targeting them is not just about destroying iconic symbols of a culture (and thus destroying morale) but also about destroying potential future tourism revenue. Hitler's Baedeker raids were followed by another strategic mobilization of the interwar tourism culture when the British government appealed to the public for much-needed information about the physical characteristics of potential landing beaches at Normandy in advance of D-Day:

> While the British were considering invasion sites, the BBC broadcast an appeal for information on tides, defences, and enemy presence along the coast from Norway to Spain. The public response was overwhelming: more than 10,000,000 postcards and vacation photographs provided data, from which detailed maps of unusual accuracy were constructed. (Berman 1994, 470)

Figure 13 shows the beach at Anselles in Normandy, just east of Arromanches, and is one example of the millions of holiday postcards the British

TOURS OF DUTY, TOURS OF PLEASURE 95

FIGURE 13. Holiday postcard showing panoramic view of the beach at Anselles-La-Plage. Cat. No. HU 81694. Courtesy of the Imperial War Museum Archive, London. Copyright IWM.

public sent to the government in advance of D-Day. This postcard, and millions like it, enabled the Inter-services Topographical Department, itself a division of the Admiralty, to strategically reframe the holiday beaches of Normandy into military landing zones (in this case, Arromanches became part of the Gold Beach sector). After five years of conflict, British citizens were more than willing to contribute to the war effort by sharing their personal photographs and postcards; indeed, to do otherwise would have been considered unpatriotic and self-defeating.

What is interesting about both these examples is the way that crucial military decisions relied on the everyday tourism experiences expressed in guidebooks, postcards, and personal photographs. This suggests that during times of war, governments and militaries are able to discipline the lifeworlds of tourism—from industry infrastructure to individual memories—and put them to work in aid of the war effort. However, that explicit hierarchal relationship does not cohere when we examine the experiences and everyday practices of Allied soldiers serving abroad during the Second World War. The growth of mass tourism during the interwar years and the widespread consumer culture that sustained it were so powerful that they did not disappear when war broke out in 1939.

Soldiers on Vacation: Militourism and the Circuits of R&R

Building on the experience of the First World War, official R&R rotations were embedded even further within military logistics during the Second World War. Soldiers were regularly rotated out of frontline combat duty in both the European and Pacific theaters of war, and where travel home was not possible, military personnel were transported to nearby sites where leave had been arranged. For example, when Allied soldiers acquired short-term combat leave in Europe, many used their three-day passes to see famous landmarks that had been publicized during the tourist boom of the 1920s and 1930s. Thus, at various times from 1939 to 1945 (depending on how the war was progressing), Allied soldiers visited famous sites in Rome, Venice, Nice, Athens, London, Paris, and the French Riviera. Official guidebooks were published to help soldiers make the most of their brief stays; for example, in *How to See the Côte D'Azur* (1940), enlisted men were provided with a map of the area and a guide to the services available to troops on leave (e.g., doctors, pharmacies, dentists, Laundromats, dry cleaning and religious services) as well as recreational opportunities (e.g., movies, sightseeing tours, portrait sketches, swimming, tennis, and roller skating) (Commissariat au Tourisme and Franco-Allied Good Will Committee 1940). These were supplemented by unofficial guidebooks written by soldiers themselves that listed hotel, club, and restaurant recommendations and provided useful tips for soldiers on leave (e.g., book accommodation well in advance; bring your ration book; bring your own soap) (Courtenay 1941, 4). Occupied Paris, of course, was one of the main centers for German R&R from 1940 to 1944, when Hitler and many senior figures in the Nazi Party enjoyed excursions to the city (Baranowski 2004; Gordon 1998; Koshar 2000, 150–55; Semmens 2005; Torrie 2011). However, once Paris had been liberated in August 1944, it became the largest hub of Allied R&R activity in Europe, followed closely by the French Riviera, which the Americans renamed the "United States Riviera Rest Area" and proceeded to divide between Nice, which catered to enlisted men, and Cannes, which catered to officers (Endy 2004, 19–23;

Goldstone 2001, 33–34). When soldiers arrived in designated leave areas, they were met by a complex array of military, public, private, and volunteer organizations. These included official welcome centers providing information; nationally designated clubs, restaurants, and shops, which separated officers from enlisted men (as well as white troops from black); American Red Cross clubs and other welfare centers run by volunteer groups such as the YMCA; and hundreds of local businesses (e.g., theaters, clubs, restaurants, cinemas) that catered to Allied forces on leave (Commiserat General Au Tourism 1945, inside cover). As a 1945 guidebook for Allied soldiers in liberated Paris claimed, they "poured in an uninterrupted stream to lose themselves in the ocean of joy that was Paris free at last" (Commiserat General Au Tourism 1945, 132). Indeed, it was these experiences of R&R that gave Americans the taste for postwar European tourism: "GIs established personal relationships in other countries where Recreation and Recuperation (R&R) facilities were situated in areas with normal tourism appeal—scenery, beaches, shopping, and access to entertainment" (Smith 1998, 212; see also Endy 2004, 19–23).

In non-European battlefields across North Africa, the Middle East, South Asia, Southeast Asia, and the Pacific, Allied troops took leave in a variety of locations from large and well-established urban command centers like Cairo, Hong Kong, and Sydney to small Pacific islands and beaches. These R&R itineraries are politically significant because they operated within still-functioning empires and colonial outposts. Though R&R encounters between Allied soldiers and local populations in Europe were certainly framed through long-standing cultural differences,[8] the leisured encounters that took place within a colonial context were more explicitly scripted by racial, civilizational, and gendered asymmetries. In other words, the privilege of Allied soldiers on leave in colonized territories was intensified and amplified by the prevailing context of colonial asymmetry. Certainly the condition of war enabled soldiers on leave to claim that privilege more easily, but in many non-European battlefields, that privilege was normalized by the codification of racial inequality into law, the administration of local populations through institutions of colonial rule, and the techniques of governance that ordered local populations according to the hierarchy of empire.

Once again, Cairo functioned as British headquarters during the war, and once again, officers circulated through Shepheard's Hotel's famous terraced front while all enlisted men frequented the red-light districts and brothels behind the hotel. Indeed, on December 14, 1942, *LIFE* magazine ran a story on the role of Shepheard's Hotel in the war and included a number of images by photographer Bob Landry. Capturing the familiar image of the front terrace of Shepheard's, the *LIFE* caption read, "Beyond is Cook's tourist office, which still does a rushing business in wartime" (Humphrey 2012). While India functioned as a British command center for the war in Southeast Asia and the Middle East, it was also a geographical haven where Allied officers, soldiers, and pilots could recover from battle and enjoy the benefits of leisure established by the British colonial administration. This was especially the case with the Raj-built hill stations in northern India, which operated as scheduled R&R stops for Allied troops circulating through Burma, Malaysia, and Singapore. As Figure 14 shows, the hill stations provided Royal Air Force (RAF) pilots with opportunities for trekking, hiking, and camping while on leave. Taken by an official RAF photographer, this image certainly reveals the positive benefits of R&R for RAF soldiers. The cool air and refreshing activities of the hill stations kept soldiers away not only from the sapping tropical heat of the front line but also from the vices and sins of colonial cities like Calcutta and Hong Kong. However, this image also inadvertently reveals the conditions of empire that underscored these hiking and camping expeditions in the Himalayas. On the bottom right of the photograph are six figures, partially hidden by the grass, who appear to be local guides or laborers. These are the subjects who enabled the RAF Aircrew Mountain Centre—the military unit running the R&R centers—to function by guiding soldiers up the mountains, carrying camping equipment, setting up camp, cooking meals, negotiating with local populations, and striking camp at the end of the holiday. In foregrounding the leisured experience of RAF pilots on leave over the working lives of the laborers who constructed and facilitated the R&R camp, Figure 14 succeeds in visualizing the colonial logics that continued to underscore the adventures of Allied officers and soldiers in India during the Second World War. The problem with these logics, of course, is they negate the complex negotiations over nationalism, loyalty,

FIGURE 14. RAF officers look out over Sonamarg trekking and climbing camp in the Kashmiri Himalayas. Cat. No. CI 1523. Courtesy of the Imperial War Museum Archive, London. Copyright IWM.

and empire that were developing at this time in South Asia, including the anticolonial, independence, and nationalist movements that were using the war as a catalyst to end British colonial rule. In this sense, Figure 14 represents a double escape: certainly RAF soldiers were enjoying a brief respite from battling the Japanese, but they were also avoiding the growing anticolonial sentiment that threatened their privileged position of "Imperial vacationers" in the Himalayas.

These colonial logics were especially intense in the Pacific theater of the Second World War. Allied soldiers—mostly American—were rotated on and off of aircraft carriers and in and out of secure island bases, but some, like U.S. Air Force pilots, were sent back to special rest homes on Honolulu for longer stretches of R&R. Hawaii was an absolutely central intersection for the practices of war and tourism between 1939 and 1945: not only was it a major American military base but its popularity as a tourist destination during the 1920s and 1930s made it ideal as the preferred R&R destination for American forces in the Pacific. In urban spaces like Honolulu, as well as sites adjacent to the American military base, a complex mixture of subjectivities encountered each other throughout the war, including regular tourists, soldiers on R&R from the Pacific theater, soldiers off duty from the local military base, American women employed in the war effort (e.g., nurses, secretaries, service workers, prostitutes), indigenous communities, local Japanese communities, American citizens who had settled in Hawaii, and the families of American servicemen who arrived in Hawaii to share R&R leave with their loved ones. As Vicuña Gonzalez (2013, 13) explains, the Allied soldiers stationed in and circulating through Hawaii

> brought a particularly sexualized version of the tropics-as-paradise into the American national consciousness. In Hawaii and the Philippines, militarism jump-started the first tourist establishments on the islands: catering to military and colonial personnel, zones for rest and recreation cropped up, exploiting fantasies—if not always realities—of the exotic.

For me, the intermingling of tourism and militarism in R&R sites like Hawaii cannot be disentangled from the competing colonial logics they mobilize, for example, by the Japanese seeking to extend their empire throughout the Pacific and by the Americans seeking to consolidate their rule over an indigenous Hawaiian population. In that sense, the everyday practices of soldier-tourists (taking pictures; collecting souvenirs; visiting famous landmarks; and making use of local bars, clubs, and brothels) are constituted by "exploiting fantasies" and therefore cannot be understood as benign.

What happens when the persistence of a tourist sensibility in wartime—when a "tour of duty" becomes a "tour of pleasure" through R&R—resonates through these colonial logics? How do modes of domination intrinsic to the practices of war and tourism intensify and amplify the experience of colonialism? For Carolyn O'Dwyer (2004, 35–36), this conjunction is revealed most clearly when the tourist gaze and the military gaze fold into one another during the experience of R&R:

> The *militourist gaze* [is] a visual point of violence where the scopophilic gaze of the desiring tourist meets the eye of military surveillance. The consuming gaze of leisure strategically collapses into the perceptual logics of surveillance. Concomitantly, the soldier comes dangerously armed not only with weapons, but with the preconceptions and aspirations of the pleasure seeking tourist.

O'Dwyer traces this conjunction through a particular photographic archive from the Second World War and demonstrates how one American soldier—Henry "Rip" Yeagar—contrasted his experience fighting and killing "Japs" with familiar tourist tropes of the "seductive South Seas." O'Dwyer's study of wartime Hawaii is significant because it demonstrates how the conjunction of the tourist gaze and the military gaze reinforced rather than overturned deeply entrenched power relations between races, genders, and classes. As she argues, tropes of exoticism, pleasure, and paradise popularized by the Hawaiian tourist industry in the 1920s and 1930s rendered the local population of Hawaii innocent and its landscape feminine so that they *required* the protection of a paternal American military force (O'Dwyer 2004; see also Bailey and Farber 1992; Vicuña Gonzales 2013, 49–82). Of course, Hawaii was not being protected for the local population—it was being protected for serving American forces to enjoy its tourist resorts while on R&R and for millions of future American and international tourists—including, eventually, Japanese tourists—to experience this "paradise in the Pacific."

For O'Dwyer, the parallel gazes of militarism and tourism share similar logics of power and therefore become mutually reinforcing in specific sites like Hawaii. As she explains, "the unequal relations of power fundamental to the structure of the tourist gaze were exponentially magnified in the racist and masculinist environment of war, not least by the sheer volume of the mobile service population" (34). Though I share O'Dwyer's central claim, I want to argue that the intertwining of tourism and militarism is never totalized; rather, it is always riven with fractures, slippages, and contradictions that can never be resolved. Indeed, it is this *lack* of coherence between tourism and militarism that needs to be interrogated further to discover the everyday practices of reordering, improvisation, and resistance that are always taking place. With this in mind, it is worth revisiting how experiences of R&R were made visible during the Second World War and what those expressions simultaneously foregrounded and concealed. Allied militaries, and the official photographers and journalists attached to them, promoted a benign account of R&R in which soldiers took advantage of their postings overseas and behaved like regular tourists (e.g., consulting their guidebooks, enjoying local food, speaking with locals, visiting famous tourist attractions) (Tanner, n.d.). What these images conceal, of course, are the much less picturesque actions of soldiers on leave in which local populations were exploited by troops pursuing relaxation, recuperation, and pleasure. Here the constitutive logic of differentiation shared between tourism and war is made clear: battles need Others to function as threatening enemies, just as tourism needs Others to function as exotic hosts. With respect to R&R, that shared logic of differentiation and domination is important because it allows the norms that legitimate, condone, and justify acts of killing on the battlefield to slip into the experience of off-duty leave. When soldiers transition into periods of R&R, their hypermasculine dispositions of aggression, violence, and hostility are dispersed through a variety of micropolitical acts that subordinate and exploit local populations.

Pleasure as Propaganda: Edward Steichen and the War Effort

Alongside the strategic deployment of radar, sonar, photography, and cinema, modern militaries were also using the visual technologies of consumer culture for propagandist purposes. Indeed, if images could mobilize consumers to buy goods, they could certainly inspire young men to enlist and encourage citizens to support the war effort. Photographer Edward J. Steichen is a particularly interesting figure in this transition. During the First World War, Steichen led the Photographic Division of the American Expeditionary Forces in Europe and supervised aerial reconnaissance photography (Bachner 2004, 6; Hüppauf 1993; Niven 1998; Phillips 1981; Signal Corps, n.d.). After the war, Steichen went on to become the most famous—and most expensive—commercial photographer of his time, directing major fashion and advertising campaigns in the 1920s and 1930s and producing several iconic celebrity portraits (Phillips 1981, 12–15). At age sixty-one, Steichen was too old to enlist in the Second World War, but after the attack on Pearl Harbor he convinced the U.S. Navy that his combination of photographic talent—both aerial reconnaissance and fashion photography—could be utilized in the war effort. He was put in charge of the Naval Aviation Photography Unit (NAPU), which was to "document the activities of the Navy for recruitment, training and other

Office of War Information purposes, primarily providing images for newspapers and magazines rallying support on the domestic front" (Bachner 2004, 7; also Phillips 1981, 17–22). In effect, Steichen was employed to run an advertising campaign for the American military: his unrivalled expertise in styling, editing, and choosing photographs that mobilized the American public's desire to purchase consumer goods could be directed at mobilizing support for the war (Heppenheimer 2006; Phillips 1981, 22). Steichen assembled a group of distinguished photographers and photojournalists, who traveled with the U.S. Navy all over the Pacific theater of war from 1943 to 1945.[9] Steichen himself was a busy man during the war: along with taking his own photographs of American navy pilots aboard the USS *Lexington* and coordinating the entire NAPU project in Washington, D.C., he also curated a photographic exhibition about the war at the Museum of Modern Art in New York City titled *Road to Victory* and directed the Academy Award–winning documentary *The Fighting Lady* about the aircraft carrier USS *Yorktown* (Phillips 1981, 17–20; *Time* 1945). Despite his many commitments, Steichen exercised a high level of editorial and stylistic control over the NAPU photographs. To achieve the kinds of images that would work best as advertisements, Steichen made sure that his photographers were able to use their own equipment (i.e., Rolleiflex cameras, Kodachrome film) rather than the cumbersome Speed-Graphic cameras issued by the navy; he arranged for all negatives to be sent to his personal lab in Washington for development and printing; and he explicitly favored photographs that mimicked his own style of classical compositions (e.g., heavy use of shadows, dramatic contrasts between light and dark) (Heppenheimer 2006; Phillips 2006, 27–29). He personally developed, selected, and edited all NAPU images that were sent out to the press and the public and helped write the important captions that accompanied the photographs.

What makes these images significant for me is their deliberate foregrounding of leisure and tourism amid war. Steichen was charged with documenting the everyday life of soldiers and sailors "as they relaxed, trained, went about their lives, prepared for the next battle, and waited" (Bachner 2004, 7–8). In the navy, of course, much of that waiting occurred on aircraft carriers in the Pacific, and the NAPU photographers were on board to capture the different ways that soldiers and sailors entertained themselves while at sea (e.g., sunbathing, athletics, volleyball, weight lifting, reading, writing, sewing, card games). It is here, in the NAPU's images of leisure, recreation, and relaxation aboard the Pacific aircraft carriers, that the interwar tourist sensibility emerges most clearly. Indeed, it is easy to see why Alex Danchev (2005, 25) has argued that "from this collection one might well think that hell in the Pacific is a poor tan." Figure 15 is a typical NAPU image showing three sailors doing acrobatics while stationed aboard a submarine tender. Although this photograph was taken by Horace Bristol, the composition reproduces Steichen's own style of dramatic contrasts between light and dark, explicit lines and angles, and careful arrangements of foreground and background objects. Given Steichen's professional experience, it is unsurprising that many of the NAPU images are identical to the carefully staged fashion shots he took in the 1920s and 1930s, only now it was the masculinity of soldiers and sailors rather than the beauty of female models and celebrities on display. By replacing conventional scenes of war with leisured images that tapped into already circulating discourses of tourism and consumer culture, these photographs worked to connect soldiers and sailors to fellow citizens on the home front. Images of sunbathing, relaxation, fitness, and male horseplay were familiar to American audiences who participated in similar leisure activities themselves, but they also convinced audiences that American forces were winning the war in the Pacific—otherwise, why else would they have the time, energy, and permission to engage in such larks?

The NAPU images were not only about life aboard aircraft carriers: the photographers also went ashore with the troops and captured more scenes of soldiers relaxing on the beaches of the Pacific islands. The beach, of course, is an important liminal space between nature and culture that is dominated by discourses of leisure and tourism—a place where societal conventions can be easily discarded, individuals can adopt different identities, and feelings of freedom and liberation produce a "carnivalesque" atmosphere (Inglis 2000, 36–54; Lěncek and Bosker 1998; Preston-Whyte 2004; Shields 1992, 73–116). But beaches are also central to military strategy as sites of amphibious landings, fierce battles, troop coordination, communication hubs, logistic headquarters, and mass

FIGURE 15. Crewmen exercising aboard a submarine tender. National Archives photo 80-G-472362. Courtesy of the Still Picture Branch, National Archives and Records Administration.

slaughter. This strange conjunction is nowhere more apparent than on the Normandy beaches: they were used by "thermal" bathers in the 1930s who came to swim in the supposedly medicinal waters of the English Channel; fortified by German soldiers trying to protect their newly conquered territory during the Second World War; contemplated and studied by Allied commanders planning the D-Day invasion in 1944; and strewn with corpses after the invasion—and ever since, the Normandy beaches have been "littered with carefree, suntanning bodies" resting from their tourist excursions to war memorials (Diller + Scofidio 1994, 278–95).

The juxtaposition between militarism and tourism on beach landscapes involves multiple temporalities: as military troops occupy and secure beaches for strategic reasons during the war, they are also territorializing the beaches for future tourism. This is certainly the case with Figure 16, Charles Kerlee's photograph of navy men relaxing on the beach in Guam. These figures are shorn of signs that would identify them as sailors or military personnel: they are in swimming trunks (or boxer shorts) and framed through the prominent "exotic" signifier of the palm tree. Not only are they mobilizing a tourist sensibility amid the rhythms of war, they are also foreshadowing future acts of sunbathing, relaxation, and leisure tourism on more peaceful postwar beaches. Kerlee's photograph, as well as many others in the NAPU archive, draws explicitly on the iconic tourist photographs, postcards, and advertisements of Hawaii that circulated before the war, while simultaneously offering the viewer the promise of future tropical holiday destinations after the war. It comes as no surprise, then, that Steichen himself worked on tourist and cruise advertisements for Hawaii just before the Second World War: his stereotypical images of hula dancers, beaches, and sunsets were "highly regarded and widely displayed" in popular periodicals such as *National Geographic* from 1939 to 1941 (Desmond 1999, 102–3).

Central to the juxtaposition of tourism and militarism in the NAPU archive is a particular form of colonial nostalgia. These photographs depict the Pacific as an empty land that is simply awaiting occupation—by famous colonial explorers in the past, by military forces in the present, and by tourists in the future. Certainly NAPU photographers, soldiers, and audiences made sense of this region by drawing from the same arsenal of iconic images in which the South Seas were depicted as the "paradise in the Pacific." Many popular cultural representations circulating before the war (e.g., *Mutiny on the Bounty*, the adventures of Captain Cook, the stories of Robert Louis Stevenson, the paintings of Paul Gauguin, 1930s Hollywood films such as *Waikiki Wedding* and *Hawaii Calls*) suggested that the Pacific was populated by primitive cultures untouched by modernity and progress (Kahn 2000; Manderson and Jolly 1997; Rennie 1995; Vicuña Gonzalez 2013, 7–9; Wilson 2000). However, the NAPU images signified the familiar Edenic paradise of the Pacific not by recourse to culture (i.e.,

FIGURE 16. Navy men relax and swim at bathing beach on Guam. National Archives photo 80-G-474328. Courtesy of the Still Picture Branch, National Archives and Records Administration.

primitive tribes) but rather by recourse to nature—by evacuating local Others from the frame and focusing instead on the dramatic landscapes, lush flora and fauna, and intense contrasts between idyllic beaches and sublime mountains. This enforced absence of local subjects was a common trope in colonial visualization: new lands were routinely cleared of

108 TOURS OF DUTY, TOURS OF PLEASURE

inhabitants so that supposedly "untouched" areas could be rescripted, reoriented, and reterritorialized to fulfill the desire of the colonizer. The NAPU photographs of South Pacific beaches construct a form of militarized *terra nullius* by suggesting these spaces as uninhabited and apparently unused by locals. Signifiers of "native" presence are absent on the beaches, and any material remnants that do appear in the frame are detritus from the present modern war (e.g., empty supply boxes, ammunition shells, stray fuselages). When signs of local habitation do emerge (e.g., seaside villages, beach houses), they are rescripted into the Allied story of success in the Pacific as soldiers and sailors colonize destroyed villages and make them "operational" (e.g., constructing showers in abandoned buildings, using bomb craters as bathing and swimming holes, rigging up laundry and shaving facilities from scattered debris).

There is a careful balance struck in the NAPU archive between including enough signifiers of difference to confirm that soldiers and sailors are operating in an exotic setting made familiar by a prewar tourist culture but not enough to suggest that they are actually shirking their military duties. This balance is achieved most clearly in images that adopt the conventions of tourist photography. For example, Figure 17 by Wayne Miller depicts two American sailors visiting a Buddhist temple in Ceylon (Sri Lanka). This image is familiar because it looks like a holiday snapshot; indeed, it reproduces amateur photographs taken by tourists on the prewar circuit of the Pacific. There are, however, important differences here. The NAPU photographs are professional holiday snapshots taken by experienced photographers and submitted to Steichen's keen editorial eye. The conventions of tourist photography are disciplined by the documentary ethos underscoring the NAPU project, for example, the two main figures are not looking at or posing for the camera the way tourists would. More to the point, the militarized identities of these figures are immediately and deliberately signified by their sailor uniforms. By presenting a professionalized and militarized formulation of regular tourist photographs, the NAPU photographs of soldiers on R&R in the Pacific—sunbathing, swimming on sandy beaches, visiting cultural monuments, taking in historic sights—tell audiences that American forces have successfully colonized the Pacific and made local cultures serve both their strategic

TOURS OF DUTY, TOURS OF PLEASURE 109

FIGURE 17. Sailors from the USS *Saratoga* (CV-3) on liberty in Buddhist temple grounds at Anurodapura, Ceylon. National Archives photo 80-G-474022. Courtesy of the Still Picture Branch, National Archives and Records Administration.

and leisured needs (Edwards 2003; Mitchell 2005b, 145–68; Ryan 1997, 140–82). But the NAPU photographs also tell us something else: they tell us that American military elites were not just successful at governing all aspects of their soldiers' lives, including their leisure time; they were also successful at mobilizing those lives and putting them on display for propagandist purposes. Toward the end of the war in 1945, however, the propaganda coordinates of the NAPU project shifted. As the enemy retreated, the NAPU photographers introduced local subjects in more "interactive" shots of soldiers laughing with local children or sailors buying fruit from local food stalls. This was yet another mobilization of a convention within tourist photography: capturing colorful local hosts alongside the exotic signifiers of a strange destination. By visualizing and popularizing "benign" encounters between American troops and "grateful" hosts, the NAPU images normalized a particular understanding of the Pacific: it was only *because of* American military success in the region that local people were able to carry on with their everyday lives—laughing, playing, buying, selling—without being oppressed by the Japanese Empire.

It is difficult to dislodge the NAPU photographs from their propagandist framing: these image makers were advertising the U.S. Navy and selling American victory in the Pacific to an American audience back home. Steichen's commercial photographic style was perfect for the job; indeed, he was not just a willing participant in the propaganda effort, he was an enthusiastic architect of its aesthetic norms. Using his experience as a fashion photographer, Steichen mobilized a particularly dramatic style to convey the robust masculinity of the U.S. Navy and its confidence in the face of Japanese aggression. Images of sailors and soldiers effectively on vacation in the Pacific convinced readers that the American military had everything in hand; so successful was their military campaign that their soldiers were able to take time off to enjoy themselves and see the sights in the Pacific. The propagandist framing of the NAPU project is clearest in its production and visualization of Hawaii. For example, Figure 18, an unattributed image of two sailors on leave in Waikiki, exemplifies how the preexisting culture of leisure, tourism, and consumption that Steichen helped to manufacture during the 1920s and 1930s was central to the NAPU project.

The relaxed pose of the sailors under the palm tree positions them within the same circuit of leisure as the swimmers in the background; indeed, both soldiers and tourists appear entirely at home on the beaches of Diamond Head. The NAPU images of Hawaii (e.g., U.S. Air Force pilots playing tennis at dedicated R&R rest homes, wrestling with each other on a manicured lawn, or dancing with their respectable and well-groomed "dates" in Honolulu) reproduced the conjoining of militarism and tourism as entirely innocent. The framing of Hawaii did not allow for photographs of soldiers and sailors interacting with "exotic" local populations because

FIGURE 18. Two U.S. sailors on leave near Diamond Head discuss the sights under a palm tree. National Archives photo 80-G-422057. Courtesy of the Still Picture Branch, National Archives and Records Administration.

both NAPU and the American military were invested in rendering Hawaii as an entirely American playground: a place to rest, relax, and play for both American forces and the wider American population. By referencing the "exotic" interwar tourist imagery of Hawaii largely through familiar objects (e.g., palm trees, beaches, tropical flora, swimmers, sunsets) rather than through local people, the NAPU photographs helped facilitate an important depoliticization: they securitized and Americanized Hawaii for the purposes of a future tourism market by effacing the palpable and long-standing tensions over its sovereignty. These photographs helped to silence those indigenous, alternative, and disruptive voices that resisted Hawaii's primary valuation as a military command center and desirable tourism destination. As the visual productions of Hawaii suggest, this was a robust nationalist envisioning that rendered all overseas landscapes and populations subordinate to the adventuring spirit of America's military forces. While mainstream photographers, journalists, and cameramen documented America's incremental military encroachment in the Pacific, NAPU showed how this colonization happened simultaneously through usually unseen practices of leisure and tourism. What interests me most about the NAPU archive is that no matter how robust its propagandist framing, the juxtaposition of tourism and war was too jarring to be contained within its parameters. The benign leisure and tourist activities that these photographs depict did not square with the extremely violent, racialized, sexualized, and dehumanizing character of war in the Pacific. By further interrogating that moment of excess, it is possible to see how NAPU's confident propagandist message starts to unravel.

The Excesses of Sex and Death: Tourism, Voyeurism, and Dehumanization in the Pacific

With Steichen's experience in advertising, respected war record, recognizable style of bold shapes and simple contrasts, and insistence on strict editorial control, he was crucial in making sure the NAPU images signified within the propaganda framework he advocated. As Allan Sekula (1975, 35) argues, his willingness to take charge of such an exercise reflected a professional life that was uncritically and unreflexively geared to aestheticizing the status quo:

> The only consistent vectors in Steichen's career were sentimentalism, opportunism, and a fierce dedication to craft; the first two lead directly into his becoming a benign ideological agent of corporate political power. Throughout the larger part of his career, in his advertising and fashion work and his monumental "photo essays," Steichen contributed to a falsified image of the family, of women, of consumption, of war and international politics, and of cultural freedom. A "global vision of life," even in its "humanist" and liberal manifestations, may serve only to mask another vision, a vision of global domination.

Certainly Sekula's framing of Steichen helps us to politicize the simple propagandist framing of the NAPU images by prompting us to ask what is seen (i.e., American presence, confidence, and success in the Pacific) and what is unseen (i.e., the colonial asymmetries and unequal class, race, and gendered relationships that made American military success possible). To be sure, Steichen was more willing to use his photography to serve power than he was to critique it, and in this sense I think Sekula is right. But this positioning of Steichen as a "benign ideological agent" committed to producing American war propaganda is problematic because it invokes notions of an uncontested truth. To suggest that Steichen's photographs offer a "falsified" image of life suggests that propagandist images such as the NAPU collection actually lie—and that what we need to do is uncover and reveal the truth underneath those lies. This further suggests that there is some kind of *better* image that could have been taken by the NAPU photographers that would have documented the truth and conveyed it—in toto—to its audience. That, of course, is impossible— no photograph, no representation whatsoever, visual or otherwise, can ever do this. So while a propagandist framing helps to demonstrate that the NAPU images present a sanitized version of American military life in the Pacific (and, indeed, shows us how Steichen's vision and skill brilliantly aestheticized this sanitation), it does not help to make visible the constitutive power relations that enabled American forces to proceed through the Pacific or the multiplicity of alternative lives that were effaced, ignored, or actively subordinated in that march to victory. To create a space in which the range of asymmetries usually closed off by a propagandist framing are able to articulate themselves, it is necessary to reread (and deliberately misread) these photographs. All images always signify beyond the register of their production and framing and thus always tell us more than they mean to. For me, the NAPU images are particularly interesting because they are saturated with glaring silences, competing articulations, and ambivalent meanings that undermine their official propagandist framing. With this in mind, I want to supplement Sekula's critique of Steichen with a further series of deconstructions that pay particular attention to the erasure of local populations, the ambivalent sexualities on display, and the confrontational images of the enemy that appear regularly toward the end of the war.

The numerous depictions of leisure and tourism in the NAPU archive suggest that when American soldiers were on leave in the Pacific, they engaged in healthy sporting activities, went sightseeing, took tourist photographs, and enjoyed the friendship of their fellow soldiers. Such a benign account completely effaces the less salubrious activities that soldiers have always engaged in when on leave, namely, drinking, vice, and prostitution. Cynthia Enloe (2000, 68) has argued that the tourism industry is central to the military's use of prostitution and is a key factor in forcing women into prostitution: "In many parts of the world, in fact, the presence of brothels for male soldiers has laid the groundwork for the development of brothels for male tourists. That is, militarism and tourism may not be polar opposites after all." Feminist scholarship on the "comfort women"—the two hundred thousand mostly Korean and Chinese women who were used as sexual slaves by the Japanese military—tells us much about the wartime intersections of militarism, travel, power, and sex in the Pacific (Hicks 2011; Min 2003; Soh 2009; Tanaka 2002; Yoshiaki 2001). Building on those feminist insights, I want to focus more specifically on how preexisting circuits of tourism and institutional structures of R&R helped to entrench militarized prostitution for Allied soldiers in the Pacific, especially in Hawaii. The link between prostitution, militarism, and tourism can be discerned in the marketing of Hawaii as a tourist destination during the 1920s and 1930s: it was depicted as different from the rest of mainland America, a place to forget ordinary life and indulge in leisure, pleasure, and hedonism (Desmond 1999, 79–121). Hawaii's status as somehow different from the rest of America (and thus as an ideal site for tourism) was transposed into wartime so that the rules and regulations governing the home front of America—including the treatment of women—somehow did not apply to this "foreign base." Bailey and Farber (1992, 17–18) argue that Hawaii during the Second World War was a *liminal* space, not quite home front and not quite front line—a "highly charged arena in which the individual dramas of cultural contact were played out." The suspension of norms, the threat of war, and the now well-entrenched pursuit of pleasure encouraged by the tourist industry meant that prostitution for American troops in Hawaii during the Second World War was not just widely accepted; it was also openly and jointly organized by brothel owners, military elites, public officials, and the tourism industry (Bailey and Farber 1992, 95–131; Enloe 2000, 64; 1993, 145–47). Hawaii's liminal character did not make it a neutral space; indeed, as Bailey and Farber (1992) argue, Hawaii during the Second World War was an intensely racialized, sexualized, and colonized site in which local Hawaiian, Japanese, and female bodies were subject to harassment, violence, and discrimination—acts that were excused or justified in the name of the war effort. That schema of multiple, intersecting, and powerful asymmetries is effaced in the NAPU photographs that depict R&R activities in Hawaii as wholesome, benign, and celebratory. By sanitizing the experience of R&R and ignoring the practice of militarized prostitution, the NAPU project helped entrench a colonial logic that privileged the bodies, lifeworlds, and needs of Allied soldiers above those of women, indigenous Hawaiians, and other subaltern subjects (e.g., migrant laborers, resident Japanese communities).

This effacement of militarized sex does not extend to the subsequent interpretive frames through which these photographs have been read. Indeed, the recent reissue of these images in two coffee-table photograph books—*At Ease* (2004) and *Men of WWII* (2007)—has foregrounded the lingering homoeroticism and ambivalent formations of masculinity at work in the NAPU photographs. Focusing mainly on images of enlisted men aboard navy ships and relaxing on Pacific islands, these two books transform NAPU's propagandist effort—to show men "at ease" during war—into a series of beefcake shots in which the almost always topless, heavily muscled, and sweating bodies of sailors and soldiers are on display. The photographs on board naval ships show male bodies working on or resting near often phallic machinery (airplanes, gun turrets, machine guns), doing physical exercise (wrestling, weight lifting, calisthenics, swimming), or relaxing in the sun (e.g., reading, sunbathing while playing cards). The photographs on Pacific beaches depict mostly naked marines swimming, showering, washing, and bathing. Certainly these images fulfill NAPU's remit of documenting the everyday lives of men at war, but they do much more than this: they foreground the intimacy, closeness, and tenderness produced between men when they are thrown together in large groups far away from the heteronormative structures of family and society. The positioning of these male bodies in close proximity and often in contact with each other suggests a number of potential transgressions of the heteronormative order. Photographs of men lazily napping together, combing each other's hair, sunbathing with entwined limbs, roughhousing, and grooming each other contain a sexual charge that exceeds

Steichen's framing of these activities as innocent homosocial bonding.

The ambivalence of the masculinities and sexualities on display emerges clearly in the group shots of men engaged in collective activities and seemingly unaware of (or deliberately ignoring) the camera. Because these subjects do not challenge the viewer with their direct gaze, the isolated world within the frame produces a feeling of voyeurism rather than spectatorship. Viewers are looking into the usually hidden world of soldiers off duty—a secret world for most of us—rather than consuming a familiar tourist photograph or fashion advertisement.[10] Given the conservative norms of sexuality and masculinity that prevailed during the Second World War, it is unsurprising that the NAPU images attempt to secure ambivalence, uncertainty, or deviance by directly signifying the heteronormative order, for example, by showing tattoos of female figures, positioning figures next to wall posters of pinup girls, and referring to traditional family structures back home. Those efforts fail, of course, and what these reissued photographs suggest is that the bodies of sailors and soldiers were not entirely constrained by the prevailing norms of heterosexual masculinity. The experience of being away at war in the Pacific—and, indeed, the experience of being photographed while off duty—allowed the familiar patterns of masculinity, sexuality, and militarism to be somewhat reordered. My point is that the leisured and touristic sensibilities that prevailed during off-duty moments greatly facilitated this reordering by creating an alternative disposition through which multiple and sometimes oppositional gendered identities, relations, and sexualities could appear. Because the soldiers and sailors were relaxing while off duty (and thus unshackled by the restrictive norms of duty, labor, and home), their usually private, intimate lifeworlds and relations were on display for the camera. This act of making visible what is usually unseen does not, as Danchev (2005, 25) suggests, make the two recent collections of NAPU photographs "snapshots of a world of unfeigned innocence." This claim negates both the direct interventions of the photographer who poses the subjects, constructs the scene, and frames the action and the willing, vibrant, and enthusiastic dispositions of those bodies who actively courted and enjoyed being on display for the cameras. Moreover, to suggest that these images are innocent underestimates the threat that alternative masculinities and sexualities posed to wartime heteronormativity and effaces all of the unseen laboring bodies that enabled these troops to experience leisure time in the Pacific during the Second World War.

While NAPU's propagandist frame is certainly troubled by a focus on gender and sexuality, it starts to explicitly unravel in the later photographs of the Japanese enemy—both dead soldiers and live prisoners of war (POWs). Unlike the official war photographers and photojournalists who captured the progress of battle and thus visualized the enemy at a distance, the NAPU photographers arrived after the battle and were therefore able to capture images of the dead and mutilated bodies of Japanese soldiers left behind as their armies retreated. Some of the dead are dismembered—Steichen, for example, took a famous image of a stray hand amid the rubble of a bomb blast—and some are completely unrecognizable as human figures. These photographs fully dehumanize Japanese subjects by equating their dead bodies and body parts with the exotic objects usually framed by the tourist gaze. For example, O'Dwyer (2004, 39, 45) documents how U.S. Navy pilot "Rip" Yeagar took many photographs of violent death—both of individual Japanese soldiers and also mass graves-with "apparent casualness": "[his] camera bore witness to a disturbing degree of violence—a violence sometimes accidentally recorded by the photographer but as often gratuitously perpetrated by him in the course of his hobby." The desire to trivialize enemy death by incorporating it into an established iconography of tourist photography—a palm tree, a pyramid, a dead soldier—is the same desire that prompted American soldiers to collect Japanese skull trophies as souvenirs of their time in the Pacific (Janowski 2007; Weingartner 1992). The level of depersonalization, disaggregation, and dehumanization enacted by Allied soldiers in the Pacific—and, more importantly, the touristic sensibility that enabled such relations—is exemplified in the famous photograph of marines on Guadalcanal boiling a Japanese POW's head and behaving as if they were at a weekend BBQ (Harrison 2006, 822).[11]

For me, the NAPU images of dead Japanese soldiers are the ultimate expression of the mode of domination shared by war and tourism—a mode that, when followed to its logical conclusion, dehumanizes enemies and renders them equivalent to objects. That shared mode of domination is facilitated by, and works to reproduce, the powerful discourses and practices of racism, patriarchy, and imperialism that prevailed during the war in the Pacific. For example, O'Dwyer connects Yeagar's tourist portraits of dead Japanese soldiers with his representations of local women and children:

> The photographs mark out a field of representational and physical violence, a site where the structures of power expressed through colonial relations and the expectations and desires typical of the island tourist intersect with the racist and masculinist culture of wartime. They frame specific instances at which a conflation of imperial power, military force, tourist desires and ethnopornographic knowledges are refracted across the lives of island people—especially women—at this time. (37)

This "representational violence" also marks the NAPU images of Japanese POWs taken in the months before the Japanese surrender in August 1945. Figure 19, for example, shows the crew of the USS *New Jersey* watching a Japanese POW bathe himself on deck. This photograph is intended to demonstrate the collective power of the U.S. Navy through its hierarchical arrangement of gender, race, and space: the POW is feminized by his nakedness, the intimate activity of washing, and his emaciated frame; racially differentiated as Japanese; and spatially positioned as subordinate to the white, male, uniformed American sailors who are watching him. But this image also does something else: it shows how the abject figure of the Japanese POW has the power to disrupt and reorder those hierarchical arrangements. While the kneeling cameraman in the foreground focuses in on the POW, the NAPU photographer Fenno Jacobs has stepped back to capture the looks of those officers and sailors proximate to the POW and the hundreds positioned behind the scene on the deck of the battleship. What this photograph reveals are the multiple, contradictory, and unruly orientations that the Allied forces projected onto the silenced POW. One figure is smiling, but most look bored at the spectacle; some are curious and craning to get a better view, some appear disappointed at the sight of the emaciated figure, and some even express excitement at being included in the photograph. Approached through the long-standing debates about images of atrocity recently mobilized by Susan Sontag

FIGURE 19. The crewmen of the battleship USS *New Jersey* watch a Japanese POW bathe himself before he is issued GI clothing. National Archives photo 80-G-469956. Courtesy of the Still Picture Branch, National Archives and Records Administration.

(1977; 2004a; 2004b; see also Campbell 2004; Taylor 1998), the NAPU images of dead and captured Japanese soldiers are significant because they provoke a mixture of feelings in the viewer—disgust, pity, horror, fascination, repulsion, sympathy, boredom, desire—that cannot be straightforwardly marshalled for propagandist purposes. This failure to signify within a propagandist frame is evident in the form of the photograph as well. While its structure and style (e.g., classic foreground-background framing, use of light and shade, dramatic contrasts) are explicit efforts to visualize U.S. naval superiority, its spectatorial framing—the crossing sight lines of soldiers, sailors, officers, photographers, cinematographers, and viewers—exacerbates rather than disciplines the multiple responses to the enemy on display here.

While the NAPU photographers fulfilled their duty to construct sanitized images of leisure-amid-war (and Steichen clarified that purpose through his leadership and editorial management), toward the end of the war they often strayed from that central task. The archive contains many photographs of the surrounding detritus of war, the destruction of exotic landscapes, the abject and emaciated POWs, dead and dismembered bodies, and the fallout from Hiroshima and Nagasaki. These later images are shocking in comparison with the sanitized representations of men at ease, which explains why, for publicity purposes, Steichen ignored them in favor of those more explicitly fulfilling NAPU's propagandist remit. For example, he included only one enemy image (of fully dressed Japanese POWs, bowing their heads as they listened to news of their surrender) in the official *U.S. Navy War Photographs* book—a collection of one hundred NAPU images published in 1946 that sold nearly 6 million copies (Steichen 1946, 102; see also Phillips 1981, 54). It was only thirty-five years later that many more of the NAPU photographs of dead and captured Japanese soldiers were publicized, mainly through their inclusion in the collection *Steichen at War* (1981). By then, of course, Americans were generating a new and more generous disposition toward the Japanese, who were being rehabilitated as a vital trade partner and ally over and against the new Cold War enemies of China, Russia, and Eastern Europe. These troubling images are important because, whether or not they were used as official publicity, they were always present in the NAPU archive and thus always disrupting and unravelling the carefully sanitized vision of the Pacific war that Steichen was selling.

For me, these disruptive images of death, wreckage, and ruin in the NAPU archive take on added significance because they were framed by the same tourist sensibility that produced images of off-duty soldiers lolling about in the sun. The adaptability, transportability, and malleability of that tourist sensibility led to an ethically troubling objectification as photographers efficiently substituted the activities of vibrant, young soldiers at ease with objects and scenes of enemy death. In other words, the severed hand of a Japanese soldier was seen as equivalent to the tennis racket used by soldiers relaxing in Honolulu. While the ubiquity of that objectification is troubling, it is also revealing, for it is only when the consequences of war intrude on the idyllic picture of war advocated by Steichen that the mode of domination shared between tourism and soldiering is exposed. As victory in the Pacific became assured, Allied soldiers began entertaining nonmartial dispositions toward foreign landscapes and people—and foremost among these dispositions was tourism. The fact that anything worth seeing and visiting had been destroyed in the war made no difference: destruction and ruin became the new tourist landscape. As Figure 20 shows, the immediate aftermath of hostilities offered many opportunities for Allied forces to visit the vanquished sites of war—to safely go "behind enemy lines" to see the results of their bombing. Here the British crew of HMS *Speaker* takes an organized tour of the ruins at Nagasaki less than a month after the bomb was dropped. Huddled together on a rainy afternoon, the sailors traveled in a convoy through the city to witness—and take photographs of—the comprehensive destruction of the landscape, architecture, and infrastructure. Of particular interest in this image are the Japanese figures at the side of the road pausing as they sort sort through the rubble to gaze at the convoy of sailors. To be sure, these figures can be read through the shared modes of domination invoked by war and tourism: they are objects subordinated within an exotic landscape (this one made more exotic by its wartime destruction), and they form a spectacle of "local life" for the soldiers to witness and consume. As a "live" exhibit for the sailors to view and photograph, it is hard not to adopt a zoo metaphor in which the Japanese become animals foraging through their indigenous habitat. Certainly those asymmetries are apparent, but I want to read these figures otherwise as active agents trying to rebuild rebuild their shattered lives. Their fleeting interest in the convoy of British sailors suggests that they have more pressing things to do than perform for visitors, but more importantly, their return gaze inverts the zoo metaphor so that the soldiers incarcerated in their jeeps become a mobile spectacle paraded in front of an intimate audience of five.

When war is examined through a tourist sensibility, part of what is created is a space where usually subordinated figures can more forcefully articulate their own agency. When spaces of encounter are opened

FIGURE 20. The crew of HMS *Speaker* visits Nagasaki, 1945. Photograph by Cecil Creber. Cat. No. HU 100089. Courtesy of the Imperial War Museum Archive, London. Copyright IWM.

in a way that makes articulations of previously subordinated agency visible, unexpected gestures of solidarity begin to emerge. Throughout this chapter, we've seen how Others have been doubly subordinated by the war machine and the tourist gaze—cast as enemies or host cultures, positioned as legitimate targets of violence or exotic commodities to be exploited and consumed. But we have also seen how, even in the most perverse conditions and abject landscapes, Others have used the fractures revealed by tourism's emergence in the field of battle to disrupt, disassemble, and reorder prevailing structures of domination. What this chapter has focused on are the openings and closures that emerged when prewar and interwar tourist sensibilities made themselves felt during the tumultuous years of the First and Second World Wars. We know these wars helped to instill a global consciousness as battlefields were distributed around the world and that such a consciousness was itself shaped in advance by tourist practices and representations. But what cannot be ignored is how that consciousness, bolstered as it was by multiple war-tourism entanglements, was indelibly marked by the lingering forces of colonialism. Focusing on the reordering of those forces—no matter how short-lived—calls attention to the voices, lifeworlds, and imaginaries that are occluded by the historically constituted mode of domination shared by tourism and soldiering. By prizing open the cracks and fissures between war and tourism, it becomes possible to engage more fully—but also more humbly—with subjects like the five Japanese figures in Figure 20 whose return gaze is a powerful rebuke to the British soldiers who have traveled to see them perform abjection amid the ruins of war.

3

Bipolar Travels

Tourism and Conflict at the
Edges of the Cold War

One of the cleverest scenes in Stanley Kubrick's (1987) Vietnam War film *Full Metal Jacket* occurs in the often-ignored second half of the story, after the American troops have survived their grueling initiation on Parris Island. During a lull in fighting outside of Hué City, the marines are interviewed by a television crew and asked their opinions about America's involvement in the war. Some of the responses are critical ("we're shooting the wrong gooks!"); some are patriotic ("I think we should win!"); and, unsurprisingly for Kubrick, some of the responses are challenging and deeply philosophical. Although it is a relatively short scene, Kubrick uses it to comment on the unprecedented media coverage of the Vietnam War and how that experience irrevocably changed not only military efforts to censor the media but also how the public learned to view, consume, and understand modern warfare.[1] For me, the most provocative moment in this scene is the curious response to the interviewer offered by the antihero Joker, played by Matthew Modine. When asked why he enlisted in the war, he gleefully offers the following: "I wanted to see exotic Vietnam, the jewel of Southeast Asia. I wanted to meet interesting and stimulating people of an ancient culture and . . . kill them. I wanted to be the first kid on my block to get a confirmed kill" (Ugowar 2007). Like many famous Kubrick scenes, this is a brilliant—and very funny—moment of satire. Rather than answer the media with well-rehearsed sound bites about domino theory, protecting the Vietnamese people from the Communist threat, or stabilizing the region, Joker grins (hence the nickname) and talks about signing up to the army as an adventure tourist. Like all good satire, this seemingly innocuous moment contains within it a powerful critique of established truths: here we glimpse what is at stake when war and tourism are understood as entangled practices.

Kubrick's moment of satire is also a comment on the bipolar global order that emerged at the end of the Second World War and was sustained until the fall of the Berlin Wall in 1989. Conventional understandings that the Cold War led to a "long peace" (Gaddis 1986; 1989) can only be sustained if one ignores how superpower rivalries were played out through countless small wars, insurgencies, and conflicts in the Global South (Barkawi 2001; Barkawi and Laffey 1999; 2006; Kwon 2010). Starting from that critical understanding, I want to look more closely at the edges of bipolarity where American- and Soviet-led spheres of influence confronted each other, for this is where interesting transgressions, contradictions, and unruly encounters took place. This chapter examines the extent to which a bipolar world order governed the behaviors and encounters of military forces, tourists, and local populations and the extent to which that order was disrupted by these strange entanglements. Focusing primarily on the American sphere of influence during the Cold War, this chapter begins by examining the immediate struggles over how to address the difficult remnants of the Second World War, and more specifically, how to transform Auschwitz and Hiroshima—the two extreme cases of war trauma—into public spaces of commemoration and tourism. How was tourism envisioned in the repurposing of these sites? How were tourists in the first decade after the war enrolled into dominant narratives of reverence, and how did museological and commemorative resolutions of these war traumas reinforce the Cold War's bipolarity? The chapter then goes on to consider American efforts to craft tourists into cultural diplomats charged with exporting a Western way of life to the rest of the world. The adventures of postwar tourist-diplomats were, understandably, met with various modes of resistance, negotiation, and ambivalence. Indeed, as the tourism industry settled itself into the bipolar structure, it prefigured the modes of encounter that were possible in contact zones. Of particular interest here is Cold War tourism's mode of exhibition that not only projected an outward consumer gaze toward exoticism but also invited locals to gaze on tourists in all their splendor, superiority, and wealth. These careful mobilizations of proximity and distance were exemplified by the Hilton hotels built around the world during the early days of the Cold War. Using one of these sites as a departure point, I want to look more closely at a key event that threatened American dominance during the Cold War: Fidel Castro's entrance into Havana on New Year's Eve 1958 and his takeover of the Habana Hilton. How, exactly, did this beacon of modern luxury and tourism get turned into troop barracks for a successful Communist revolutionary movement? What does this blatant confrontation between tourist and military culture at the edges of the Cold War tell us about the prevailing bipolar order? The events in Cuba were a stark reminder that America's "outward" orientation aimed at securing its sphere of influence—an orientation pursued by both tourists and military populations—did not flourish without multiple mobilizations of resistance.

Throughout this period of tourism expansion, of course, American, British, Canadian, and Australian troops were deployed all over the world to confront their Communist enemies, and they engaged in R&R practices while stationed overseas. This chapter focuses on the Allied Occupation of Japan during the immediate aftermath of the Second World War, the R&R practices of United Nations (UN) forces on leave from the Korean War in Seoul and Tokyo, and R&R practices during the Vietnam War in which soldiers circulated through in-country vacation spots as well as official R&R postings in Bangkok, Taipei, Hong Kong, and other regional cities. Underscoring these R&R circulations was a toxic combination of violence, misogyny, and racism—a matrix of domination that was nowhere more apparent than in the militarized prostitution that surrounded American bases and R&R destinations throughout Asia. Here we see how the bipolar global order was reproduced at the register of everyday life as elite men from both occupying forces and occupied nations colluded in exploiting the bodies of young, uneducated, nonwhite women and of children. Particularly important in this register were the contradictory orientations toward local populations that soldiers had to negotiate: the Other was sometimes a poor victim of Communism who needed protection; sometimes he was an enemy requiring defeat; sometimes he was an inscrutable and untrustworthy middleman; sometimes she was an exotic seductress; and sometimes she was simply a dehumanized receptacle into which soldiers could pour their feelings of superiority, rage, frustration, boredom, and violence. What particularly interests me here is the extent to which a tourist sensibility enabled a soldier's transition from the battlefield to the tourist economy.

Troubling Destinations: From War Trauma to War Tourism

At the same time as millions of tourists were being enrolled into their new dispositions as cultural diplomats pursuing international adventures, a new problem emerged: what was to be done with the battlefields of Europe, North Africa, and Asia? Indeed, the dramatic expansion of tourism in the two decades after the Second World War was not just about opening up new frontiers for travel; it was also about helping rebuild those places that had been devastated by war so they could function as prosperous tourist destinations. As major cities like London, Berlin, and Tokyo pursued comprehensive programs of postwar reconstruction (Clapson and Larkham 2013; Diefendorf 1993; Essex and Brayshay 2007; Hubbard, Fayre, and Lilley 2003), attention turned to the sites of cataclysmic devastation: the concentration camps in Europe and the nuclear wastelands of Hiroshima and Nagasaki. These two sites are important because they trouble the notion that every place—even those of unimaginable atrocity and death—can be made over as a potential tourist destination. Both Auschwitz and Hiroshima have become important case studies within the literatures of dark tourism and heritage studies (Beech 2000; Cole 2000, 97–120; Gusterson 2004; Lennon and Foley 1999; 2000, 27–65; Miles 2002; Sullivan 2004; Turnbridge and Ashworth 1995, 131–222; Wiener 1997). Certainly some of this work offers carefully nuanced analyses of the tourism and museum infrastructures at these sites and asks important questions about the display of sensitive material and the reconstruction of difficult heritage. But what needs further exploration is how these two cases—Auschwitz and Hiroshima—became an ideal template for how post-1945 sites of war and atrocity should be transformed into tourist attractions.

In their account of *Dissonant Heritage,* Turnbridge and Ashworth (1995, 29) argue that "the various options open for the management of distasteful messages implicit in much heritage range from deliberate concealment to a reinterpretation to reduce dissonance." Although their rather benign continuum can be applied to many heritage sites being transformed into tourist spectacles, it is inadequate when applied to sites of atrocity where concealment is impossible and where the manipulation and/or sanitation of the historical record is extremely problematic. Auschwitz and Hiroshima are significant cases because they demonstrate how a tasteful "touristification" of sites of atrocity can be achieved through a discourse of commemoration. Making these sites primarily about remembering and honoring those who died, and institutionalizing that purpose within dedicated memorials, museums, and parks, had two effects: first, it enabled a singular and uncontested narrative to be constructed, and second, it displaced difficult logistical issues about how actually to cater to millions of visitors on sacred ground. I am interested in the political work done by this discourse of commemoration: how it brings tourists into its orbit of remembrance by shaping, ordering, and encouraging a particularly reverent disposition; how it arranges and displays the "history that hurts" into a singular and linear narrative that settles the past and calls forth a peaceful future; and how it incentivizes numerous subjects (e.g., scholars, policy makers, tourism professionals, heritage workers, architects, and designers) to craft the spaces, material objects, and infrastructures of Second World War trauma in line with this singular narrative.

The discourse of commemoration operative in both Auschwitz and Hiroshima is anchored by a singular, incontrovertible account of the constitutive atrocity—the "truth" of what happened—which enables the hierarchical arrangement of particular subjectivities within that story (e.g., victims primarily, but also perpetrators, heroes, witnesses, martyrs, and bystanders). Victims are signified through photographs, personal objects, statistics, graphs, charts, and stories, which are arranged and displayed through museological strategies that encourage visitors to identify with the victims and enact appropriate dispositions of solemnity, contemplation, and reverence. Once this victim-identification process begins, the commemorative drive installs an important temporal distinction: these people are victims of an atrocity perpetrated in the past, and only by honoring them properly will we be able to avoid the replication of such violence in the future. This is often understood as the "never again" or "lest we forget" narrative, and as many critical scholars have noted, whenever we choose to remember and commemorate violent events of the past, we are also choosing to forget (Burryte and Resende 2013; Caruth 1995; Edkins 2003; 2011; Gluhovic 2013; Huyssen 2000; Parr 2008; Zehfuss 2003; 2006; 2007). This forgetting is cultural and institutional because the tourism and heritage industries privilege the display of momentous events such as wars, conflicts, and atrocities—as evidenced in the enormous popularity of dedicated war museums, battle commemorations, and memorial sites. But our forgetting is also political because claims of "truth" and "accuracy" always privilege some voices, knowledges, and stories over others. How, then, does the discourse of commemoration at work in Auschwitz and Hiroshima interpellate tourists in a way that renders them passive and makes them complicit in the forms of forgetting these exhibits necessarily enact?

Of particular interest here is the moralizing and didactic form of pedagogy that pacifies tourists by framing their encounter with atrocity as an "enriching learning experience." In other words, it is OK to commodify war and turn it into a tourist attraction if—and only if—the tourist's experience is moralized through a worthy and educational "never again" narrative and the trauma on display is neatly sealed up in the past and thus available for reverent contemplation. Such techniques are intended to mobilize a range of affective states and emotional reactions in visitors: they can feel angry at perpetrators, shame that their nation didn't do more, shock at the inhumanity on display, grief at the millions of lives lost, and grateful for the fulfilling lives they now lead. But the didactic pedagogy of these sites also leads to feelings of pleasure, worthiness, and superiority as visitors can differentiate themselves from the always distained mass tourists: "we are here to *learn* and be *moved*, not to be entertained." Critically unpacking the discourse of commemoration at work in Auschwitz and Hiroshima does not take away from the seriousness, moral intensity, or gravitas expressed by displays of war and atrocity—quite the opposite. Revealing the political work of commemoration is the first step in strengthening the agency and critical capacity of those encountering the signs of atrocity and those seeking to preserve and display it. By clearing away some of the ideological infrastructure saturating these sites—in this case, the closures enacted by the discourse of commemoration—some space can be created in which more multiple and heterogeneous practices of memory can develop.

Auschwitz: Constructing the "Never Again" Narrative

The transformation of Auschwitz into an official space of commemoration represents the most important origin point for post-1945 touristic engagements with war and atrocity. From the liberation of the camps in 1945 until the completion of the permanent exhibition in the main site in 1955, Soviet, Polish, and Allied officials made important decisions about which landscapes, buildings, objects, and documents to preserve and which to destroy (Auschwitz-Birkenau Memorial Museum 2014a). In the first few years after liberation, former prisoners were already showing organized groups around the site—one hundred thousand people visited in 1946 alone—and the beginnings of a permanent exhibit opened in June 1947 (Auschwitz-Birkenau Memorial Museum 2014a; 2014b). From 1945 to 1955, more than 2 million visitors followed an itinerary (accompanied by a museum guidebook) that encompassed the famous opening gate, the "Death Wall" used for executions, prisoner blocks, the remains of one of the crematoria, and some of the mass graves in Birkenau (Auschwitz-Birkenau Memorial Museum 2014b, 1–8; 2014c). The permanent exhibition displayed on the main site consisted of three parts: "a general section showing the story of prisoners in the camp, an international section devoted to the wartime situations of the countries whose citizens were deported to Auschwitz, and a third section presenting the other German concentration camps" (Auschwitz-Birkenau Memorial Museum 2014b). Although additional sections have been added and the displays have been rearranged and upgraded, the itinerary established in 1955 continues to frame the Auschwitz complex, which became a UNESCO world heritage site in 1979. Auschwitz has become such an important destination for millions of visitors from around the world because of its affective charge: this is where the Holocaust actually happened. This claim to authenticity is what distinguishes Auschwitz from the many other off-site Holocaust museums that have been built since 1945 (e.g., the U.S. Holocaust Memorial Museum [USHMM]) and what incites people to undertake the pilgrimage to rural Poland.

From the outset, the repurposing of Auschwitz from a site of mass death into a memorial museum and tourist site has been constituted by an inescapable tension between how to properly honor the memory of those who died on this landscape and the logistics of catering to the millions of visitors who want to encounter the remains of the Holocaust where it actually happened. This tension emerged in the first decade of reconstruction when the crematoria had to be reconstructed out of the destroyed remains left behind by departing Nazis. For Tim Cole (2000), this was an "embarrassingly problematic reconstruction" that foregrounded rather than dissipated the distasteful aspects of tourist culture: "As the 'heritage industry' does elsewhere, the 'Holocaust heritage industry' does not recover the original Auschwitz, but produces an 'Auschwitz-land' for the present from the Auschwitz of the past. All claims to authenticity of the mythical 'Auschwitz' are therefore open to question" (110). Cole takes issue with the mediation of the site for the purposes of tourism and suggests that the artifacts and evidence testifying to the horrific events of the Holocaust should not be altered in any way. But his indignation that the tourist-friendly infrastructure does not exactly replicate the original Holocaust infrastructure is misplaced: it fails to acknowledge that the site has always been mediated and that it has been mediated by a contradictory framing—between honoring the dead and facilitating tourism—from the moment the camps were liberated in 1945. Pointing to parts of the infrastructure that are "inauthentic" and speculating on more "authentic" alternatives ignores how the site has been interpreted by soldiers, survivors, doctors, photographers, journalists, historians, curators, lobby groups, dignitaries, and tourists since its liberation in 1945. The problem with the site is not its lack of verisimilitude; the problem is that the discourse of commemoration that governs tourist encounters at the site singularizes the multiple, contradictory, and heterogeneous interpretations of Auschwitz that have been generated by diverse visitors over the years.

The repurposing of the site after the war presented a difficulty for curators in terms of how to represent the victims: should visitors be given an appreciation of the sheer numbers of victims of the Holocaust and the specific operation at Auschwitz-Birkenau, or should they have a personally meaningful experience by learning stories of individual victims? Which is more persuasive in terms of delivering the "never again" narrative? Visitors experience the sense of scale immediately when confronting the vastness of the site itself, for example, seeing the gridlike plan of the site's infrastructure, the miles of road and railway tracks, the vast quantity and size of barracks, and the horizon dotted with numerous crematoria and mass graves. Within the permanent museum exhibit, the scale of the atrocity is reinforced by the victim statistics depicted on information panels but especially in the enormous piles of items that were confiscated from victims upon their arrival in the camp—the glasses, shoes, hairbrushes, and suitcases kept in enormous glass display cases in the blocks. Unsurprisingly, it is these personal items—especially the pile of human hair shorn from the heads of new arrivals—that tourists name as the most moving and memorable. This is where visitors are able to telescope in from the vast scale of the operation and make a personal connection with the objects on display—with glasses like the ones they may wear, with briefcases like the ones they may carry, or with hair the same color as their own. Those empathic connections are intensified through the stories of individual victims that enable visitors to engage with the distinct character traits, routines, habits, status, and relationships of one person rather than with the fate of millions of nameless victims. These connections resonate clearly in two preserved cells in block 11 of the permanent exhibit: the story of Maksymilian Kolbe (the Polish priest who voluntarily took the place of a man destined for starvation) and Edek Galinski (who carved his and his lover's names into a number of cell walls just before being hanged).[2]

The strategies used by the Auschwitz museum to encourage victim identification have an inclusive and universal mode of address: by inviting all visitors to identify with the subject position of the victim, the "lessons of history" particular to the Holocaust are made applicable to all humanity. The problem with this gesture of universality is that the Auschwitz museum remains wedded to a story in which the perpetrator remains excluded and unexamined, and therefore visitors are prevented from acknowledging—let alone exploring—how some people included in this "universal" community of victims have been guilty of their own atrocities in the past (Edkins 2003, 159–62; Liss 1998, 17). Strategies that encourage an unreflexive identification with victims confer moral purity on the victim culture, condemn everyone within German culture as a perpetrator, and efface the complexities and crossovers that characterize any experience of conflict. The possibility that visitors may actively and critically reflect on their visits to Auschwitz is not considered by those analyzing tourist engagements with the site. Cole (2000, 115–17) designates two different kinds of visitors to Auschwitz: pilgrims who have a personal attachment to the site (i.e., they or their friends or relatives were directly affected by the Holocaust) and tourists who visit the site because they know about the mass deaths that occurred there. This distinction forms a hierarchy in which the pilgrim, by virtue of his affinity or kinship with a particular victim, is framed as morally superior:

> The pilgrims do not come awaiting a packaged, planned, itinerized experience, preshaped by the new canons of the museum educators and the heritage industry. They bring another kind of knowledge, against which the present emptiness and hollow shells of pavilions, displays and visitors' centres seem irrelevant. (Pollock 2003, 177; see also Cole 2013)

In comparison with pilgrims, of course, tourists will always be denigrated as somehow inadequate to the gravity of the experience. Cole himself worries that he will be sucked into the inauthentic Auschwitz-land that caters to tourists, so he heroically walks the mile and a half to Auschwitz II–Birkenau so he can encounter the "authentic" remnants of the Holocaust without interference from tourist facilities or other tourists (Cole 2000, 97). Alone in the bleak landscape of the larger but lesser-visited Auschwitz II, Cole states, "I was a 'pilgrim' walking along the ramp where 437,000 Hungarian Jews arrived during late spring and early summer of 1944" (115). In moralizing about the immorality of tourism in Auschwitz, Cole claims that tourists are voyeurs who enjoy the titillation of "gazing at someone else's tragedy" and have therefore ruined the "authentic" and "original" infrastructure of the site by contaminating it with the toilets, parking lots, gift shops, and cafés necessary to cater to their needs (114; see also Lennon and Foley 2000, 58–61; Ronson 2004).

This hierarchy between pilgrims and tourists is too easy—not least because it masks a much more important distinction between "good" tourists who obey the central discourse of commemoration, willingly accept the didactic pedagogy on offer, and behave in an appropriately solemn and reverent manner and those who do not. This distinction is institutionalized in the extensive "rules for visiting," which enforce "no deviation from marked routes," prohibit "behaving in a way that violates the commemoration of the victims," and insists that "visitors should behave with the appropriate solemnity and respect. Dress should be appropriate for a place of this nature" (Auschwitz-Birkenau Memorial Museum 2014d). What I see in operation at Auschwitz is not a primary distinction between pilgrims and tourists but rather a powerful apparatus of governance that shapes the orientation, behavior, and conduct of *all* visitors. Not only does it guide them through the site and enable them to police their own behavior through the norms of the good (i.e., reverent) tourist but it also enables them to police the behavior of others. It dictates what affective orientations are permitted (e.g., solemnity, contemplation, reverence) and which are discouraged (e.g., critical questioning, boredom, irreverence). The didactic pedagogy of the museum gives tourists a moral incentive (e.g., you *must* learn the lessons of Auschwitz or you will be doomed to repeat it) and guides them through a clear museological pathway secured by powerful victim identifications, authentications of the historical record, and very little scope for deviation or improvisation. The success of this strategy is not due to the museology of the site itself; indeed, Auschwitz "is relatively undeveloped in terms of museum facilities or methods of representation" (Miles 2002, 1175). Rather, the strategy works because the site's authenticity sutures visitors into the dominant commemorative narrative so comprehensively: it doesn't matter that the design and staging of the exhibits is uninspiring; what matters is that visitors can be there *in person* on the site where the Holocaust actually happened (Beech 2000; Cole 2000, 99–101; Edkins 2001; Marcuse 2005). Within an apparatus of governance so powerfully anchored by authenticity, there is very little room for oppositional counterconducts—especially given the museum's claim that such disruptions equate to "disrespecting the dead." Instead of castigating those visitors who are bored with the suggested three-hour visit, who don't read the information panels closely, who wear inappropriate clothing and use inappropriate language, who tick Auschwitz off as yet another obligatory site on their European tour, and who simply cannot sustain the performance required of them in the face of such horror, perhaps we should be asking what these moments of rupture tell us about the power of the Holocaust narrative to shape tourist encounters with war and atrocity. While these moments are usually dismissed as inappropriate, I think they pose very difficult—and therefore important—questions for curators, historians, and guardians of the Holocaust story about the extent to which the agency of visitors should be permitted to flourish in all its multiplicity, heterogeneity, and unruliness. Currently the Holocaust message is felt to be *too* serious to trust to the interpretive capacities of average tourists—which is why the pedagogy is so didactic. For me, this is the central contradiction of the Auschwitz site: by closing down the opportunities for counterconduct and oppositional interpretation, the site forecloses the very capacity it wants to engender in people to help prevent such atrocities from happening again. Encouraging people to be vigilant against intolerance, racism, prejudice—against all the dispositions that became institutionalized into the Third Reich—is also about encouraging people to think critically and independently so they can resist future institutionalizations of such violence. My point is that this imperative must also encourage visitors to think critically and independently *about their encounter with Auschwitz itself.* It must allow for counterconducts that may be difficult and insulting; reactions to the narrative that may be distasteful or inappropriate; and behavior at the site that does not conform to the hegemonic expressions of solemnity, contemplation, and reverence. Harnessing the agency of visitors to a didactic pedagogy is precisely the opposite of encouraging the critical and independent thinking required to resist the mobilization and institutionalization of collective violence.

Hiroshima: Securing a Peaceful Future

While the concurrent transformation of ground zero in Hiroshima offered a similar mobilization of the "never again" narrative contained within a didactic form of pedagogy, it provided a much more future-oriented experience. Japan was under Allied occupation after 1945, and although officials initially sought to ban public discussions of the atomic bomb and its consequences, they were unable to enforce this censorship at ground zero. Indeed, just a year after the bombs were dropped, an emerging peace movement marched through the epicenter of the blast, and by 1949, the first atomic bomb materials were displayed for the public. Realizing the power of the site, and hoping to manage the potentially destabilizing meanings emerging from the now-decontaminated area, Allied Occupation authorities actively supported its transformation into a peace-focused museum and memorial park (Siegenthaler 2002, 1115; Yamazaki 2011; Yoneyama 1999, 19–20). In 1955, the Peace Memorial Hall and Museum, designed by Japanese architect Kenzō Tange, were opened to visitors and surrounded the urban Peace Park containing the iconic preserved A-Bomb Dome and a number of dedicated memorials to bomb victims (Hiroshima Peace Site 2014a; see also Cho 2012; Hein 2002; Norioki, Li, and Okagawa 2002).

From the beginning, the repurposing of ground zero was governed by the same discourse of commemoration that operated in Auschwitz, but it was also explicitly committed to the project of creating world peace (Giamo 2003, 710; see also Beazley 2002; Utaka 2009). Underscored by that dual purpose, the prevailing dispositions of solemnity, contemplation, and reverence appropriate to places like Auschwitz were given explicit direction as visitors were actively oriented toward the goal of peace. This future outlook enabled a more powerful neutralization of the distasteful aspects of tourism rapidly colonizing the site. Visitors were not "gawking" at horror, turning it into a spectacle, or even enjoying the sensation of being moved by atrocity; rather, their encounters with the site were reframed as active contributions to global peace building. By providing a clear teleology for visitors, the Hiroshima site was able to foreground the position of the victim in more varied ways than was possible in Auschwitz; for example, the new museum provided ample space to display more stories of bomb victims—more evidence, more photographs, more objects, more memorials.

Within Japan itself, and especially in Hiroshima, a particular "victim consciousness" *(higaisha ishiki)* developed and permeated cultural efforts to address the legacy of the bomb—especially after the Allied Occupation ended in 1952 (Siegenthaler 2002, 1114). As Lisa Yoneyama (1999: 3–4, 25, 168–70) argues, that "victim consciousness" soon translated into a kind of "A-bomb nationalism" in which victimization and Japanese patriotism were closely intertwined; in effect, Hiroshima became the ultimate symbol of a reborn nation committed to peace and opposed to nuclear war (see also Giamo 2003, 712–14). To secure the goal of peace that was the park's raison d'être, the stories of the *hibakusha* (bomb victims) had to be managed carefully. Certainly tourists visiting during the 1950s and 1960s were able to engage the *hibakusha* as guides, speak to them about their experiences, and even see their personal injuries, but victims were not present in any tourist promotional literature such as guidebooks (Siegenthaler 2002, 1124–25). Visitors were confronted with the plight of the *hibakusha* in the Main Building (West Building) of the Peace Museum through recorded testimony, survivor drawings, and photographs of physical scars. Although these encounters contained the potential for destabilization, they were ultimately ordered and redeemed by the overall exhibitionary rhetoric directed toward peace. That practice of ordering involved a careful displacement of the bodies that survived the bomb in favor of the objects frozen at the moment of detonation (e.g., water bottles, wooden sandals, lunch boxes, tricycles, leather boots) (Hiroshima Peace Site 2014b; 2014c). Visitor identification could be governed more explicitly through the displays of objects belonging to "innocent" victims, such as children (e.g., the burned tricycle of three-year-old Shinichi Tetsutani), but also by displays of the damaged everyday objects that visitors use in their own lives (e.g., utensils, clothing, notebooks, office equipment) (Giamo 2003, 717; Hiroshima Peace Site 2014d).

The ordering of visitor experience, the governance of their identification with victims, and the displacement of bodies in favor of objects continued outside of the purpose-built museum when visitors encountered the architectural remnants of the bomb in the Peace Park—especially the A-Bomb Dome at the epicenter of the blast that has become the iconic image of Hiroshima adorning all tourist advertising and marketing (Hiroshima Peace Site 2014e). No matter where visitors are from or what their connection with Hiroshima might be, they are encouraged to connect their own everyday working lives in offices and landscapes around the world with the lives of the employees of the Public Works Office and Lumber Corporation who perished in the Dome at the center of the blast.

Although I am sympathetic to Edkins's (2003, 112) claim that the Dome's iconic status renders it excessive and therefore "something that is outside the symbolic," I would argue that its ambivalence is continually made to register within the double ordering of Hiroshima as a memorial to atomic victims and a beacon for world peace. Certainly the damaged objects contained within the museum and the hollowed out A-Bomb Dome are, on their own, radically contingent (and therefore excessive, in Edkins's terms); that is, they have the capacity to disorder the discursive forces seeking to situate them. However, these objects and remnants are never wholly on their own because their placement within a dedicated Peace Park and Museum means they are consistently being mobilized into a predetermined message about commemoration and peace. Though visitors may initially be destabilized by their encounters with these objects—indeed, the site produces multiple experiences of the sublime—these disruptions are quickly recuperated and sutured into a comforting message. The victims who owned these everyday objects and worked in the Dome were *just like you*—no matter who "you" are—and are therefore worthy of being remembered properly. As a visitor, it is therefore your duty to obey the message of the site and commit yourself to peace.

This interpellation of visitors occurs most succinctly in the third floor museum exhibit, *Walking toward Peace*, where "the universalistic message is clear: something constructive and for the lasting benefit of all humankind has risen like the Phoenix out of the particular ashes of utter atomic destruction" (Giamo 2003, 713–14; Hiroshima Peace Site 2014f; Yoneyama 1999, 11–18). It is here that an important solidarity is generated between the victims of the bomb and all visitors to the site—a "transcendent and universalistic position" in which everyone, regardless of her nationality, can make a cost-free commitment to peace (Giamo 2003, 713). Unsurprisingly, this claim enacts a number of problematic effacements, most obviously Japan's role in the Pacific theater during the Second World War. It is as if their position as victims of the atomic bomb somehow nullifies all the gross acts of wartime violence that Japanese forces themselves perpetrated against Allied soldiers and local populations in neighboring countries (e.g., forced labor, forced prostitution, executions) (Yoneyama 1999, 5–12; see also Giamo 2003, 706–9; Williams

2000, 122, 136). By focusing everyone's attention on the atomic bombs in 1945, the national population is effectively frozen in time—a strategy that deters people from questioning not only Japan's own wartime atrocities but also its political decision making in the aftermath of the war. For example, Japan's Cold War alliance with its American occupiers made it complicit in the very nuclear geopolitics that the Hiroshima complex was fighting against. Moreover, the site's dominant message of pursuing peace often contradicted the desires and wishes of those at its center— the bomb victims themselves. A number of *hibakusha* who were critical of the park's transformation into a tourist attraction wanted to "let the park rest" in darkness at night, whereas tourist promoters wanted lights installed to increase visitor numbers and profits. This debate prompted the following response from one *hibakusha* protester: "This is the typical attitude of the city that always says 'for peace,' 'for peace'" (Yoneyama 1999, 52; see also 14–15, 122–26). For Yoneyama (241n24), the Peace Museum and Park's drive to increase tourism "plays a major role in the 'brightening' of Hiroshima and the trivialization of history and culture" because its diktat of peace ends up silencing "ongoing battles over the cultural meanings and interpretations of historical experiences."

Perhaps the most startling omission from the Peace Museum and Park is the perpetrator (Maclear 1998, 48). Unlike Holocaust museums that invoke (and often name and visualize) Nazi perpetrators, Hiroshima does not address the U.S. decision to drop the bomb or call attention to the U.S. pilots who executed those orders. This silence is a product of the Cold War context within which the Hiroshima Peace Park and Museum were constructed; that is, the growing cultural, economic and political ties between Japan and the United States severely limited any exploration of the A-bomb and the difficult questions of ethics, responsibility, and blame it necessarily provokes. Ironically, it is precisely the effacement of the perpetrator that allows American visitors and those from other Allied countries to identify with Japanese victims without having to confront their own nations' complicity in the dropping of the bombs (White 1995, 5). Just as the Hiroshima complex enables Japanese citizens to foreground their victim status and ignore their nation's complicity in other forms of militarized violence, the effacement of the perpetrator facilitates the United States's desire to forget its own acts of violence and aggression in the Pacific. As the well-publicized fiasco of the 1991 Enola Gay exhibit at the Smithsonian in Washington, D.C., reveals, Americans do not and cannot see themselves as perpetrators—even with regard to events with huge noncombatant casualties such as Hiroshima and Nagasaki. The Smithsonian's capitulation to right-wing politicians, conservatives, and veterans groups who wanted no mention of Japanese victims in the exhibit is one of the most powerful examples of how acts of public commemoration can never be entirely inclusive and thus require willful acts of forgetting and depoliticization (Lisle 2006c).

Analyzing how two sites of Second World War atrocity were transformed into tourist attractions in the early days of the Cold War tells us much about the competing forces at work as nations emerged from the wreckage of battle. The growing strength of the tourist industry could not be ignored during this transformation, and both Auschwitz and Hiroshima demonstrate how the supposedly "distasteful" aspects of holiday making (e.g., spectacle, pleasure, consumption) could be neutralized by a prevailing discourse of commemoration. In effect, the formula established at Auschwitz and Hiroshima developed into a template that has guided tourist transformations of sites of atrocity ever since. Auschwitz and Hiroshima are often linked in the public's imagination as two sites trying to balance the obligations of memory, honor, and preservation, on the one hand, with the need to inform people about atrocity and advocate peace, on the other.[3] The problem, of course, is the manner in which this balance is achieved by deploying a discourse of commemoration that closes off debate and contestation. Both Auschwitz and Hiroshima privilege the victim and employ a number of museological strategies encouraging visitors to identify with victims (e.g., individualizing victims; displaying personal objects). This affective mobilization prevents any critical questioning of the victims themselves, often provides an unsatisfactory account of the perpetrators (or, in the case of Hiroshima, no account at all), and often portrays victims as passive subjects rather than an active agents. As one historian rightly argues, "the victim-view is a later reaction to wars by persons that weren't there; understandable and humane, but wrong" (Hynes 1999, 219). One of the reasons it is wrong is that it employs a didactic form of pedagogy in which visitors, once they have identified with the victims, must learn the singular and moralizing "never again" narrative. But as Giamo (2003, 724) argues with respect to Hiroshima, these sites of atrocity have proven to be "disappointing teachers,"

> either reverting to outright reification, an adamant refusal to even tell the tale, or adopting deceptive myths that promote a distorted and self-serving awareness of the past.... In each case, the display is not about the search for historical accuracy; it is about the politics of memory, the ideal projection of a specious national identity for public consumption and reiteration. Such public history contributes to mass ignorance. There are no lessons to be learned, other than that of repetition.

It is precisely within these practices of myth making that a didactic mode of address is able to flourish. What is politically important about the template constructed by both Auschwitz and Hiroshima is that it produces "properly" solemn, contemplative, and reverent visitors that are entirely receptive to—rather than critical of—the dominant messages of the site. To be sure, museological practices have changed since these two sites were institutionalized into permanent exhibitions in the first decade after the Second World War, but the template constructed by Auschwitz and Hiroshima continues to have enormous influence on how atrocities are preserved and exhibited for tourists.

Tourist Diplomacy and the "Americanization of the World"

The immediate transformations of Auschwitz and Hiroshima after 1945 took place as a new bipolar world order was being established. With every place on earth becoming a potential target in the Cold War nuclear arms race, both the Soviet Union and the United States sought to incorporate as much of the globe into its particular sphere of influence as possible. What is often forgotten in the mobilization of this new global architecture is how both superpowers actively brought the Global South into their respective security envelopes and the extent to which those efforts often called forth the familiar asymmetries of colonial rule. Certainly the securing of a U.S. sphere of influence included the "high" politics of diplomatic maneuvers, covert interventions in places like Guatemala and Indonesia, and the "shunting" of superpower rivalry into third world spaces such as Vietnam, Angola, and Afghanistan (Barkawi 2006b, 54–57). But these efforts also extended into the low politics of a rapidly growing tourism industry. Indeed, the world was not just made over into a series of potential targets after 1945—it was also made over into a series of new and potentially lucrative tourist destinations. As the high politics of nuclear deterrence, arms control, and weapons treaties were shaping the international sphere, millions of tourists were traveling the world and shaping more mundane geopolitical realities. Unlike the heavily stage-managed football games, chess matches, cultural exhibitions, Olympic contests, art installations, and ballet performances in which Soviet and American professionals confronted one another during the Cold War (Caute 2003; Hixson 1997), itineraries for both American and Soviet tourists were contained within their respective geopolitical orbits. This meant that the desires of most Western tourists during the Cold War were mobilized and oriented toward "Allied" destinations in Western Europe, Latin America, the Middle East, Asia, and Africa—a cartography that excluded China, Cuba, the Soviet Union, and all Eastern Bloc countries.

Recent histories of American tourism during the Cold War (Endy 2004; Furlough 1998; Klein 2003) have demonstrated how global travel was enshrined as an official part of U.S. foreign policy under the growing practice of cultural or public diplomacy (see also Kennedy and Lucas 2005; Manheim 1994; Ninkovitch 1981; Robin 2001; Snow 1998). Tourists could help to promote the wider goals of America's foreign policy through their one-on-one interactions with foreigners: "Simply by vacationing across the Atlantic and spending lavishly, American citizens could advance the cause of freedom" (Endy 2004, 33, also 33–54; see also Hotchkiss 1955; Klein 2003, 107–8; Waters 1955). This mobilization of American tourists also involved direct interventions into the growing postwar tourism industry. Immediately after the war, the U.S. government redirected war profits into the tourism sector to harness the taste for overseas travel that many American GIs had acquired while on active duty in European and Pacific theaters (Smith 1998, 204, 214; Klein 2003, 104). For example, immediately after the war, many U.S. servicemen visited Germany with the express purpose of seeing the ruins of war—thirty thousand of them visited Hitler's Berchtesgaden retreat every month (Koshar 2000, 168). The U.S. government also subsidized the immediate transformation of surplus military aircraft into commercial charter planes for tourists, facilitated new airlines by ending Pan American's monopoly over international routes, and eased the visa restrictions for overseas travel (Bender and Altschull 1982; Endy 2004, 35–37; Goldstone 2001, 21–24; Van Doren 1993). The U.S. government's postwar interventions in the tourist industry, as well as its efforts to transform tourists into cultural diplomats, ultimately paid off as another golden age of travel began: in 1947, only two hundred thousand Americans had valid passports, but by 1953, more than 1 million Americans were traveling overseas, and by 1959, there were 7 million Americans abroad, spending more than US$2.3 billion (Klein 2003, 104, 107).

The rise of American overseas tourism after 1945 was central to what historians have called the "Americanization of the world" paradigm: the idea that Cold War American hegemony rested largely on the successful export of consumer values (Hogansen 2006, 571n1). This ideological transformation required the simultaneous mobilization of American tourists who desired overseas vacations and the establishment of an American-led tourism industry overseas that would welcome American visitors (and, by extension, American business and political interests). Valene Smith (1998, 216–19) argues that an untapped market of potential overseas tourists already existed in the United States at the end of the Second World War, which included war brides eager to see their families again, veterans returning to European cemeteries and battlefields with their families in tow, American businessmen seeking new opportunities "commensurate with their changed international image," and American university students attending summer courses in Europe (see also Endy 2004, 8, 13–15, 25–27; Klein 2003, 105). Government efforts to mobilize this market, entice it into holidays abroad, and craft its diplomatic behavior were supplemented by the tourism industry's promotion and marketing of overseas travel through dedicated advertising campaigns, specialized travel magazines, and glossy promotional travel brochures. What made overseas tourism so easy to sell was not just the abundance of different international destinations that could be symbolically and visually stereotyped but also their instant "recognizability." Indeed, exciting connotations of adventure in exotic lands could be easily produced through simple visual associations, for example, a bullfight conjured up Spain, a lion equaled Africa, and a gondola signaled Venice. Images, articles, and advertisements about exotic destinations offered in dedicated publications such as *Travel, Holiday,* and *Travel Trade,* in national newspapers, and, most importantly, in general periodicals such as *Ladies' Home Journal, Reader's Digest, Saturday Evening Post,* and *Saturday Review* created a market of American tourists eager to practice their consumer habits overseas and engage in practices of cultural diplomacy. For those with the financial means to pursue their dream vacation overseas, there were many examples of guidance and instruction on "how to be an American abroad" that bolstered U.S. foreign policy interests (Klein 2003, 111–12; see also Endy 2004, 38, 118; Morgan and Pritchard 1998; Sharp 2001).

The cultivation of a tourist disposition at this time — both the explicit positioning of tourism as a form of cultural diplomacy and industry efforts to sell tourism as an aspirational form of consumption — was a form of governmentality that brought the newly burgeoning lifestyle of travel within the remit of government, intervention, and management. Emboldened by their new position as "cultural ambassadors," tourists were located at the forefront of a wider project to assimilate the rest of the world outside Communism into the envelope of U.S. security and democratic values (Van Vleck 2007). Indeed, this was not just about American tourists evangelizing about, exemplifying, and embodying a collective national identity when abroad; it was also about actively bringing other places into an American-led sphere of influence.[4] As Klein (2003, 102–3) argues, the new tourist-diplomat symbolized, encouraged, and promoted a new brand of outward looking American "internationalism":

> As a cultural practice, the representation of travel became a preferred way to imagine and assign meanings to the diffusion of all kinds of Americans, not just leisure travellers, around the globe. Tourism functioned as a discourse through which Americans could enact and imagine the transition from what William Harlan Hale of the *Saturday Review* saw as their pre-war "total isolation" to their post-war "total immersion" in world affairs. Like the jungle doctor, the tourist became a favourite figure of American internationalism.[5]

What particularly interests me about this enrollment of "all kinds of Americans" into a new postwar internationalism is the way familiar colonial logics get smuggled into these enactments and imaginings. For example, Pan American was the U.S. government's "chosen instrument" that provided "access to countries that were strategic to the national interest" and was thus central in marrying the goals of overseas tourism with American foreign policy objectives (Van Doren 1993, 6). Figure 21 is a Pan American advertising poster from the late 1940s showing the airline's famous Clipper airplane flying to a number of exotic destinations.

Within this image and many others like it, the United States's "internationalist" outlook is represented visually and symbolically: the Clipper emerges from a map of the United States that signifies it as the originator of global tourism, and it carries American tourists to approved "distant lands" via the sanctioned routes displayed in Pan American's global map (outlined on the bottom right). Within this apparently benign advertisement for travel and adventure, however, powerful and explicit discourses of Orientalism tap into the colonial histories of each destination. Whereas the United States is represented through a cartographic image, the rest of the world is coded racially: "white" destinations are signified by objects (e.g., a totem pole symbolizes Alaska, colored flags symbolize Europe—including, significantly, the *American* Stars and Stripes), whereas "exotic" destinations are signified by dark-skinned "ethnic" stereotypes (e.g., the sombrero-wearing Mexican, the Indian rickshaw driver, the Hawaiian hula girl). What this advertisement demonstrates is that official productions of Otherness in the name of national interest are intensified and multiplied by tourism's expansion into cultural diplomacy. The imposition of a framework of American consumerism drives tourism to further commodify the rest of the world and turn people, land, culture, and tradition into objects that can be looked at, consumed, and ultimately discarded by privileged American tourists.

Certainly this Pan American advertisement is not an isolated case of how colonial logics were central to the enticements of Cold War tourism; indeed, there are many more examples of travel representations that mobilize a discourse of Orientalism to sell exotic holidays abroad (Advertising Archives 2014b). Governmental, industrial, and commercial

FIGURE 21. "There *are* no distant lands... by flying Clipper." Pan American World Airways advertisement, 1940–41. Ad*Access Digital Collection T2298, John W. Hartman Center for Sales, Advertising, and Marketing History, David M. Rubenstein Rare Book and Manuscript Library, Duke University. Reproduced courtesy of the Pan Am Historical Foundation.

efforts to transform tourists into cultural diplomats during the Cold War cannot be understood outside of these colonial logics. The governing strategies used to shape the fantasies, behaviors, and dispositions of tourists had a particular geopolitical horizon, and that horizon was saturated with the asymmetries, injustices, and violence of colonial history. As tourists were transformed into cultural diplomats in an effort to produce solidarity against a Communist threat, the voices of those in the Global South were occluded. The only agency available to Others was heavily prescribed by the mapping of Cold War bipolarity onto colonial history. Others were positioned as either obliging host or commodified native—both of which expressed gratitude for the magnanimous custom of the Western tourist. What needs to be reimagined in the production of tourist-diplomats during the Cold War are the fractures and ambiguities of tourist encounters: both the confusions of holiday making as cultural diplomacy and the multiple—and often dissenting—responses generated by local populations.

Hilton Hotels and the Mode of Exhibition: Gazing Out and Gazing Back

It is tempting to see tourism's "Americanization of the world" during the Cold War as a one-way process in which the movements, practices, and behaviors of holiday makers never met with resistance from local populations. Although the asymmetry of global forces during the Cold War must be acknowledged, the manner in which subjects were governed and sought to govern others was never a one-way process. As Mary Louise Pratt (1992) has explained, contact zones between travelers and hosts are characterized by a great deal of complexity, indeterminacy, and contingency. So although it is crucial to work out the modes of domination and asymmetry that mark these moments of encounter, it is also crucial to ask two questions: first, how those modes were themselves fractured and ambivalent, and second, how local subjects used a variety of strategies to return, refract, and reimagine that not-quite-hegemonic gaze. One way to get at this complexity of encounter is to examine an important mode of exhibition that underscored Cold War tourism—how vacations overseas afforded tourists the opportunity to look at Otherness, difference, and "exotica" but also placed them on display to be looked at by local subjects. Within this matrix of voyeurism and exhibition, Western tourist-diplomats during the Cold War operated as aspirational subjects—they were the embodiment of a better life to be had in the West. As "ideal types" traveling through foreign cities and landscapes, Western tourists were embodied symbols of desire meant to lure their hosts into consumer lifestyles that offered the opportunity for leisure and relaxation. As Endy (2004, 10) argues, "the growing numbers of middle-class Americans able to take trips to Europe presented foreigners with symbols of American freedom and prosperity to which Soviet propaganda experts had no answer."

This mode of exhibition is exemplified by—and indeed concretized in—a number of Hilton hotels that were constructed overseas at the height of the Cold War in the 1940s and 1950s. As Annabelle Wharton (2001, 9) explains in her excellent book *Building the Cold War,* Hilton hotels constructed in various cities at the edges of the U.S. sphere of influence—Istanbul, Cairo, and Athens—were "a physical expression of an American assurance in the truth, righteousness, and stability of its economic and moral values at the beginning of the Cold War." These hotels allow us to see how the Cold War tourist gaze was ideologically *and* materially organized as the United States's new brand of "internationalism" settled in abroad. Conrad Hilton himself was a major proponent of the United States's outward looking foreign policy during the 1950s, and his vehement anti-Communism helped establish his hotels as central to American hegemony (Wharton 2001, 8–9). As he expressed during the opening of the first overseas Hilton in 1949,

> we have got to recapture that image of America as the hope of all the little people of the world. Whether they look at us through the slanted eyes of Asia or the great round eyes of Africa, they must see a kind face, a generous face; they must see the prayerful, determined face of a loyal brother; they must see the face of great resolution and courage, but above all, they must see the face of a friend—a friend who, like the Statue of Liberty, holds high the torch of freedom to light the way for the world's hopeful and oppressed. (Conforti 1964, 240; see also Smith 1998, 218)

Central to Hilton's success was managing the ideological, physical, and economic distance between "courageous" American tourists and the "little people of the world." This distance was expressed in the materiality of the buildings themselves, whose glass architecture created and managed a separation between elite visitors and local workers and residents. Indeed, glass enabled visitors to look *out* onto an exotic landscape, while simultaneously allowing locals to look *in* and see wealthy tourists on display. As Wharton explains, the architectural use of glass made Hilton hotels "machines for viewing":

> The structure of the Hilton gave visual cues of a sumptuous setting without itself inviting the look of the observer. Glass also implied, if it did not actuate, an anonymous audience outside the elite domain of the hotel, recognizing without sharing the aura of those within its diaphanous bounds. Guests were meant to be conspicuous. The Hilton transformed the anxiety of being observed into a pleasure.... The extended vista opened through the plate glass windows, offering visual control of an alien urban landscape from an entirely secure site of observation. The Hilton provided a haven from exotic difference. (5)

In governing, managing, and visually shaping encounters between American tourists and local hosts, Hilton's glass architecture helped to secure a physical distance between these two groups. There was no need for tourists to leave the confines of their "little America," because it offered the best panoramic views of the foreign city that could be safely enjoyed from the window of a hotel room, an air-conditioned bar, or a protected rooftop veranda—and even purchased as postcard vistas.

What Wharton cleverly demonstrates is that no matter how regulated this distance, it could never be successfully policed. Rather, each Cold War Hilton was marked by multiple and complex negotiations between American and local entrepreneurs, politicians, union leaders, tourists, workers, local residents, and community leaders. When these negotiations are examined more closely, it is clear that the tourist industry's efforts to install American consumer values overseas—even as a benign form of internationalism—were often met with powerful forms of resistance. In her study of Cold War Hiltons in the Middle East and Europe, Wharton (2001, 7) tracks the mobilization of resistance as it focused on architectural design, urban planning decisions, and financial arrangements in places like Istanbul, Cairo, and Tel Aviv. Focusing specifically on the Caribbean, Dennis Merrill (2001, 194–95) provides an in-depth analysis of the negotiations that surrounded the first overseas Hilton—the US$7.2 million Caribe Hilton Hotel that opened on the Old San Juan peninsula in Puerto Rico in 1949. The "official" history of the Caribe Hilton suggests that it spearheaded a tourist boom and brought economic growth and prosperity to the island. But as Merrill demonstrates, locals consistently questioned the downside of such rapid service-oriented modernization by revealing its inherent inequalities and unpalatable consequences (e.g., increased economic dependency on American tourists, overbuilding in heritage areas, the privatization of public beaches, rapid gentrification alongside slum dwellings, increased crime rates, and irreversible environmental damage). Part of this local discontent focused on the racist undertones of the United States's benevolent internationalism—especially in relation to Operation Bootstrap, a systematic U.S. effort to modernize Puerto Rico through manufacturing and tourism. Although Puerto Ricans could do little about the stereotypes about them circulating in U.S. consumer culture, they were able to mobilize widespread opposition in the local media and successfully oppose the Caribe Hilton management when they threatened to bring in Jim Crow laws and implement the color bar (Merrill 2001, 204-6). What both Wharton and Merrill suggest is that the "anonymous audience" of locals gazing in through Hilton windows did not accept the promissory logic of U.S. Cold War ideology—the idea that if they worked hard enough, they, too, could enjoy the pleasures of a Western consumer lifestyle. Locals were well aware that the presence of a Hilton hotel in their homeland reoriented their local economies irrevocably toward serving Western interests and that the economic disparity of the global tourism industry meant they would forever be subordinate hosts rather than privileged guests.

The Habana Hilton, New Year's Eve 1958

Perhaps the starkest example of the return gaze breaking out of these asymmetrical structures was the transformation of the Habana Hilton in the two years after its opening in 1958. Although Cuba was an important part of the "hemispheric solidarity" promoted by Nelson A. Rockefeller and the U.S. government during and after the Second World War, its fading 1920s tourist infrastructure could not compete with the glittering new hotels in

Puerto Rico or the up-and-coming resorts in Acapulco and Montego Bay (Schwartz 1997, 106–9; Goldstone 2001, 21–44). Thus, President Batista created something different: his "free-wheeling, laissez-faire" policies produced a more hedonistic form of tourism based on casinos, nightclubs, horse racing, and prostitution (Merrill 2001, 201). As Rosalie Schwartz (1997, 126–27) argues, "exciting, cynical, sinful Havana wooed and won its northern neighbours... wonderful and foreign, the city became the 'coolest' place because it was the hottest. Havana cultivated its reputation for sinfulness and capitalized on the customer's willingness to pay for prurience." Such licentiousness could not be explicitly marketed in the United States's prudish postwar culture, so a more sanitized version of Cuba's hedonism was disseminated through a number of prominent cultural formations such as tourist advertisements, television shows, and films (Advertising Archives 2014a; johnjohn, n.d.). For example, tourist advertisements convinced viewers of the American sitcom *I Love Lucy* (1951–57) that a vacation in Cuba meant encountering *in person* the exotic Latin American rhythms of the rumba and the mambo they heard Desi Arnaz play every week. Likewise, the popular film *Guys and Dolls* (Mankiewicz 1955) demonstrated how even straitlaced and "proper" women can let loose in Havana and fall for (but ultimately redeem) inveterate gamblers like Sky Masterson (Schwartz 1997, 119–22).

Such Hollywood images did not, of course, show the consequences of Cuba's tourism policy on local residents; indeed, visitors who stuck to the well-entrenched tourist trail (e.g., horse racing at Oriental Park, dancing at the Tropicana nightclub) remained secure within the tourist enclave of "mythical" Havana. But as Merrill argues, the inequalities entrenched and exacerbated by Batista's laissez-faire tourism policies "intensified domestic dissent, fed anti-Yankee sentiment, and undoubtedly contributed to Fidel Castro's Communist revolution" (Merrill 2001, 201). From 1955 to 1959, Cuba's guerrilla movement increasingly targeted a number of highly visible leisure and tourist establishments (e.g., movie houses, hotels, nightclubs, casinos) in its effort to destabilize the Batista government, but tourists were not especially deterred until a failed assassination attempt on Batista in 1957 killed one American tourist, injured another, and forced several holiday makers to take cover in nearby casinos and hotels (Schwartz 1997, 164-79). In this context, the grand opening of the Habana Hilton in March 1958 was Batista's effort to restore Cuba as a desired holiday destination and lure back wary American tourists: "the name [Hilton] signalled both the tangibles and intangibles of stability and safety. Even timid tourists would recognize the distinctive logo and know that modern comforts and familiar amenities (such as chambermaids) would put them at ease" (Schwartz 1997, 178). However, not even the well-publicized and star-studded Hilton opening could detract journalists and photographers from turning their gazes toward the emerging revolution. As a result of such "bad" publicity, there were not many American tourists left by the time an advance group of rebels—or Fidelistas—entered Havana on New Year's Eve 1958. It is at this moment that a curious entanglement developed in which the Cuban rebels took over the Habana Hilton, displaced the remaining American tourists, and transformed the hotel from a site of leisure into the revolution's headquarters. As the rebel soldiers began to occupy Havana, more than twelve hundred of them set up camp within the Hilton, and by January 2, the grand ballroom had become their administrative headquarters. Diplomats continued to liaise with the hotel to get the remaining tourists out of Cuba and posted messages such as the following: "U.S. Embassy requests that our guests be ready to move with their luggage. The official departure point is the Nacional. No transportation from there. Now lack Gas! No definite info re: more flights today. Next report 1/2 hr" (Cole 1959c). R. Caspari, the Hilton labor councilor present at the time, was forced to organize meals for both the soldiers and the few remaining tourists; otherwise, as one rebel leader politely announced, "he would put a machine gun in every strategic spot of the hotel to make sure that it would be done" (Lefever and Huck 1990, 16). In a way, the transformation of the Hilton on New Year's Eve 1958 represents an inversion of what happened in Auschwitz and Hiroshima: there landscapes of war were turned into tourist attractions; here a tourist landscape was reterritorialized into the headquarters for a revolutionary war.

American photographer Lester Cole was present in Havana on New Year's Eve 1958, and along with capturing the revolution in the streets, he also recorded the overnight transformation of the Habana Hilton from a leisure hotel into troop barracks for the rebel soldiers. His black-and-white Hilton images, approximately fifteen in total, are situated amid a larger archive of the revolution that includes formal portraits of the rebels (e.g., Fidel and Raul Castro) and street shots of crowds awaiting the arrival of the soldiers (Cole 1959b). Most of the Hilton photographs are formal group portraits of the rebels taken on New Year's Day 1959, but there are also some informal snapshots of the off-duty soldiers resting and recuperating in the expansive hotel lobby. At first glance, Cole's documentation of the Cuban rebels making themselves at home in the Habana Hilton on New Year's Eve 1958 appears trivial and fleeting—a curious juxtaposition of leisure and revolution, but nothing more. This initial interpretation is secured by Cole's rendering of a central opposition between the gleaming modernist design of the new hotel (e.g., the geometric sofas, patterned wallpaper, oversized lamps, marble floors, recessed lighting, glass infrastructure, and large central atrium) and the rough appearance of the young solders. As Figure 22 illustrates, after weeks on the road, Castro's Fidelistas were happy to relax in such salubrious surroundings, attending to their daily routines (e.g., cleaning their rifles) while recuperating from fighting. This photograph in particular exemplifies how the clean lines, muted palate, and geometric order of the hotel's 1950s design motif (e.g., the lamps, the curtain, the pillar) are thrown into relief by the unkempt soldiers (e.g., the worn and dirty soles of their boots, their unwashed uniforms) strewn about the lobby in improvised configurations. Cole is able to mobilize a number of visual binaries through this central opposition—light and dark, in focus and out of focus, foreground and background, cluttered and empty—all of which work to reinforce the strangeness of these dirty rebel soldiers colonizing such a cosmopolitan and sophisticated leisurescape. With further reflection, however, the presence of these soldiers in the Hilton doesn't seem strange at all; indeed, hotels have always been requisitioned as troop barracks for soldiers either advancing to or retreating from battle. What interests me most about Cole's Hilton images are the way they convey familiarity and, in doing so, help to visualize the long-standing entanglements between tourism and war.

Cole's Hilton images deploy the conventions of classical photography

FIGURE 22. Cuban rebel soldiers cleaning their rifles, Habana Hilton lobby, Havana, Cuba, 1959. Copyright Lester Cole/CORBIS.

to aestheticize the rebels and make them knowable, familiar, and unthreatening. These conventions confer on Cole and his subjects certain pregiven dispositions that obey the regulations of classical portraiture. In the more posed group portraits in the front lobby of the hotel, the soldiers' faces are proud and serious rather than smiling, they often stare directly at the camera, and they hold their guns aloft like trophies. As Figure 23 shows, their bodies are carefully arranged into classical positions of differential heights that are offset by the geometric modernism of the hotel's design and architecture. Here the soldiers have chosen to pose amid the foliage of the hotel atrium—possibly hoping to bring some of the landscape they have traversed into the sterile environment they now inhabit. This is a classical composition that works wholly within the regulations of the

FIGURE 23. Cuban rebel soldiers at the Habana Hilton, 1959. Copyright Lester Cole/CORBIS.

photographic canon: highly contrasting shades of light and dark, asymmetrical focal points and diagonal lines guiding the viewer's eye into the image (e.g., the pointed guns) (Lisle 2011). By adhering to these conventions so closely, both Cole and the soldiers reproduce the central conceit of the form—that the artistic and creative input of the photographer is effaced when photographs are understood primarily as evidentiary documents. The soldiers pose and behave the way they do because (1) they want to convey the seriousness of the revolution (especially given their leisured surroundings) and (2) they understand Cole to be *recording this moment for posterity*. His images say, "This happened, I was there, this is proof." Cole is not making art; he is simply documenting a crucial moment in

Cuban history, and as such, the endeavor requires discipline and serious comportment on the part of his subjects. I want to read Cole's archive against this rather obvious claim by suggesting that the reterritorialization of the Habana Hilton was not just a serious affair requiring the gravitas of photographic subjects. Rather, the event was also prefigured by existing discourses of tourism, leisure, and pleasure that find their way into these images in unexpected ways. For example, many soldiers cannot help but smile when positioned in front of the camera, and the serious faces central to the posed images are belied by a number of grinning and smirking soldiers, including a surprising portrait of Castro himself grinning at the camera (Cole 1959a). Though some subjects appear bored and disinterested in Cole's presence (perhaps succumbing to exhaustion after the long march to Havana), many more embrace a "carnivalesque" atmosphere and happily arrange themselves around dogs, machine guns, palm trees, and homemade Cuban flags as they pose for the photographer (Cole 1959b). These images belong to the everyday register of personal photography—even tourist photography—in which the hierarchical relationship between photographer and subject is rearranged (Haldrup and Larsen 2003; Larsen 2005). Certainly these reorderings have the potential to produce new asymmetries and hierarchies, but the presence of joviality, celebration, and relaxation—dispositions more familiar to tourist experiences—render these soldiers familiar, friendly, and innocent rather than threatening revolutionaries. Remove the military fatigues and serious expressions and these photographs are simply beautifully constructed postcards—some more posed than others—that reveal how behavior is transformed by its spatial and material environment. These rebels may be off duty in terms of soldiering, but they are enrolled into new dispositions afforded by the modernist aesthetic of an international hotel. What makes Cole's images of the initial occupation of the Habana Hilton important is the way they capture the oscillation between these two positions: the rebels are simultaneously soldiers and tourists.

As a modernist citadel, the Habana Hilton was a prominent symbol of the privileged political system and tourist economy the revolution was working against. As Caspari recounts, the occupying soldiers were curiously respectful of its infrastructure: "The lobby smelled like a stable and everything was in an indescribable state of dirtiness, although the hotel had been protected and the rebels behaved well. They had not even broken an ashtray" (Lefever and Huck 1990, 16). This respect for the building and its new purpose as the revolution's headquarters spread outside of its walls as well, for example, Habana Hilton employee passes guaranteed workers safe passage in the streets of the city. As the remaining tourists were evacuated and the soldiers settled into the Habana Hilton, its days as a modern tourist paradise were numbered. Castro's revolutionary army struggled to govern Cuba's sprawling, mafia-infested tourist industry throughout 1959, and by June 1960—eighteen months after the rebels entered the Habana Hilton—they nationalized the hotel and renamed it the Hotel Habana Libre (Lefever and Huck 1990, 17–18; Hunt 2014). The revolution's effect on tourist arrivals from the United States was unsurprising, as one local newspaper reported at the time: "Sr. Castro long ago blew the whistle on tourism when he roughed up Americans, hurled insult after insult at the U.S. and behaved in general like an anti-social host. The touring public reacted like any guest might. It went away and didn't come back" (Lefever and Huck 1990, 18). With the nationalization of the Habana Hilton only two years after its grand opening, Conrad Hilton's ideological dream that his hotels could "show the countries most exposed to Communism the other side of the coin—the fruits of the free world" was no longer (Wharton 2001, 8). If the "fruits of the free world" included the hedonistic and privileged American tourism that kept Cubans in servile and subordinate positions throughout the 1950s, Castro was not interested. It is unsurprising, then, that tourism languished in Castro's Cuba for much of the 1970s and 1980s. However, as the revenues from sugar production plummeted and the Soviet Union collapsed in the late 1980s, Cuba once again turned to tourism as the main generator of national income. As Americans were banned from visiting Cuba, Castro's government courted visitors from Europe, Canada, Central and South America, and Japan throughout the 1990s, and the country is now running a multi-billion-dollar tourist industry often referred to as Club Red (Avella and Mills 1996; De Holan and Phillips 1997; Goldstone 2001, 95–123; Jayawardena 2003; Lasansky 2004; Schwartz 1997, 204–12).

While New Year's Eve 1958 in Havana is only a moment in the long arc of the Cold War, it is an important one in terms of revealing how bipolarity shaped the entanglements of war and tourism. It shows us first and foremost that spaces of leisure, such as hotels, can also become theaters of war. Indeed, the rebel takeover of the Habana Hilton troubled the Cold War's imaginary of clear front lines and demarcations between spheres of influence: here was a revolution in a hotel lobby (rather than a battlefield) and in the United States's backyard (rather than on distant killing fields). Moreover, this event illustrates how the design of modern hotels like the Habana Hilton and the tourist dispositions they encourage are powerful enough to reorient even the most unlikely subjects—in this case Castro's rebel soldiers. What must these Fidelistas have thought as they marched into the gleaming marble and glass atrium of the Hilton? How quickly, and in what ways, were their martial dispositions reoriented toward touristic ones? When the Cold War ended and Cuba reengaged in tourism in the 1990s, the Hilton Habana Libre was once again reterritorialized by foreign tourists. As non-American Western visitors wander across the expansive tiled lobby of the hotel, they are also moving through the haunting traces of Fidelistas cleaning their guns, resting amid the potted palm trees, and sleeping on appropriated sofas. It can only be hoped that these ghosts make a reappearance in the future transformation of the hotel—perhaps by displaying Cole's photographs in the central lobby that the rebels once occupied.

Cold War Militourism: R&R Itineraries In and Out of Asia

As the postwar battlefields of Europe and Asia were preparing themselves for the future influx of tourists, military forces all over the world were being demobilized and redeployed. During this transition, an important shift took place in which the martial framework through which soldiers made sense of their fighting experiences gave way to a touristic one in which they were suddenly on leave in an exotic and now peaceful environment. So as sites of wartime atrocity such as Auschwitz and Hiroshima transformed themselves into tourist attractions, demobilized soldiers went on permanent R&R and became tourists keen to enjoy their release from the pressures of fighting. The effects of this immediate postwar transition were felt in every city in the major theaters of the Second World War but were most acute in Tokyo. After Emperor Hirohito surrendered in August 1945, thousands of American soldiers who had been fighting all over the Pacific theater were relieved of active duty and traveled to Japan. By the end of the year, 350,000 U.S. troops were in the country—a force that would eventually become the official Allied Occupation (Elderidge 1997; Kristof 1995). Examining the interactions between demobbed American soldiers and local populations in postwar Tokyo tells us a great deal about the entanglements between tourism and militarism; indeed, it is a paradigmatic case of how both practices facilitate new forms of governance, violence, and exploitation. Even before Japan's official surrender was announced, government, city, and military officials in Tokyo were making plans to cater to the expected influx of American soldiers on leave. Acknowledging links with the "comfort women" system organized by the Japanese army during the war, Japanese and U.S. officials at all levels organized and facilitated a number of "comfort facilities," including dance halls, restaurants, clubs, bars, and, most importantly, brothels. This initiative was known officially as the Recreation and Amusement Association (RAA), and it lasted from the end of August 1945 until the end of January 1946. Although the central purpose of the RAA was to organize, manage, and control prostitution, it was often promoted through the benign language of tourism. For example, while the chief of the Metropolitan Police for Tokyo officially welcomed U.S. soldiers and wished them an enjoyable stay, he also argued that to protect "our wives and daughters and sisters" from the sexual advances of the soldiers, the city must "form a central association which would cater to the amusement of the Americans" (Lie 1997, 256–57). The problem with this tourist framing of "enjoyment" and "amusement" is that it required the bodies of local women to become objects available for tourist consumption. Off-duty soldiers took in the sights of Tokyo during the day and purchased souvenirs of their visit, and extended that mode of touristic consumption into the evening when they purchased the bodies of prostitutes for their "enjoyment" and "amusement."

The RAA is a powerful example of biopolitical governance in which police forces, city politicians, bureaucrats, military officials, businessmen, recruiting agents, street associations, public health workers, and the Japanese and U.S. governments colluded in a strategy to control the bodies and sexual interactions of two intersecting populations: American soldiers and local women. It allowed Occupation forces and local officials to exceed their normal remit of governing the working and professional lives of soldiers and citizens—now they were able to extend their modes of surveillance and intervention into the intimate lives of these populations. This was especially acute in the area of public health as regulated prostitution enabled U.S. and Japanese officials to control venereal disease and ensure the physical fitness of both soldier clients and prostitutes. Here, the Japanese medical profession was enrolled into the RAA because U.S. military officials instituted VD Control Laws and mandatory health checks for prostitutes. To ensure the widespread distribution of penicillin to both soldiers and prostitutes, a vast network of clinics, laboratories, and hospitals, as well as hundreds of health workers, became part of the extensive machine of governance (Tanaka 2002, 155–60). However, when the RAA was shut down in January 1946, gonorrhea and syphilis were rampant throughout both populations, with some military units reporting infection rates of higher than 50 percent (155–56). As Cynthia Enloe (2000, 58) argues, the Allied Occupation force expressed a "taxonomic urge" in their support of the RAA by making sure, once again, that only "certain kinds of men have certain kinds of sexual relationships with only certain kinds of women." So while the extension of biopolitical governance through militarized prostitution is an effort to police the intimate lives of intersecting populations, entrenched cleavages of class, race, and gender shape that policing; for example, certain brothels were reserved for white officers, whereas others were reserved for black soldiers (Enloe 2000, 49–107). The Japanese government reproduced this "taxonomic urge" not just because the RAA provided much-needed employment and income for a vanquished population but also because it allowed the government to more efficiently divide and control the bodies of Japanese women. As Molasky (2001, 109) argues, "the RAA was to serve as a 'Female Floodwall' *(onna no bōhatei),* channeling this foreign male desire into designated (lower-class) female bodies, thereby protecting the pure women of Japan's middle- and upper-classes" (see also Koikari 1999; Kovner 2012; Lie 1997; McClelland 2012; Soh 2009; Tanaka 2002). Indeed, "elite men of power looked to prostitutes and would-be-prostitutes to serve as new sexual 'soldiers,'" who, at the height of the RAA, numbered seventy thousand (Lie 1997, 257). Although these women were not coerced into becoming RAA prostitutes in the same way the comfort women were, the context of deprivation, defeat, and unemployment in Tokyo in 1945 meant that many Japanese women did not have any other choice. For example, many young women responded to ads promising office work for "women of the New Japan," but when they arrived for the interview, they were told that the only positions left were for comfort women, and many applicants were not in a financial position to refuse (Lie 1997, 257; Elderidge 2007).

Whereas feminist scholars have provided excellent analyses of how the RAA involved collusion between male military and government officials from both Japan and the United States, I am interested in how a preexisting tourist sensibility contributed to the normalization of militarized prostitution at this time. For the American soldiers arriving in Tokyo in 1945, the city was understood through contrasting frames: it was both a "liberated" enemy city (indeed, many American soldiers would have taken part in the intensive bombing raids of 1944–45), but it was also remembered as a popular tourist destination in the 1930s that was especially welcoming to North American and European visitors (Leheny 2000). In the very short time between the cessation of fighting and their arrival in Tokyo, these soldiers had to accomplish an affective transfer in which the previously dehumanized Japanese enemy was transformed into the welcoming and obliging Japanese host. As the victorious occupying force, U.S. servicemen enjoyed institutional support for the multiple ways in which they enacted their privilege and superiority—an arrangement that turned the entire city into a "pleasure playground" oriented toward servicing their needs. Part of what enabled U.S. soldiers to objectify and commodify an entire population and an entire urban infrastructure was a familiar tourist sensibility. Because Tokyo was there to provide "enjoyment" and "amusement," visiting servicemen were able to equate their experiences consuming exotic cultural monuments and local meals during the day with their experiences "consuming" local prostitutes at night. In effect, the bodies of prostitutes became the ultimate tourist attraction for American soldiers—the definitive "exotic experience" from which they derived enjoyment and through which they exerted power over the foreign culture they had just vanquished. What is particularly striking about the RAA in this experiential landscape is how the logistical arrangements of prostitution mimicked those of popular tourist attractions. For example, the sheer volume of U.S. servicemen pouring into the city meant that brothels had to be hastily arranged and rearranged (e.g., futons and beds had to be purchased). The first RAA brothel—the Komachien (Babe Garden)—was populated with thirty-eight prostitutes, but when five hundred to six hundred soldiers were waiting in line on the street, officials increased the number to one hundred (Elderidge 2007). Here, women's bodies were reduced to the simple calculus of supply and demand: increasing the number of "objects" in demand from soldiers increased profits and turnover because it satisfied more paying customers.

At the beginning of 1946, the U.S. government ended the RAA, in part because of complaints that institutionalized prostitution was immoral and antidemocratic, but mostly because the levels of VD were so high among troops (Tanaka 2002, 160–66; Lie 1997, 257–58). Immediately, thousands of Japanese women were unemployed and were forced to become unregulated streetwalkers. Although there is evidence that these pan-pan girls (usually overly made up and dressed in Western clothing) self-organized and exhibited solidarity and political agency (e.g., by teaching each other self-defense), the levels of violence against prostitutes rose dramatically when sex work was deregulated, as did VD infections (Kovner 2009, 782–88; Lie 1997, 257–60). As Sarah Kovner (2009, 779) argues, the end of the RAA did not end prostitution in Occupied Japan, nor did it end the various ways in which the bodies of Japanese women were regulated and controlled for the use and pleasure of elite American and Japanese men:

> Bodies of Japanese women became a key site of political and cultural contestation during Allied Occupation. Deregulated sex markets shaped the built environment and economy of Japanese cities. But it also spurred many people to reimpose order by constructing elaborate taxonomies, cartographies, health regimes, and moral codes to give meaning to this most conspicuous sign of their occupied status.

Whether institutionalized or deregulated, prostitution in Tokyo during the Allied Occupation illustrates the comprehensive and pernicious character of biopolitical governance. Its capacity to impel or restrict behavior derives not only from its ability to police intimate encounters between subjects but also from its capacity to track and control the spread of disease throughout a population. Certainly this mode of governance was constituted and enabled by multiple imaginaries in which colonialism, patriarchy, misogyny, nationalism, patriotism, and militarism intersected and reinforced each other. What interests me here is that within that mode of governance, American servicemen understood their time in Japan through a powerful and familiar tourist sensibility: they were privileged bodies away from the pressures of home and stationed in an exotic land during peacetime. Though Japan was only a transit point for most soldiers who returned to their lives in America (and thus functioned as a brief tourist excursion), many soldiers remained in Japan until 1952 as part of the formal occupying force. During the Occupation, a tourist sensibility continued to shape how American soldiers engaged with their "hosts": Japan was racially and culturally different (i.e., it was exotic and therefore perfect for tourist adventures); its vanquished status strengthened the occupiers' privilege (i.e., American soldiers resembled colonial rulers in that they were able to afford luxury, decadence, and vice); and this privilege enabled a complex production of racial and gender differences (i.e., the male bodies of mostly white occupiers romanticized, desired, befriended, used, and exploited the bodies of Japanese men and women).

The tourist framing of the Allied Occupation shifted once again in 1950 when new Allied troops joined the occupying forces in Japan as they collectively mobilized for the Korean War. Behind the front lines in Korea, there were R&R provisions such as mobile libraries and exchanges for soldiers to purchase souvenirs as well as more formalized R&R provisions in Seoul that sought to "replicate domestic cultures" by offering films, sports events, and celebrity concerts (Lee 2001, 69). There was, of course, organized military prostitution in Seoul as well, but for the most part in-country prostitution was located on the outskirts of U.S. military bases (Lee 1991, 79–80; Lie 1995). Given that the Allied Occupation of Japan had been in place since the end of the Second World War and had given rise to a highly developed prostitution industry, most R&R rotations during the Korean War were to Tokyo. Indeed, starting in December

1950, approximately fifteen thousand troops per month took advantage of five-day R&R visits to Tokyo (Lee 2001, 70). For historians like Bevin Alexander (1991; see also Moon 1997, 28–29; Yea 2003), the encounters between American servicemen on leave and Japanese people were framed as benign and beneficial for both because they were part of a wider effort to rehabilitate Japan from an enemy to an ally:

> Although the reconciliation of the Japanese people with the American people began in the years of the occupation before the Korean War, it was the war itself, with its hundreds of thousands of young American men who briefly visited Japan and briefly encountered Japanese people in bars, clubs, hotels and on the streets, that slowly turned a World War II–spawned antagonism for the Japanese into an affection for the Japanese. It was a rare American who visited Japan, even on a five-day R&R, who came away with anything but admiration for the Japanese people. (426)

For Alexander, American servicemen were heeding the call of foreign policy advisors at the time and behaving like tourist-diplomats; that is, they were serving American interests by cultivating feelings of "affection" and "admiration" for the Japanese. What is missing in this account, of course, are the asymmetries and exploitations that underscored these person-to-person diplomatic efforts to rehabilitate Japan. Because the terms of rehabilitation were set by the American occupiers, Japan was kept in a permanently abject position. As Rey Chow (2006, 37–38) argues, American practices of banning international travel and controlling media information were enabled by continually framing Japan as guilty for the Second World War—and, by extension, of course, framing themselves as innocent. So while UN and U.S. soldiers renamed their five-day R&R rotations to Tokyo as I&I (intercourse and inebriation) and A&A (ass and alcohol), media reports at the time (including newspaper, magazine, and television news reports) as well as subsequent mainstream histories like Alexander's and novels such as James Salter's (1956) *The Hunters* continued to avoid the issue of prostitution by depoliticizing these encounters through a benign discourse of reconciliation.[6]

Images of R&R during the Korean War were further popularized during the 1970s and 1980s as Western audiences watched the popular film and then television program *M*A*S*H* in which characters were always trying to get leave passes to Tokyo. Of course, as these cultural expressions were being consumed on the home front, American soldiers in Vietnam were experiencing their own respite from active combat duty. R&R during the Vietnam War operated in three registers: the daily pursuit of leisure, relaxation, and sightseeing; in-country leave arranged at stand-down and official R&R beach resorts; and an official five-day leave rotation to a designated regional city. As Meredith Lair (2011) makes clear, many American forces in Vietnam held supporting or administrative roles and therefore did not see combat during their tours. Unlike the grunts in the field, these troops—known as rear echelon mother fuckers (REMF)—oriented themselves to their foreign surroundings through a much more explicit tourist sensibility. For those Americans stationed in Saigon, for example, there were familiar tourist opportunities on bus tours of the zoo, racetrack, and markets as well as the ubiquitous entertainment at various bars, restaurants, hotels, and brothels in the city (Lair 2011, 191–92). Because it catered to so many soldiers either stationed in or transiting through the city, Saigon became the site for the first overseas USO center opened in a combat zone in 1963. Throughout the war, a further seventeen USO centers were opened in Vietnam, as well as six additional centers in Thailand, which coordinated tours of American entertainers, singers, and dancers and served more than 1 million servicemen a month (Coffey 1991; United Service Organizations, n.d.). Outside of Saigon, Long Binh Post (twenty miles north of the city) was the largest U.S. base in size and population and catered to thousands of troops stationed in or transiting through Saigon during the war. Certainly the base offered a variety of amenities and recreational opportunities for troops, but it also amplified the ever-present tourist sensibility by constructing and maintaining its own museum. The *Nature of War* exhibit aimed to depict the "enemy environment" for incoming troops, journalists, and visiting dignitaries and displayed a full-scale hut, a temple, a variety of weapons, and a simulated village (Lair 2011, 35–36). It was on bases such as Long Binh Post, as well as other military-run post-exchanges (PXs), that soldiers purchased personal cameras to document their adventures overseas:

> Cameras were ubiquitous in Vietnam, enabling soldiers to snap away on their tours of duty as middle-class excursionists had done since the early 20th Century.... Slipping momentarily into tourist mode, soldiers snapped pictures—aerial shots from helicopters, blurry stills from moving trucks,

close-up studies taken during idle moments on the ground—that captured a million variations of these scenes. (Lair 2011, 215, 192)

In a much more explicit manner than Korea or even the Second World War, a soldier's experience in Vietnam was explicitly framed by a tourist sensibility from the outset: even before any R&R was taken, troops transiting through Saigon or stationed in rearward bases treated Vietnam as a tropical holiday destination. They may have been sent to fight or facilitate combat, but in their off-duty time they would behave as tourists in an exotic Asian land.

Once soldiers entered the field of combat, they still had several opportunities for leisure, recreation, and tourism at various stand-down centers both inland and on the coast. These locations varied in their amenities but served as interim sites for R&R in addition to official leave taken in-country or abroad. Leave to these centers was granted on an ad hoc basis by the commanding officer, and many catered to specific military units, for example, the 101st Airborne managed Eagle Beach on an island across from Hué City (Lair 2011, 114). Logman's Beach in Qui Nhon was the largest and most popular stand-down center in the country and received not only troops for interim R&R but also weekend visits from administrative and support staff stationed nearby. Here troops engaged in a variety of activities in direct opposition to practices of combat:

> On the beach, soldiers could enjoy boating, inner tubes, water skiing, surfing, and scuba diving lessons. Just inland, a miniature golf course, driving range, horse-shoe pits, badminton, volleyball, basketball, a craft shop, and a music room with instruments for check out were available for soldiers to pass the time. (Lair 2011, 116, also 193)

Those ad hoc experiences of tourism-amid-combat were eclipsed by the experiences of officially scheduled in-country leave. These three-day episodes, arranged in advance by the commanding officer, took place in two official U.S. Army R&R sites: the mile-long China Beach (Bac My An) in Da Nang, which catered to troops stationed farther north, and the half-mile-long Vung Tau Beach (eighty miles south of Saigon), which catered to troops stationed farther south. In 1968, at the height of the war, more than twenty-nine thousand American troops visited the facilities at Vung

FIGURE 24. The beach at Vung Tau R&R center. Cat. No. CT 205. Courtesy of the Imperial War Museum Archive, London. Copyright IWM.

Tau, depicted in Figure 24 (Lair 2011, 112). This aerial shot of the resort in 1970 resembles a photograph of many Asian beach resorts at the time: there are holiday makers swimming, sunbathing, frolicking, and otherwise enjoying the beach; service staff working in bars, restaurants, gift shops, and other services; and even a lifeguard to ensure the safety of beachgoers. Indeed, "in-country R&R folded the tourist experience directly into the war's milieu, for soldiers fresh from combat did not have to travel far to exit the war and enter a tropical playground" (Lair 2011, 113). These official coastal resorts had all the amenities of the stand-down centers as well as bus tours, movies, and regular floor shows. It was in Vung Tau and China Beach that many Western soldiers took up surfing, making their own surfboards in beachside huts and forming the China Beach Surf Club and the Allied Surf Association of the South China Sea.[7] At the height of the war, soldiers fortified R&R beaches with barbed wire and machine guns to protect the surfers, but they also brokered deals with enemy troops in the area: the North Vietnamese soldiers could enjoy wave-riding privileges in exchange for a cease-fire during the day (Warshaw 2005, 671; see also Ponder 2008; Scott 2008).

Over and above the opportunities for tourism and leisure in-country, troops were also eligible for official five-day R&R passes after ninety days in-country. Pan American World Airlines, which already had the contract to fly supplies from the West Coast of the United States to Vietnam, also had the contract to fly servicemen on R&R trips throughout Southeast Asia (Periscope Film LCC Archive 1967). Soldiers could travel to Bangkok, Taipei, or Honolulu, but at the height of the war in 1968–69, they could also travel to Hong Kong, Kuala Lampur, Penang, Manila, Singapore, Sydney, or Tokyo (First Battalion, Fiftieth Infantry Association 2002; Lair 2011, 110; *Time* 1967). At the peak of troop deployment in Vietnam in 1970, seventeen thousand soldiers were participating in out-of-country R&R excursions every month (Lair 2011, 111). Speaking specifically about the seventy thousand American soldiers who chose Bangkok and Pattaya for R&R in 1969, Suntikul (2012, 95) argues, "R&R destinations were chosen by virtue of specific attributes, including proximity to the combat zone, social stability, and friendly political alignment. By these criteria, Thailand was an ideal R&R destination." The process of exiting Vietnam for an official R&R tour involved traveling to Camp Alpha just outside Saigon for showers, processing, vaccinations, and instructions, before being flown out of Tan Son Nhut Airbase. This initial transition ensured that "a GI's transformation from soldier to tourist began even before he got on the plane" (Lair 2011, 111). Once they arrived at their chosen R&R destinations, American soldiers on leave did not have to distinguish between friendly or hostile natives: they simply entered into an economy of leisure "which was single-mindedly devoted to the pursuit of pleasure" (*Time* 1967). These R&R excursions during the Vietnam War are important because they intensified a long-standing mythology of the Pacific as a tourism paradise that had marked both the itineraries of previous soldiers on leave from the Korean War and the routes of Western tourists in the 1950s and 1960s seeking a taste of the "exotic."

Of course, by claiming that soldiers on leave are just like any other tourist in the region, official and media accounts of R&R made sure to highlight the financial and cultural benefits for host countries as a direct result of the influx of American servicemen. As *Time* magazine reported in 1967, the modern U.S. serviceman is better educated, more sophisticated, more curious about alien cultures, and better behaved than any of his predecessors—and he has more money to spend. On the average, he spends roughly $200, making a total yearly tourist bonanza for the area of some $72 million.

Indeed, the experience of American R&R in Thailand throughout the Vietnam War is considered one of the major catalysts for that country's postwar tourist success (Ouyyanont 2001; Suntikul 2012). More generally, the American experience of R&R throughout the region not only gave soldiers "the opportunity to behave as tourists in Asia, stockpiling souvenirs and memories of a once-in-a-lifetime adventure"; it also incentivized and encouraged practices of consumerism that were the lynchpin of the postwar U.S. economy (Lair 2011, 110). In other words, the frenzy of tourist consumption experienced by young men on R&R overseas not only generated a tourist economy abroad but was also the entry point into a lifetime of consumerism at home. This benign framing of R&R as an economically productive force throughout Asia extends to the depiction of prostitution as simply one of many consumer experiences available to soldiers on leave. As *Time* magazine reported in 1967,

> among single men, the favorite city is Bangkok. Its Pechaburi Road [sic] offers the neon-lit Goldfinger Massage Parlor, the Whisky A Go-Go Club and some 50,000 bar girls, but also impressive temples for inspection during the recuperative hours. The companionship of a girl who also numbers English among her several skills can be secured for $11 a day or $50 for a full five days.

Here the relative economic power of the soldier enables him to equate the leisure experience of visiting an "impressive temple" with the consumer experience of buying a girl—both perfectly "valid" activities of soldier-tourists in exotic lands. In all three registers of R&R during the Vietnam War—stand-down centers, in-country resorts, and official R&R leave—prostitution was a central part of the tourist experience. Institutionalized and militarized prostitution existed within Vietnam to service both the stand-down centers and in-country resorts: these "pleasure belts" were orchestrated by officers in the U.S. military, government officials, and a variety of local and global entrepreneurs. As Enloe (2000, 67) argues, "prostitution was not simply a matter of personal choices or of private sexual desires. There were institutional decisions, there were elaborate calculations, there were organizational strategies, there were profits" (see also Barry 1995). These institutional arrangements spread out across R&R destinations in Asia so that militarized and industrialized prostitution began to shape the urban fabric of major regional cities. For example, the bars, nightclubs, and massage parlors on Bangkok's Petchburi Road expanded for five miles and became known as the American Strip, dedicated to serving soldiers on R&R.

The experience of R&R during the Vietnam War is important because it intensified and further disseminated a logic of hedonism–objectification in which American soldiers indulged in all manner of excess at the expense of local populations and landscapes. Because R&R released soldiers from both the confines of home *and* the dangerous labor of combat, it produced a "carnivalesque" atmosphere in which soldiers "indulged their appetites and tried on new personas, safe in the knowledge that their behaviour would likely go unchecked" (Lair 2011, 194). As Lair (2011, 211) goes on to say, "feasting, drinking, fucking, killing—it was all okay there. The Nam was a wonder-land of possibilities, and service therein was a once-in-a-lifetime chance to break taboos and indulge the flesh." As sex with prostitutes during R&R became a normalized leisure experience to be expected, enjoyed, and repeated, like sunbathing, surfing, or water skiing, the bodies of Asian women became commodified objects to be consumed, enjoyed, and discarded. Their bodies were equated with other tourist services—gift shops, bars, restaurants, nightclubs—whose sole purpose was to provide pleasure, leisure, and entertainment for troops. As one American soldier explained, these women were reduced to "Little Brown Fucking Machines," and the experience of R&R was routinely referred to as "rape and run" or "intoxication and intercourse" (Enloe 2000, 69; Inglis 2000, 140–41; Lair 2011, 207; Moon 1997, 34; Truong 1990, 161–67).

It is certainly the case that the pleasure belts of militarized prostitution around military bases and in R&R destinations could only be created and maintained by institutional collusion between the U.S. military, regional governments, and other male elites, and that profits from such collusion were not shared with the women providing the sexual labor (Chang 2001, 628; see also Brock and Thistlewaite 1996). Although it is important to call attention to the macropolitical decisions about infrastructure and economy that enabled prostitution to flourish within the wider experience of R&R, this tells only part of the story. What interests me is how a familiar tourist sensibility was central to the everyday practices of mobilization, production, and governance within military culture that *prepared* American soldiers for their tourist experiences and *sanctioned* their exploitation of Asian women. Scott Laderman's (2009, 47–85) analysis of the military-produced Pocket Guides that were issued to American soldiers in 1963, 1966, and 1971 suggests one way that a tourist sensibility directly bolstered military actions during the Vietnam War. Like all travel guidebooks, these provided soldiers with tourist information about where to go sightseeing in Vietnam and contextualized those excursions with general information about the culture and people of Vietnam. Unlike regular guidebooks, however, the military Pocket Guides were overtly ideological documents that persuaded troops of the necessity of U.S. involvement in Vietnam. The first edition (1963) was framed explicitly through a tourist sensibility; indeed, "the general impression a casual reader might have received from the flowery descriptions in the pocket guide was that southern Vietnam in 1963 was more of a holiday destination than a war zone" (52). By the final edition (1971), however, the "flowery" tone had been replaced by the looming possibility of defeat, and the tourist sensibility had been jettisoned in favor of a clear focus on "martial responsibilities" (85).

The Pocket Guides were part of a wider network of governmentality in which the bodies of American soldiers were prepared for their encounters with the landscape of Vietnam and the Vietnamese themselves. Central to that network were the military's efforts to educate troops about public health and personal hygiene, especially with respect to VD. A 1967 television documentary about R&R titled *A Holiday from Hell* shows how this mode of governance worked to prepare soldiers on their first leave to Taipei (Periscope Film LCC Archive 1967). While on the bus from the airport to the R&R center, soldiers are given a lecture from a seasoned U.S. Marine Corps sergeant who covers issues of personal security, general conduct, and girls—the "good ones and the bad ones." After explaining that girls with a circular pin on their lapels can be hired, the sergeant then expresses the objectification of Asian women that underscores the experience of R&R: "She's what we call a thoroughbred. She's got plenty of practice—she's been in operation since January... she can be hired out of the bar, but in order to hire her you must sign a contract for it, just like buying a car" (Periscope Film LCC Archive 1967, 12:35–13:05). Once the laughter has died down, the sergeant goes on to list all the especially seedy bars where soldiers have to watch out for themselves and their belongings—the very bars that all the soldiers are interested in. These official instructions to soldiers are, of course, internalized and performed by more seasoned troops who offer advice, tips, and suggestions to their younger colleagues, such as "do not purchase the company of a girl for more than 24 hours at a time; they seldom look as good in the morning" (*Time* 1967; see also Lair 2011, 207–8). The documentary frames the local population in contrasting ways: on the one hand, they are members of an ancient culture that soldier-tourists on R&R should visit; but on the other hand, they are depicted as "wily" Asians looking to fleece the rookie soldier of all his money. This contrast is more specific with respect to the women working in the bars and nightclubs: on the one hand, they are sexualized as exotic objects of desire (with the camera lingering on their faces, gestures, and comportment), but on the other hand, they are described— almost distastefully—as too "businesslike" in their intimate transactions.

While the exotic character of Asian women and Asian cities is foregrounded in the experience of R&R, there is always a threat right under the surface of leisure and tourism—the threat of VD carried and spread by Asian prostitutes. While they were concerned about the spread of VD throughout their troops (indeed, in 1969–70, at the height of American deployment, 50 to 60 percent of prostitutes working in Vung Tau and China Beach were infected with gonorrhea), the American military were also hesitant to place too many restrictions on the intimate interactions between soldiers and local women lest they disrupt the profitable arrangement of militarized prostitution (Sun 2004, 86n34). An important mechanism that allowed military authorities to inform soldiers about VD but not intervene in their behavior was the military health-education film shown to all incoming troops. The most famous of these is Miller's (1969) U.S. Air Force film *Where the Girls Are—VD in Southeast Asia,* a narrative public service film about an innocent soldier (Collins) whose moral resolve weakens in Vietnam; he succumbs to two sexual encounters (one in a bathhouse in Saigon, one on R&R), fails to use a condom, contracts syphilis, and thus jeopardizes a life of future wedded bliss with his innocent fiancée back home. Aside from the moralizing tone of the film and the obvious manner in which it tries to turn didactic instruction into a compelling story, its importance lies in the way it represents gender, militarism, leisure, and prostitution. For Sue Sun (2004, 67), the film is important because it articulates a "strategy of prophylactic venereal-disease management based on instilling fear of Vietnam—and Vietnamese women—in the minds of American soldiers." Rather than the robust, masculine soldier conquering Communism on behalf of grateful Vietnamese subjects, *Where the Girls Are* suggests that soldiers are vulnerable—especially when they are off duty and enjoying the tourist and leisure opportunities of Asia. This complex trafficking of threat suggests that the fear instilled by the Vietcong is replicated during the experience of R&R as soldiers are taught to fear the specter of disease contained within Asian women's bodies. The difference here is certainly spatial: the threat of the VC can be contained on the battlefield, but the threat of VD is so pernicious that it infiltrates the everyday spaces and circuits of pleasure, leisure, and tourism. That distinction, of course, is highly gendered. Unsurprisingly, the productions of fear and desire articulated in *Where the Girls Are* operate through a familiar binary between the Madonna (i.e., the "pure" fiancée waiting back home) and the whore (i.e., all of the Vietnamese women represented in the film). However, the Vietnamese women are depicted as *so* sexualized, feminized, and available that they are irresistible to the protagonist. It is not Collins's fault that he succumbs to their seductive charms; rather, he is the innocent victim of their alluring, exotic, and ultimately dangerous sexuality. Like all militarized modes of governance aimed at managing the intimate lives of soldiers and Others, this film is solely concerned with the bodies and capacities of American soldiers rather than with those of Vietnamese women (see also CBC 2007). As Sun argues,

> the prostitutes in the film appear as aggregated sexual phantoms, without names, personal histories, or spoken dialogue. They are simply visual representations of the unpredictable dangers posed to American servicemen abroad.... The portrayal of these women as purely sexual beings creates a shopping mall-style

fantasy that obscures the cash-driven reality of the illicit market funded by the labour of these women. (78–79)

My point here is that the "shopping mall–style fantasy" that subordinates and exploits Vietnamese women during the war is part of a wider tourist sensibility operating throughout the region. That one of Collins's sexual encounters takes place on R&R is no coincidence: the bodies of women all over Asia were reduced to tourist commodities to be consumed by soldiers on leave.

The objectification of women's bodies—and, indeed, the bodies of all Vietnamese subjects—is even more explicit in a medical-hygiene film produced by the U.S. Army (1969) titled *Personal Hygiene in a Hot Climate*. Shot in black and white, the film aims to help soldiers take care of their bodies while overseas as they confront severe heat and humidity, dehydration, contaminated food and water, disease, insects, and all manner of bacteria and viruses. The film depicts the country of Vietnam as an unhygienic cesspit that threatens the health and well-being of American troops, and it offers instruction to soldiers about how to prevent contamination, disease, and illness. The Vietnamese themselves are represented as either a threatening absence (i.e., the enemy) or as an ignorant, backward, and unenlightened population that doesn't understand the basics of public and personal hygiene. Over images of open sewers, untreated rubbish, children defecating in the streets, and locals happily consuming unfiltered water and unwashed food, the sarcastic voice-over urges soldiers to eat only in U.S. military messes and approved restaurants ("meat and potatoes—that's the ticket!"). Certainly the film objectifies, racializes, and subordinates the Vietnamese Other in multiple ways, but that objectification is only the precursor to depicting Vietnam and all its subjects as a looming threat. This is especially clear in the section on VD, in which the bodies of Vietnamese women are equated with the threatening, disease-filled, contaminated landscape of Vietnam. Framed as "another hazard to stay away from," Vietnamese women are depicted as seductive and toxic figures bent on luring innocent U.S. soldiers into a lifetime of disease. Over scenes of soldiers entering bars, massage parlors, and nightclubs and fondling Vietnamese women in the street, the voice-over argues,

> Now a lot of you guys are going to like the look of these pretty little honeys. They're young, slim and sexy. Forget it! You may think these are just like the girls back home, gone a little wrong. They're not! They're professional hustlers whose business it is to sleep with as many men as they can every day.... Some of these girls have the kinds of VD you have never even heard of. Don't fool around with them! They've got VD—and they'll give it to you! (U.S. Army 1969, 1.04:42–1.06:54)

While there are a few depictions of Vietnamese women as silent and innocent victims in traditional dress who need the protection of the American military, a majority of Vietnamese women depicted in these public information films are hypersexualized figures in Western dress who speak English, work in bars and nightclubs, and want to lure American soldiers into a world of vice, hedonism, and pleasure. The representations of gender and power are complex here: while soldiers are "lured" by these "pretty little honeys," they are also intensely critical of the overly "businesslike" approach these women have to sex because it sullies their desire for a silent, exotic, and abject woman.

Over and over again, American soldiers objectify Asian women within Vietnam and throughout regional R&R destinations: when they share information on the best "deals" for prostitutes, when they routinely pay for sex while on R&R, when they listen to medical-hygiene films about VD, and when they read in their Pocket Guides about the necessity of protecting Vietnamese women from the Communist threat. Over and over again, the agency of these women is effaced, ignored, and silenced. Certainly I agree with feminist scholars that militarized prostitution enacts a relentless and violent objectification of local women, and I am especially interested in the work of Trinh-T. Minh-Ha (1989) because it carves out critical and creative spaces within which the multiple voices of Vietnamese women can be articulated. However, I want to insist that the violence enacted by militarized prostitution is actively facilitated by the "exotic lens" of tourism and that the tourist sensibility that operated during the Vietnam War was absolutely central in shaping and directing the asymmetrical encounters between occupying forces and local populations. The multiple productions of Otherness—as threats, victims, enemies, and objects of sexual desire—have always constituted practices of tourism, and these productions are certainly amplified and intensified during war. This matters because a preexisting tourist sensibility justifies and excuses institutionalized violence: it becomes OK for occupying soldiers to exploit local women because these women are simply part of the objectified landscape produced, normalized, and secured by decades of tourist adventures in "exotic" Asia.

This seductive entanglement of tourism, war, and sex has populated many representations of the Vietnam War within Western popular culture—from countless barroom, brothel, and prostitute scenes in Vietnam War films to Broadway musicals such as *Miss Saigon*. American television audiences watched a version of this entanglement in the popular American television show *China Beach* (1988–91), which portrayed the interactions between American soldiers, entertainers, medical staff, and Vietnamese locals at an R&R center during the war (Ballard-Reisch 1991; Rasmussen 1992). In all of these representations, the official framing of R&R as an innocent experience of cultural encounter was questioned; indeed, the late 1960s and early 1970s gave rise to a number of critical voices that questioned the racist, patriarchal, and colonial discourses that sustained the Vietnam War. Importantly, this critical questioning was linked to the increased presence of American women serving in Vietnam (mostly as nurses) and the continuing racial desegregation of American forces (Enloe 2000, 224–29, 280; Dornfield 1995). This connection between diversity on the front lines and countercultural forces at home was fertile ground for American writers and filmmakers throughout the 1970s and 1980s who helped to construct a new consensus over their loss in the Vietnam War (Anderegg 1991; Aufderheide 1990; Dittmar and Michaud 1991; Levine 1999; Melling 1990; Porteous 1988). However, just like the military personnel shooting medical-hygiene films about VD during the 1960s, subsequent filmmakers—even critical ones—were concerned primarily with how participation in the war affected Americans and American identity rather than how it affected the local Vietnamese population or those in the red-light districts of Bangkok, Manila, or Tokyo. For example, Vietnam War films such as Oliver Stone's *Platoon* (1986) and Brian De Palma's *Casualties of War* (1989) that were critical of American soldiers' behavior toward local Vietnamese people consistently recuperated a better vision for *America*. Certainly there were "bad apples" in the forces who did terrible things (i.e., rape or torture Vietnamese people), but they were always punished accordingly by justified revenge (e.g., *Platoon*) or by the U.S. military's judicial system (e.g., *Casualties of War*). Overwhelmingly, the cinematic consensus constructed about the Vietnam War in the 1980s was held together by the redemption of American veterans and American citizens rather than an acknowledgment of the harm done to Vietnam and the Vietnamese population. When Vietnamese subjects do appear, they are only there to facilitate the recuperation and redemption of American figures and thus are partitioned out into an array of abject positions including unredeemable enemy, sacrificial martyr, and innocent victim. In other words, they are reduced to signifiers of an exotic theater within which American struggles over identity take center stage.

Lurking within this post hoc cinematic and cultural consensus over the Vietnam War is, of course, a powerful tourist sensibility that continues to shape the manner in which tourists interact with Vietnam. As many have argued, Vietnam itself has become an important theater for staging American memory and identity (Laderman 2009; see also Alneng 2002; Henderson 2000). Certainly this includes the many organized tourist excursions for Vietnam veterans themselves, but it also includes the backpacking itineraries of a younger generation of Western adventurers who grew up watching films like *Platoon* and television shows like *China Beach*. As Alex Garland's (1996) novel and Danny Boyle's (2000) film adaptation *The Beach* depict, the Vietnam War (and the subsequent struggles over national identity it provoked) have shaped the way an entire generation of American citizens understand Southeast Asia. This is a place of danger, exoticism, and seduction that can be easily and cheaply accessed through the experience of tourism. In this sense, the Western cultural consensus that was built over the Vietnam War throughout the 1980s unleashed a new population of occupying subjects. As American forces departed in a cloud of failure in 1975, they were gradually replaced by tourists throughout the late 1980s and 1990s who were interested in seeing the land that had caused so much painful national introspection. The problem, of course, was that the violent asymmetries that characterized the Vietnam War—its racism, misogyny, and paternalism—were recuperated through a new "liberating" and "productive" tourist industry whose benign face seemed capable of generating new global solidarities by erasing past injustices.

Cold War Continuities

I began this chapter with Joker's mischievous retort to the camera in *Full Metal Jacket* because it neatly overturns the commonsense hierarchy between war and tourism. For all its brilliance, however, this scene still leaves the Vietnamese silent as the viewer's gaze remains fixed on the soldier-tourist protagonist. In this sense, *Full Metal Jacket* reproduces the same conceit of much Cold War popular culture—cinema, photography, journalism, fiction—that refuses to examine the lingering Orientalism underscoring America's foreign policy decisions and tourism's complicity in reproducing that unequal framing. By ignoring the asymmetries of power that underscored Cold War geopolitics, the terrain of culture established a powerful continuity between a tourist sensibility that was established in the Cold War of the 1950s and its subsequent manifestations in the 1970s and well into the twenty-first century. Indeed, tourism's capacity to envision the world through prevailing geopolitical discourses—in this case the Cold War's bipolar "architecture of enmity"—is not disrupted or compromised by revolutions, wars, or conflicts; rather, these monumental events become pivotal moments for a tourist sensibility to recalibrate, adapt, and reposition itself within a transformed geopolitical landscape. This is important because, although the friend–enemy geopolitical coordinates may differ between the Cold War of the 1950s and the War on Terror of the 2000s (i.e., from a Communist enemy to an Islamic fundamentalist), tourism's ability to *envision* the world within these coordinates of enmity remains as robust and clear-sighted as ever.

To try to unpack that continuity, it is important to show how the Cold War stabilization of the war–tourism hierarchy is consistently overturned when we understand these practices as entangled, complicit, and co-constitutive. With that in mind, I want to end this chapter with a series of satirical postcards by Vietnamese artist Dinh Q. Lê titled *Untitled from Vietnam: Destination for the New Millennium* (2005). The postcards use familiar images of "exotic" Asia to critique the Vietnamese government's

2000 campaign Vietnam: Destination for the New Millennium, which intentionally evacuated the experience of war in an effort to attract wealthy tourists. Lê's images, like the Vietnamese government's campaign, are directed specifically at American holiday makers. In one postcard image of a blue sky and sandy beach, Lê's caption is "*Come back to My Lai...for its beaches.*" As Figure 25 illustrates, another postcard juxtaposes the "exotic" image of women in traditional Vietnamese áo dài outfits with a deliberate reference to the U.S. struggle to accept its defeat in the Vietnam War.

Though much of Lê's art examines the cultural construction of Vietnam under globalization, he explains the specific issue of tourism that led him to produce these postcard installations:

> In a way, Vietnam is trying to reinvent itself. The world has only known it for its war. Is it possible to reinvent the country as a tourist destination known for its beaches and natural beauty? I don't think it's possible. I think we can move forward and rejoin the world, but I think we have to acknowledge the past. I thought the tourist marketing campaign in 2000 that used the line "Vietnam: Destination for the New Millennium" was problematic. On one hand, it promoted our beautiful beaches, but on the other it ignored other tourist sites such as the DMZ and the Cu Chi tunnels. It is a conflict of messages, but this is where Vietnam is: we are grappling with the old and the new Vietnam. (Choron-Baix 2009, 68; see also Lê 2005; Miles and Lê 2003)

Lê's postcards are powerful cultural responses to the way Vietnam is traditionally "seen" by Western audiences as a silent backdrop to their own privileged experiences. Indeed, not only was Vietnam the exotic theater within which the U.S. military struggled to contain Communism in the 1960s and 1970s; it currently plays host to thousands of tourists and travelers seeking the same "jewel of Southeast Asia" that Joker was looking for in Kubrick's *Full Metal Jacket.* What I like about Lê's work is that it refuses to accept Vietnam's traditional silence and instead offers a critical response to the combined forces of military strategy and global tourism. While Joker's retort in *Full Metal Jacket* demonstrates the entanglements between a dominant tourist gaze and military strategy, Lê's art goes one step further by forcing viewers to see Vietnam differently—to recognize their own complicity in constructing Vietnam as a convenient "exotic" backdrop for the continual resuscitation of privileged

FIGURE 25. Dinh Q. Lê, *Untitled from Vietnam: Destination for the New Millennium*, 2005. C-print, 30 × 40 inches. Courtesy of the artist and PPOW Gallery, New York.

Western identities. In this, he echoes Alneng's (2002, 482) claim that the "meta-war" of cinematic images has made Vietnam the ultimate empty signifier for Americans: "We have turned Vietnam into a mirror—a place without a place. Gazing at Vietnam, We see Ourselves where We are not—a self-affirmation deceivingly disguised as an ego-escape." While Lê's postcards operate in the same satirical register as Joker's retort to the television cameras in *Full Metal Jacket*, I think Lê's work is harder to dismiss because it offers something more jarring, more confrontational. To paraphrase Roland Barthes (1993), both responses—Joker's and Lê's—make us laugh, but it is only Lê's that "punctures" our complicity, that "shoots out like an arrow" and disturbs our familiar ways of looking at Vietnam. It is precisely Lê's spirit of confrontation that needs to be foregrounded in future critical explorations of how tourists and military populations occupy foreign lands.

4

Global Interventions

Contested History and the Rise of Dark Tourism

If we understand war and tourism to be shaped by historically specific geopolitical architectures, then the post–Cold War landscape is particularly significant because the foundational us-them binary of the Cold War was disaggregated into multiple animosities, threats, enemies, and risks. This moment was centrally shaped by a debate over whether the supposed benefits of liberal rule (i.e., systemic peace, enhanced freedom, economic growth and the protection of fundamental rights) could be extended around the world or whether that exportation was just another form of Western imperialism to be enjoyed by elites at the expense of the rest of the world (Doyle 1983a; 1983b; Fukuyama 1989; 1993; Huntington 1993; 1996; Kaplan 1994; 1997). This debate became especially heated with respect to the humanitarian and military interventions staged (or not staged, or badly staged) in response to violent ethnic conflicts in places like Bosnia, Somalia, Rwanda, Kosovo, and Sierra Leone. Throughout the 1990s, this structuring debate changed the orientation of armed forces in combat zones: no longer simply "fighting the enemy," soldiers were now deployed on a multilateral basis as peacekeepers mediating between different ethnic groups and facing complex humanitarian emergencies. Moreover, multilateral forces weren't the only figures intervening in such war zones: they now had to engage in peacekeeping operations alongside a 24/7 global news media, charity groups, volunteers, a range of non-governmental organizations (NGOs), and, of course, tourists.

In part, the post-1989 geographical expansion of tourism was a response to the supposed inauthenticity of traditional tourist resorts and itineraries: people wanted to visit new destinations, encounter new cultures, see new cities, and explore new landscapes that hadn't already been commodified and packaged by the forces of mass tourism. Importantly, destinations considered previously "untouched" or "forbidden" by Western tourists during the Cold War became central to the post–Cold War tourist imaginary. The globalization of tourism also increased the diversity of travel itself: the model of package tourism that dominated throughout the 1970s and 1980s was now supplemented by forms of independent travel that gave people more autonomy to choose not just their destinations but also the types of vacations they wanted (e.g., backpacking, hosteling, city breaks, nature tourism, clubbing holidays, food tourism, cultural tourism). Independent travel is an important component of what Nikolas Rose has identified as the rise of the modern, self-governing liberal subject: rather than passively accept the authority of paternal institutions, individuals now seek out expertise to help cultivate a resilient self, acquire and expand particular skill sets so as to compete in the global job market, and develop a lifestyle that balances individual fulfillment with the obligations of collective relations (e.g., family, friends, community) (Rose 1989; 1996; Rose and Miller 1998). Independent global travel is a central experience for the modern subject because it signals a cosmopolitan rather than a parochial disposition (i.e., one is "worldly'), enables the acquisition of cultural capital that is easily measured and expressed (e.g., knowledge of "foreign" food, culture, language), and secures the prized value of autonomy by denigrating mass tourism (i.e., independent travel rather than package tourism). At a more structural level, of course, the globalization of tourism after the Cold War—its drive to cross borders and colonize new destinations—is central to the neoliberal policies of economic expansion that were being consolidated throughout the 1990s. Tourism is understood as an industry that can generate huge profits, expand markets (in terms of both producers and consumers), and bring much-needed investment to a multitude of destinations. In this sense, independent travelers in the 1990s were simply doing what American tourists did to economically rejuvenate Europe in the 1940s and 1950s—only now tourism diplomacy was truly global because it contributed to the economic development of millions of "new" destinations around the world.

As they traversed the globe in their millions, Western tourists were encouraged to act as cultural diplomats consolidating the foundation for a truly global collectivity. Their encounters with different cultures, communities, and landscapes were not a prelude to colonialism or inequality but rather an expression of the commonalities and solidarities that united everyone around the world. Indeed, during the 1990s, tourism studies scholars, policy makers, and industry practitioners were keen to promote tourism as an engine for global peace—a form of people-to-people diplomacy that functioned as a "catalytic force for tension reduction and peace-building" (Yu and Chung 2001, 37–38; see also Higgens-Desboilles 2006; Lollis 2013; Moufakkir and Kelly 2010; People to People International, n.d.). New travel magazines (e.g., *Wanderlust, National Geographic Traveler*), travel guidebook series (e.g., The Rough Guide), Internet travel sites (e.g., Travelocity, Lonely Planet's Thorn Tree forum), television networks (e.g., Travel Channel, Discovery Channel), and television programs (e.g., PBS's *Going Places,* BBC's *Holiday,* ITV's *Wish You Were Here*) promoted tourism as a force for productive and peaceful cross-cultural understanding that helped to break down barriers, create powerful moments of recognition, and bring diverse groups together. Tourism's contribution to soft power was always understood as secondary to diplomacy's hard power—these are activities that support the more important encounters of statesmen, officers, diplomats, and businessmen (Nye 1990; 2004; Leonard 2002). Louis D'Amore (1988a, 38), for example, argues that "tourism operates at the most basic level of 'track two' diplomacy by spreading information about the personalities, beliefs, aspirations, perspectives, culture and politics of the citizens of one country to the citizens of another." D'Amore himself is an important figure in the post–Cold War resuscitation of tourism as a driver for peace; indeed, his International Institute for Peace through Tourism advocates the power of tourism diplomacy to "shatter the isolation and 'fear of the other'" and achieve "the oneness of humanity" (Schwarz 2006; see also International Institution for Peace through Tourism, n.d.; Visscher 2007).

What particularly interests me about the imbrications of tourism and conflict throughout the 1990s is a shared normative ethos—a belief that the widespread dispersal of both soldiers and tourists around the world would help to build peace. Multilateral militaries arrived in war zones to maintain cease-fires between ethnic groups and pursue peacekeeping missions, while tourists engaged in cross-cultural encounters in far-flung places to reduce tensions, focus on commonalities, and increase global harmony. I am particularly interested in the forms of violence, domination, and exclusion that operate under these supposedly unified efforts to construct peace. These are particularly difficult to tease out because the shared normative ethos is so difficult to question, let alone critique—who can be *against* military force used to stop violence and bloodshed or *against* mundane acts of tourism that contribute to global peace? My point is that the shared normative ethos of building, exporting, and securing peace is sustained by a powerful but problematic geopolitical imaginary in which a global, cosmopolitan community awards itself the right to intervene in cultures, landscapes, and nations deemed unable to look after themselves. That intervention takes many forms, from the supposedly "benign" actions of tourists spreading their wealth, volunteers distributing aid, or multinational companies investing in emerging markets to the more violent actions of military occupation. Drawing on critical and postcolonial scholars, this chapter explores how multilateral deployments of military force and the dramatic increase in global tourism are complicit in the global expansion of liberal rule throughout the 1990s and 2000s (Dillon and Reid 2009; Duffield 2007; Inayatullah and Blaney 2003; Jabri 2010; 2012; Muppidi 2012; Riley and Inayatullah 2006; Shilliam 2010). In this sense, the chapter contributes to a larger concern about how cosmopolitan claims about inclusion, diversity, difference, and tolerance work to mask their own boundary-making practices—those often pernicious acts of violence and domination that are effaced in the name of achieving world peace. To uncover the constitutive hierarchies and asymmetries of globalization, the chapter starts by examining how the professionalization of Western military forces in the 1990s amplified and strengthened the manner in which a tourist sensibility shaped the off-duty activities of soldiers. The first Gulf War exemplifies some of the new techniques used by military institutions to produce, manage, and regulate the entirety of a soldier's life, from her skills deploying weapons to her mental health and well-being while on leave. Following on from these shifts in military culture, the chapter examines how dark tourism functioned in postconflict spaces such as the Middle East, Cyprus, South Africa, and Northern Ireland. What becomes clear in these cases is the impossibility of confining conflict to an unenlightened past that can be easily commemorated in the peaceful present of liberal rule. I am particularly concerned with how overarching terms like *peace* and *reconciliation* are deployed in contested sites where dark tourism is emerging—how these supposedly inclusive terms work to efface historical enmities, mobilize new asymmetries, and find new ways to silence dissenting voices.

Professionalizing R&R and the Reordering of Military Life

As the world moved into the more uncertain multipolar landscape of the 1990s, Western militaries were no longer fighting a static bipolar enemy; rather, they now had to defend the values of a liberal democratic order that was busy arranging itself against multiple potential threats. This required the moralization and professionalization of military forces so they had a clear sense of just actions during war, a desire for cooperation with other nations alongside a commitment to national interest, a more modern understanding of diversity both within and outside their own ranks, a capacity to punish their own wrongdoers, and a desire to learn from Cold War "mistakes" such as Vietnam. Institutionally, this transformation was achieved by two powerful interlocking discourses: humanitarianism and egalitarianism. All major post–Cold War interventions (e.g., the Gulf War, Bosnia, Somalia, Kosovo) were justified, to some extent, through the moral claims and rhetorical imagery of humanitarianism—multilateral international forces were "liberating" and "saving" victimized populations from immoral and undemocratic tyrants. The overarching framework of humanitarianism was so powerful because it was able to harness a range of supplementary discourses such as democratization, the protection of human rights, and the expansion of freedom. At the same time as this mobilization of humanitarianism, all modern Western militaries responded to the festering issues of institutionalized sexism, racism, and homophobia by reorganizing their internal structures around egalitarian norms. All soldiers, no matter what gender, race, sexual orientation, religious affiliation, or belief, were to be treated equally and legally protected from discrimination. This combination of humanitarianism and egalitarianism led to a number of education and training techniques aimed at reorienting soldiers into new societal and workplace norms (e.g., preventing discrimination on the basis of gender, race, sexual orientation, age, or religion). These had an internal dimension aimed at changing the culture of the institution (e.g., mandatory workshops on diversity, sexual harassment, and discrimination) as well as an external dimension aimed at changing the way militaries interacted with their host cultures (e.g., extensive "cultural sensitivity training" before deployment so soldiers could treat "friendly" civilians abroad with respect) (U.S. Army 2011; see also Brooks 1991; Dandeker and Mason 2009; Moore 1990; Nelson 1990; Salmoni 2006). I am interested in how the professionalization of Western militaries in the immediate post–Cold War era shaped the practices, behaviors, and experiences of soldiers on leave from active duty. In the U.S. military, traditional rotations of R&R continued to operate during most of the multilateral interventions of the 1990s, but their frequency was increased to approximately fifteen days R&R for every six months served. However, the inherited traditions of R&R (i.e., leisure, hedonism, prostitution) were seen to be incompatible with humanitarian, egalitarian, and professional modern militaries—how can soldiers save foreign women and children from violence, poverty, civil war, and drought one minute and sexually exploit women from this population, or their own female colleagues, the next (Enloe 1993, 172, also 142–60; 2000, 49–152)? Unsurprisingly, no matter how many mandatory workshops on diversity, sexism, or cultural sensitivity soldiers attended, the experience of R&R continued to produce racist, sexist, and exploitative behavior. Though the humanitarian and egalitarian values that were transforming professional militaries may have increased the number of serving women and ethnic minorities, they did not disrupt the institutionalized combination of masculinity, aggression, racism, and misogyny that fueled dispositions of combat as well as soldiers' behavior when they left the combat zone and confronted local Others in spaces of leisure, rest, and relaxation.

The U.S. military's efforts to impose humanitarian and egalitarian values on the practice of R&R began during the Gulf War in 1991. One of the conditions King Fahd laid down for the U.S. presence in Saudi Arabia was a "no-brothels" policy (Enloe 1993, 182). Combined with a ban on alcohol in this Islamic state, U.S. military elites faced a problem: how were they to provide troops with "expected" forms of traditional R&R when their "safe enclave" behind the front line—Saudi Arabia—banned both prostitution and alcohol? Recognizing this difficulty, King Fahd donated two hotels to U.S. forces—Hotel California and The Oasis—so that both male and female GIs could relax, swim, and sunbathe for short R&R breaks without offending Islamic leaders or the local Muslim population. Because these hotels were both surrounded with high walls—like "a space capsule set in the middle of a forbidding land"—whatever soldiers got up to with one another on their time off was invisible to local Saudis (Kirk 1991, 25). As visual and material enclaves, these two hotels permitted only minimal interactions with the local culture (e.g., the procurement of food, water, and medicine). Recognizing the limitations of an alcohol-free R&R rotation, U.S. officials developed another solution: they rented out the *Princess Cunard* luxury cruise ship, docked it nineteen miles off the northern coast of Bahrain, and provided three-day R&R trips for nine hundred soldiers at a time. Because the ship was outside of the visual, moral, and territorial orbit of the surrounding Islamic culture, the soldiers could drink alcohol, swim, sunbathe, play sports, have sex with each other, use the fitness rooms, and watch uncensored films without fear of offending their hosts (Wines 1990; Cohen 1993, 839). Stand-up comedian Jill Turbow was booked to entertain soldiers aboard the *Princess Cunard* and subsequently turned her experiences into a one-woman stage show—*Between Iraq and a Hard Place*—in which she recounted some of the exploits aboard the ship:

> They drank the entire ship dry in the first two days—completely. There wasn't a drop of liquor left on the boat. They were bringing in beer by the *thousands of cases*—literally unloading truckloads. They couldn't get it on there fast enough.... At first they tried to curtail fraternization. Some of them hadn't seen a woman in a year.... We had some dancers who made some extra cash. The opportunity was immense.... I've never had that type of attention before or since. (Deni 2002)

By rendering R&R invisible behind hotel walls or sequestering it on a floating cruise ship, the U.S. military was able to provide traditional R&R opportunities for its forces while still maintaining a policy of "cultural sensitivity" toward its Islamic hosts. The problem, of course, was that these enclave opportunities did not satisfy the tourist sensibility of soldiers, so the military also organized heavily supervised hotel stays, shopping tours, "cultural orientation tours," golf packages, and other tourist excursions in the Gulf region (Cohen 1993, 839). For example, from the decks of the *Cunard*, soldiers could arrange to go on supervised outings into Bahrain itself, in which they participated in traditional tea ceremonies, enjoyed camel rides, visited mosques, and otherwise contributed to a newly established Bahrain tourist economy (Hollier 1991, 2–4).

Of course, not all experiences of R&R during the Gulf War were successfully kept invisible or disciplined by the twin rhetorics of humanitarianism and egalitarianism. Other tourist encounters between soldiers and locals harkened back to earlier wars when male soldiers and officers didn't have to worry about their behavior toward local women or, indeed, fellow women soldiers. On the way home from active duty in the Gulf War, the aircraft carrier USS *Midway* made an unscheduled stop at the Thai beach resort of Pattaya, which had been one of the preferred R&R destinations for American soldiers during the Vietnam War. As the *Midway* website demonstrates in its collection of "Liberty Port Souvenirs," the seven thousand sailors who stopped at Pattaya enjoyed a number of sex shows (e.g., "Pussy Ping Pong Show"), massage parlors, and other forms of militarized prostitution (USS *Midway*, n.d.). In a sex-tourist resort suffering from the onset of AIDS in the 1980s, bar owners and entrepreneurs in Pattaya welcomed the carrier's visit and hoped they could recoup lost revenues by selling the services of Thai girls and women (Chang 2001, 628; see also Barry 1995, 145; Erlanger 1991, A9). Navy officials were under no illusion about the purpose of rerouting the USS *Midway* to Pattaya; indeed, they organized lectures on sex education and VD prior to the stopover and handed out condoms "as if they were Hallmark Cards" (Chang 2001, 631; Moon 1997, 37). Once again, as Enloe (2000, 71–72) argues, the USS *Midway*'s "spontaneous pit stop" in 1991 was explicitly sexualized and simply more evidence that a male soldier's access to sex in the form of prostitution with local women is—and has always been—an institutionalized part of military policy.

In the ethnic conflicts that followed the first Gulf War, the practice of R&R became the object of further efforts to professionalize military forces and regulate encounters with local populations. The ban on prostitution and the limited access to alcohol established during the first Gulf War continued throughout deployments in the 1990s and enabled U.S. military leaders to argue that their forces were better, fitter, healthier, and more prepared for combat than ever before (Masko 1991; O'Connor 1996; Tharp 1991; Wilkinson 1991). However, efforts to keep troops segregated from local populations did not mean that a soldier's tourist sensibility disappeared. For example, when operations and scheduling permitted, UN forces serving in the Bosnian conflict (1992–95) took breaks on the Dalmatian coast, and UN forces in Somalia (1992–93) made use of the beaches surrounding Mogadishu and the tourist resorts in nearby Mombasa. Aside from these short-term and/or opportunistic experiences, the primary form of R&R experienced by Western soldiers throughout the 1990s was a scheduled fourteen-day break at home with family and friends (U.S. Army 2010; see also Pincus 1996; Tilson 1996). This policy produced a complicated reordering of the military's public–private distinction. On the one hand, encouraging soldiers to return home for R&R (rather than facilitating organized vacations to places like Pattaya) enabled militaries to respond to growing critiques of militarized prostitution. Releasing soldiers into the private sphere of home and family meant that the military could relinquish its responsibility for the private behavior of its troops and employees. In other words, what a soldier gets up to during his R&R stay at home is his business: if a soldier visits a prostitute, or shouts racist abuse, or gets in a fight, the military—as an institution—cannot be held accountable. On the other hand, relinquishing soldiers for R&R rotations back home was accompanied by new techniques of governmentality in which every aspect of a soldier's life—including her "off-duty" time—was made available for surveillance and intervention by the military. Institutionally, this shift was facilitated by bringing R&R into newly created welfare structures aimed at supporting the health, well-being, and morale of troops. Within the U.S. military, for example, R&R was brought under the Office of Morale, Welfare, and Recreation (MWR), a

> comprehensive network of quality support and leisure services that enhances the lives of Soldiers, Civilians, Families, military retirees and other eligible participants. Family and MWR's vision is to be the driving force for programs

and services that provide the foundation for the Army's home by (i) increasing soldier and family resiliency; (ii) restoring balance; and (iii) enhancing recruitment, readiness and retention for Soldiers and Families. (U.S. Army Family, Morale Welfare, and Recreation Programs 2014a)

In effect, soldiers were trained for field operations, but they were also trained how to behave while off duty—how to relax and recover from time on operation and how to prepare for subsequent deployment. For example, following the first Gulf War, the MWR provided detailed instructions on what to expect emotionally and physically when shifting suddenly from the combat zone to the home front and provided soldiers with an institutionalized support structure comprising a variety of contact points (i.e., mentors, counselors, chaplains, vets) to help them transition in and out of their R&R home leave (Brown 1997, 78–82; see also Anderson 2004; Inigo 2004). Crucially, this support structure was not limited to serving military personnel but also extended to spouses and families dealing with the expectations and aftermath of R&R rotations (Military One Source 2014).

Though these efforts to support troops on R&R appear benign (and, indeed, are framed primarily through the language of well-being), they are examples of how institutions mobilize techniques of self-management to further disperse their capacity to survey, discipline, and control their subjects. "Instructing" and "guiding" soldiers on how to take responsibility for their own well-being is about getting soldiers to internalize institutional norms and oversee their own self-management—to become the kind of soldier the military wants them to be. The result is a simultaneous alleviation of institutional responsibility (which is devolved to the individual) and an extension of military norms into the areas of mental health, family life, domestic routines, and intimate relations. As soldiers willingly and enthusiastically adopted these tools of self-management both on and off the battlefield, they effectively militarized their entire lives and the lives of their families, friends, and relations. This pervasive militarization of everyday life also underscored the rebranding of R&R as family-oriented leisure time—a transformation that had the added bonus of banishing the negative stereotypes of R&R that had arisen during the Vietnam War. Military authorities recognized that troop cohesion, military culture, and general morale could be enhanced further if soldiers and their families could spend their R&R break *on holiday* together. Thus the MWR developed a range of incentives and rewards encouraging soldiers and their families to spend their R&R breaks at any of the five Armed Forces Recreation Center Resorts (AFRCs) in Virginia, Germany, Florida, Hawaii, and Korea. Nonprofit AFRCs dedicated wholly to the U.S. armed forces have been in operation since 1946, but the current resorts differ from previous incarnations in that they explicitly "promote strong family values" (U.S. Army Family and Morale, Welfare, and Recreation Programs 2014b; see also McEnany 2008). Gone are the days of militarized prostitution, binge drinking, and all-night parties: now R&R involves organized family outings (e.g., Disney World, Munich Zoo), family-sized swimming pools and recreation areas, dedicated children's programs, and family-friendly restaurants. The AFRC resorts operate through both incentive and reward: they are much more affordable in comparison to other holiday options (making it easier to take the whole family); they are dedicated to members of the armed forces rather than the general public (which means spending leisure time with like-minded military families); and they offer the comfort and familiarity of an institutionalized setting with organized events, excursions, and recreational opportunities (thus alleviating the shock of adjusting to noninstitutional life for a two-week R&R rotation). As the wife of one American soldier explained of the Edelweiss resort in Germany, "I know it's an army hotel, but it doesn't feel like it" (Coon 2006). So keen is the U.S. military to publicize the family-friendly type of R&R made available at AFRCs that incoming soldiers and their families are issued with detailed instructions on how to deal with media interest in their vacations—interest that the military itself generates (U.S. Army in Europe, n.d.).

The rebranding of R&R that began after the Cold War—keeping soldiers apart from local populations in the area of operation or heavily supervising their tourist encounters; releasing soldiers into their home environments for scheduled R&R; and providing opportunities for military families to enjoy holidays together at family-themed AFRC resorts—may have been a public relations success, but it did not necessarily alleviate the "bad behavior" associated with traditional R&R pursuits. The masculinity, misogyny, and racism that reigned on the battlefield did not disappear once soldiers embarked on their R&R rotations; indeed, the ban on alcohol and prostitution while on duty may have increased the hedonistic tendencies of soldiers on leave. Moreover, the normalization of masculinity, misogyny, and racism within military operations abroad led to difficulties when soldiers transitioned back home, especially with respect to domestic violence (Basham 2008; Bowling and Sherman 2008; Laufer and Gallops 1985; McCarroll et al. 2003; Meis et al. 2010; Nelson 2007). In short, no matter how forcefully the military seeks to professionalize its troops into the norms of humanitarianism and egalitarianism, off-duty soldiers carry with them the competing norms of masculinity, misogyny, and racism. In R&R rotations, these norms justify the soldier's disregard for—and indeed violence against—various host communities as well as family members (Allred 2006).[1]

Reimagining Dark Tourism

Places like Kuwait, Bosnia, Somalia, Rwanda, the Democratic Republic of the Congo, Sri Lanka, and Sierra Leone became 24/7 media spectacles, objects of moralizing foreign policy discourses, and spaces of intervention throughout the 1990s, but they also became part of a new cartography of global tourism that reframed every part of the world as a potential tourist destination. Not even war could stop the inexorable rise of independent travelers who distanced themselves from the "hordes" of tourists by seeking out authentic and never-before-seen sites that had been prized open by the forces of globalization. In many cases, sites of war, conflict, and atrocity were precisely the objects of attraction: no natural wonder or man-made amusement could compete with the sheer authenticity of a site where mass death had occurred in the past or violent ethnic conflict was still occurring. If a tourist sensibility shaped the behavior of soldiers and nonmilitary personnel intervening in post–Cold War ethnic conflicts, then we can also say that a peculiar *martial* sensibility shaped many tourists who eschewed the beaten path in favor of more "dangerous" destinations emerging from conflict. Indeed, what could be more real, and therefore more of a draw for independent travelers, than the mass fatalities caused by war?

Much of the newly coined "dark tourism" that arose after the end of the Cold War was a response to the perceived loss of authenticity as a result of globalization. If the entire world was now knowable (through media and communications) and visitable (through an expanded tourism industry), then it was increasingly impossible to have a "real" encounter with something previously undiscovered or unseen. As I have argued elsewhere (Lisle 2006b, 337),

> sites of recent conflict—war zones, battlefields, mass graves, camps—function as the last remaining "real" in an otherwise commodified world. For what is more "real" than death, atrocity, warfare and violence? In short, tourists are motivated to see places like Belfast, Beirut and Cambodia because these are the *only places left* where it is possible to experience an unmediated and authentic encounter with "the real."

Unsurprisingly, scholars turned their attention to the phenomenon of tourists visiting "black spots," and very quickly a growing literature on dark tourism—or *thanatourism*—came to include the encounters with war and atrocity that are of particular interest here (Blom 2000; Dale and Robinson 2011; Dann and Seaton 2001; Kamin 2014; Lennon and Foley 2000; Logan 2008; Pierkarz 2007; Rojek 1993, 138; Seaton 1996; 1999; 2000; Sharpley 2005; Sharpley and Stone 2009; Slade 2003; Stone 2005; 2006; Stone and Sharpley 2008; Strange and Kempa 2003; Tarlow 2005; Uzzell 1992; Uzzell and Ballantyne 1998; White and Frew 2013; Wight 2006; see also the dark tourism Forum at https://www.facebook.com/darktourism). A. V. Seaton (1996, 240) provides the clearest definition of thanatourism as "travel to a location wholly, or partially, motivated by the desire for actual or symbolic encounters with death, particularly, but not exclusively, violent death which may, to a varying degree be activated by the person-specific features of those whose deaths are its focal objects." While the literature on dark tourism is often useful in providing details of particular sites, its foundational categories reproduce problematic assumptions about the geopolitics of danger (i.e., a safe "here" and a dangerous "there") and the progressive direction of modernity (i.e., a teleology privileging the inevitability of liberal rule). That spatiotemporal foundation is important because it shapes the interpretive frameworks and museological strategies that are employed in dark tourist sites, particularly with respect to the commemoration of past conflicts.

The central problem with the literature on dark tourism is its uncritical reproduction of the geopolitical imaginary of liberal rule that took hold throughout the 1990s and 2000s. Dark tourism is understood entirely within this geopolitical logic: globalization opens up possibilities for newly enlightened communities to transform their "difficult" heritage into viable tourist attractions (thus generating income) and create new—and above all authentic—destinations for tourists to visit. This suggests that those of us living in liberal, democratic, and capitalist systems have become, to paraphrase Francis Fukuyama, "caretakers" to human history in two senses. First, because we have evolved out of the ideological struggles that led to war and conflict (i.e., we have reached the end of history), we are caretakers to our own stories of struggle, which we duly craft into the "lessons of history" to be exhibited in museums, at tourist attractions, and in memorials. Second, we are also caretakers to those unfortunate populations who are still "mired" in the ideological struggles of history: we exemplify how the central values of liberalism, free markets, and democracy can lead civilizations out of intractable struggle; we make military, economic, and diplomatic interventions to thwart those who are opposed to such a transition; and we seek to protect those cultural and natural artifacts on the ground that will be of value to future tourists. In this way, the literature on dark tourism helps to secure an "us" (i.e., enlightened, civilized, peaceful tourists who are interested in the "lessons of history") over and against a threatening "them" (i.e., those still mired in ideological struggle that could "spill over" into our secure communities). These antagonistic constituencies are mapped onto global terrain by positioning truly dark sites (i.e., the still smoldering remains of atrocity) in backward, unenlightened zones "over there" and more popular, developed, and safe heritage sites (i.e., institutionalized displays of historical violence) in modern, democratic territories (Bowman and Pezzullo 2010, 190).

In their book *Dark Tourism,* Lennon and Foley (2000) dismiss the voyeuristic "adrenalin disaster tourists," "hot-war tourists," and thrill seekers who arrive during battle, or in the immediate aftermath of an atrocity, to gaze on the detritus of recent conflict (see also BBC 2005a; Pierkarz 2007, 154, 164–65; Seaton 1999). They privilege the category of "serendipitous" tourists who take in war zones as part of a much wider vacation itinerary and who arrive well after an atrocity when the infrastructure has been repaired and the site has already been turned into a tourist product (9, 23–25). Those who make serendipitous visits to historic battlefields to encounter the memorabilia of war are precisely the demographic to which Valene Smith (1998, 202) was referring with her claim that "war-related tourism attractions are the largest single category known." For Lennon and Foley, this population of tourists is statistically more relevant (because millions of visitors arrive to sites of war once they have been transformed into proper tourist attractions) and morally acceptable (because these visitors are commemorating past atrocities rather than gawking at them). Because the literature defines dark tourists primarily by *when* they travel to war zones (i.e., during battle, in the immediate aftermath of battle, or once a battlefield has already been turned into a tourist product), it uncritically adopts the tourism–peace model in which there are clear distinctions between war (when tourism stops) and peace (when tourism prospers). Such a blunt temporal demarcation fails to address how a tourist sensibility is operative in powerful ways during war and how war's production of threats, enemies, and Others frames postwar activities of tourism and commemoration. As this book argues, these two practices are deeply entwined, enmeshed, and juxtaposed and cannot be contained within particular time periods. The efforts of dark tourism literature to address the connections between war and tourism are entirely superficial and apolitical: authors do not reflect on the foundational categories of world order that produce, on the one hand, a progressive view of modernization in which barbarous populations emerge out of darkness by embracing liberal rule and, on the other hand, a bifurcated cartography in which safe spaces over here encourage tourism to historical sites of war, while dangerous places over there are engulfed in struggle and therefore deter all but the most intrepid (and morally questionable) dark tourists.

In the dark tourism literature that examines how the sites themselves have been transformed into viable tourist attractions, we encounter the same tension between commemoration and entertainment that so vexed the battlefield tours in the aftermath of the First World War. All of the literature, more or less, acknowledges the tension between horror/atrocity/death, on the one hand, and leisure/tourism/entertainment, on the other, and often denounces tourism as "an inappropriate and even immoral vehicle for the presentation of human suffering and troubling events" (Strange and Kempa 2003, 387; see also Seaton 1996, 234). This moral posturing is misplaced and unhelpful: the reconstruction, preservation, and display of sites of atrocity and conflict is a multi-billion-dollar industry that is incredibly lucrative for local communities. So the question is not whether tourism *should* be present in the aftermath of atrocity (indeed, it is always present) but rather how and in what form tourism can operate sensitively, ethically, and reflexively in sites with a contentious past. I want to argue that the dark tourism literature seeks to resolve the difficult and intractable juxtaposition of tourism and atrocity by framing it positively within a discourse of commemoration. As we saw with Auschwitz and Hiroshima, any site of atrocity, no matter how horrific, can be transformed into a viable tourist attraction by sequestering its entertainment value within serious commemorative messages about honoring the dead, remembering victims, and projecting a peaceful future. While the dark tourism literature recognizes the tension between tourism's demand for entertainment value and the requirement of commemoration in these sites, it claims that the "theme park" characteristics of tourism can be nullified by interpretive strategies that encourage pious commemoration of the past and enthusiastic support of a peaceful future.

By failing to interrogate the political work that commemoration does, the literature on dark tourism cannot address how these sites harness the coordinates of remembering and forgetting to exclusive claims of national identity, loyalty, and belonging and silence those stories that trouble or subvert the conventional trajectory from violent conflict into peaceful unity. In this sense, I agree with Ashworth's (2002, 191) claim that the argument in Lennon and Foley's *Dark Tourism* (such as there is one) is "theoretically limited." For example, Lennon and Foley argue that dark tourist sites like Auschwitz are important because they introduce doubt and anxiety about the larger project of modernity (11–32), but they fail to examine how the interpretations of atrocity at tourist sites sanitize violence by comforting the visitor. Tourists acknowledge the horrors ushered in by the modern project (which can, at times, be uncomfortable), but that confrontation is quickly alleviated by sealing violent acts in an unenlightened past (or locating them in a foreign country), foregrounding the "lessons of history," commemorating heroes and victims, and idealizing a peaceful future of unity and reconciliation. By positioning themselves as "defenders of historical truth and against the commodification of 'dark tourism' sites" (Smith 2002, 1189), Lennon and Foley construct a problematic normative framework in which "good" dark tourism sites are those that promote commemoration and reconciliation (and thus further the progressive aspects of modernity) and "bad" dark tourism sites are those that commodify horror and disrespect the dead (and thus foreground modernity's distasteful progeny—postmodernity, with its privileging of surface, superficiality, play, and relativity) (Smith 2002, 1189; Wight 2006, 122–23). Lennon and Foley are unable to see how the practices of "good" dark tourism they advocate (i.e., those that help visitors learn about the past so as not to repeat it) enact their own exclusions, effacements, and silences, nor are they able to recognize how the voyeuristic practices of "bad" dark tourism they castigate may contain moments of ethical reflection, transnational solidarity, and active politicization.

The dark tourism literature that develops Lennon and Foley's initial arguments (Pierkarz 2007; Sharpley 2005; Stone 2006; Stone and Sharpley 2008; Tarlow 2005) is even more problematic because it seeks to counter the normative framework of "good" and "bad" dark tourists by resorting to "marketing research and Positivist ambitions of scientific labelling" (Löfgren 1999, 267; see also Bowman and Pezzullo 2010, 199). This work suggests that all scholars need to do is construct more detailed and accurate charts that locate the phenomenon of dark tourism and the motivations of dark tourists within an already settled positivist framework (e.g., on a fixed continuum of dark to darker or hot to hotter). While Lennon and Foley claim that reverent commemoration is the *right* choice for dark tourist attractions, and the subsequent positivist scholars claim to neutrally record a new tourism phenomenon according to accepted universal criteria, none of this research questions the political and ethical foundations upon which all of these claims rest, namely, a problematic geopolitical division between liberal spaces of peace and illiberal spaces of conflict and a progressive teleology in which peaceful, enlightened liberal spaces function as the ideal toward which all other nations must work. Without an interrogation of these constitutive logics, the detailed accounts of specific dark tourism sites remain both superficial and ethically problematic. Ashworth (2002, 191), for example, suggests that the dark tourism literature does not offer the "careful reflection" that these sites require: "It neither raises the ethical issues which are central to many of the current debates about heritage nor even the impact of these upon the practical choices inherent in the management of such sites."[2] Indeed, despite its abundance, the dark tourism literature fails to address the complex performance of the tourist encounter itself and the possibility that both tourists and hosts might reflect critically on their experience, subvert conventional scripts of pious reverence, reject the sanitized account of innocent victims, consider feelings of uneasiness and disappointment, and reflexively question their desire to confront death and atrocity in the first place. As Bowman and Pezzullo (2010) argue, the dark tourism literature is entirely silent on the actual performances, actions, and behaviors that take place in these sites, because such encounters are thoroughly ambivalent and therefore cannot be understood within static normative frameworks, positivist methodologies, and reductive scientific labels.

What is desperately needed in the debates about dark tourism is a meta-conversation that reveals how scholars, practitioners, and policy makers are complicit in reproducing the prevailing geopolitical imaginary of liberal rule. This conversation is beginning with critical scholars both within and outside of tourism studies who call attention to the way tourism mobilizes entrenched global power relations (e.g., nationalism, neoliberalism, patriarchy); restricts the flourishing of agency in host sites; and generates new techniques of governance, management, and control for intersecting populations of hosts and guests (Bianchi and Stephenson 2014; Hollinshead 1999; Hollinshead and Jamal 2001; Minca and Oakes 2006; Werry 2011). With specific reference to dark tourism itself, Bowman and Pezzullo (2010, 199) suggest that "it may be time to abandon the term 'dark tourism' insofar as it may present an impediment to detailed and circumstantial analysis of tourist sites and performances in all their mundane or spectacular particularity and ambiguity" (see also Sather-Wagstaff 2011; Wight 2006). Indeed, applying a more critical framework to the micropolitical and everyday registers within which tourists encounter the remnants of war refutes both Lennon and Foley's normative framework and the supposedly neutral taxonomies offered by positivist scholars, and it contests the drive to bring "dissonant" sites centrally into the confines of liberal rule. For me, the troubling ethical and political issues that abound in any effort to represent the "history that hurts" (e.g., the role of perpetrators, the closures of victory culture, the marginalization of Others) will never go away and, indeed, should be constantly interrogated rather than resolved or neutralized through hospitable gestures of inclusion. Only by constantly foregrounding those intractable difficulties does it become possible to unpack the seductive mobilizations of commemoration that prevail in so many dark tourist sites. Indeed, my efforts to keep the political open, contest the way tourism seeks to resolve complex histories of conflict, and distance myself from the positivist foundations of the dark tourism literature lead me to use *political tourism* rather than *dark tourism* when referring to tourism's encounters with conflict.

The Consolations of Enmity: Ideological Incarceration in the Middle East and Cyprus

In societies with endemic divisions, such as the Middle East and Cyprus, tourism and war are not mutually exclusive and therefore do not follow the conventional tourism–peace model. Here tourism thrives amid a permanent political conflict in one of two ways: it is either traditional (i.e., nonpolitical) tourism that functions as a central driver for employment and economic growth or it is political tourism that represents a partisan account of the division from one side of the conflict. The first formation plays down political divisions by foregrounding the peace, security, and stability of its extant tourism industry and includes, for example, traditional sun, sand, and surf holidays; luxury resorts; religious tourism and pilgrimages; and visits to ancient ruins. The second formation rests entirely on selling conflict to visitors—on enrolling tourists into a partisan narrative of victimization, oppression, and injustice—and includes various walking tours, bus tours, conflict museums, and memorial sites. However, traditional forms of nonpolitical tourism cannot help but be shaped by surrounding political divisions. For example, tourist attractions in the Middle East aimed at religious pilgrims (e.g., Rachel's Tomb in Bethlehem) have become contested within the rigid coordinates of the Israeli–Palestinian struggle, and their viability as tourist attractions has been threatened by the material imposition of the Separation Barrier (Selwyn 2011; Shachar and Shoval 1999). Drawing explicitly on critical approaches to tourism and conflict, I want to focus specifically on how political tourism in the Middle East and Cyprus enrolls visitors into partisan narratives that reproduce prevailing orientations of enmity, antagonism, and conflict.

The Middle East: Ideological Incarceration

Given the entrenched and comprehensive nature of the Israeli–Palestinian conflict, opportunities for political tourism in the region are many, largely because positions of neutrality on the part of both tour operators and tourists are impossible: willingly or not, actively or passively, everyone is positioned by the conflict. This antagonism is mobilized across the landscape of political tourism from the official museum exhibits justifying Israel's claims to territory to the alternative walking tours through Palestinian neighborhoods under occupation. In the divided city of Jerusalem, a majority of political tourism is pro-Israeli—a situation created in part by the many international groups that arrange tours for those visitors already sympathetic to Israel's position. For example, the Israeli government is involved in the Taglit: Birthright Israel program, which offers fully subsidized two-week visits for eighteen- to twenty-four-year-olds from Jewish communities from around the world (Brin 2006; Taglit 1999). The pro-Israeli story is further enshrined in prominent state-funded museums and memorials in Jerusalem, including the Yad Vashem memorial to the Holocaust, the Israel Museum, and the Tower of David (Museum of the History of Jerusalem). These institutions provide a convincing message to visitors that the Israeli claim to both the city of Jerusalem and the state of Israel is historically legitimate and politically justified. Critical scholars have begun the process of analyzing how this pro-Israeli narrative is materialized in curatorial decisions, exhibits, and architecture as well as examining the extent to which visitors accept or question this dominant story (Abdallah 2002; Benevenisti 1998; Cohen 2011; Katriel 2001; Krakover 2002; 2005; Noy 2011; Oren and Shani 2012).

Outside of institutionalized museum space, the pro-Israeli message is reproduced most clearly in the walking tours that cleverly arrange spatial itineraries, foreground particular objects (and ignore others), and claim the status quo of Israeli occupation as a neutral position.[3] For example, in pro-Israeli walking tours of Hebron, guides establish "the near-continuous Jewish presence in the city" by harkening back to the era of King David, ignoring the Jewish community's minority status in a largely Palestinian city, and justifying the presence of the Israeli army by constantly invoking the threat of "Arab attacks" (Clarke 2000, 17). Backed by state authority, the pro-Israeli narrative mobilizes a singular and undisputed historical trajectory (i.e., an ancient and biblically enshrined Jewish claim to territory), reinforces a powerful victim status through continual reference to the Holocaust, effaces the equally ancient presence of Palestinian communities in the city, and justifies the contemporary signs of state security and militarization that segregate urban populations into either Israeli or Palestinian communities. So powerful is the pro-Israeli narrative that it has produced its own version of political tourism for local Israelis: "extreme tours" in which ex-Israeli military officers take visitors to illegal Israeli settlements, espouse the values of Zionism, and teach them "the excitement and enjoyment of shooting" terrorist (i.e., Palestinian) targets (Carr 2012). These experiences dovetail with the picnicking Israelis who gathered on a hill overlooking Gaza City during the conflicts in 2009 and 2014 to watch a "live show" of the Israeli Defense Force bombing select Palestinian targets (Gregory 2012; Mackey 2014; Middle East Eye 2014; Turn Off Your Television 2011; Withnall 2014).

Given the asymmetry of the conflict with respect to statehood and recognition, political tourism sympathetic to the Palestinian position does not have the institutional presence or financial support of its Israeli counterparts. One exception is the Islamic Museum on Temple Mount, which includes a display of the blood-stained clothing of Palestinians killed during the 1990 Temple Mount riots alongside historical artifacts from Islamic history (Israel Museums 2011; see also Brin 2006, 232). This anomalous display demonstrates how pro-Palestinian political tourism is mobilized outside of institutions and more directly linked to activism against the Israeli state, solidarity building among victimized and oppressed groups, and global consciousness raising about the plight of the Palestinian community under occupation (Isaac 2009, 248; Isaac and Ashworth 2012; Lanfant and Grayburn 1992; Pearce 1992).[4] For Palestinians, political tourism—sometimes called *justice tourism*—is an opportunity to show local and international visitors the consequences of Israeli political occupation on the everyday lives of Palestinians and to articulate Palestinian claims to statehood, territory, and political representation. Primarily operating through walking and driving tours, pro-Palestinian political tourism is not limited to the streets of East Jerusalem but more commonly takes visitors further afield into Hebron, the West Bank, and the Gaza Strip (Brin 2006, 230–32). Although these tours are keen to establish a historical Palestinian presence and therefore a legitimate claim to territory (and in this sense mimic their pro-Israeli counterparts), their focus is much more on demonstrating how the everyday life of Palestinians is constrained by the material manifestations of Israeli sovereignty with its overwhelming security apparatus (e.g., checkpoints, barriers, restrictions, urban infrastructure, and surveillance networks). Historic buildings, established Arab neighborhoods, and iconic Palestinian monuments take a backseat to contemporary features of the conflict that highlight "alleged injustice caused to Palestinians by Israel" (232). For example, a popular tour to Hebron explains the encroachment of Jewish settlements into majority Palestinian areas (e.g., the three-hundred-strong Jewish community in the heart of the city), takes visitors through the al-Aroub refugee camp, shows them the Mosque of Ibrahim where twenty-nine Muslim worshippers were massacred in 1994, and constantly refers visitors to the large security fences and structures bisecting the city (Clarke 2000, 15–16). Central to all pro-Palestinian tours is a visit to the controversial Separation Barrier that divides Israel from the West Bank. Palestinians are largely opposed to the barrier not only because it encroaches beyond the 1967 cease-fire line and annexes territory within the West Bank but also because it prevents Palestinians from access to farmlands, schools, hospitals, social services, and employment. Typically, these tours include visits to various sections of the wall itself, discussions with Palestinians directly affected by the barrier (especially in Bethlehem and East Jerusalem), and in some cases discussions with Israeli settlers in the area (Isaac 2009, 251). During many of these tours, visitors are encouraged to leave graffiti messages on the wall expressing their opposition to such an extreme manifestation of Israeli sovereignty, and in this way, political tourists place themselves alongside a number of high-profile graffiti artists, such as Banksy, Blu, and Ron English, who have painted numerous images on the Palestinian side of the wall opposing its divisive presence (Krohn and Lagerweij 2010; Parry 2010). Recognizing the strange juxtaposition of art, tourism, and occupation, Banksy labels his Palestinian images "Holiday Snaps" and has stated that the Separation Barrier is the "ultimate activity holiday destination for graffiti writers" (Guardian 2011; Parry 2005).

As these accounts suggest, political tourism in the Middle East reproduces the same binary composition of identity, territory, and loyalty that has prevented a lasting political settlement from emerging. This is "dissonant heritage" at its most strident: there remain two divergent accounts of the conflict; both sides claim victim status while casting the Other as the perpetrator (e.g., terrorist, suicide bomber, oppressor, occupier), and both sides mobilize a security apparatus aimed at keeping the Other out of specified territory. More often than not, tourists arrive already inculcated into this well-publicized legacy of enmity and make expected choices in terms of political tourism. Within such an entrenched context of animosity, tourists and visitors are given a prepackaged account of the conflict that frames commemoration, reflection, and engagement within the reductive coordinates of Israeli versus Palestinian. For example, pro-Israeli political tourism constructs history and territory through three originary accounts: first, that the Jewish people have lived on the land since biblical times and therefore have a right to continue living there; second, that Jews have been persecuted throughout history, especially during the Holocaust, and therefore deserve a secure homeland; and third, that the Israeli state charged with protecting Jewish people is justified in defending itself against aggressors. All three accounts mobilize a powerful victim narrative that frames collective modes of commemoration—including those performed by tourists—within the parameters of Israeli statehood.

In other words, Jewish victims can only be properly commemorated, and the contemporary Jewish community can only take care of its own history, within institutions and rituals protected by the sovereign state of Israel. The problem, of course, is that such a reductive and exclusive orientation toward history, territory, and identity justifies contemporary acts of aggression against those with competing claims, namely, Palestinians and other Arab nations. The originary story framing pro-Palestinian political tourism is a much more contemporary one that focuses on the victimization of Palestinians under Israeli occupation. As such, its modes of commemoration are sutured to the experience of being oppressed, and its future horizon is oriented toward achieving sovereign statehood in the region. Here the overwhelming condition of oppression justifies and excuses retaliatory acts of violence against its occupier. So while political tourism is thriving in the Middle East, it operates entirely within the parameters of the region's central enmity: it is either pro-Israeli or pro-Palestinian. In this sense, the forms of commemoration, mobilizations of history, and efforts to educate visitors are ideologically incarcerated and beholden to an overarching ethos of opposition and antagonism.

The extent of this ideological incarceration is such that it frames even those progressive efforts of political tourism promoting peace building and coexistence. Certainly there are examples of less dogmatic tours that advocate impartiality and objectivity, seek to show visitors how both communities have always lived and worked together, and point out where the city of Jerusalem is unified rather than separated.[5] But while Jewish-Israeli guides and Palestinian guides seek neutrality rather than partisan advocacy in their presentation of the conflict, their own positions are always clear. As one guide to the Separation Barrier confessed,

> I try to maintain objectivity and impartiality in my portrayal of the city's geopolitical realities; still, it doesn't take much to guess my opinions when I show participants the outraging differences between a Jewish neighbourhood, with all its amenities, and a Palestinian neighbourhood, which enjoys none. (Brin 2006, 236)

A good example of how a prevailing architecture of enmity shapes efforts to promote coexistence is the transformation of the Turjeman Post Museum in East Jerusalem. It began as a museum commemorating its former function as an Israeli army post on the Jordanian border (1970–97); became a more interactive exhibition promoting tolerance, understanding, and coexistence within Jerusalem (1999–2005); and has recently become the Museum on the Seam, a politically focused contemporary art museum with exhibits on human rights, homeland, nature, and protest (Museum on the Seam 2009a). The many long and fierce battles over how to make such a one-sided story of Israeli Army heroism more respective of Jerusalem's diversity does not reveal the complex work of collaboration between two communities; rather, it reveals internal struggles *within* the Israeli community about whether and how to permit Palestinians into "their" already determined story (Ben-Se'ev and Ben-Ari 1999; see also Abowd 2007). For example, managers of the temporary Museum of Tolerance (1999–2005) were interested in encouraging Palestinians to visit the museum but were not interested in involving Palestinians in the curation of the exhibition story itself (Ben-Se'ev and Ben-Ari 1999, 125–27). Similarly, the art exhibit *Right to Protest* frames dissent as an Israeli problem rather than something that all societies contend with: "Israeli society is divided in its protest; it seeks a solution for its difficulties, it is split and fractured, with profound rifts both within itself, and vis-à-vis its Palestinian neighbours" (Museum on the Seam 2009b). There is no sense, here, that Israeli society *includes* Palestinians and other ethnic groups and that they too may be engaged in protest. Certainly the reframing of tourist institutions around issues of human rights is to be welcomed, but it is important to acknowledge how the ideological incarceration of the region powerfully shapes even those efforts to think more productively about peace and coexistence.

Perhaps it is in spaces of leisure and tourism not explicitly framed as political that the region's ideological incarceration can be more profoundly questioned. Rebecca Stein (2008, 149; see also Maoz 2010) documents how during the Second Intifada (2000–2005), Israeli-Jews understood the tourist resorts of the Sinai desert as an exceptional space outside of the familiar coordinates of antagonism and therefore enabled Israeli tourists to stage an alternative encounter with their Arab hosts:

> Amid the renewed politics of regional enmity that had followed the second uprising, Sinai's serene coastline appealed as a different kind of Middle Eastern place where Arab cultures and persons could be enjoyed in other ways,

unmarked by the terms of the Arab-Israeli conflict. Sinai was perceived as an uncanny place, both within the Arab Middle East and thus affording tourists its cultural pleasures, yet outside the landscape of regional politics.

Although such encounters are important disruptions to the status quo of antagonism, they are often only temporary moments; indeed, this particular idyll was shattered when the Sinai Hilton hotel was bombed in 2004, killing thirty-four Israeli tourists, and again in 2015, when a terrorist bomb exploded on a chartered tourist flight departing from Sharm el-Sheikh. More generally, the possibility for alternative encounters between Israelis and Arabs in leisured space doesn't obviate the more fundamental asymmetry between host and guest—in this case, the socioeconomic privilege of Israeli tourists compared with their Arab hosts locked in a service economy. This inequality is even starker when the question of regional mobility is examined, for example, when the free movement of Israeli tourists is compared with the restricted movement of Palestinian subjects enforced by the militarized Israeli state (e.g., checkpoints, borders, encroaching settlements, roadblocks, road closures). A useful counterpoint to Klein's study of Jewish-Israeli tourism is Laura Junka's photographic study of Palestinians camping on Gaza Beach during the Second Intifada (Junka 2006). By showing Palestinian agency at its most varied, foliated, and complex, Junka seeks to go beyond the two dominant stereotypes of Palestinians as either militant warrior (e.g., suicide bomber) or passive victim of Israeli aggression. In visualizing the multiplicity of Palestinian agency, Junka shows how a tourist sensibility pervades even the most restricted, militarized, and occupied spaces. For example, the foreground of Figure 26 shows a Palestinian child holding a rubber ring preparing for a swim in the ocean, while a number of children in the background are already in the water or playing in the sand.

Formally, it is a beautifully balanced photograph that uses the surrounding frivolity and bright colors to counterbalance the anxiety and anticipation on the child's face. Many of Junka's photographs show Palestinian families engaged in familiar beach behavior—swimming, playing volleyball, barbequing, sunbathing, building sand castles—and could have been taken on any sun-drenched beach in the world. But lurking in all of

FIGURE 26. Morning swim. Courtesy of Laura Junka.

these photographs are signifiers of Israeli occupation, for example, UN refugee tents repurposed as holiday beach huts or bombed-out ruins of the surrounding urban architecture. In Figure 26, for example, the singularity of the child in the foreground is set against a collection of adults gathering in front of a UN refugee tent (top right). By focusing on familiar experiences of tourism, leisure, and holiday making, Junka is not suggesting that the Israeli state has reduced its violent incursions into Gaza or that frolicking Palestinians are somehow not as committed to achieving independence and statehood. What her images offer is insight into how the routines and habits of everyday life—in this case the activities of leisure, tourism, and camping—always trouble and exceed the macropolitical architectures of enmity that seek to contain them. They are visual reminders that life, joy, tourism, and fun thrive in the unlikeliest of places, and paying attention to these unexpected moments is part of a wider effort to create more space for Palestinian agency to flourish. Junka's photographs are useful in helping us understand what is missing from accounts of political tourism in the Middle East. What would political tourism look like if it were to *begin* with the heterogeneous texture of everyday life; accept agonism as a general condition (not just between Israelis and Palestinians but between all communities); and prompt visitors to reflect on their own complicity in structures of power, injustice, and violence?

Cyprus: Stalemate

Whereas the Middle East is characterized by ongoing antagonism and violence, Cyprus remains in a nonviolent stalemate in which Greek Cypriots and Turkish Cypriots have largely reconciled themselves to the UN-patrolled Green Line and Buffer Zone that has bisected the island since 1974. To some extent, this inertia suits both communities, who rely on traditional and nonpolitical forms of tourism as their main source of revenue (e.g., sun, sand, and sea packages but also clubbing, nature tourism, and antiquities). Still, both communities offer opportunities for political tourism—walking and driving tours as well as museums and memorials—that explore the legacy of partition and consider the prospects for reconciliation (Connery 2008; Farmaki 2013; Ioannidis and Apostolopoulos 1999; Lennon and Foley 2000, 129–44; Timothy, Prideaux, and Kim 2004; Warner 1999; Webster and Timothy 2006). Although there are a few instances of political tourism on the east coast of the island adjacent to the abandoned town of Varosha, a vast majority of these opportunities operate within the divided capital of Nicosia.[6] Although the division on Cyprus is not marked by explicit outbreaks of violence, its tourism industry remains as ideologically incarcerated as its Middle Eastern neighbors. Each side claims rights to sovereignty and territory, crafts a history of victimization and justified aggression, and enacts narratives of commemoration that reinforce nationalist claims (Lisle 2007). Both communities on Cyprus seek to enroll tourists into their partisan account by carefully foregrounding particular historical events (e.g., massacres, uprisings, killings) and even more carefully effacing long histories of entanglement, cooperation, and coexistence. What makes Cyprus different from its Israeli and Palestinian neighbors is the long-standing presence of foreign troops on the island: UN forces that have been patrolling the Buffer Zone since partition and U.K. forces that are stationed at the two British sovereign base areas of Akrotiri and Dhekelia. These military populations are important to the question of political tourism because, although they occupy a potentially disruptive space between tourists and residents, their presence actually produces, reinforces, and ultimately secures the structuring enmity of the conflict.[7]

Although it is possible to arrange private tours along the Northern borders of the Green Line, including a visit to the Sehitlik Martyrs Memorial "to the unarmed and defenseless victims of Greek thugs," the most popular and explicit opportunities for political tourism in Northern Nicosia are the Museum of Struggle and the Museum of Barbarism (Dubin 2002, 300). The first tells the chronological story of Turkish presence on the island and their fight for independence, starting with their efforts against the British (1878–1955), focusing mainly on the long-standing conflict with Greek Cypriots (1955–74), and culminating with a small section addressing life under partition (1974 to the present). The narrative trajectory, museological strategy, and exhibitionary rhetoric are unashamedly partisan, with displays of handmade Turkish weapons, images of Turkish Cypriot heroes and martyrs, and unapologetic demonizations of Greek leaders and Greek Cypriots (Lisle 2007, 99–100; see also Papadakis 1994, 407–9). The story of violence and struggle culminates in the final room, which juxtaposes a memorial to Turkish Cypriot martyrs (complete with hundreds of names) with an overtly positive and celebratory account of local life symbolized by photographs of smiling children. Across town at the Museum of Barbarism, the larger story of the Cypriot struggle is told through one event: the murder of a Turkish Cypriot family at the hands of Greek Cypriots. Displays of blood-stained clothes, damaged furniture, and framed bullet holes are juxtaposed with international press clippings documenting the atrocity, as well as various memorials, paintings, and poems commemorating it. Both institutions feel anachronistic in terms of their displays and museology, but even more so with respect to the overt partisanship of their message. Such explicit constructions of the Other as an unredeemable and demonized enemy, and of "us" as heroes, martyrs, and victims, sits awkwardly with international tourist populations who are used to encountering displays of war that culminate in a celebration of peace and an acknowledgment of lessons learned (e.g., the Hiroshima Peace Park). Tourists' discomfort at encountering such explicit displays of partisanship is exacerbated when they emerge from the museums into a city that is changing its material infrastructure to accommodate the possibility of future reconciliation. For example, the recent reconnection of Lidhra Street, the main thoroughfare between the capital's Northern and Southern sectors, is at odds with the museum narratives of violence, antagonism, and enmity. What results is a rather confused agenda for political tourists: for the most part, they are confronted with didactic and uncompromising accounts of the "barbaric" Greeks and the "heroic" Turks, but other times, they are encouraged to ignore the conflict entirely in favor of celebrating the growing signs of reconciliation and economic regeneration.

In Southern Nicosia, there are many more opportunities for tourists to encounter the struggle, but these possibilities are formulated quite differently than they are in the Northern sector. The South has its own Museum of National Struggle, but it only recounts the Greek Cypriot anticolonial struggle against the British from 1955 to 1960. Unlike the Northern museum, which imposes outdated museology on an up-to-date story (1878 to present), the Museum of Struggle in the South uses contemporary museological techniques and architecture (e.g., glass, steel, open plan rooms, large photographic montages, interactive displays) to tell a story firmly rooted in the past (1955–60). What emerges clearly is an identity constructed through nostalgia: Greek Cypriots are produced as an oppressed community fighting for liberation and independence from their British colonial occupiers. The problem is how that backward looking narrative shapes the contemporary struggle in Cyprus even though the museum story ends in 1960. Visitor understandings of Greek Cypriots being oppressed by the British are transposed outside of museum walls by substituting Turkish Cypriot oppressors for British ones (Lisle 2007, 103–5; Papadakis 1994, 405–7). This substitution is enacted most explicitly outside of museum space when tourists take advantage of the opportunities to encounter the Green Line and peer into the Buffer Zone. For example, the official Green Line Tour run by the Cyprus Tourist Guides Association focuses on the everyday life of the city adjacent to the Buffer Zone and visits many of the small businesses that operate in the old buildings at the edge of the border (e.g., cobblers, jewelers, tailors, cafés). However, what makes the tour so popular are the encounters with

FIGURE 27. In the Buffer Zone, beside Holy Cross Catholic Church, Nicosia. Photograph by the author.

the border itself: the opportunities to look through windows to the other side; walk beneath one of the UN posts; and confront the many sections of barbed wire, fortified walls, and shuttered buildings that constitute the border itself. Figure 27 shows one of the more militarized sections of the border just outside of the Holy Cross Catholic Church, where tourists constantly gather to get a glimpse of the "other side."

Close to this section of the border was the visitor platform that enabled tourists in Southern Nicosia to look across the ten-meter-wide Buffer Zone into the Northern sector (Jacobson et al. 2010). Before it was demolished in 2007 in the ongoing effort to reunify Lidhra Street, the platform was patrolled by Greek Cypriot soldiers who simultaneously explained the reason for the border to curious tourists and prevented them from taking pictures. The purpose of the platform was expressed in the overarching sign, in English and Greek, which read, "Nothing is gained without sacrifices and freedom without blood." That message was further secured by a memorial installation at the base of the platform that displayed large emotive photographs commemorating Greek Cypriots who had been missing since independence. Similarly partisan framings are also present outside of Nicosia. For example, the displays at the Famagusta Gulf View Point, a purposely built viewing platform and museum on the east coast of Cyprus, are as didactic and one-sided as the museums in Northern Nicosia (e.g., the Turkish population are invaders who "loot, rape, murder, uproot and desecrate") (Famagusta Gulf View Point, n.d.; Lisle 2007, 105). Like the memorial adjacent to the viewing platform on Lidhra Street, the focus in Famagusta is primarily on constructing Greek Cypriots as victims by highlighting what they have lost as a result of the struggle (i.e., not just friends and family members but also farmland, property, family heirlooms, and beach access).

Cyprus exemplifies the ambivalence at the heart of any effort to transform sites of conflict into viable tourist attractions and commemorative spaces. On the one hand, both sides are unwilling to let go of privileged forms of remembering and forgetting that designate homogenous victims and perpetrators and continuously replay past atrocities in the present. Indeed, that seductive narrative is often the most appealing for tourists who don't have the background knowledge to suggest otherwise. On the other hand, neither side in the conflict is willing to embrace a more heterogeneous form of remembering that constructs a shared narrative of the conflicted past for all communities. Indeed, the great risk in Cyprus is that in the urge to embrace reconciliation, the violence perpetrated during the conflict will be forgotten, sanitized, or transformed into anodyne and depoliticized tourist displays. Neither of these options is satisfactory: the first reproduces the same architecture of enmity that sustained the original violence (and, indeed, is the current status quo), but the second effaces difficult episodes of violence by locating them firmly in the past and gesturing to a bland and general future in which sacrifices are forgotten as the island embraces an "inevitable" unification. What makes Cyprus particularly interesting is not just that it has stalled between two unsatisfactory modes of commemoration but that its ambivalence has a physical manifestation in the eerie chasm of the Buffer Zone—the liminal space between northern and southern Cyprus in which artifacts from the partition in 1974 have been left to decay. Along with the hundreds of derelict buildings that frame the Buffer Zone on either side, dozens of cars lie abandoned in parking lots and automobile show rooms; the ghost town of Varosha consists of the concrete skeletons of holiday homes and apartments; and the old Nicosia International Airport located beside UN headquarters—including aircraft from the early 1970s—is slowly deteriorating. When tourists peer over the sandbags at the top of viewing platforms, look through the empty oil drums and barbed wire set up along the Green Line, and gaze across the plains toward the deserted beaches of Varosha, they do not see some menacing Other returning their curious gaze—they see dust-covered objects, derelict structures, and decaying ruins. In effect, the Buffer Zone has become the ultimate dark tourist destination: a much-coveted open-air museum that can be glimpsed from afar but never entered, encountered, or experienced.

The stalemate shaping opportunities for political tourism on Cyprus assumes, of course, that the Buffer Zone has been empty since 1974. In fact, for the last forty years, it has been patrolled by successive UN forces, traversed by Greek and Turkish military personnel, toured by visiting dignitaries, studied by local and visiting academics, and farmed by approximately nine thousand local residents from both communities. Indeed, the somewhat invisible history of the Buffer Zone has produced its own tourist culture in which those with access have collected, preserved, and interpreted the ruins that lay abandoned as partition took hold in 1974 (Lisle, forthcoming). For example, Canadian forces stationed at the Maple House UN post at the top of Lidhra Street from 1964 to 1993 had a dedicated room where they displayed the local objects and artifacts they had collected in the Buffer Zone, including old photographs of the city, television sets, radios, paintings, sewing machines, and assorted household items (United Nations Peacekeeping Force in Cyprus 2010, 10). Perhaps a more poignant example of how the urge to collect, preserve, and commemorate penetrates even the most inhospitable spaces is the yellow Morris Minor that was abandoned near Lidhra Street in 1974. As Figure 28 shows, successive UN forces have annually repainted the car's original bright yellow coat, pruned and tended to the plant life that threatens to engulf it, and adorned it with a makeshift museum label reading "Yellow Car." This carefully tended object is now used as a reference point for

FIGURE 28. Morris Minor abandoned in the Buffer Zone during the events of 1974. Courtesy of UNFICYP.

UN patrols of the Buffer Zone, a meeting point for negotiations between Greek and Turkish delegations, and a key feature of the exclusive tours of the Buffer Zone run by the UN for visiting dignitaries (United Nations Peacekeeping Force in Cyprus 2014). Although the Maple House museum and yellow car are not museums or memorials in the traditional sense, they are important because they remind us that communities other than Turkish and Greek live on the island, have their own account of the conflict, and seek to commemorate their own particular encounters with Cypriot life. What makes these examples different from the museums and walking tours in Nicosia is that they are not available to locals or tourists. The position of the Maple House museum and the yellow car within the restricted Buffer Zone means that their successive curators and caretakers do not have to negotiate the difficulties of displaying these objects to a public that is still very much divided. Out of the spotlight, these amateur curators simply gather and tend to whatever objects and artifacts remain inside the parameters of the Buffer Zone without any regard for whether it may be owned, claimed, or remembered by either community (Lisle, forthcoming).

As the pressure for reconciliation increases in Cyprus, debates over the future of the Buffer Zone will intensify: some groups will seek to destroy all signs of partition to further reconciliation, whereas others will seek to safeguard the ruins as a memorial to the divided island (Constantinou 2008). Central to this reimagination will be the cross-border and bicommunal groups who have long been working together to make sure that moves toward reconciliation do not end up reproducing and entrenching old divisions (Constantinou and Papadakis 2001; Loizos 2006; Occupy the Buffer Zone 2014; Scott 2012a; 2012b; Scott and Topcan 2006; Ungerleider 2001). Whatever direction the process of reconciliation takes in Cyprus, it will be important to consider the role of tourists—not just the majority who visit beach resorts and generate the most gross domestic product but also the increasing number of political tourists who want to see the signs and symbols of the conflict up close. Indeed, whatever matrix of preservation–regeneration is decided on for the 3 percent of the land mass that constitutes the Buffer Zone, it is hoped that at least some part of its ghostly presence will remain intact. For me, the decayed objects, abandoned buildings, and derelict spaces littering this border constitute the most appropriate kind of memorial to the conflict because they do not lend themselves easily to the ideological mobilizations that continue to reify partition. Rather, the rusting cars, empty hotel rooms, sunken balconies, and buckling Tarmac create an appropriate space of contemplation within which both locals and tourists can reflect on how prevailing architectures of enmity are produced and sustained.

The Tyranny of Reconciliation: South Africa and Northern Ireland

If political tourism in the Middle East and Cyprus remains ideologically incarcerated within a mode of antagonism, and therefore reifies a predetermined, homogenous, and singular form of remembering and forgetting, how does political tourism operate in postconflict societies that have supposedly embraced a peace process? South Africa and Northern Ireland differ from Cyprus and the Middle East because the opportunities for political tourism are being managed by a future-oriented discourse of reconciliation rather than a past-oriented discourse of commemoration.

Rather than arranging the coordinates of remembering and forgetting around reductive accounts of innocent victims, guilty perpetrators, and unjust atrocities, the discourse of reconciliation unifies those coordinates around a future of agreement, forgiveness, and nonviolence. This does not mean that narratives of struggle and episodes of violence are forgotten; rather, it means that they are definitively placed in the past and narrated in such a way that peace and reconciliation are the inevitable outcome. In South Africa, for example, the multiple, complex, and contradictory histories of the apartheid era are smoothed into a single trajectory of righteous struggle against, and liberation from, majority white rule. Unsurprisingly, this has generated many opportunities for political tourism whose popularity derives from the positive and empowering nature of the central narrative: a just struggle of the masses against unjust rule by the minority. Northern Ireland does not offer such clear winners and losers and thus cannot mobilize such a clear trajectory of victory or liberation. Instead, its heterogeneous history of sectarian conflict is reduced to a "two communities" model that has achieved peace through consociational power sharing. Unsurprisingly, the resulting opportunities for political tourism in Northern Ireland are not as consensual or numerous as they are in South Africa.

Paul Williams (2000, 112) argues that postconflict memorial museums are "the most effective allocation of resources for the purpose of reconciliation" because they make an authoritative statement about a past atrocity, but they also allow visitors to engage in a plurality of interpretive practices around that event. Though I agree with Williams that the number of interpretations available in postconflict sites is potentially infinite, I am particularly concerned with how those possibilities are being closed off by an increasingly hegemonic discourse of reconciliation. In many postconflict sites, difficult debates about commemoration (e.g., what to preserve, how to display it, who should decide) are being neutralized and displaced by an overarching goal of reconciliation that *everyone*—locals and tourists included—must sign up to. As a result, long-standing and intractable differences are forced aside, repressed, or ignored: reconciliation is positioned as the *only* way to secure peace, and political tourism's participation in this process is contingent on it arranging and narrating the conflict to support inevitable unity. Like the *hibakusha* in Hiroshima, I want to ask what is done *in the name of* peace and reconciliation in the postconflict sites of South Africa and Northern Ireland and how political tourism becomes complicit in new constructions of remembering and forgetting.

One of the difficulties in comparing the postconflict situations of South Africa and Northern Ireland is the temptation to arrange them chronologically in terms of how far along the road to reconciliation they have traveled. Thus, places like the Middle East and Cyprus cannot be considered as postconflict cases because they remain divided and have not yet embraced a peace process; Northern Ireland is well into a peace process and beginning to engage in the difficult question of how to commemorate its divided history, whereas South Africa has succeeded at reconciliation (thanks largely to the Truth and Reconciliation Commission [TRC]) and currently enjoys healthy tourist revenue from those attractions that celebrate the liberation from apartheid. I want to reject the developmental teleology inherent in that comparative process—indeed, in comparative politics in general—and look instead at how the discourse of reconciliation shapes political tourism in these sites regardless of how "reconciled" they appear to be. Reconciliation is never an innocent or neutral objective that all members of a postconflict society can sign up to; rather, it is a political imperative that achieves widespread support precisely because it disavows all the hierarchies, exclusions, and effacements it inevitably constructs. Unlike traditional comparative politics (especially that which seeks to explain, understand, and ultimately solve deeply divided societies), I want to start from a more critical position that is concerned with how reconciliation operates as a mode of governance aimed at managing both local and tourist populations more efficiently. In this sense, I agree with an ex-combatant in Northern Ireland who states, "I am not really interested in reconciliation. It is a term that has been so used and abused; it's a dirty word as far as I'm concerned" (McEvoy, McEvoy, and McConnachie 2006, 81). The central issue here is how the ultimate goal of peace embedded in reconciliation works to efface still-lingering animosities of conflict and produce new asymmetries of its own.

Although the differences in South Africa and Northern Ireland are important (and, indeed, lead to very different experiences of political tourism), they are similar in that a discourse of reconciliation operates to confirm a collective identity, invite visitors in to encounter and learn about that identity, and exclude dissenting subjects who challenge the future-oriented promise of peace. These dissenting subjects are constructed as a serious threat to the body politic—as if allowing them to be heard will automatically plunge everyone back into previous forms of endemic violence. To prevent such backsliding, reconciliation also offers the promise of a peaceful future to all those who have signed up: they will benefit from the economic regeneration instigated by new forms of tourism. Following on from Wendy Brown's work on tolerance, I want to explore the new authorities, hierarchies, and asymmetries that are produced when reconciliation is constructed as a wholly benign collective goal toward which everyone can strive. What Brown (2006, 4) does so well is expose the depoliticizing and undemocratic functions of tolerance: she shows how it operates normatively while simultaneously rendering its normative foundation "oblique almost to the point of invisibility." Like tolerance, reconciliation too often goes unchecked and uncriticized because it operates with "the aura of pure goodness" that masks the exclusions it invariably produces (10). How are local, national, and international visitors pacified by messages of reconciliation and peace that consign violence to the past (and, indeed, enclose it within museum walls and display cases)? What is hidden, silenced, and marginalized in the generalized messages of national harmony? What actions are excused in the name of pursuing peace, and how are tourists enrolled into that narrative?

South Africa: Consensus

The opportunities for political tourism in South Africa are important because of the widely held consensus they reproduce. At the heart of these experiences is a powerful anti-apartheid master narrative of liberation that documents the justified struggle against oppression undertaken by the masses (from incarcerated African National Congress [ANC] leaders to Soweto schoolchildren) and celebrates South Africa's transition into a peaceful and unified "rainbow nation." This message abounds in the many museums, memorials, and institutions that emerged after 1994, such as the

Apartheid Museum in Gold Reef City, the Hector Pieterson Museum in Soweto, Freedom Park in Pretoria, the Walter Sisulu Square in Kliptown, and the Constitution Hill Museum in Johannesburg (Meskell and Scheermeyer 2008; Newbury 2005; Rankin and Schmidt 2009). However, by far the most popular political tourism attraction in South Africa is Robben Island, the prison where Nelson Mandela and other political activists were incarcerated for eighteen years. The immediate transformation of Robben Island from a prison to a viable tourist attraction indicates the prevailing belief in the 1990s that, like the TRC, Robben Island would function as a catalyst for nation building, a "cathartic mechanism designed to pave the way for political and cultural transformation" (Strange and Kempa 2003, 394), and a "cultural showcase for new South African 'rainbow nation'-style democracy" (Williams 2000, 16). Established in 1997 as a museum and national monument, Robben Island achieved UNESCO world heritage status in 1999 and national heritage status in 2006. A standard visit to the island includes a bus tour of the surrounding lime quarry, gardens, churches, mosques, former leper colony, and cemetery, but the most popular feature of the tour is undoubtedly Mandela's cell in the maximum security prison. As Strange and Kempa argue, tourists' encounter with such a small and sparsely furnished cell resonates so powerfully because it is framed within a narrative about the "broader resilience and power of the human spirit" in overcoming apartheid (394; see also Phaswana-Mufaya and Haydam 2005; Shackley 2001). Upon encountering Mandela's cell, tourists "regulate their bodily comportment through feelings of spatial trepidation and deference to the memory of those who spent time there"—not just because the anti-apartheid narrative is so powerful but also because the museum encourages tourists to view political prisoners as "blameless victims of a malevolent state" (Williams 2000, 90). Indeed, it is hard to imagine dispositions *other* than reverence toward the political prisoners in a condition where Robben Island has become "a world-wide icon of the universality of human rights, of hope, peace and reconciliation" (Shackley 2001, 362).

Central to the Robben Island experience is a carefully constructed balance between authenticating, documenting, and displaying the hardships suffered by political prisoners under the apartheid regime and emphasizing the values of justice, equality, and collective action that were mobilized to overcome apartheid. That balance is achieved by the manner of its delivery: tours are led by former political prisoners who were incarcerated in Robben Island. Indeed, tourists routinely cite their interaction with the political prisoner guides as the quality that makes Robben Island so popular: not only does it lend a personal touch to the experience, it also generates "an authentic 'spirit of place'" (Shackley 2001, 356). Guides can illuminate the hardships they suffered (e.g., working at the infamous lime quarry, restricted diets, limited visits, censored communication, solitary confinement) but also embody the forgiveness central to the new South Africa. As one visitor explained,

> one of the most moving experiences of the tour was to hear the former political prisoner guides speak in such gentle tones, without bitterness, about their hopes for reconciliation and the need to build a new South Africa that would include rights for all its citizens. The idea, the guide said, is to remember the past yet also move past it. (Nanda 2004, 381)

The anti-apartheid liberation story is told not through artifacts and objects on Robben Island (in part because prisons are not spaces where objects are collected or preserved) but rather through the "intangible heritage resource" of the political prisoner guides' own stories (Ka Mpumlwana et al. 2002, 252). Curators claim that the different types of interaction made possible within the open-ended guide–guest encounter are what prevent Robben Island from being an "emotions factory" that locks visitors into a didactic and singular message (Shearing and Kempa 2004, 70). For example, curators are adamant that the guides should not follow a preset script but simply tell their own personal stories in a way that facilitates questioning, interaction, and dialogue. This is especially important when dealing with visitors who are already hostile or negative (e.g., Afrikaaner groups), and guides speak eloquently about how to "read" their audience and calibrate their story so as to get the central message across (Shearing and Kempa 2004, 70–72).

What interests me is how Robben Island has become an important site of governance that inculcates both locals and visitors into a single and agreed narrative of the triumph over apartheid and the creation of a "rainbow nation." The political prisoner guides are crucial figures in this mode of governance, for even though they are not given an agreed script to follow, they are "unanimous in the expression of their own desire to communicate a narrative of inclusion, tolerance, and the triumph of the human spirit" (Shearing and Kempa 2004, 70–71). What Robben Island suggests is that reductive and didactic forms of commemoration don't just emerge from partisan narratives; they also emerge from the imposition of consensus—especially when that consensus is forged through wider discourses on tolerance, diversity, and freedom of choice. For Shearing and Kempa, Robben Island is an important institution of governance because it promotes "certain ways of thinking and therefore acting across the population" (65). Unlike partisan museums, which are "intentional vehicles for shaping consciousness," Robben Island is understood as a positive example of "public hope" because of its nondidactic and inclusive nature (65). Shearing and Kempa conclude that Robben Island's museological strategies are normatively desirable: they *do* employ techniques of governance, but these are beneficial because they inculcate a "hope sensibility" (76). Certainly Robben Island, like all museums, is an institution of governance aimed at ordering, managing, and directing both local populations and international visitors, but I disagree with Shearing and Kempa's claim that its inclusive narrative somehow obviates the more distasteful effects of governance. A commemorative narrative of choice, diversity, and freedom may be enabling (and, indeed, may allow multiple agencies to flourish), but it is also disciplining, disempowering, and, at times, authoritarian. No museum narrative commemorating the past— especially a past of conflict and struggle—operates without imposing limits on who can be included in the story and who cannot or shaping the behavior of visitors who confront that story. What is so difficult to discern on Robben Island are the silences produced by the anti-apartheid narrative: with such a powerful and widespread consensus in place, it is hard to tell who has been left out of the story and why.

Robben Island's mode of governance does not work in the same way as the other post-1994 museums in South Africa. Indeed, many of the sophisticated visual and museological techniques used in the newer postapartheid museums—especially photography and mixed media—outclass the Robben Island experience in their ability to mobilize the emotions, sensations, and empathy of visitors (Marschall 2006; Newbury 2005). Robben Island works instead through a much more conventional mode of address: it mobilizes authenticity—especially around Mandela's story—and foregrounds the aura of the site for visitors. This is not a new museum building, a replicated site of atrocity, or a relocated infrastructure; this is the *actual* prison used during apartheid and thus exudes an aura of realism that is reinforced by the political prisoner guides who were *actually* incarcerated there. Unsurprisingly, the authenticity of the site is anchored by Mandela's cell and the fact that tourists can actually encounter, feel, and be a part of that space. In effect, Robben Island doesn't need sophisticated museological techniques or complex visual representations: the power of the site speaks for itself and is amplified by the narration of the political prisoner guides. As visitors are governed within Robben Island's authentication of the anti-apartheid story, the difficulties of the liberation struggle itself are lost. The centrality of Mandela and the ANC to the story effaces the many disagreements between different groups opposing apartheid, for example, disputes over the use of violence, the collaboration with liberal white activists, and the future of the Afrikaaner population under black majority rule. As Teeger and Vinitzky-Seroussi (2007, 67) argue with regard to the Apartheid Museum, Mandela's story is "given prominence even at points when history does not call for it." As a result, when curators at Robben Island tried to give prominence to the forgotten stories of women and other marginalized groups at the prison, they found it "difficult to depart from the triumph narrative without appearing to betray the 'new' South Africa" (Strange and Kempa 2003, 400). The dominance of a sanitized anti-apartheid story, and Mandela's centrality to that story, is becoming increasingly problematic as the cracks of the "rainbow nation" begin to show. Despite its geographical and political isolation from the everyday struggles of post-apartheid life, Robben Island has been forced to respond to charges that, like the TRC, it "overstated the completeness of the reconciliation process" (Strange and Kempa 2003, 400–401; see also Shackley 2001). As Ali Hlongwane (2008a; 2008b), former curator of the Hector Pieterson Memorial and Museum, argues, for a South African museum to respond to the needs of its local community it must trouble the narrative of black liberation that underscores its very raison d'être. In other words, it must celebrate the success of black liberation in overcoming apartheid while simultaneously pointing to its internal disagreements, post-apartheid failings, and ongoing exclusions.

That critical questioning is embraced more explicitly by some of the modes of interaction and engagement on display at the District 6 Museum in Cape Town and the Constitution Hill Museum on the site of the Old Court complex in Johannesburg. Both institutions are insistent that they are "living museums" whose primary constituency is the local community they are commemorating. An important part of how they both use and contest the dominant anti-apartheid narrative is the way they understand the relationship between museums and conflicted history. Following Neil Postman's (1990, 58) argument, a museum should first and foremost be a timely argument with its *present* society—an argument that is not afraid to bring up difficult, uncomfortable, and painful truths about both the past *and* the present. The District 6 Museum, for example, commemorates how a vibrant multicultural and multiracial community was forced out of their neighborhood when the apartheid government declared it a "White Group Area" in 1966 (Ballantyne 2003; Beyers 2008; Douglas 2011; Julius 2008; McEachern 1998a; 1998b; Rassool 2007; Soudien 2006). However, in their efforts to collect oral histories, memories, and artifacts from the displaced community, museum curators are extremely wary of "uncritical frameworks of triumphalism and celebration" (Rassool 2000, 19). This anxiety is especially acute with respect to visiting academics who position District 6 as a "convenient field site for the study of culture and the politics of transition" but also with respect to the South African tourist industry that positions the museum as a convenient and safe "'space of apartheid' for tourists to witness" (Ka Mpumlwana et al. 2002, 256). Being alive and attentive to these risks means understanding the District 6 Museum as a "generative space for working with and interpreting memory" that is explicitly oriented to the local community it serves (Julius 2008, 113–16). In this sense, District 6 is not a finished story because curators are constantly encouraging former residents of the area to visit and share their experiences, connecting the forced removals of District 6 with similar apartheid displacements, and linking the local experience to global examples (District 6 Museum, n.d.; Julius 2008). Similarly, the museum complex at Constitution Hill does not restrict its narrative to the apartheid past but instead asks about how the past continues to produce some of the more difficult aspects of contemporary life. For example, it has recently responded to homophobia in South Africa by hosting public discussions, poetry readings, and art installations and by organizing a pride walk in the city (Constitution Hill Museum 2013). Its spatial location beside the new Constitutional Court means that visitors cannot look back on past abuses of human rights without considering the ways in which such abuses continue in the present day. Moreover, it continually renews its commitment to the local community by making itself available for political dialogue, problem solving, and network building as well as for parties, raves, and celebrations.

Certainly both District 6 and Constitution Hill engage with the antiapartheid master narrative, but they are able to carve out spaces of interaction in which that narrative can be troubled and enlarged. Their insistence on being "living museums" rather than conventional institutions that place history behind glass suggests that they are constantly reinventing themselves as they respond not only to the stories about apartheid they keep uncovering but also to the pressing contemporary issues that their local communities face (e.g., curators at Constitution Hill insist that all their exhibits are temporary and changeable) (Madikida, Segal, and Van Den Berg 2008; Segal 2004). What makes these institutions critically interesting is the way they force visitors to contemplate their own relationship to memory—especially the potentially traumatic memory of violence, repression, and power. It is more difficult for visitors to remain passive when confronted with curatorial gestures of welcome that ask direct questions and challenge them to think about their own positions vis-à-vis structural violence. While I am not claiming that District 6 and Constitution Hill somehow avoid being institutions of governance (for this is surely impossible), I am claiming that they create more space within which those techniques of governance can be troubled, redirected, and reimagined. In this sense, they go some way to puncturing not only the naive and depoliticizing discourse of reconciliation that shapes so much political tourism in South Africa but also the "consensual political culture" bequeathed by the TRC (Teeger and Vinitzky-Seroussi 2007, 71).

Northern Ireland: Evasion

Since the Good Friday Agreement was signed in 1998, issues of commemoration in Northern Ireland have become an increasingly important aspect of the peace process, and tourism—especially in Belfast—has been positioned as a key driver of the region's economic regeneration. Given the lack of tourism in the region during the Troubles, opportunities for visitors to encounter remnants of the conflict only began to develop seriously after the cease-fires in 1994. Indeed, as Dépret (2006, 143–44) argues, the Northern Ireland Tourist Board has had to play catch-up since then—a process that was helped enormously by European and national funding (see also Leslie 1996; 1999; O'Neill and Fitz 1996; Rolston 1995; Wall 1996). As the Good Friday Agreement was being implemented in political institutions, more and more visitors took a red double-decker bus tour titled "Living History" that visited the famous political murals on the Falls and Shankill roads, the Peace Wall, and the Crumlin Road Gaol. Even more popular were Black Taxi Tours that offered a more intimate experience (five-person maximum per taxi), whereby a knowledgeable guide would show visitors their own personalized itinerary of the murals, memorials, and "black spots" of West Belfast (Dépret 2006, 149; Lisle 2000; 2006d). As these diverse opportunities to encounter remnants of the Troubles were developing, the Ulster Museum—the official repository of the region's heritage—remained relatively silent on recent struggles, preferring instead to fold the Troubles into a longer historical narrative and display more generic scenes of nature, technology, and society. Indeed, for much of the post-cease-fire period, formal and official efforts to commemorate the Troubles remained "off limits" (Flynn 2011, 385). Dépret (2006, 138–47) suggests that while officials were not keen to position remnants of the Troubles as "prime motivators" for tourism, local and community groups were much more enthused by the opportunities created by "curious tourists" who wanted to see the sites of sectarian violence. I think Dépret's argument partly holds with respect to the late 1990s and early 2000s, and many scholars and tourist workers continue to frame the developments of political tourism through an official–community distinction. For example, some would claim that the official Red Top City Bus tours offer sanitized accounts of the Troubles, whereas the community-run Black Taxi Tours offer something more "authentic" because they are more interactive (Causevic and Lynch 2005; 2006). For me, that framing is extremely problematic because it implies that there is a "true" narrative of the Troubles to which only local communities have access (and which officials get wrong), and only locals who lived through the Troubles have the legitimate right to tell that story to tourists. McDowell's (2008, 406) more nuanced account suggests that official promotions of the economic potential of political tourism combine with local promotions of partisan stories in a way that "effectively— and perhaps inadvertently—leads to the international legitimization of sectarian politics and sectarian landscapes." Conversely, Dépret (2006, 146) argues that a deep-set ambivalence about marketing the history of the Troubles for tourists means that the question of *who* can tell Belfast's history is answered by a "cacophony of voices." What interests me is how the overarching discourse of reconciliation driving the peace process in Northern Ireland has largely failed to shape that cacophony of voices into a consensus and has therefore failed to impose agreed coordinates for remembering and forgetting. The result has been that efforts to commemorate the Troubles—from official institutions, community groups, civil society, and individuals—remain isolated, dispersed, and often more susceptible to reproducing the sectarian politics of the past.

This is not to say that Northern Ireland has not tried to mobilize an official narrative of peace and reconciliation that operates locally by way of inclusion and assimilation, and internationally by inviting visitors to learn about the hard road to peace. However, those efforts have largely failed because they have insisted on a framework of neutrality that gives visitors from around the world multiple (and often bewildering) points of connection so as not to alienate local Republican, Nationalist, Loyalist, and Unionist communities. This framework of neutrality is based on a universal mode of address: it offers to educate visitors with radically different levels of knowledge about the Troubles but also allow locals from both sides of the sectarian divide to safely learn about the adjacent communities with which they have been in conflict for several decades (Dépret 2006, 160–61; Jarman 1998). For example, the "Living History" bus tours of Belfast "potentially allow anyone to ride the tour bus without feeling alienated" largely because the guides pride themselves on not giving away their own political sympathies.[8] However, the representations that most embody this claim to neutrality are the two postagreement installations staged by the Ulster Museum. In *Conflict: The Irish at War* (December 2003–December 2006), the Troubles were contextualized within a centuries-long framework of animosity in which visitors were told that the Irish have always been at war with one another and the Troubles are simply the latest manifestation of that antagonism. The exhibition's more contemporary section provided oral testimonies from a variety of people involved in the Troubles and displayed a number of objects from both sides of the sectarian divide (e.g., Orange Lodge banners, letters smuggled from the Maze Prison, a Royal Ulster Constabulary officer's helmet damaged in fighting, an Irish Republican Army Roll of Honor, and British Army bullets) (Crooke 2001; Leonard 2008). Whereas advocates of the exhibition were thankful that the Ulster Museum was finally addressing the Troubles and displaying its artifacts, critics like myself were unhappy with how the central framing of "ancient hatreds" reified sectarian divisions and obscured both the heterogeneity of Northern Ireland and the complexity of the struggle itself.

After its three-year, £17 million refurbishment, the Ulster Museum reopened with a long-overdue permanent exhibition on the Troubles. Located on the first floor at the back of the building, the exhibition displays large photographs arranged on the mocked-up gable ends of houses, black-and-white video footage, and text panels explaining the development and cessation of violence. Many visitors appreciate the chance to learn about the Troubles in a familiar museum atmosphere, and the installation won Best Exhibition 2004 at the Museum of the Year Awards (Meredith 2009). However, the overwhelming sense from local communities and from visitors is that the Troubles Gallery is "bland, safe and strenuously non-controversial" (Meredith 2009; Reming 2011). Indeed, as the head of human history at the museum concedes, "the result is a coherent but limited treatment of the subject" (Blair 2011, 3; 2012). The Troubles Gallery tries to remain neutral primarily through a minimalist approach that leaves most interpretive work up to the visitor. For example, its informative wall panels are factual, few, and strenuously impartial, leaving the visitor to spend more time wandering through the blown-up photographs and watching the looped video installations. One of the most striking things about the exhibit is that all the visuals and text are black and white. Not only does this locate sectarian violence firmly in previous decades when black-and-white documentary news photography reigned, but it also leeches the displays of their meaning and texture. Over and above this minimalist aesthetic, the most problematic aspect of the Troubles Gallery is the complete lack of objects, artifacts, or relics from the period. It is as if the curators felt that blown-up black-and-white images would be safer because two-dimensional photographs would not ignite the same passions as bullet casings or prison uniforms. Indeed, the initial plans to include blood-stained clothes, guns, and controversial works of art were shelved in favor of a "small, muted and evasive" exhibit that uses black-and-white photography to avoid the conflict (Jones 2010). As John Grey (n.d.) argues,

> how the museum now treats "The Troubles" in the light of past criticism of evasion has to be something of a litmus test. Here a museum exhibition that does not include a single original artefact fails at first base. Visitor centre style wall panels bombard us with facts at the expense of illumination. Different panels tell us that the Troubles started in October 1968, or, alternatively, in 1969, and none of them explore why the Troubles started at all. Richard Kirkland's 1996 criticism that "absence acknowledges unfinished business just as it bespeaks a form of timidity" still stands.

Tucked away at the back of the new building, the Troubles Gallery is isolated not only from the preceding sections of Irish history (which do, of course, display objects) but also from the entire museum. No wonder many visitors inadvertently miss the whole thing.

The Troubles Gallery's commitment to impartiality effaces the important structural asymmetries of the Troubles themselves (e.g., state vs. nonstate actors, legitimate and illegitimate uses of force); isolates Northern Ireland from other sectarian struggles around the world (e.g., the Middle East, Bosnia, Cyprus); and ultimately fails to encourage visitors to reflect on global issues of human rights, national identity, coexistence, and tolerance. Moreover, the exhibit's anodyne conclusion negates the lingering difficulties of power sharing (e.g., the ongoing problems with parade routes, flags, and paramilitary activities) and therefore reproduces the problematic official line that Northern Ireland is exemplary in its embrace of the peace process and should thus act as a template for other conflicted regions. Responding to critics of the exhibition, the director of National Museums Northern Ireland claimed that "the impact of the Troubles is unresolved—so the gallery is unresolved" (Meredith 2009). But this is absolutely not the case: for this exhibit to remain unresolved would be to invite reflection on how the Troubles continue to resonate in Northern Ireland; stage interactive encounters asking visitors to work through the difficulties of a continuing peace process; confront visitors with the difficult ethical decisions involved in displaying a "dissonant heritage" that nobody agrees on; and ultimately leave visitors with more questions, anxieties, and curiosities than certainties. *That* kind of exhibit would be a more honest reflection of unresolved tensions in Northern Ireland, but instead the Troubles Gallery hides in false neutrality and ultimately avoids all the difficult questions it was supposed to address in the first place. In the end, an overarching commitment to neutrality and impartiality prevents engagement with the difficult but necessary debates that any postconflict society must have with itself about how to sensitively and ethically represent a divided history (Graham and Whelan 2007).

Northern Ireland's evasion of its difficult past is exemplified even more clearly in the debates over the future of the Maze/Long Kesh Prison located ten miles south of Belfast. This 367-acre sprawling institution was home to more than ten thousand Republican and Loyalist prisoners during the Troubles, including the ten Republican hunger strikers who died protesting British rule. The last prisoners left in 2000, and the undersecretary of state MP Ian Pearson established the Maze Consultation Panel, whose mission statement was

> to undertake a meaningful, focused and transparent consultation process with the aim of bringing forward innovative and sustainable development proposals for the former Maze Prison/Long Kesh site, so that this site, which symbolised the period of conflict, can become the engine for economic and social regeneration. (Reinvestment and Reform Initiative 2003; see also Flynn 2011, 390; McAtackney 2014; Purbrick 2006; RPS Planning and Development 2003, 1)

Tourism, of course, was always envisioned as part of Belfast's wider notion of "economic and social regeneration," and the cross-party panel reviewed fifteen key proposals, which included plans for a sports stadium, a shopping complex, a motor racetrack, and more housing (*Belfast Newsletter* 2003, 1, 5; *Belfast Telegraph* 2004; Connolly 2004; Dykes 2003; Hill 2004; McDonald 2003; McHugh and Gordon 2004). One of these proposals, put forward by ex-Republican prisoner group Coiste Na n-larchimí (An Coiste), included a ten-acre museum of conscience that would preserve at least one of the H-blocks and the hospital wing within a wider peace park (Coiste Na n-larchimí 2003). An Coiste's proposal drew on the increasing success of political tourism (especially their own Political Tour operating in West Belfast) as well as the development of memorial museums around the world. Indeed, their proposal drew explicitly on the work of the International Coalition of Historic Sites of Conscience (ICHSC), which was set up in 1999 to preserve "places where human rights and democracy itself were cruelly attacked, bravely defended, or hotly debated" (Centre for Human Rights, Social Justice, and Democracy 2002, 1; International Coalition of Historic Sites of Conscience 2014). Their involvement with the ICHSC was strategically important because it sought to place the Maze/Long Kesh alongside other museums of conscience such as the District 6 Museum in South Africa, the Gulag Museum at Perm-36 in Russia, and the Maison des Esclaves in Senegal. As Graham and McDowell (2007, 356–57) argue, Republican groups in Northern Ireland drew explicitly from South Africa when making their case for a museum at the Maze/Long Kesh because they wanted to construct a popular narrative about overcoming state violence and oppression (see also Crooke 2005). Unsurprisingly, An Coiste's proposal was strongly contested by Loyalist and Unionist groups who refused the assumption that Republican forces had been "liberated" from state oppression. Moreover, they felt that *any* museum at the site—especially one that preserved the hospital wing where the hunger strikers died—would effectively become a "shrine to Republicanism" (RTE 2003; see also Graham and McDowell 2007, 351–53; Robinson 2013).

The final report of the Maze Consultation Panel was submitted in 2005 and proposed a multiuse site including a sports stadium as well as an International Centre for Conflict Transformation (ICCT) located in one of the H-blocks and the hospital wing (Maze Consultation Panel 2005). What is striking about the recommendation for an ICCT is the decision to omit the word *museum*. While this undoubtedly appeased Loyalist and Unionist groups, it also downgraded the role of tourism at the site—an odd decision, given that that the public felt that tourism was the strongest pull factor in any redevelopment of the Maze/Long Kesh (Maze Consultation Panel 2005, 43). The problem, for Graham and McDowell (2007, 355–56; see also Dixon 2002), is that this nonmuseum is framed in exactly the same way as a museum:

> The ICCT will be housed in structures that include the iconic physical elements of Long Kesh and thus, in practical terms, raises precisely the same questions as would a museum: who will define the terms of "conflict transformation"?; whose representations will be included?; whose meanings will dominate? Both the Report in general and the specific proposal for an ICCT are marked by the same "constructive ambiguity" that characterizes all the "key documents of the peace process" which can "be interpreted in various ways to suit the receiving audience."

This ambiguity is symptomatic of how the discourse of reconciliation has failed to mobilize a shared idea about how to commemorate the Troubles in Northern Ireland. Again and again, official bodies opt for anodyne and neutral frameworks that either sanitize the history of the Troubles or seek to match the atrocities on both sides to achieve some kind of forced impartiality. This unsatisfying answer also resonates in the panel's understanding of the kinds of tourists likely to visit the regenerated Maze/Long Kesh: these visitors will travel to see a sports match, shop in the leisure complex, or ride in the equestrian center, but will only visit the ICCT if it can be easily incorporated into that traditional tourist itinerary. Very simply, naming this memorial complex an ICCT rather than a museum downgrades its role as a tourist attraction and instead envisions "a neutral, inclusive and constructive 'place apart,' to be used by organizations and communities to further the cause of conflict transformation" (Maze Consultation Panel 2005, 14). Although the final report does make oblique references to proposed "visitors," it does not position tourists as primary stakeholders in the ICCT: those positions are reserved for communities, practitioners, academics, and international partners.

Though the sentiments of neutrality and inclusivity sound convincing—and, indeed, the final report bends over backward to foreground these two characteristics—they actually mask how the ICCT is directed toward specific ideological goals and thus envisions specific kinds of visitors. The ICCT's main role is to promote a "shared society" through local endeavors (i.e., offering "dialogue and confidence" to the different communities within Northern Ireland) and international outreach work (i.e., "allowing others to learn from the problems Northern Ireland has experienced, and how we are seeking to resolve them") (Maze Consultation Panel 2005, 14-17). To the extent that the ICCT envisions tourism at all within this framework, it is primarily as a form of pedagogy—as the final report suggests, "much could be achieved in terms of educating visitors to the Centre as well as promoting peace and reconciliation" (Maze Consultation Panel 2005, 15). This is problematic because it places the Troubles in the past as something we can learn from and thus prevents an exploration of present-day struggles and unforeseen social cleavages that remain part of the legacy of the Troubles. In this sense, the ICCT proposal reflects Graham and Whelan's (2007, 493) wider claim that "the 1998 Peace Agreement is built on the unsustainable assumption that the burdens of the past can somehow be set aside in a consociational society." Any tourist entering the ICCT will be led to believe that the Northern Ireland within which he is currently traveling is now a reconciled community that deals with any lingering sectarianism through proper democratic channels. Moreover, the mandate of the ICCT positions individuals from Northern Ireland—especially academics—as "experts" who can provide the "answers" to conflict transformation and show other divided societies how to deliver themselves from entrenched violence. This claim rests on the reductive theoretical horizon of comparative politics that disavows specific and complex conditions of hierarchy, asymmetry, and exploitation in favor of generalized categories such as political institutions, civil society, media structures, and ethnic identities. But comparative politics is not a neutral framing, and the comparative ethos that grounds the entire mandate of the ICCT—that it is there to *help* and *instruct* other sites coming out of conflict—teaches visitors that Northern Ireland is "successful" in relation

FIGURE 29. Daniel Libeskind's design for the PbCRC at the Maze/Long Kesh. Courtesy of Studio Libeskind.

to other divided societies. With such a hierarchy in place, visitors will be encouraged to ignore the specificities of each conflict—especially those in the Global South—and look out from the Northern Irish Troubles to Sri Lanka, the Middle East, or Kosovo and ask, "Which ones are the Catholics, and which ones are the Protestants?"[9]

Despite the Maze Consultation Panel's decision to disavow the ICCT's museum status to avoid partisan mobilizations of the Troubles, its central features of conflict transformation and reconciliation began to impose their own limitations on how the site subsequently developed. A Maze Long Kesh Development Corporation was established to oversee the site's transformation, £18 million in Peace III funding was secured from the European Union, and planning permission was granted for world-renowned architect Daniel Libeskind and local company McAdam Design to implement the newly named Peace-Building and Conflict Resolution Centre (PbCRC) envisioned in Figure 29. In July 2013, Libeskind's proposal was unveiled, showing similarities with his previous work on the Jewish Museum in Berlin and the Ground Zero memorial (Crownshaw 2008; Derrida 1992; Huyssen 1997; Libeskind 1992; Stead 2000; Williams 2000, 96–97; Young 2000a). Although there is, of course, no precise detail on what will be housed inside the PbCRC, Libeskind's signature features of abstraction, emptiness, and reflectivity are well suited to the values of neutrality and inclusivity so favored by official efforts to commemorate the Troubles (Stott 2013). William Neill (2006, 117) argues that the raw memories embedded in the Maze will make it difficult to "neuter" the space in the same way the government has recently sanitized the urban fabric of Belfast. But this underestimates the power of the discourse of reconciliation to write over contested history and determine what gets included and excluded in the center. For example, the Maze Consultation Panel's final report proposed that the PbCRC should simply display "straightforward factual information"—as if "the facts" themselves are uncontested and their simple unadorned display will somehow avoid any unpleasantness arising from competing accounts of the Troubles (Maze Consultation Panel 2005, 17). Similarly, there is an assumption that if objects and artifacts are to be included in the PbCRC, the overall focus on peace and conflict resolution will prevent visitors from treating the space like a museum. Those overseeing the PbCRC envision potential visitors to be so *in agreement* with the goals of peace, reconciliation, and conflict transformation that they will interpret any displays appropriately, that is, passively and in accordance with the values of peace and reconciliation that frame the center. There is no sense in which visitors will be forced to question these values or contemplate the exclusions and effacements that such a consensus might mask. Because it is framed *in advance* by a discourse of reconciliation, it has already shut down the possibility that radical, critical, and confrontational ideas about commemoration might emerge. In the end, Loyalist and Unionist worries that the PbCRC will become a "shrine to terrorism" are unfounded—a more likely scenario is that it will present an anodyne, sanitized, and flaccid account of the Troubles that will satisfy no one.

As the transformation of the Maze/Long Kesh continues to languish in a political stalemate, people in Northern Ireland have continued to develop multiple forms of commemoration that attract political tourists. Murals continue to be painted and repainted all over Northern Ireland; new Black Taxi Tours continue to show visitors infamous scenes from the Troubles; and smaller memorials, artifact collections, rituals, and festivals continue to reflect on the legacy of the Troubles. Scholars are engaged in wide-reaching surveys that document artifacts and memorials to the Troubles, and the thriving cultural scene in Belfast continually offers alternative approaches to commemoration that do not reinscribe sectarian boundaries (Brown 2008; Conflict Archive on the Internet, n.d.).[10] Perhaps the most prominent advocate for alternative forms of remembering is the Belfast-based cross-community group Healing through Remembering (HTR). Along with initiatives such as a Day of Reflection, HTR outlined proposals for a Living Memorial Museum project in 2007 titled *Without Walls*. This was not a formal call for architectural proposals but rather an open call for ideas from the public that was followed up by a series of public workshops in Enniskillen, Dundalk, London, Armagh, Dublin, Belfast, and Derry/Londonderry (Purbrick 2007, 10). At first glance, this process looks similar to the official public meetings held by the Maze Consultation Committee in 2004, but the results of these two consultations couldn't be more divergent. Unlike the Maze/Long Kesh proposals, the submissions to HTR were not restricted to official application forms but instead took a variety of shapes from professional architectural drawings and DVD proposals to poetry, sculpture, sketches, collages, and letters. Whereas the Maze/Long Kesh proposals were always wedded to a traditional site-specific institution, the HTR proposals included much more open-ended and reflexive ideas that emphasized the direct involvement of local communities in curating (e.g., a tent museum, a museum on wheels, a jigsaw museum) (Purbrick 2007, 23–29). For Louise Purbrick, a member of the Living Memorial Museum subcommittee and author of its final report, the richness and multiplicity of these submissions "in no small way re-defined what a museum, and particularly a conflict museum, should be" (12). It is unclear what the future of these proposals—currently contained in a number of display books—might be, or whether tourists will ever get a chance to see them. But I think they are an important counterweight to the inertia that prevents governing bodies from publicly commemorating the Troubles and thus keeps Belfast stuck as a "deeply divided city that is afraid of expressing its tensions" (Neill 2006, 119). Efforts such as those by HTR keep the fraught debates over commemoration in Northern Ireland alive and away from the temptations of political closure—both the sectarian closure advocated by

Republican/Nationalist and Loyalist/Unionist groups still wedded to a divided culture but also the anodyne closure advocated by officials keen to use the discourse of reconciliation to neutralize all forms of dissent.

Visiting Emptiness: Despair, Anxiety, and Hope

Reflecting on the difficulties of constructing memorials to the Holocaust, James E. Young makes a convincing argument about countermonuments. For him, memorials and monuments should never offer a "final solution" to the debates over commemoration and in this sense should discard didactic, authoritarian, and patriotic motifs in favor of absence, emptiness, and abstraction that invite active reflection (Young 1993; 2000b; see also Dickenson, Blair, and Ott 2010; Edkins 2003; Lupu 2003; Stubblefield 2011; Vinegar and Otero-Pailos 2012). From his participation in the Holocaust memorial debates in Berlin, Young initially suggested that the most fitting memorial would be "a thousand years of memorial competitions" rather than a finally-final permanent monument (Young 2002; see also Young 1992; 1997; 1999). It is clear that artists and architects currently working on memorials are taking Young's arguments seriously, and it is no coincidence that he was invited onto the jury for the new Ground Zero memorial in Manhattan (Lower Manhattan Development Corporation 2004). Speaking about the trend in countermemorialization, Paul Williams (2000, 3) argues,

> Without positing that older memorial conventions have been eclipsed or abandoned, it is clear that the critical consensus now favours minimalist and abstract design over that which is grandiose and authoritative; decentered and incommodious space over that which is central and iconic; bodily visitor experiences that are sensory and emotional rather than visual and impassive; interpretive strategies that utilize private, subjective testimony over official historical narratives; salt over stone, perhaps.

This new form of memorial design is also shaping the way museums are addressing contested histories, prolonged conflict, and episodes of atrocity. As Williams goes on to argue, this has produced a new kind of visitor experience: "the current ideal is that subjects will physically engage with the form in order to arouse some sensory mode, rather than standing back to contemplate a semi-realistic representation" (94). This new trend in commemorating through absence, emptiness, and reflection does not rely primarily on displaying the facts of an atrocity, the names of the dead, or the relevant objects of violence. Nor does it rely on mobilizing emotions through a narrative arc of violence → struggle → peace or through carefully chosen (and often dramatically enlarged) images. Rather, in their best arrangements, the conditions of absence, emptiness, and reflection force the visitor to viscerally embody her encounter with historical violence and ultimately question her desire to confront it. Insisting on that kind of physical presence makes it difficult for tourists to remain passive in the face of atrocity and instead forces an engagement—sometimes an uncomfortable and anxious engagement—with the events being depicted. Very simply, the conditions of absence, emptiness, and reflection do something that traditional museum narratives do not: they create a larger space of contemplation within which it becomes possible for visitors to understand how the conventional logics of identity/difference underscoring their everyday lives can, in some cases, lead to conflict. For such insights to be encouraged, conflict cannot remain locked in the past and forever kept there by legitimations of the present as peaceful, enlightened, and democratic. Rather, visitors must be encouraged to make connections between how specific atrocities occurred in the past, how atrocities are *still* occurring, and—crucially—how the culture of tourism and spectacle in which they are currently participating is actually complicit in securing the asymmetries from which atrocities sometimes emerge. These insights are by no means automatic, and indeed, many visitors will refuse the challenge entailed in conflating the past with the present and pointing to the anxieties shared across both time periods. But opening up more spaces of contemplation for political tourists is one way to write not only the past but also the rest of the world back into the picture by insisting that logics of "dark" and "light" do not entail a reductive geopolitics in which "backward" nations are continually at war with each other while "enlightened" nations enjoy the democratic peace of liberal rule.

Because the rise of political tourism since the end of the Cold War is the result of intensifying forces of globalization, it bears the same underlying asymmetries between the privileged who enjoy its benefits (e.g., those who can take holidays) and the majority who must serve its needs (e.g., those who must accept diminished working conditions to secure employment). And of course, those asymmetries map onto and reinforce the prevailing geopolitical imaginary of safe/democratic/ peaceful versus dangerous/authoritarian/conflict ridden. Too often, the opportunities for political tourism that emerge in postconflict spaces simply reproduce this geopolitical imaginary without question. Narrative trajectories that go from conflict to peace, commemorations that sequester violence in the past, and exhibitions that isolate individual conflicts from global structures of power all contribute to a bifurcated geopolitics of enlightened versus unenlightened populations. Moreover, the dark tourism literature that insists on empirically proving how light or dark an attraction is simply compounds the problem. Opportunities for tourists to encounter conflict and atrocity can certainly be superficial, depoliticizing, and anodyne, but they also have the capacity to confront visitors with profound questions about how to ensure human rights in a global condition of intense cultural, religious, and political difference. But the only way those deeper questions can be asked is if curators, academics, policy makers, designers, and tourists themselves question the prevailing geopolitical imaginary that enables smug and risk-free contemplations of historical conflict and atrocity. The proposition of encountering the remnants of conflict is a difficult one: difficult for those deciding what to preserve and how, difficult for local communities who feel their history is being taken away from them, and difficult for victims and survivors who have to relive their traumas in commodified form. The least that can be done is to make it equally difficult for visitors by forcing them to recognize their own complicity in the global asymmetries that can lead to conflict in the first place.

5

Connecting Tourism and Terrorism

Milblogs, Soft Targets, and the Securitization of Travel

Following a decade of dispersed ethnic conflicts, complex military interventions, and a changing world order, the events of 9/11 ushered in a familiar architecture of enmity expressed by American president George W. Bush's claim that "either you are with us, or you are with the terrorists" (Bush 2001a). Through an array of political interventions, military deployments, and cultural disseminations, the fluctuating geopolitical landscape of the new millennium was rearranged into a reductive binary in which fanatical terrorists emanating from an "axis of evil" threatened all global citizens who valued freedom, democracy, and liberty (Bush 2002). Western powers reproduced this bifurcated world order by constructing a terrorist threat that was both exceptional and extreme, which in turn enabled them to launch a widespread War on Terror characterized not only by its high-profile external deployments (e.g., military involvement in Afghanistan and Iraq) but also by pernicious internal interventions aimed at habituating populations to a permanent state of emergency (e.g., increased surveillance measures, security checks, and government monitoring) (Amoore 2006; Amoore and De Goede 2008; Aradau and Van Munster 2007; 2009; Dillon and Neal 2008; Dillon and Reid 2009; Evans 2010; Ingram and Dodds 2009; Jabri 2006). With respect to foreign policy, those pursuing the War on Terror identified a number of dispersed but threatening populations (e.g., the Taliban, al-Qaeda, al-Shabab) and sought to infiltrate and stop their networks by explicit military engagements (e.g., interventions in Afghanistan and Iraq) as well as the widespread circumvention of sovereign borders and international law (e.g., drone surveillance and extraordinary rendition). Crucially, Western powers understood that terrorist enemies were dispersed throughout complex global networks, which meant that anywhere in the world could potentially become part of the War on Terror's battlefield—including domestic territory. In effect, Western governments used the exceptionality of the terrorist threat to launch unprecedented interventions not only into foreign territory but also into the everyday lives, patterns, and habits of their own citizens. As highly technologized and asymmetric modes of combat developed overseas, new modes of surveillance enabled governments to access the travel patterns, financial transactions, religious practices, and online behavior of citizens so as to more comprehensively "root out enemies within."

Though the War on Terror's bifurcated architecture suggests a nostalgia for bipolar geopolitics, clear enemies, and calculable defense strategies, it operates on a completely different terrain. Its *deterritorialized* character does not disaggregate enemy populations and map them onto unchanging sovereign spaces; rather, it operates within and through conditions of flux, multiplicity, mobility, and contingency. Indeed, what makes this particular geopolitical construction different from its predecessors is its reach: its ability to construct any person or any space on the planet as a potential threat and its capacity to intervene in the most private registers of everyday life in the name of fighting that threat. Those pursuing the War on Terror are well aware that porous borders, multiple loyalties, and free mobility are absolutely central to the neoliberal economic conditions securing their privileged ways of life. By forcefully producing a bifurcated architecture of enmity out of the contingent character of global politics, they are able to protect the attributes of globalization sustaining their privileged ways of life while simultaneously identifying and pursuing enemies who oppose those ways of life. What interests me is how the War on Terror uses a powerful civilizational discourse to mobilize solidarity within a diverse global collective that is positioned against the supposedly insular, homogenous, and dogmatic terrorists. We know, of course, that the construction of global collectivities (us) and entrenched enemies (them) within any architecture of enmity is never as simple as dominant discourses would have us believe and, more to the point, always requires a series of depoliticizations and erasures. With that in mind, I am interested in the work that the War on Terror's architecture of enmity does in our deterritorialized geopolitical landscape. What practices go into sustaining and reproducing it? What complexities and contingencies does it seek to cover over? What new exclusions does it mobilize, and how does it justify its actions in the name of "fighting terrorism"?

This chapter starts by tracking how a tourist sensibility shaped the deployment of U.S., U.K., and coalition forces in Afghanistan and Iraq after 9/11 and pays particular attention to how these tours of duty were disseminated through visual technologies, social media, and online communication. Certainly contemporary soldiers mobilize the same tourist sensibility as their predecessors when they rely on familiar Orientalist tropes to distinguish between exotic hosts and dangerous enemies. However, the widespread use of the Internet to share stories of foreign deployment changes both the dynamic of the soldier's encounter with his or her foreign hosts and the manner in which resulting images and stories are interpreted and remediated. What requires further scrutiny is how the tourist sensibility underscoring these military adventures is mediated through digital technologies and how that mediation works to reinforce a growing physical and moral distance between occupying forces and local populations. The chapter then moves on to consider how the travel patterns and practices of tourists all over the world were transformed by the "ever-present terrorist threat" that emerged after 9/11 and the many efforts to counter that threat at home and abroad. Although not a new phenomenon, the explicit terrorist targeting of tourists and tourist resorts took on a new significance in the aftermath of 9/11 because tourists were seen as hugely symbolic of the diverse collectivity arranging itself against a predetermined terrorist threat. Indeed, the interpersonal connections forged by tourism—between tourists themselves, between tourists and hosts, and between hosts trying to maximize tourism revenue—were seen as central to the effort of building a "coalition of the willing" to defeat terrorism. What particularly interests me is how the bodies of Western tourists and the resorts in which they gather have become central battlefields in the War on Terror. Focusing on the aftermath of 9/11 and the terrorist targeting of tourists in Bali and Mombasa in 2002, I want to explore how the global tourist industry has been doubly mobilized by the War on Terror—on the one hand, it is the soft target of choice for terrorists, and on the other hand, it is central to the cross-cultural solidarities needed to combat the threat of terrorism. Of particular interest here is how the material infrastructure and labor force of the global tourism industry have become securitized to such an extent that they are now considered to be on the front line of the War on Terror. To this end, I examine the changing behavior of travel under a condition of permanent war by looking at both the increasing surveillance of travelers themselves (e.g., airport security measures) and the efforts to mobilize tourism's labor force to identify and monitor "suspicious" travelers (e.g., counterterrorism training programs). Certainly scholars are asking important questions about civil liberties, private spheres, and legal rights with respect to these new modes of surveillance and governance (Bigo 2010; Lyon 2007), but what I want to show more generally is how the privileged experience of travel is now explicitly underscored by serious geopolitical concerns that make it increasingly difficult for it to fulfill its central fantasy of escape.

Dispatches from the War Zone: Isolation, Objectification, Dehumanization

The deployments of U.S., U.K., and coalition forces to Afghanistan (2001) and Iraq (2003) revealed an important tension in the way tourist sensibilities are now being mobilized by modern militaries. On the one hand, opportunities for troops to interact with local populations were being curtailed by a no-fraternization policy that aimed to protect coalition soldiers from spiraling urban violence and shield the surrounding Muslim population from the potentially offensive antics of Western troops (Engber 2006). As a consequence, off-duty soldiers were effectively confined to military bases that were turned into havens of leisure, relaxation, and consumerism. On the other hand, soldiers arrived in Iraq and Afghanistan equipped with personal digital technologies—smart phones, laptops, notebooks, cameras—that enabled them to record and disseminate their overseas adventures. While coalition military leaders initially struggled with issues of confidentiality, censorship, and security with respect to their troops' use of digital technologies, they soon installed Internet access on military bases and enabled the use of personal devices provided soldiers did not compromise operational security by revealing details of specific missions or troop positions (Dao 2010; Wall 2010; Wendle 2011). Unsurprisingly, this tension between the physical incarceration of soldiers on bases and their proliferating modes of communication is changing the well-established tourist sensibility of modern militaries. Soldiers have less opportunity to encounter foreign cultures through off-duty leave or regional R&R rotations (i.e., fewer chances to eat local cuisine, engage in local traditions, and view nonstrategic foreign landscapes) but more opportunity to record and disseminate their experiences of foreign deployment. Inevitably, the isolation of troops produced a much richer account of the everyday life of modern soldiering (e.g., its long stretches of boredom alleviated by the many leisure opportunities of military bases) but a much reduced account of how occupying soldiers negotiate their foreign surroundings and encounter host populations. Consequently, new technologies of representation (e.g., camera phones, digital cameras, laptops) and modes of media dissemination (e.g., milblogs, social media posts, Flickr images) potentially provide more access to the ways in which soldiers are shaped by a tourist sensibility, but these representations are limited because they predominantly reveal experiences of leisure and adventure within the enclave of the military base rather than within a foreign city, landscape, or resort.

That solipsistic disposition was also entrenched by the experience of official R&R, which, geographically, culturally, and psychologically, contained soldiers within a militarized circuit with almost no opportunity for spontaneous tourist experiences. Indeed, the familiar recruitment strategy of "join the army—see the world" has become largely redundant as soldiers are now managed within militarized enclaves from the moment they deploy to the moment they return home. For example, American troops in Afghanistan and Iraq did not escape that enclave during official R&R breaks because they were flown back to the United States for their annual leave and distributed to their domestic airport of choice through the Onward Travel program (Jontz 2004; U.S. Army 2010; U.S. Central Command 2007). The only sustained opportunity for soldiers to engage in tourist behavior within the general area of operation was during three- to four-day short-term breaks at rearward operating bases in Qatar, Kuwait, and Bahrain. These bases were equipped with comprehensive fitness facilities; swimming pools; saunas; bowling alleys; driving ranges; mini-golf courses; movie theaters; Internet cafés and/or wireless capability; Xbox and PlayStation rooms; music rooms; opportunities for manicures, pedicures, and massage; and familiar restaurants such as Burger King, Chili's, and Subway (Edgar 2007; Yde 2007). One of the most popular of these R&R destinations was Camp As Sayliyah, near Doha, which also offered soldiers the choice of six supervised day trips into Qatar, including camel rides, boat trips, Jet Skiing, falconing, deep-sea fishing, sand dunes, and beach barbecues (Smith, n.d.; Stan, n.d.; Zimmerman 2004). Unlike the R&R provisions of previous conflicts, these tourist excursions were tightly organized, heavily managed, and highly supervised so as to maintain the no-fraternization policy of the overall operation. Within such a tightly controlled geography of battlefield–military base–home, soldiers were not able to deploy a tourist sensibility on unsupervised foreign excursions, nor were they able to relive the infamous pub crawls and militarized prostitution of their predecessors (indeed, American soldiers were limited to three beers a day during their visits to regional R&R facilities).

While the Qatari R&R Pass Program appeared to offer soldiers a wholesome mini-break and the opportunity to experience local culture, it was eventually closed down in 2011 owing to lack of use (Jontz 2011). To be sure, this closure was partly about the overall drawdown of coalition troops in the region, but the more acute reason for closure was that soldiers were being explicitly encouraged to spend their short-term R&R breaks with their units at newly refurbished in-country military bases. In replacing the regional R&R Pass Program with the rest-in-place policy, the U.S. military concentrated its efforts on making in-country military bases havens for safety, leisure, relaxation, and fun. The MWR division in charge of transforming these bases provided a standard package "including video games, recreational games such as foosball, televisions and exercise equipment," and, where possible, an Internet café system (Burke 2012). By importing forms of suburban American culture directly onto the front lines of the war, these familiar pastimes, modes of communication, and cultural products were meant to comfort soldiers until their full R&R rotation back home (Gillem 2007, 73–172). All in-country bases had logistical and support relationships with the surrounding population (e.g., acquisition and delivery of goods, outsourcing of some services), which included select—and vetted—local entrepreneurs who were permitted on these military bases to sell souvenirs to visiting soldiers (e.g., traditional clothing, utensils, postcards, toys) (*Time,* n.d.). One of the most famous in-country bases in Iraq was an officer's club in Baghdad previously used by Saddam Hussein's former Republican Guards. Soldiers on three- to four-day breaks from combat enjoyed the benefits of a "fitness centre, swimming pool, game room, Internet café, TV and movie room, indoor and outdoor movie theatres, outdoor basketball, tennis, and volleyball courts and a field for flag football and soccer" (Edgar 2007; Stanis 2003; Yde 2007). Elaborating on the transformation of former Ba'athist estates into R&R centers for coalition soldiers, Meredith Lair (2011, 231) explains,

> Many of these manses sat on the Tigris River, offering scenic views and slightly cooler breezes. Their marbled halls opened onto grand patios, swimming pools, and elaborate but poorly tended gardens newly amended by volleyball nets and horseshoe pits. Inside, MWR personnel—the Special Services troops of the twenty-first century—carved gift shops, eateries, weight rooms, screening rooms, game rooms, computer labs, phone centres, saunas, and sleeping quarters out of ornate salons and bedroom suites. The scenes conjured by T-bone steaks, crystal chandeliers, and uniformed Iraqi or TCN attendants were more Gatsby than grunt, making Iraq a strange war indeed.

These adapted-for-use enclaved spaces in Iraq served a dual purpose: primarily, they were architectures of containment that secured the no-fraternization policy and produced physical, moral, and experiential distance between occupying troops and their hosts (Turner 2007; 2010). But to make life inside the wire palatable, these adapted bases were also architectures of leisure and consumption; indeed, both the previous leisure pursuits of the Ba'athist regime and the current leisure pursuits of occupying soldiers were efforts to offset their condition of immobility and isolation.

These leisured landscapes were central to a particular calculus employed by the U.S. military in Iraq—what Lair has called the "comfort-for-morale equation"—in which soldiers, wherever and whenever possible, were rewarded for their service with comfort and luxury (e.g., high-quality food such as Alaskan crab, down comforters, just-released films and video games) (Lair 2011, 229). The result of this calculus was a further distancing of soldiers from the surrounding local population who rightly resented the abundance afforded to soldiers contained in enclaved bases while they suffered shortages in food and water supplies, electricity, and medical services. The confinement of R&R to well-stocked and secure in-country military bases needs to be understood as part of a wider mode of distancing in asymmetric warfare in which occupying forces rely on technology (e.g., unmanned aerial vehicles, simulation training) to physically and morally remove themselves from their enemies, who become thoroughly dehumanized into pixels, data, and digitally rendered targets (Der Derian 2009; Gregory 2011; Robben 2011; Singer 2010). The consequence of technologically rendered distance and dehumanization is that foreign bodies are much easier to kill because they are not considered equivalent moral agents. What particularly concerns me is how distance and dehumanization are mapped onto the off-duty and everyday lives of soldiers stationed abroad. When they are isolated from the local population within the leisured enclaves of military bases, soldiers conceive of the "enemy" as even more remote, unknown, and threatening. Because the no-fraternization policy prevents sustained encounters and interactions with local populations, occupying soldiers find it more difficult to think of their hosts as equivalent human agents with full, complex, and rich lifeworlds. The mode of isolation at work in modern military occupations is changing the tourist sensibility of soldiers in such a way that they are only able to conceive of their local hosts in highly reductive ways: as either implacable enemies or invisible servants.

This mode of distancing is belied by the increased access to, and use of, digital technologies that aim to bring audiences closer to the "real" action of war. The media-saturated interventions in Afghanistan continually documented, disseminated, circulated, recirculated, scrutinized, and debated the actions of soldiers both on and off the battlefield. While media saturation characterized the first Gulf War (e.g., real-time reporting, the onset of twenty-four-hour news networks), the use of digital technology and Internet dissemination were only in their infancy at that time, and the use of such technologies by amateurs—including soldiers and civilians—was minimal. The subsequent conflicts in Afghanistan and Iraq, however, were mediated not just by journalists using traditional visual and narrative formats (e.g., television, radio, newspapers) but more and more by journalists, governments, soldiers, civilians, terrorist groups, concerned citizens, and activist communities who disseminated digital images and narratives through websites, milblogs, podcasts, photo-sharing sites, and social media feeds. It is not hard to see how the access to reasonably cheap communication technologies (e.g., smart phones, digital cameras, tablets, laptops) and the widespread ability to distribute images and narratives horizontally through the Internet is destabilizing the professional cultures of journalism and the traditional relationship between the media and military press offices. With respect to the interventions in Afghanistan and Iraq, this has produced serious tensions between Western military elites who want to produce a univocal story of strategic success and individual soldiers who want to use digital technologies to tell their personal stories.[1] This tension is especially evident in popular milblogs—Internet diaries written by individual soldiers (both on tour and discharged) that include narrative, photographic, and video documentation of their deployment (Hockenberry 2005; Kennedy 2008; 2009). As John Hockenberry (2005) argues, "milbloggers offer an unprecedented real-time real-life window on war and the people who wage it. Their collective voice competes with and occasionally undermines the DOD's [Department of Defense's] elaborate message machine and the much-loathed mainstream media" (see also Finer 2005). More importantly, while traditional media institutions struggle with citizen journalism in war zones, and military elites struggle to control how serving soldiers disseminate their experiences online, neither has any control over the way terrorist groups use the Internet to increase recruitment and radicalization, disseminate their message to wider audiences, and provide visual evidence of their actions through hostage and suicide videos (Conway 2006; Conway and McInerney 2008; Freedman and Thussu 2011; Kavoori and Fraley 2006; Kenney 2010; Seib and Janbek 2010; Tsfati and Weimann 2002).

What is particularly interesting about the widespread availability and use of digital technologies in war is that *all* aspects of a military operation can now be seen—including troop activities both on and off the battlefield. Whereas technologies such as helmet-cams enable soldiers to record their experiences of battle (McSorley 2012), more familiar personal recording devices such as camera phones are ubiquitous on in-country military bases where soldiers' antics are widely documented and disseminated. How does this increased opportunity to share one's experience of war change the tourist sensibility that has always shaped soldiering? How do these new technologies enable soldiers to strike a balance between a strategic view of their foreign surroundings and a touristic one? One milblog, titled *My Vacation in Iraq,* often drew comparisons between the activities of war and tourism. As the author Sergeant Lucas Port mused while standing on a volleyball court within a secure military base, "it is right under a palm tree and if you try real hard you can pretend you are on vacation back there if you shut out the occasional pop of gun fire across the road at the firing range" (Port 2005; see also Ballard 2005; Freeman 2007; Kave 2005; Old Blue, n.d.; Rassler 2010). While many of Port's blog posts detail his boredom and the activities he pursues while confined to his base (e.g., hours of playing Xbox), he also posts pictures and comments of the leisure pursuits that shape his excursions outside the wire. In one photograph (see Figure 30), Port and his colleague pose in front of a foreign monument—in this case, the Monument to the Unknown Soldier—in central Baghdad. Here the incongruity of the war-tourism entanglement is clearly visualized: a familiar tourist pose (i.e., visitors arranged in front of a monument) is militarized by the soldiers' desert camouflage and military equipment (e.g., guns, ammunition). Images such as these reaffirm Struk's (2011, xv) argument that "touristy pictures" have always made up a bulk of soldiers' personal photographs taken during war. The question, for me, is how that tourist sensibility has changed as a result of the heavily managed distance between soldiers and local hosts and the digital media practices that soldiers now use to record and disseminate their overseas adventures. Lair (2011, 234–35) suggests that a new and fortified distance forged during the interventions in Iraq and Afghanistan changed the familiar tourist tropes of American soldiers' personal photographs, for example, ubiquitous shots of the "exotic" desert landscape and the everyday life of locals in Iraq were mostly framed by

FIGURE 30. Tomb of the Unknown Soldier, monument 9. Courtesy of Sergeant Luke Port.

the window of the military jeep from which the soldier-tourist safely took his or her picture. Unsurprisingly, the no-fraternization policy meant a dramatic increase in "buddy" photographs of soldiers teasing, roughhousing, and joking during the long stretches of boredom that characterized their confinement to base (Lair 2011, 234). As Lair goes on to say, "many Americans spent a year in-country without ever meeting an Iraqi person, which tended to reduce the locals to off-screen abstractions in soldiers' visual diaries" (234).

Liam Kennedy (2009, 14–15) is much clearer about the tourist sensibility that underscored American soldiers' Web-based accounts of their tours of duty in Iraq and Afghanistan:

> Certain visual tropes and categories of photograph are apparent. A tourist frame is very common, with images depicting smiling soldiers posing in the desert, or in front of ancient monuments, or murals, or statues. There are also many images devoted to natural landscapes—desert sunsets are a favourite—and to animals (mostly camels and lizards) and insects. In the photographs in which soldiers pose for the camera they adopt conventional postures of tourist

photography, but there is some incongruity in their wearing full military uniforms and carrying weapons.

Augmenting Struk's (2011, 52–62) claims about soldier photographs and photograph albums of the First and Second World Wars, Kennedy suggests that these milblogs represent a new kind of visual travelogue in which the distance between soldier and foreign surroundings is secured primarily by an imperial gaze. Like Kennedy, I think the tourist sensibility underscoring milblogs can, and often does, work to reinforce the "more imperial gaze of a victorious, occupying force" (15), but I think the relationship between touristic and strategic modes of encounter is much more complicated than he suggests. Certainly milblogs and other Internet accounts of soldiering in Afghanistan and Iraq reinforce a moral, physical, and visual distance between the occupying force and local Iraqis and Afghanis—but this distance is never as overdetermined as a simple imperial gaze suggests. In short, there is more contained in that distance than a colonizer–colonized hierarchy allows. The circuits of leisure that operate within and outside the combat zone are fueled by competing and contradictory desires: on the one hand, there is a strategic desire to remain apart from (and superior to) surrounding foreign cultures—a desire enabled by dehumanizing enemy populations and enacting a no-fraternization policy with noncombatant civilians; on the other hand, there is a touristic desire to get closer to the "real" exotic—a nostalgic desire to inhabit foreign landscapes and encounter a "real" Afghani or Iraqi person who is not the enemy. These competing desires *can* align to reinforce an imperial gaze, but their multiple productions of difference (e.g., enemy, host, combatant, civilian, local) suggest a much wider and richer range of possible encounters between occupying forces and local populations. What soldiers' online narratives and visual accounts of war demonstrate is the irresolvable contradiction in the logics of difference connecting war and tourism: they *simultaneously* mobilize a touristic desire for managed proximity to difference and a militaristic desire to eradicate the difference embodied in targeted enemies. What I am interested in is how these two desires constantly unsettle each other—how the relentless jostling between touristic and strategic modes of encounter, not to mention the multiplicities of difference produced across these two frames, always has the potential to trouble colonizer-colonized hierarchies as soon as they emerge. To explore that disruption in more depth, I want to foreground the tourist sensibility that underscored the documentation and widespread dissemination of the photographs of American torture practices that took place in Iraq's Abu Ghraib prison in 2003 (Hersh 2004a; 2004b; 2004c; 2005; Leung 2004; Salon Staff 2006). Much has been written about what these images say about American identity and how they undermine the government's efforts to justify the War on Terror (Amis 2007; Bennett 2007; Danner 2005; Eagleton 2007; Eisenman 2007; Hitchens 2005; 2007; Rajiva 2005; Sontag 2004b). While issues about responsibility, military culture, and racism were central to these debates, what interested me most were the discussions of the photographs themselves: who took them, how they were disseminated, how they were interpreted, and, most importantly, what photographic conventions they invoked. Errol Morris's (2008) film *Standard Operating Procedure* does much to reveal Sabrina Harman's complex reasons for taking the photographs (see also Gourevitch 2008; Struk 2011, 1–20). Formally, there was an obvious pornographic framing to the images that revealed the constitutive and combined forces of racism, misogyny, and violence in American culture (Baudrillard 2006, 86–88; Camon 2004; Tétreault 2006). While many commentators felt that this was a new and terrible chapter in American foreign policy, a number of scholars and curators—including Susan Sontag (2004b)—revealed important historical and visual connections between the Abu Ghraib torture scenes and the early-twentieth-century practice of lynching in the American South (Allen et al. 2000; Allen and Littlefield 2005; Apel 2003; 2005; Campbell 2004; International Centre for Photography 2004). For me, the lynching-torture connection is forged not only in the formal poses enacted by the subjects—both perpetrators and victims—but also in how the resulting images were disseminated. As Dora Apel (2003, 92–93) argues,

> when lynching photographs were transformed into souvenir postcards, they were sent to friends and family with the senders' proud boasts of having been in the mob, making blackness an exotic spectacle and privileging the "look" of whites over blacks.... At Abu Ghraib, compact discs, videos and computer

files of digital images performed the role of the postcards, and were meant to circulate only within the community of American military personnel, their families, and friends.

It is crucial that both lynching photographs and the Abu Ghraib images were used as postcards (i.e., Internet files to be circulated and souvenirs to be collected), yet in all the discussions about how the Abu Ghraib photographs reproduced familiar tropes of pornography, misogyny, and racism, what is missing is how these images both visualize a tourist sensibility and resonate through a tourist framing. The exception here is writer and critic Luc Sante (2004), who draws from the tagline of Morris's *Standard Operating Procedure*—"I wouldn't recommend a vacation to Iraq anytime soon"—to suggest that the Abu Ghraib images resemble the colonial tourist photographs of hunters on safari: "The pictures from Abu Ghraib are trophy shots. The American soldiers included look exactly as if they were standing next to a gutted buck or a 10-foot marlin." Sante rightly argues that both frames—the tourist and hunter—seek to prove, legitimate, and display the protagonist's superiority over a thoroughly dehumanized and objectified Other-animal. But as he acknowledges, his referencing of the colonial hunting photograph is rather outdated. For me, the Abu Ghraib images are not nostalgic or archaic but are instead *entirely familiar* because they resemble billions of banal, everyday tourist snapshots collected in albums, stored in smart phones, backed up in the cloud, and posted on blogs and social media sites. Indeed, Susan Sontag (2004b) argues that "today's soldiers instead function like tourists, as Rumsfeld put it, 'running around with digital cameras and taking these unbelievable photographs and then passing them off, against the law, to the media, to our surprise.'" Gourevitch (2008) inadvertently invokes this tourist framing when discussing Sabrina Harman's photographs from Iraq:

> Much of Harman's photo album from Al Hillah looks like a fantasy travel brochure for post-Saddam Iraq: here she is, skin aglow, beaming, amid swarms of joyous Iraqi children—children clambering into her lap, throwing their arms around her, mobbing her in the streets; here she is welcomed into local homes by mustached men in dishdashas bearing tiny cups of tea; here she is visiting the antiquities, with a Bedouin and his camel at the ziggurat of Borsippa, and

with fellow-soldiers at the Ishtar gate of Babylon; and here she is in camouflage, with her arm around a pregnant woman swathed in black, her hand on the future-full belly, the woman grinning.

Certainly the American personnel of the 372nd Military Police Company stationed in Abu Ghraib were soldiers, torturers, and amateur pornographers, but they were also *tourists,* and the torture photographs they took were visual accounts of their holiday in Iraq. In this sense, Lynndie England's grin as she points to the naked, hooded prisoners says, "Look at what we get up to at work!" but it also says, "Look at what I found on my holiday in Iraq!"

The most insightful commentaries on the Abu Ghraib photographs acknowledge that the tourist frame is at least a part of how we make sense of these images, but I want to argue that its centrality has not been fully addressed or explored. I find this omission quite astonishing because tourism is absolutely central to our understanding of how these photographs were imagined, constructed, disseminated, and interpreted. The Abu Ghraib images show privileged guests (American military personnel) posing alongside exotic Others (Iraqi prisoners) whom they have encountered in faraway lands. Western audiences immediately recognize the poses enacted by the torturers at Abu Ghraib because they are the *same* poses Western tourists have been producing on their holidays for more than a century. How many of us have, like Sabrina Harman, Lynndie England, and Charles Graner, leaned into a photograph to grin and point and give a thumbs-up at a valued exotic object—in their case an Iraqi prisoner, in our case a statue, a monument, or a tourist attraction? How many of us have, like Harman, England, and Graner, grinned and posed for the camera as we bestride a famous landmark—in their case a human pyramid of naked Iraqi prisoners, in our case a sacred mound of earth, a revered historical object, or a marker of hallowed ground? Like the torturers at Abu Ghraib, we *know* what to do when placed in front of a camera in faraway lands: we stand upright, we grin, we point, and, above all, we *pose.* Such posing signifies the asymmetrical power relations inherent in both tourist and military encounters: the privilege of the posing subject (the tourist, the soldier) is secured by the exoticism and abjection of her surroundings, including—and especially—objectified Others. The tourist framing of the Abu Ghraib photographs is unsettling because it forces audiences to reflect on their own actions as tourists in foreign lands. Have I, too, objectified, dehumanized, and degraded foreign hosts? Are my actions as a privileged tourist part of a wider set of asymmetries that culminates in Abu Ghraib?

Civilizing Travel: Protecting Tourists from the Terrorist Threat

While the tourist sensibility of coalition soldiers in Afghanistan and Iraq was simultaneously confined to military bases and extrapolated through digital disseminations, tourists themselves were being drawn into the War on Terror as the soft target of choice for terrorists. The deliberate targeting of Western tourists by terrorist groups certainly predates the events of 9/11; indeed, when a radical Islamic group killed fifty-eight Western tourists in Luxor, Egypt, in 1997, governments and tourism professionals understood that issues of security in tourism required much more attention (Hall, Dallen, and Duval 2004). The paucity of those efforts was revealed on 9/11 when the hijackers instantly transformed airplanes from technologies of travel into airborne bombs. In the aftermath of those events, however, the tourism industry became absolutely central to the burgeoning security apparatus being mobilized to combat terrorism. Think, for example, of the dramatic increase of surveillance and security at airports, the move to biometric passports, and the intensification of pretravel screening. Suddenly terrorism was directly impinging on the everyday practices of millions of tourists after 9/11: it limited not only *where* one could "safely" travel (i.e., certainly not Iraq or Somalia) but also *how* one traveled (e.g., with restricted amounts of liquid). I am particularly interested in how the intense securitization of the tourism industry after the events of 9/11 made the bodies of tourists and the consumer landscapes of the tourist industry (e.g., resorts, monuments, attractions) central objects in the wider security apparatus of the War on Terror.[2] Although practices of tourism and terrorism seem antithetical—one devoted to travel and leisure, the other to political violence—their entanglement is revealed most clearly in the counterterrorism responses to 9/11. The tourism industry became central to the far-reaching practices of securitization, governance, and regulation that were made possible when Western governments rendered the terrorist threat exceptional in its scope, irrationality, and intensity (Amoore and De Goede 2008; Aradau and Van Munster 2009; Dillon and Neal 2008; Huysmans 2006a; 2006b; Jabri 2006; Neal 2009; Odysseos and Petito 2007; Van Munster 2004; Walker 2006). Responding properly to such an exceptional threat meant that the everyday lives of tourists and tourism workers, as well as the material infrastructure of the tourism industry, became mobilized as objects of security and thus available for a variety of political interventions. What I am particularly interested in is how tourism operates within the War on Terror's matrix of exceptionality and securitization—how the trivial lifeworlds of leisure, travel, and relaxation are subject to pernicious acts of surveillance and intervention that are then justified as the most appropriate response to an exceptional terrorist threat.[3] To understand how the tourism industry facilitated its own securitization, it is necessary to examine its central role in the reconstitution of a cosmopolitan global community after the events of 9/11—a process that erased important asymmetries within that community (e.g., between privileged tourist guests and their local hosts).

In his most famous speech in response to the events of 9/11, George W. Bush (2001a) made the famous claim, "Either you are with us, or you are with the terrorists." Discursive analyses of the speech illustrate how the reductive binary through which Bush framed the events of 9/11 helped to produce and secure a global community of "civilized" people who were being attacked by "uncivilized" terrorists (Collet 2009; Graham, Keenan, and Dowd 2004; Oddo 2001). I am particularly interested in how tourists were positioned within this binary framing as symbols of a cosmopolitan celebration of cultural difference, diversity, and inclusivity—but also crucially as diplomatic agents helping to forge solidarity between diverse members to present a unified response to an exceptional terrorist threat. As Vicuña Gonzalez (2013, 218) explains, "in the post 9/11 world, tourists were reentrenched as the universal liberal subject whose mobility, modernity and gift of economic hope needed to be secured against the encroachments of barbarism." This distinction resonated clearly in Bush's us-versus-them worldview but also in the expert and academic communities seeking to develop the tourist industry's comprehensive response to the exceptional threat terrorism posed (Blake and Sinclair 2003; Bonham, Edmonds, and Mak 2006; Fall and Grey 2005; Fainstein 2002; Floyd et al. 2003; Goodrich 2002; Mansfield and Pizam 2006). Peter Tarlow (2006a; see also Tarlow 2006b), an expert on the relationship between tourism and terrorism who frequently advises the U.S. government, provided the most succinct and unapologetic distillation of this binary view: terrorists are those who engage in violent acts (including the targeting of tourists) because they come from uncivilized, "medieval societies," whereas innocent tourists are targeted because they come from modern, civilized, Western societies. The sociological characteristics of the "medieval societies" that give rise to terrorists are the debasement of women, a xenophobic fear or hatred for the Other, the discouragement of travel, a rejection of capitalism, and a rejection of individualism. By contrast, the sociological characteristics of the modern societies from which tourism arises are the exact opposite: "we" embrace other cultures, encourage travel, promote capitalist forms of economy, encourage individual expressions of choice, and, of course, allow women to play a major role in the tourism industry (Tarlow 2006a, 82–83; see also Schwarz 2006; Sönmez 1998; Sönmez, Apostolopoulos, and Tarlow 1999).

These expert voices fed into government and policy debates on how to resuscitate a tourism industry that flatlined after 9/11. Mimicking a program that took place after the Second World War, the U.S. government introduced a number of structural and financial incentives to get Americans traveling again, restore the industry's pre-9/11 profit levels, and help rebuild the global alliances that had perished in the ruins of the Twin Towers (Blake and Sinclair 2003; Endy 2004, 33–54; Fanstein 2002; Goodrich 2002; World Tourism Organization 2001, 26–30). These economic incentives were explicitly framed by wider foreign policy goals: U.S. policy makers were unapologetic about politicizing tourism and utilizing its capacity as a soft power (Nye 2004) to pursue foreign policy objectives. As an ideological, cultural, and noncoercive force capable of persuading other cultures into an American worldview, global tourism became a highly effective form of people-to-people cultural diplomacy that cemented the values of a global community united against an exceptional terrorist threat. For example, George W. Bush (2001b) added holidays and vacations to the list of other consumer practices that were considered the "ultimate repudiation of terrorism." In his famous "Let's Roll" speech in November 2001, Bush declared, "Those who travel abroad for business or vacation can all be ambassadors of American values. Ours is a great story, and we must tell it—through our words and through our deeds" (Bush 2001b). Bush's appeal suggested that it was incumbent upon Americans to travel abroad to demonstrate the desirable values of "their" culture to Others (e.g., freedom, tolerance, diversity, a love of travel and cultural exchange) and—to paraphrase Nye (2004)—to convince well-disposed global Others that they wanted the same things that Americans did. As Americans openly wondered after 9/11, "Why does the world hate us?" those 21 percent of Americans with passports—especially members of the cosmopolitan elite who had actually traveled abroad—could ask this question with greater force: "Why *us,* who have made the effort to learn about your cultures, stay in your hotels, visit your tourist attractions, and get to know you?" (Granitsas 2005). Within this logic, the events of 9/11 actually *strengthened* the diplomatic role of American tourists: their claim of solidarity ("we are just like you: we, too, have been subjected to terrorist violence") made them the most convincing proselytizers of a cosmopolitan global community united against terrorism.

On October 12, 2002, a busy Saturday night in Kuta Beach on Bali, many Western tourists were drinking in Paddy's Pub or partying across the street in the Sari Nightclub when a suicide bomber from the militant Islamic group Jemaah Islamiyah detonated a car bomb in the intersection between the two establishments. Many tourists managed to escape the carnage and find help in local clinics and hospitals, but many did not; 202 people were killed in the Bali bombing, 80 percent of the casualties being international tourists in their twenties and thirties, with more than half from Australia and Britain (Hitchcock and Darma Putra 2007, 137). Just over a month later, an all-terrain vehicle driven by members of al-Itihaad al-Islamiya, a radical Islamic group linked to al-Qaeda, crashed through the front gates of the Paradise Hotel Resort in Mombasa, Kenya, and blew up in the lobby. A few kilometers away at Moi International Airport, two surface-to-air missiles were launched at a charter plane returning holiday makers to Israel. The missiles missed their runway target, but thirteen people were killed in the lobby of the Paradise Hotel: three Israeli tourists and ten local Kenyans. These events threatened the tourism industry's fledgling recovery from 9/11 and challenged the nascent global solidarity that had been mobilized by tourists in the previous year. While similar efforts were made to reassure tourists of the safety of these destinations, the scale of the Bali bombing intensified Bush's "with us or against us" discourse so that the terrorists were *even more* exceptional and dangerous, and all members of the global community were *even more* vulnerable (Gurtner 2007). With headlines such as "Nabbed Bali Bomber Still Laughing at the Dead," the mainstream Western media depicted the perpetrators as having no recognizable humanity and their acts as exceptional cases of evil (Post Wire Services 2002; see also Kabir 2006; Noble 2008). Even media outlets considered more progressive in their editorial stance took part in this reductive framing:

> [Bali] was, whichever way it is looked at, an inhuman deed by people who, whatever their convictions and motives, demonstrated *a lack of common feeling that places them beyond the pale of any concept of society*.... Defeating terrorism must be the shared work of all humankind—for all humankind is its prey. Our common humanity demands that it be so. (*Guardian* 2002, 19, emphasis added; see also Buruma 2002, 5; *Times* 2002, 25)

The limits of the global community are quite clear: by placing terrorists outside of the "common feeling" shared by "all humankind" (i.e., beyond the pale), terrorists are rendered exceptional in their "inhumanity." This framing enabled the Australian media and government to claim the "peaceful" island of Bali for itself rather than leave it to perish in the increasingly militant brand of Islam developing in Indonesia. Within the dominant Australian discourse, the Bali bombing constituted "not only mass murder, but also an attack on the thin sovereignty extended over Bali by (mainly) Australian tourists and the destruction of an idyll central to a certain *Australian* way of life" (Philpott 2005, emphasis added). As then Australian prime minister John Howard warned, "people should get out of their minds that it can't happen here; it can, and it has happened to our own on our doorstep" (Agence France Press 2002; see also Hitchcock and Darma Putra 2007, 137; Pedlar 2002).

Given the exceptional nature of the terrorist threat, the job of fighting terrorism could not just be left to Western and American citizens traveling abroad: this fight required everybody from around the world who was committed to the values of freedom, travel, and cultural exchange—including all those who work in the tourism and leisure industries. Thus, Western and American tourists were placed *on the same side* as those "exotic" hosts who served them meals, cleaned their hotel rooms, danced for them, had sex with them, and sold them souvenirs. However, because that inclusive "we" was marked by such obvious differences in wealth, privilege, and power, it required a further production of solidarity to suture otherwise incommensurate and radically unequal subjects into a coherent and unified collective. For example, it was common for media representations to focus on what united the victims:

> They were all different. But what they shared transcended the particulars of colour, language and belief. All were innocent of any offence, oblivious to any threat. All were unsuspecting of any conspiracy, all unprotected and at their ease.... Such inhumanity makes victims of us all. (*Guardian* 2002, 19)

The democratization of victimhood after 9/11 (what Philip Roth famously referred to as America's "gratuitous victim mentality") was enabled by focusing on what the victims shared (i.e., their innocence) as opposed to the differences that might separate them (Leith 2002, 21; see also Hitchcock and Darma Putra 2007, 141–49). This forging of victim solidarity was even more explicit in mainstream media accounts of the Mombasa attack, which portrayed Israeli tourists as *doubly* victimized—first by the "Palestinian militants" who target their everyday lives at home, and now by terrorists who target their holidays abroad (Clayton and McGrory 2002, 1; Fisher 2002, 1; Moore 2002, A01; Seenan 2002, 2).

As Bush's "with us or against us" framing resonated in expert, government, and media responses to Bali and Mombasa, tourists were continually positioned *within* a cosmopolitan global community fighting terror. As people-to-people diplomats—indeed, as Bush's "ambassadors of American values"—tourists were best placed to generate solidarity between themselves and their hosts all over the world and thus help solidify the external boundaries and internal identity of liberal rule. The problem, of course, is that neither tourism nor terrorism can be contained by reductive framings such as "with us or against us" because the heterogeneity, multiplicity, and complexity of the subjects gathered into an "us" or a "them" will always exceed the limits imposed on them.

Tourism, Terrorism, and Deterritorialization

While Bush's "with us or against us" framing continued to resonate a year after 9/11, the explicit targeting of tourists in the bombings of Bali and Mombasa troubled this binary. As documented by *Guardian* political cartoonist Steve Bell (2002) on the day after the Mombasa bombing (see Figure 31), neither tourism nor terrorism could be contained by Bush's dyad. Like all of Bell's cartoons, this one operates in several registers (Dodds 2007). While it plays on Bush's persona as a simpleton easily confused by weighty geopolitical matters (Bush is often depicted as a monkey), it also represents the genuinely difficult problem of how to address the unwanted aspects of globalization (e.g., terrorism) without sacrificing its benefits (e.g., tourism, cultural exchange, open borders). Bush's confusion between "Turrrism" and "Turrism" is an explicit acknowledgment that tourists and terrorists occupy the *same* global spaces and traverse the *same* routes and networks. Starting from Bush's confusion, I want to suggest that properly understanding the deterritorialized conjunctions of tourism and terrorism requires two things: first, that we interrogate the political work that is done by reductive framings such as Bush's "with us or against us," and second, that we engage in critiques that foreground what is *political* about these deterritorialized practices.

The first move exposes the liberal orthodoxies and cosmopolitan fantasies that sustain benign accounts of a global community held together in solidarity against terrorism. As critical scholars of cosmopolitanism rightly argue, such a reductive category can only be sustained by (1) effacing long-standing structural inequalities between those privileged subjects who set the terms for membership within the global community and the rest of the world who are invited to join and (2) constituting the liberal order through repeated deployments of violence against illiberal forces both within and outside the community (Bigo and Tsoukala 2008; Calhoun 2002; Cheah and Robbins 1998; Clifford 1997, 35–36; Derrida

CONNECTING TOURISM AND TERRORISM 261

FIGURE 31. Steve Bell's "Turrism" cartoon from the *Guardian*. Courtesy of Steve Bell.

2001; Douzinas 2007; Harvey 2000; Hindess 2008; Jabri 2007; Neal 2009). It is within this critical framework that tourism can be politicized for its reproduction of dominant geopolitical imaginaries (e.g., us vs. them) and further entrenchment of long-standing global inequalities. The potent cocktail of solidarity, innocence, and victimhood that was mobilized after terrorists targeted holiday makers on Bali and Mombasa stripped Western tourists of any agency or responsibility in sustaining the material inequalities between them and their hosts. As Bianchi (2007, 69) rightly argues, "the assumption of the tourist's unquestioned innocence implies that the phenomenon of tourism itself is somehow suspended above or external to the machinations of state power and geopolitics" (see also Nicholson-Lord 2002, 22–24; Phipps 1999; 2004, 83; Vicuña Gonzalez 2013, 218). It is precisely this "suspended" position that allows any unpalatable behavior of Western tourists—the kind that might exacerbate global inequalities—to be excused in the name of creating solidarity and countering the exceptional terrorist threat. For example, while Indonesians might despair at "drunk young infidels from Sydney and Billericay barfing all over ancient Asian culture," they put up with such distasteful behavior to receive the benefits of being included in a global community that will protect them from terrorism (Buruma 2002, 5).

These constructions of solidarity, innocence, and victimhood covered over the fact that the Balinese waiters, bartenders, cooks, and maintenance staff who perished in the Sari Nightclub bombing were working in a disco that otherwise excluded Indonesians (Buruma 2002, 5; see also Robinson 2002, 16). They also silenced important moments of complexity, struggle, and resistance within the Balinese community itself, for example, the Sari Nightclub at the center of the bomb was owned and managed by a Chinese businessman and had been the site of interethnic tensions between local Balinese and migrant workers who were operating in both the formal and informal tourist economies (Hitchcock and Darma Putra 2007, 121, 129–30; see also Tarplee 2008). Moreover, local groups were increasingly vocal against a government campaign luring tourists back to the island with the slogan "Bali for the World," arguing that Bali was not just for the enjoyment of rich global tourists but also for those who lived and worked there (Hitchcock and Darma Putra 2007, 125). The local context of Mombasa demonstrated similar erasures of tension and complexity as it was assimilated into the dominant construction of global solidarity. Leaving aside the apportioning of guilt and innocence with respect to the Israeli treatment of Palestinians, the middle-class Israeli tourists who traveled to Kenya on their chartered flight exacerbated serious financial, cultural, religious, and racial asymmetries that already existed between the majority Muslim population in Mombasa and those who visited the all-inclusive resorts north and south of the city center. The Israeli-owned and operated Paradise Hotel was not anomalous in the region, as all tourist businesses in Mombasa were owned by foreign multinationals and/or non-Muslims. Like the other hotels and resorts, Paradise was one of many well-protected tourist enclaves that minimized contact between Western visitors and Kenya's Muslim population and protected wealthy tourists from having to face the endemic poverty that surrounds Mombasa itself (Bianchi 2003, 9–10). Moreover, the tensions that led to the Mombasa bombing were well established by November

2002 and were routinely exacerbated by the arrival of American soldiers stationed in East Africa who used Mombasa's beach resorts as a favored R&R site (Nahdi 2002, 24). Indeed, it is not difficult to see how the "gambling, prostitution and excessive alcohol" enjoyed by the American soldiers on leave upset the local Muslim population (Nahdi 2002, 24; Bianchi 2003, 9; Risen 2002, 11). Similar to the depictions of Bali a month previously, the international media's desire to privilege the stories of innocent Israeli tourist-victims effaced the complex demographics of Mombasa itself (e.g., Muslim neighborhoods, multiple ethnic communities, foreign businesspeople, NGO workers, ship workers, and American soldiers on leave) and further silenced the main victims of the bombing—the local dancers (Wollaston 2002, 1).

Watching and Being Watched: The Normalization of Airport Surveillance

Demonstrating how articulations of a diverse and welcoming global community—no matter how inclusive—*continue* to reproduce familiar arrangements of power is the first step in politicizing the deterritorialized practices of tourism and terrorism. It shows that the exceptional nature of the terrorist threat does not obviate, preclude, or excuse the asymmetries that have long been deeply entrenched within the global order. What the exceptional nature of the terrorist threat *does* do, however, is produce new articulations of power that circulate in affective, embodied, biopolitical, behavioral, and material registers. Thus, the second step in making sense of the deterritorialized conjunction of tourism and terrorism is to understand how our familiar binaries of power (e.g., inside-outside, self-other, identity-difference, domestic-international) have become multiple, dispersed, mobile, and heterogeneous. This fragmentation *intensifies* rather than decreases the capacity of these power arrangements to order our lifeworlds: as the singular becomes multiple and mobile, we are faced with real challenges in terms of how we resist articulations of violence that are both complex and adaptive. Scholars using Foucault's notion of a security apparatus have been at the forefront of analyzing those unseen registers where calculations about danger, risk, and threat take root and by connecting the techniques of governance mobilized within the borders of liberal rule (e.g., CCTV cameras, biometric passports) to the illiberal practices directed outward (e.g., interventions in Iraq and Afghanistan) (Amoore and De Goede 2008; Aradau and Van Munster 2007; Opitz 2011; Neal 2009; Salter 2008a). Using this work as a starting point, I want to analyze how the securitization of the tourism industry after 9/11 made itself felt most explicitly in the modes of surveillance deployed at airports. Aimed at distinguishing more accurately between safe and dangerous bodies, new techniques and technologies of surveillance enrolled traveling bodies into two dispositions: they were self-appointed *watchers* actively looking out for deviant bodies, and they were *watched* subjects passively accepting the visual and material infrastructure put in place to survey all traveling bodies. These watching–watched dispositions soon extended to the wider reaches of the tourist industry in ways that transformed the material infrastructure of international hotels and explicitly mobilized the resident labor force (e.g., cleaners, hosts, receptionists).

The widespread culture of fear that circulates through our everyday lives and affective registers (Ahmed 2004, 62–81) deploys a logic of visuality that normalizes dominant dispositions of watching and being watched. This new visuality cannot be understood through conventional or "perspectival" modes of seeing; indeed, the passive optics that carried us from the Renaissance through the Enlightenment and into modernity are problematic because they separate the privileged observer from the observed object. As Virilio (1989, 2–3) has argued, we are now operating within an "eyeless vision" in which the hierarchical Big Brother panopticon identified by Foucault has been dispersed, intensified, and amplified by our desire to watch others, our willing submission to be watched by a variety of authorities, and the new technologies that allow these watching–being watched dispositions to flourish (Caluya 2010; Friedberg 2004, 188; Haggerty 2006; Murikami-Wood 2002). As Jordan Crandall (2005, 24) has argued, this transformation throws up incredibly difficult questions about the contemporary relationship between power and visuality: "it is never quite clear who is controlling whom and to what degree we acquiesce, or take pleasure. What is the difference between observation and surveillance? When does seeing become policing? When does control turn into submission?"

One prominent site at which tourism, security, and this new logic of visuality come together most powerfully is, of course, the surveillance infrastructures and screening technologies now used routinely at major airports. These include the now ubiquitous X-ray machines that screen bodies and carry-on bags (and now shoes, belts, and coats); the biometric software used for facial recognition, gait recognition, and retinal scanning; and the backscatter machines that visually penetrate a traveler's clothing. It is unsurprising that this apparatus continues to cause much debate about the proper balance between freedom and security in the War on Terror: are these technologies eroding our civil liberties or increasing national security? Are governments using 9/11 as an excuse to increase their powers of surveillance (Lyon 2002; 2006a; 2007a; 2007b; Surveillance Study Centre 2014)? What particularly interests me is the extent to which the visual elements of this surveillance apparatus enable, disrupt, and transform the asymmetrical categorization of safe and deviant subject positions at airports. For Morgan and Pritchard (2005, 121; see also Adey 2004; Lloyd 2003; Lyon 2003; Salter 2007; 2008b),

> surveillance and security are now central to the international tourist experience. Indeed, those key gateways of transnational mobility—the world's airports—can be seen as the perfect metaphor of the new surveillance, where people who are by definition out-of-place and out-of-time, are scrutinized, identified and sorted into those who belong and those who do not.

How do the visual technologies deployed in this "sorting" process encourage their users to understand themselves and the subjects they are scrutinizing within the us–them identity categories and for us–against us political logics made familiar by the War on Terror? How does the culture of fear underscoring the War on Terror produce, categorize, and manage subjects as primarily safe or dangerous agents? While I certainly agree with the protests against passenger profiling based on gender, sexuality, and race, too often I think these arguments lapse into a reductive account of visuality and power that assumes one is either watching (and therefore powerful) or watched (and therefore powerless). I want to think a little bit more carefully about the visuality entailed in the airport screening process and how it is negotiated by tourist-subjects. For me, restricting our questions about security technology to the obvious identity categories of gender, sexuality, and race misses the extent to which the visuality at work in airports assumes a completely different kind of identity, one that "is now so fluid as to be formless—it's a pattern that coheres momentarily and then dissolves" (Fuller and Harley 2004, 84; see also Adey 2009; Amoore and Hall 2009; Wilcox 2015, 104–30).

One of the key features of this new visuality is its anticipatory quality—"a form of being seen that knows us first and faster"—that simultaneously predicts and makes plans to intervene in our future (Crandall 2005, 20; see also Amoore 2006; Anderson 2010a; Aradau and Van Munster 2008; De Goede and Randalls 2009; Virilio 1989, 3). Surveillance technologies are not placed in airports to catch terrorists after they have committed an offence; rather, as Louise Amoore (2007, 221) argues, they are "primarily about *foresight* and the anticipation of the event":

> in these systems, the assumption is that it is possible to "build a complete picture of a person," to quite literally see who they are before they board a plane or transfer money, by relating them to the norms of a wider population and identifying their degree of deviance. (see also Ewald 2002)

Those norm-deviant logics are, of course, never neutral because "normal" subjects can only be produced and secured to the extent that they can simultaneously produce and secure "deviant" subjects (Morgan and Pritchard 2005, 125; see also Amoore 2009, 28). The War on Terror's culture of fear—anything could happen, to anyone, anywhere, at any time—is precisely what creates the conditions for this anticipatory visuality to flourish in places like airports. New surveillance technologies are reassuring because they use complex algorithms to build "a complete picture of a person" who *could* potentially pose a risk, fit a "deviant" identity, and therefore commit an act of violence or a crime. Under this anticipatory logic, everyone is designated as risky: everyone is a potential suspect because all of our everyday behaviors (e.g., movements caught on CCTV cameras, recorded financial transactions, facial or gait profiles) could be reassembled to fit the already designated characteristics of a person of interest and quite possibly a "deviant" (Amoore 2014, 93). As Gillian Fuller (2003) argues, this anticipatory logic absolutely punctures the assumed innocence of the tourist: "I have been scanned, checked and made to feel guilty. I could be a body containing wrong bodies (a smuggler), a body that could explode (a 'terrorist'), or I could be a body with no rights (an 'illegal alien')... one thing is quite sure: 'the subject' is definitely in trouble at the airport."

The fundamentally anticipatory character of surveillance technology is changing not just how state and other authorities are watching us but how we are watching each other. This is why Amoore (2007, 216) argues that our post-9/11 world has produced a "vigilant visuality"—a watchful politics that encourages all subjects to *pay attention* to any "suspicious behavior" and to report anything "out of the ordinary." To avoid becoming a person of interest and designated as a potential deviant, criminal, or terrorist, you had better be the one doing the watching and the designating—you had better be *on the side* of those deploying surveillance technology. Such vigilance is much more difficult when one is traveling to a foreign destination, not just because it is hard to tell when and where simple cultural difference gets coded as deviant but also because the act of traveling after 9/11 has become fraught with uncertainty and fear. Unsurprisingly, these anxieties have, on occasion, tipped the scales from vigilant visuality into vigilante action. For example, in August 2006, several British holiday makers refused to allow their flight from Malaga to Manchester to take off until two men "they feared were terrorists" were forcibly removed from the plane (Leake and Chapman 2006, 1). As one British couple explained,

> in the gate waiting area, people had been talking about these two, who looked really suspicious with their heavy clothing, scruffy, rough, appearance and long hair. Some of the older children, who had seen the terror alert on television, were starting to mutter things like, "Those two look like they're bombers."... While we were waiting, everyone agreed the men looked dodgy. Some passengers were very panicky and in tears. There was a lot of talking about terrorists. (1)

The employees of Monarch Airlines complied with the wishes of its vigilant passengers, and the two innocent men were removed from the flight. The actions of passengers and Monarch employees were widely—and rightly—condemned by the U.K. press, Muslim leaders, and British politicians (Akbar 2006, 12; Brough and Bone 2006, 8, 12, 20; Kumi 2006, 7), but what this incident illustrates is how willing tourists are to comply with the War on Terror's agenda and become "vigilant watchers" on its behalf.

Over and above what this example reveals about racism (especially in Britain), it also tells us something important about the pleasure subjects get from exercising vigilance. The passengers of Monarch flight 613 validated each other, and were validated by the airline, as good citizens who were doing their part in combating terrorism by being extra watchful. Tourists didn't just take pleasure in watching out for "suspicious" subjects, they also *enjoyed* the moment when their watching paid off and they found a real live "terrorist." What we have to remember, of course, is that the scopophilic pleasure of watching out for deviance—a pleasure that engages our bodies as much as our desires—is always attended by a concomitant pleasure of *being watched*. In airports, tourists and travelers enjoy performing roles and exhibiting particular behaviors for the ever-present watching eyes of CCTV cameras and security personnel. What particularly interests me here are the feelings and sensations of pleasure mobilized when watching—experiences that cannot be fully understood if we ignore the physical workings of bodies and how those bodies respond to security environments (Lyon 2006b).

My own concerns about how we might understand the role of the tourist in wider networks of security, visuality, and surveillance are echoed in Jordan Crandall's (2005) claim that a primarily disciplinary understanding of surveillance technologies is limited. Certainly Foucault's account of visuality, especially his concept of the panopticon, is useful when discussing airport screening technologies, but it fails to account properly for how subjects not only willingly invest in the gazes that oppress them but also take pleasure in that subjection. Foucault's later work began to excavate the relationship between erotics, power, pleasures, and affects, but as Crandall (2005, 20–24) suggests, new visual technologies like biometrics require new kinds of thinking about the circulations of watching and being watched:

> We are talking about something that is not unidirectional but circuitous. It is not only a form of control: it is a medium of self-reflection and self-awareness. Contrary to much political discourse, it is not always seen by us as intrusive. It can be a comforting gaze, part of a new sociality and filled with erotic charge.... To be watched and tracked is to be cared for.

With respect to the airport, then, new surveillance technologies are comforting because they give us an opportunity to confirm our identities (i.e., they make us "self-aware" and "self-reflexive") and have those identities thoroughly, visually, and microscopically checked—and authorized—by the state. With this in mind, any anxiety caused by the War on Terror's anticipatory visuality is neutralized by the "comforting gaze" that surveillance technologies can provide. Indeed, such a paternal infrastructure is reassuring rather than intrusive: it suggests that along with the anticipatory anxiety provoked by the airport screening process—"it could be me! I could be a terrorist!"—there is also a powerful alleviation of that anxiety when we relinquish our agency into the caring arms of a security apparatus that can *see* and *order* everyone properly. Reading this surrender of agency through a disciplinary understanding of surveillance suggests that these visual technologies turn all tourists into "docile patriots" who are wholly governed by the screening process (Lisle 2003; Puar and Rai 2002). Such a reading misses the feelings of pleasure and relief that are experienced when we relinquish our agency to a paternal security apparatus. I use *relief* deliberately: this is precisely the moment we believe that the multiple potentialities available in the War on Terror's visuality ("it could be me!") are finally arrested. We experience a temporary pleasure because our identities are—momentarily—rendered actual rather than potential (i.e., we are confirmed as safe travelers rather than as potential terrorists).

Gillian Fuller and photographer Ross Harley carefully explore how the affective register that gives rise to such pleasures is mobilized by the surveillance infrastructure of airports. The anxieties and pleasures provoked by airport screening are not just about watching and being watched; rather, embedded in the airport's optic gaze are the sensations of touching and being touched:

> Transit space might be full of visual media (like signs), but we experience them through the processes of movement, which necessarily changes our vision. As we extend ourselves across networks we no longer see the big picture. We constantly seem to interact with fragments. Our involvement with networks is so close that our vision becomes more tactile or "haptic" rather than merely optical. (Fuller and Harley 2004, 81)[4]

Fuller explores how the collapse of seeing and touching—what they call "haptic visuality"—requires a mode of transparency that is currently expressed in the architectural preference for glass and steel. Here, watching and being watched dispositions are no longer singular: they coexist and overlap with one another in a way that makes the space of the airport both "cubist" and "remixable." Think, for example, of how we move along one glassed-in passage on our way to an airplane and look at passengers disembarking from a different plane and walking through an adjacent glassed-in walkway. For Fuller (2008, 162), this mode of transparency is a "politico-aesthetic method" that integrates bodies into the object-world—the "biosphere skin"—of the airport: "vision is no longer just spectacular, no longer just two way (either real or imagined), no longer a fleeting glance or a sustained gaze, but precise, targeted, pattern-matched, and integrated logically and practically into movement systems." These arguments suggest that connections between visuality and touch make no sense without an understanding of the mobilities that keep bodies, objects, and atmospheres constantly in circulation at airports. Of particular interest to Fuller are those moments when the skin of the body and the skin of the object-world (i.e., the airport) come into contact. These include obvious points of connection (e.g., haptic check-in screens, portable security wands) but also less obvious points (e.g., the minute movement of the optical nerve as it focuses on a shop window display or mobile phone). Indeed, "one no longer looks at the screen, one operates through it" (Fuller 2008, 167). The strange conjunction of vision, touch, and mobility at work in the airport finally dispenses with modernity's ocularcentric vision and instigates a new kind of being-with between bodies, objects, technologies, infrastructure, and atmosphere. For Fuller and Harley (2004, 82), airports constitute a new kind of pulsing relationality: "bodies and machines measure each other—scanning each other constantly, calibrating, adjusting and entwining in all kinds of new biotechnical rhythms."

Fuller and Harley are right, I think, to position the airport as a biopolitical site in which codes, networks, and flows predominate—an indispensable node in our networked society that helps to mobilize, disperse, and manage new patterns of entry and exit (82). It is here, in the trajectory from the airport microcosm out into the world, that we can begin to link the haptic visuality of surveillance technology into sites of more explicit geopolitical violence such as Afghanistan and Iraq. For Lisa Parks (2007, 192), airport screening is only one particular node in a wider global security apparatus:

> We cannot separate the practice of stateside close sensing at the airport checkpoint from the more excessive and violent versions of scrutiny and interrogation that have emerged in the midst of the US-led war on global terror.... Its most extreme version may be in Abu Ghraib prison or Guantanamo Bay where detainees have been subject to the same kinds of scanning, imaging, profiling techniques and then brutally tortured and photographed. Airport screening practices might be understood as symptomatic, then, of a broader security regime in which looking authorizes touching and touching can become torture.

This suggests that all travelers who submit to a national security regime's apparatus of surveillance at the airport are both complicit in, and connected to, the displaced acts of torture that such a security regime perpetrates in distant places like Abu Ghraib and Guantánamo Bay. This is exactly my point: the place where we abandon our anxieties and enter into the relaxed, pleasurable mode of tourism—the airport security checkpoint—is precisely where the War on Terror's culture of fear finally captures us. This is the threshold that allows us to see the long chains of association that connect privileged Western holiday makers to distant victims of torture: both are subjected to the same security apparatus, but in radically different ways. I am not saying that the haptic visuality deployed at airports is equivalent to that deployed in Abu Ghraib, but I am saying that more work needs to be done revealing the asymmetry of body–object–infrastructure–atmosphere relations that reconstructed within those long chains of association.

Hotel Battlefield: Producing and Protecting Soft Targets

What emerged out of the detailed critical examinations of airports was a heightened attention to the assemblages of human agents and the nonhuman world. By turning their attention to matter—buildings, roads, cars, phones, passports, clothing, drones—critical security scholars have shown how objects, materialities, technologies, and infrastructures are not empty receptacles of human desires but rather have their own vitality, agency, and capacity (Acuto and Curtis 2013; Adey et al. 2013; Anderson 2010b; Aradau 2010; Coward 2010; Lippert and O'Connor 2003; Salter 2015a; 2015b). The problem with official responses to the exceptional terrorist threat was their understanding that the objects being protected (e.g., critical infrastructures, cultural landmarks) were detached from and subordinate to the humans who live within and use those materialities. This subordination of materiality characterized how governments, militaries, and private security companies used the language of soft targets to securitize spaces of leisure and travel after the bombings in Bali and Mombasa. Defined as public or semi-public (some degree of restricted access) facilities where large numbers of people congregate under relatively loose security, soft targets allow terrorists to avoid the heightened security of public buildings, achieve widespread media coverage, and kill large numbers of Western citizens (STRATFOR 2009, 1–2; Eyerman 1998). Like the attack on Luxor in 1997, Bali and Mombasa revealed that mundane spaces of leisure, such as hotels, tourist attractions, heritage sites, and museums, have become some of the most desirable and easily accessible soft targets of choice for terrorist groups (STRATFOR 2009). As one tabloid headline proclaimed, "Every tourist resort around the world, within striking distance of a Muslim country, is a potential target" (Toolis 2002, 6; see also Fahdi 2002, 24). By claiming that the everyday infrastructure of tourism—hotels, tourist attractions, beaches, museums, shopping districts—had become the new front line in the War on Terror, government, academic, media, and industry experts were able to comprehensively intervene in the tourist industry to defend these soft targets, make them more resilient, and therefore ensure that "we" could continue to enjoy secure vacations all over the world. The language of soft targets became a compelling way to make sense of those out-of-the-way places that are perfect for both tourists and terrorists:

> Holiday destinations such as the Philippines, Bali and Mombasa are soft targets, their porous borders enabling easy access for al-Qaeda operatives wanting to link up with local groups. Such places may be "paradise" to tourists, but to the suicide bomber that word means something altogether different. This clash of meanings raises issues of globalisation that go beyond the war on terror. (Foden 2002, 2)

The language of soft targets was deployed to convince tourists that it was possible to order, control, and police the deterritorialized borders bequeathed by globalization. Reassured that "our" responses to terrorism were as ubiquitous, robust, and lethal as the terrorists', holiday makers could continue to enjoy vacations in destinations that were both exotic *and* safe.

The problem with the language of soft targets is that it reduces tourism and leisure's vast labor force, its wealth generation, its cultural capital, its advertising and marketing campaigns, its increasingly comprehensive insurance arrangements, and its ever-regenerating fantasy landscapes to objects of utility that can be calculated, assessed, and evaluated for their level of vulnerability in the face of terrorism. This comprehensive subordination of the entire industry to a security calculus does not just curtail the exotic fantasies of tourists; it directs, orders, and controls the possibilities of where they can and cannot move and actively transforms the materiality of those trajectories. These changes have been clearest in the entrance architecture, lobby design, reception space, software technologies, and security provisions of international hotels. These havens of leisure, pleasure, and relaxation have always featured in geopolitical landscapes and been part of wider security infrastructures. Think, for example, of how hotels are requisitioned as troop barracks during war, how they function as a "neutral" space for peace negotiations and diplomacy, and how they constantly host the "discrepant cosmopolitanisms" of tourists, diplomats, spies, protestors, laborers, and vagabonds (Fregonese 2012; see also the Hotel Geopolitics Facebook community at https://www.facebook.com/hotelgeopolitics?filter=1). After 9/11, the securitization of hotels into safe enclaves has been central to the way cities and urban infrastructures have been transformed to achieve greater resilience against terrorism (Brock and Walker 2008; Chan and Lam 2013; Clifton 2012; Coaffee and Murikami-Wood 2006; Gunaratna 2008; Mills, Meyers, and Byun 2010; Morgan and Pritchard 2009; STRATFOR 2009). Like the ring of steel constructed around the City of London, hotels have increased their perimeter security through large concrete blocks, manned security checkposts, automatic bollards, and electronic barriers that increase the standoff distance between the private space of the hotel and its public surroundings (Gunaratna 2008; Clifton 2012). These material fortifications have changed the orientation of hotels toward their local environments so that the familiar markers of luxury, hospitality, and welcome (i.e., "please come and stay!") have been eclipsed by more prominent markers of security and surveillance that extend from external perimeters all the way through the hotel's servicescape and into each individual guest room (Hilliard and Baloglu 2008). Within this trajectory, external security barriers, CCTV cameras, security guards, and metal detectors prepare hotel guests for increased security measures within hotel walls, including even more CCTV cameras and security guards, data surveillance linked to check-in, key-activated elevators, automatic door locks, increased background checks on employees, detailed evacuation plans, emergency lighting, bombproof Kevlar wallpaper, and shatterproof glass (Clifton 2012; Groenenboom and Jones 2003; Gunaratna 2008; Jungsun, Brewer, and Bernhard 2008; Sim and Jevanathan 2012; Smith 2003; Sorrell 2009). Of course, because hotels are central to the wider preemptive network implementing pretravel data surveillance and screening procedures, the securitization of hotel guests takes place well before they see the hotel's front facade, walk into its lobby, and become entangled within the building's security matrix. This network forms part of the invisible architecture through which tourists are prepared in advance to become securitized subjects; indeed, they are *already known* as prearranged collections of data (Lyon 2003; Morgan and Pritchard 2005). Traveling bodies have become so habituated to the security procedures now used in airports (e.g., body scanners, physical searches, luggage restrictions) that they *expect* similar procedures when they arrive at their hotels (Feickert et al. 2006).

Tourism and Lateral Surveillance: Risk, Privatization, and Counterterrorism

Like all efforts to bring subjects, objects, spaces, and futures into the orbit of the War on Terror, the securitization of the tourism industry is driven by a particular understanding of risk management. Critical scholars have demonstrated how calculations of risk are central to the War on Terror's security apparatus: not only do they provide precise ways of identifying and measuring threats, they also promote the belief that by managing risk, current and future insecurities can be eradicated (Amoore and De Goede 2008; Aradau and Van Munster 2007; De Goede 2008; Salter 2008). Tourism studies scholars and those seeking to provide technical and managerial solutions to the vulnerability of the industry are attentive to the need for better risk management. As Reisinger and Mavondo (2005, 212) argue, "tourism research must take up the challenge of risk assessment. If the tourism industry is going to be prosperous, then tourism researchers must make efforts to increase the industry's understanding of risk perception." The equation that drives this research is very simple: the more risky a hotel, resort, or destination is perceived to be, the less tourism it will attract and the less profit it will generate; therefore the job of researchers and experts is to calculate risk probabilities and scenarios within the tourism industry and provide workable proposals to help reduce high levels of risk. Scholars have developed risk assessment models to identify how travelers perceive risk (e.g., risk aware, risk neutral, risk averse) and then mapped those risks onto consular warning sheets, travel advisories, global risk maps, and detailed risk registers (Floyd and Pennington-Gray 2004; Floyd et al. 2003; Lepp and Gibson 2003; Reisiger and Mavondo 2005; Sackett and Botteril 2006; Wilks 2006). Similarly, risk management models aimed at decreasing perceptions of risk and increasing levels of tourism use historical examples of crisis and disaster management to show how destinations have coped, either successfully or unsuccessfully, with terrorist incidents and political violence (Blake and Sinclair 2001; Glaesser 2003; Prideaux 2003; Ritchie 2004). These examples are then used to propose best-practice solutions for how hotels, resorts, museums, and tourist attractions should implement strategies for risk assessment and management to restore consumer confidence.

One of the common strategies emerging from this literature is the provision of counterterrorism training for tourism employees, especially hotel workers. For example, regional responses to the 2002 Bali bombing coordinated the various risk management procedures adopted by governments, policy makers, industry professionals, and private companies and proposed counterterrorism training for the Balinese tourism industry (Robertson, Kean, and Moore 2006, 41–43). Similarly in the United Kingdom, the National Counter Terrorism Security Office (NaCTSO), in conjunction with the Association of Chief Police Officers, published a comprehensive information document on the counterterrorism measures to be implemented in hotels and restaurants (Association of Chief Police Officers 2008). This was folded into the wider CONTEST 2 counterterrorism strategy in March 2009 as NaCTSO began to provide "free workshops in all major towns and cities across the UK to show hoteliers how to plan, prepare, prevent and recover from a possible terrorist attack" (Jamieson 2010; National Counter Terrorism Security Offices, n.d.). Defending the provision of counterterrorism training to such a vast labor force, then home secretary Jacqui Smith commented, "That's not about snooping, that's about the widest possible range of people helping to keep us safe in this country" (Percival 2009). In the United States, the largest program for counterterrorism training within hotels is the online Eye on Awareness: Hotel Security and Anti-Terrorism Training program, developed by the American Hotel and Lodging Educational Institute (AHLEI) in collaboration with the Department of Homeland Security (DHS) (American Hotel and Lodging Educational Institute 2011a; 2013; Smith 2003). The program was designed to complement the DHS's wider post-9/11 "If you see something, say something" campaign aimed at getting American citizens to report anything suspicious to an official—a campaign that included its own dedicated section for hotel employees (Department of Homeland Security 2010; 2011; see also Amoore 2007; Marcuse 2006). In both the DHS video No Reservations: Suspicious Behavior in Hotels and the more substantial AHLEI online program Eye on Awareness, hotel employees are trained to "see something" (recognize suspicious activity), "say something" (report suspicious activity), and "do something" (respond to crisis situations) (American Hotel and Lodging Educational Institute 2011a; Department of Homeland Security 2010). As Mark Sanna, head of security at Hyatt Hotels and part of the team that developed the Eye on Awareness program, explained,

> Think of training in a different way—from the perspective of a terrorist. Terrorists train too... they run training camps to develop their skills, they produce manuals and guides, they hold webinars for their affiliated members. If they are putting so much effort into their training, can we afford to be doing any less?

That's the security training challenge we face. (American Hotel and Lodging Educational Institute 2011b)

The AHLEI program works through both an imperative command issued to tourism employees (e.g., "say something") and a threat (e.g., "can we afford to be doing any less?") that, together, imply a terrible consequence (i.e., a terrorist bomb) if proper training is not implemented and adhered to.

These training programs are one of the main vehicles through which the securitization process is distributed across the entire tourism infrastructure. They incorporate elite bodies from across government and industry as well as the everyday lives of tourism workers who clean hotel rooms, check in guests, cook meals, and do laundry. Like the security provision at airports, retail spaces, and postconflict areas, much of the actual frontline work has been comprehensively devolved to private security companies (PSCs).[5] Alongside government initiatives, many PSCs work independently to set and regulate standards of hotel security; for example, SafeHotels, in conjunction with PSCs Pinkerton Consulting and Securitas, has developed the Global Hotel Security Standard, which provides auditing, training, and certification programs worldwide (SafeHotels, n.d.). Moreover, most major global PSCs, such as G4S and Securitas, now have a section dealing specifically with the leisure, hospitality, and tourism industries. Indeed, although the AHLEI training program was initially a government initiative, it was developed in partnership with senior global security officials from the tourism industry and employed the risk management consulting firm Cardinal Point Strategies (American Hotel and Lodging Educational Institute 2011b). This is an important site for future research as the complex network of public and private actors implementing counterterrorism training programs in hotels and other tourism infrastructures multiply and extend the reach of liberal rule (Morgan and Pritchard 2005, 127). Indeed, two large sections of the global labor force—PSCs and hotel employees—are now assimilated into a mode of governance in which their behavior is both regulated by the overarching discourse of risk management and actively oriented toward dispositions of suspicion and surveillance.

Securing Future Vacations

Using the events of 9/11, Bali, and Mombasa as a starting point to explore the securitization of the tourism industry in the War on Terror is not to suggest that these events were the origin of such practices or that they represent its apotheosis. Indeed, the entanglements of tourism and terrorism have important precedents (e.g., Luxor, 1997) and have continued to intensify in the years following Bali and Mombasa (e.g., Sharm el-Sheikh, 2005; Bali, 2005; Yemen, 2007; Mumbai, 2010; Tunisia, 2015). What I have argued here is that official responses to 9/11, Bali, and Mombasa revealed an important expansion in the scope, invasiveness, and ubiquity of securitization. To be sure, this capture of the tourism industry is only part of a wider logic in which publics are made increasingly fearful and passive—and thus more easily governed—by making the terrorist threat exceptional in its scope, irrationality, and propensity for violence. What the counterterrorism responses to 9/11, Bali, and Mombasa helped to reveal was the illiberal face of liberal rule. We are living in a global order where transnational claims to solidarity can only be sustained by effacing inequalities between members (e.g., privileged tourists and exploited hosts), where the values of inclusiveness and tolerance are belied by violent actions pursued against "illiberal" enemies (e.g., interventions in Iraq and Afghanistan), and where claims to liberty and freedom are continually compromised by pernicious techniques of governance seeking to mobilize our everyday lifeworlds to combat an exceptional terrorist threat.

Taking tourism seriously as a site of securitization and governance is not just about applying a given critical framework to yet another hidden sphere in which liberal rule makes itself felt. What makes tourism such a rich analytical site is that it forces us to ask some challenging questions about the future possibilities of work that interrogate the intersections of securitization and governance. First, the securitization of tourism brings us into productive conversations with scholars in international political economy who problematize the hegemony of neoliberal practices. As the discussion of the counterterrorism training programs in hotels suggested, there are important questions to be asked here about the affective mobilization of an entire labor force and the public–private arrangements that implement such developments. Are there local variations on this sectorwide mobilization, or moments of collective dissent? Second, the securitization of tourism can't be understood outside of the debates over critical infrastructure protection, resilience, and urban security. Tourism infrastructure in cities may not be as critical as the sewage or water system, but it is increasingly significant in terms of a city's marketability, branding, and economic growth. How, then, do we account for the securitization of different kinds of tourism infrastructure, from famous urban attractions to enclave leisure resorts? Third, the changes to global tourism after 9/11 cannot be made sense of simply by tracking the rise and fall of visitor numbers or airport throughput. The securitization of tourism is never only about the implementation of policies or technologies: it is also about less tangible notions such as the economies of desire that encourage people into foreign travel, the geopolitical imaginaries that plot global destinations according to safety and danger, and the affective mobilizations of fear, anxiety, and danger that circulate in particular destinations. What we need is more research into how securitization operates in these less tangible registers of everyday life that seem, at first, to be trivial.

CONCLUSION

Touring Otherwise

The Ethical Possibilities of Entanglement

In the decade following the events of 9/11, tourists visited the Loma Malones Observation Point approximately fifteen miles south of the town of Guantánamo, Cuba, to listen to local tour guides explain the history of the anomalous bit of Cuban soil that has been in American hands since 1901 (Paterson 2002; see also Van Veeren 2014). The combination of military and prison architecture made it difficult for visitors to see anything of the infamous Camp Delta, so a telescope was provided for them "to get a closer view" (Paterson 2002). As the Loma Malones tourists gazed at Camp Delta, seven thousand American military personnel and three thousand private construction workers took advantage of the many recreational and leisure opportunities available in Guantánamo Bay. Along with the requisite McDonald's, Walmart, and bowling alley provided on most American military bases, Camp Delta also boasted a brand-new $4 million sports arena, an outdoor cinema, a nine-hole golf course, and opportunities for windsurfing and organized sea-fishing expeditions (Levin 2008; Syson and Philips 2009). With such a comprehensive leisure infrastructure, it is unsurprising that Guantánamo Bay quickly became one of the many affordable intramilitary vacation spots favored by 1.5 million American service personnel and their families (Levin 2008). To mark these leisured experiences, the gift store at the Walmart shopping mall sold an array of souvenirs for soldier-tourists and their families, including mugs marked "Kisses from Guantanamo!" and T-shirts that read "The Taliban Towers at Guantanamo Bay: The Caribbean's Newest 5-star Resort!" (Levin 2008).

Unsurprisingly, the availability of these souvenirs prompted angry responses from activists fighting for the rights of those being detained

282 CONCLUSION

within Camp Delta. As Zachary Katznelson, a British human rights lawyer representing twenty-eight of the Guantánamo prisoners, argued,

> when I see the conditions the prisoners have to cope with and then think of the T-shirt slogans, I am appalled. To say I am repulsed is an understatement.... Pretending that Guantanamo Bay is essentially a resort in the Caribbean is grossly offensive and the idea of relaxing in the sun while close by many individuals are robbed of their rights, tortured and abused is both repugnant and ridiculous. (Levin 2008)

What I find significant about the outrage expressed by Katznelson and others is not its self-righteousness but the fact that he is *surprised* at the conjunction of tourism and torture in Camp Delta. This juxtaposition has been going on for as long as soldiers and tourists have left home for the purposes of war and leisure. Indeed, tourists have *always* relaxed in the sun while nearby prisoners have been robbed of their rights and tortured: it has happened in South Africa, Cyprus, Sri Lanka, Northern Ireland, and Cuba and will continue to happen in new holiday destinations adjacent to areas of conflict. While Katznelson's moral outrage is seductive, uncritically accepting it prevents us from seeing how tourism and military violence are consistently bound up together and how the practices of holiday making and soldiering feed off each other's productions of difference and domination. While I am not against the work that activists did—and are continuing to do—on behalf of Guantánamo detainees, I want to suggest that even these "moral guardians"—the human rights lawyers, amnesty workers, and media activists—traveling back and forth to Guantánamo Bay reproduce a tourist sensibility that is itself part of the very militarization they oppose. Australian ceramic artist Penny Byrne—who is also trained as a human rights lawyer—exposes this complicity in her series *Guantanamo Bay Souvenirs*, which reinterprets and inverts the "saccharine tweeness" of traditional eighteenth-century porcelain figurines. As Figure 32 demonstrates, Byrne gives the period costumes an "extreme ideological make-over" by painting them orange in reference to the detainee jumpsuits and by blindfolding and manacling the vintage figurines (Clement 2007). Although Byrne suggests that her work is "a twist on the sort of kitsch souvenirs that people bring home from their travels," *Guantanamo Bay*

FIGURE 32. Penny Byrne, *Gitmo Bay Souvenirs—Closing Down Sale, All Stock Must Go,* 2009. Courtesy of Penny Byrne/Fehily Contemporary Gallery.

Souvenirs signifies at a much deeper level than simply kitsch or agit-prop art (Morgan 2007). As one critic astutely explains,

> Byrne has created souvenirs for armchair tourists to covet and collect. They highlight the fact that the atrocities we witness seem distant and exotic. Shielded from harm by the screen of the TV, we watch horrors happening elsewhere. Safe at home, it is easy to believe that Abu Ghraib, Guantanamo Bay and the whole mess in Iraq is someone else's problem. Penny Byrne's clever figurines are provocative symbols of our own complacency and complicity. (Clement 2007)

For me, Byrne's placement of "armchair tourists" in global networks of violence speaks directly to the long-standing entanglements between war and tourism I have been tracing in this book.

We know that war is an extreme manifestation of difference and dehumanization; what I have tried to show is that although tourism is mostly understood as a benign activity, it actually draws on similar logics of difference and, at times, dehumanization. This alignment is clearest in the sphere of geopolitics—in the historical and contemporary architectures of enmity reproduced by efforts to maintain security, order, and justice in world affairs. From the crumbling edifice of the British Empire to the new algorithms of biometric security, policy makers, industry professionals, and tourism studies scholars have reproduced a reductive tourism–peace model stipulating that tourism only occurs when war and conflict are not present. What this book has demonstrated is that tourists always exceed the prevailing geopolitical discourses keeping war and peace firmly in their place and time. Indeed, as Diller + Scofidio (1994) discovered more than twenty years ago, once the commonsense separation of war and tourism is dispensed with, the connections between these two practices begin to proliferate in unexpected ways.[1] Indeed, I was not prepared for the extent to which practices of tourism and soldiering constantly intersect and overlap, nor was I prepared for the intensity of these entanglements. More to the point, I was surprised by the energy expended by governments, policy makers, militaries, tourism industries, and tourism studies scholars to produce and maintain a moral, political, and ethical distance between these two practices. What is so threatening about the connections between war and tourism that they must be constantly effaced?

The continuing efforts to separate war and tourism enable us to ignore the many ways in which the pursuit of leisure and travel—where we go to "get away from it all"—is always complicit in structural inequality, global violence, and geopolitical conflict. Of particular interest in this book has been the way tourist itineraries and military deployments reinforce both the dominant asymmetries of particular global orders (e.g., the Cold War) and the long-standing inequalities bequeathed by colonialism. Having said that, I did not want simply to confirm tourism's complicity in war's extreme practices of differentiation and domination; rather, I also wanted to ask whether foregrounding the many entanglements of tourism and war might go some way toward disrupting the entrenched geopolitical positions linking both practices. Whenever possible, I have tried to foreground the alternative possibilities that are always at work in such entanglements—possibilities that reorder familiar asymmetries and reveal the heterogeneity, multiplicity, and contingency of intersecting lifeworlds. Certainly this includes the lifeworlds of privileged subjects (i.e., soldiers and tourists) and marginalized Others (i.e., host and civilian populations), but it also includes the less-understood entanglements between these human figures and their material surroundings, for example, how tourists choreograph museum visits and encounter preserved artifacts of war or how soldiers use cameras to document their "tours of duty" through foreign environments.

I am not suggesting that these multiple entanglements somehow neutralize or resolve global asymmetries; indeed, as I have tried to show, power will always be articulated and disseminated throughout prevailing architectures of enmity that seek to order the mobilities, behaviors, and orientations of tourist and military populations around the world. However, by paying close attention to the everyday practices and encounters of tourists and soldiers, I have tried to show that they are always already *in relation* to the Others around them, the material objects they form attachments with, and the environments that sustain them. And it is precisely this condition of being *in relation*—of being constituted by multiple relations—that creates the possibility of revealing unexpected attachments and opening new spaces of encounter outside of the given coordinates of domination. To be sure, soldiers confirm their identities in opposition to the enemies they envision prior to battle, see during combat (either up close, across a battlefield, or on a target screen), and remember upon returning home. Likewise, tourists confirm their identities in opposition to the local hosts they envision prior to departure (helped by tourist advertising and guidebooks), see during their visits to local landmarks and historical sites, and remember when revisiting their holiday photographs. My point is that the *ambivalence* of these encounters can never be contained within the prevailing architectures of enmity that seek to order and control our everyday lifeworlds. For me, the most politically interesting moments emerge when the privileged identities of "tourist" and "soldier" become dislocated. I do not just mean when soldiers on leave become tourists, or when tourists play soldier by going to war zones; I also mean those moments when the crossovers between tourism and war unleash previously unseen solidarities and create more spaces for previously unheard voices and conversations to articulate themselves.

By framing the problem as one of entanglement rather than causation, I am already signaling a different starting place that does not assume pregiven categories such as static objects of knowledge, discrete realms of activity (e.g., economics, politics, culture), or influence that can be measured and predicted. I am framing this problem as primarily relational because conditions of entanglement allow us to see the more open and heterogeneous ground on which war and tourism intersect.

I am not interested in whether and how outbreaks of war cause tourist numbers to fall or if tourism has the capacity to produce world peace. For me, such questions are reductive and politically problematic because they subordinate the register of everyday life to the privileged categories of sovereignty, statecraft, diplomacy, and profit. In posing war in relation to tourism rather than, say, great power rivalry, civilizational alliances, or peace-building efforts, I am also contributing to a larger critical project that seeks to reveal how global politics is produced and maintained where we least expect it (Sylvester 2009). In this sense, my arguments are primarily disruptive because they seek to unsettle familiar and assumed accounts of global politics and show how there are always multiple ways to frame the world. In being attentive to those multiplicities, we discover that some alternative framings do not efface or silence the register of everyday life through which practices of war and tourism intersect but instead widen, complexify, and enrich the limited horizons of knowledge produced by traditional accounts of global politics.

What I have tried to demonstrate in this book is that tourism's relentless desire for difference cannot be fully contained within prevailing geopolitical coordinates. Certainly governments, policy makers, militaries, tourism industries, and tourism studies scholars spend enormous sums of money and hours of labor trying to track, manage, and control tourists— not just making them *stay put* during times of war but also making sure that their peacetime travels reproduce established geopolitical parameters. But just as tourists always exceed the dictates of geopolitics, so too do the soldiers and military personnel deployed overseas, who cannot help but recalibrate their encounters with foreign territory through preexisting tourist sensibilities. The result, of course, is that tourist destinations can never be separated from military targets, and vice versa; indeed, connecting the practices of tourism and war is part of a wider effort to demonstrate the *deterritorialized* condition of global politics. My purpose has been to reveal the ethical, political, material, and visual consequences of maintaining the geopolitical boundaries that separate war and tourism within prevailing architectures of enmity. By showing how war and tourism are disciplined within those geopolitical frames, as well as revealing the multiple ways they disrupt, exceed, and resist those frames, my hope is that we can begin to see how the entangled practices of war and tourism tap us into the heterogeneity, multiplicity, and contingency of the world around us.

Clearing the Ground: Complicity, Agency, and Articulation

To demonstrate the difficult ethical and political questions that arise when the entanglements of war and tourism are taken seriously, I want to end by considering two artistic interventions that, in different ways, use tourism to expose the violence of the global order. For his project *Signs of Life* (part of his larger *Rwanda Project: 1994–2000*), Chilean artist Alfredo Jaar bought more than two hundred postcards that were originally issued by the Rwandan Tourist Board and the Belgian airline Sabena (Jaar 1998; 1994). The postcards depicted familiar images of "exotic" and "natural" Africa preferred by tourist boards across the continent, for example, wildlife shots of lions, gazelles, and zebras and "natives" in traditional costumes performing "ethnic" rituals and dances. All the postcards bore the Rwandan Tourist Board slogan: "Rwanda—Decouvrez 1000 merveilles, au pays des 1000 collines" (Rwanda—Discover 1000 marvels in the land of 1000 hills). As Figure 33 illustrates, on the back of each postcard, Jaar wrote several versions of the same sentence—"Caritas Namazuru is still alive!"—changing the name of the survivor each time.

Jaar sent all two hundred postcards to friends and family around the world, but as the Rwandan Post Office was not operative during his stay in 1994, he posted the cards from Uganda on his way home. Like all of Jaar's work on Rwanda, *Signs of Life* confronts viewers with their own complicity and impotence in the face of atrocities like the Rwandan genocide. As Nicholas Mirzoeff (2005, 87) argues, "by turning the postcard on its head to identify specific individuals rather than generic stereotypes, Jaar surprises Western viewers into confronting their own stereotypes." Certainly that confrontation exposes the entrenched colonial relations upon which Western stereotypes of Africa are built; indeed, "many in the West know more about the plight of Rwanda's fauna (especially Dian Fossey's gorillas in the mist) than about the slaughter of its human inhabitants" (Lévi-Strauss 2005, 90). But the confrontation provoked by *The Rwanda Project: 1994–2000* is also about the wider issue—much addressed by

FIGURE 33. Alfredo Jaar, *Signs of Life,* 1994, from *The Rwanda Project: 1994–2000.* Courtesy of Madeleine Grynsztejn and the artist, New York.

Susan Sontag and her followers—of whether to look at images of atrocity. As Frank Möller (2009; 2013) rightly argues, the themes of concealment and silence in Jaar's later work on Rwanda recognize—and thus partly circumvent—the irresolvable dilemma of looking–not looking. To look is to reduce the victims to objects, but *not* to look is to continue the world's inaction in the face of genocide.

In his account of *Signs of Life,* Möller (2009, 789; see also Michaels 1994) alludes to the latent connections between tourism, colonialism, and genocide embedded in the project:

> By using postcards, Jaar not only engaged with Africa's frequent reduction to a tourist destination and its exposure to the tourist gaze. He also critically commented on one of the most sarcastic comments reportedly made by the columnist Simon Hoggart to explain Western inactivity in response to the Rwandan genocide: "Nobody you know has ever been on holiday to Rwanda."

Although most commentators acknowledge the power of *Signs of Life* as an introduction to the much bigger *Rwanda Project,* they usually locate the ethical and emotional power of Jaar's work in his later, quieter, more conceptual Rwanda installations (e.g., *The Eyes of Gutete Emerita*). However, I think there is much more at stake in these postcards than we initially realize. I do not read the postcards as a one-note piece of conceptual art that leads to a more fully developed project later on; rather, I see these postcards as making two important—and very difficult—political connections. First, as Möller begins to suggest, the postcards make the Western tourist gaze complicit with a wider geopolitical gaze that, in an echo of imperial visuality, allows Western governments to ignore genocide. We only *see* places like Rwanda if they conform to prevailing tourist stereotypes: a land of abundant nature where visitors can encounter exotic animals, lush flora and fauna, and primitive cultures. Second, the postcards also implicate the viewer—the art spectator—into this uncomfortable complicity. Although Jaar's later and more popular work in *The Rwanda Project: 1994–2000* directly addresses the positionality of viewers and their complicity with Rwanda's continuing invisibility, the specific subject position of the tourist disappears. My point is that many of the audience members encountering Jaar's work in the galleries of Europe, Japan, and the United States are *also* Western tourists, and some of them will have been on vacation—probably a safari—somewhere in Africa. What *Signs of Life* does that the rest of the *Rwanda Project* doesn't quite manage to do is suggest that efforts to challenge the exploitative Western interventions in Africa (i.e., from mineral extraction to humanitarian intervention) *must* include a challenge to the prevailing tourist gaze. The difficulty, of course, is that the dominant tourist gaze framing visitor encounters with stereotypical "Africa" (e.g., big-game safaris) is the same tourist gaze framing visitor encounters with Jaar's work in major art galleries and museums.

Politicizing the tourist gaze is made even more difficult when tourism is held up as the one economic strategy that will save Africa from poverty, famine, disease, and "tribal warfare." As *Rwanda: The Bradt Travel Guide* (Booth and Briggs 2004, vii) suggests,

> before the genocide, Rwanda's three main earners of foreign exchange were coffee, tea and tourism, and this is still the case—with tourism seeming likely to far outstrip the other two and help to rebuild the economy. For now, it's still an unspoilt country, with no crowds and no queue for gorilla-viewing permits. This is sure to change, just because it's such a terrific tourist destination—so don't delay! Start planning your visit!

To challenge the economic importance of tourism in places like Rwanda is to trouble the global policies and governmental strategies aimed at *helping* "Africa" out of poverty, famine, disease, and "tribal warfare." It is to expose how, in Marianne Gronemeyer's (1991) words, Western forms of help— from aid to tourism—continue to reproduce long-standing colonial power relations that maintain Western privilege and subordinate communities in the Global South. Though *Signs of Life* does expose tourism's complicity in that colonial economy of "helping," its message is only circulated in a contained sphere: Jaar's friends and family who received the postcards and those cosmopolitan, "art-aware" spectators who visited his *Rwanda Project* installations in the big galleries of Europe, North America, and Japan. To be sure, some of those gallery visitors were brought up short by *Signs of Life,* but how much more powerful it would have been if Jaar's postcards had been sent to the millions of tourists who have gone on a safari or gorillas-in-the-mist tour in Rwanda.

CONCLUSION 291

A counterpoint to the way tourism was explicitly figured in Jaar's *Signs of Life* is the more explicit return gaze mobilized by Eugenie Dolberg's (2010) project *Open Shutters: Iraq*. In collaboration with Iraqi and Syrian colleagues, Dolberg arranged for women from five Iraqi cities to be trained in photography so they could create visual stories of their everyday lives in a war-ravaged country. The women operated throughout 2006–7, and the result was a touring exhibition of their photographic stories, an exhibition catalog, and a film about the project by Maysoon Pachachi (Dolberg 2010; Pachachi 2009). Bernadette Buckley (2011) has explained the political significance of these images in terms of how they reveal the everyday life of Iraqis not shown on mainstream media feeds. But Buckley also suggests another register at work in these images: by showing the ruin and aftermath of war, they also show us—by way of absence—Iraq as it used to be, "those same deserted streets, once beautiful, once pulsating with life" (83). For me, one of the most compelling photo essays in this collection, by Um Mohammed, is titled *Bitterness*. In this set of images, the city of Basra is represented as a ruin of its former self—a "crossroads of people and cultures" now characterized by its bombed infrastructure, demolished buildings, and decaying architecture. Figure 34 is one of Mohammed's photographs of the war-ravaged amusement park. Um Mohammed explains,

> The amusement park near our house was looted and all the rides destroyed by people stealing the metal and brick. Even the palm trees were set alight. The last time I passed by there, I saw that instead of children playing there were grazing sheep. And in place of the green lawn, there were heaps of garbage drowning in stagnant water. (Dolberg 2010)

These images are haunting not just because they depict how the Iraq War destroyed a once thriving city but also because they show how circuits of leisure and tourism were a central part of that destruction. Along with the former amusement park, Um Mohammed shows us the remnants of the cultural center, the Al Karnak Cinema and the waterfront Corniche—all of which used to be central meeting places for Basra residents and those visiting the city. While Um Mohammed's photographs allude to what once was, they also offer an alternative tourist gaze that originates

FIGURE 34. Um Mohammed, *Amusement Park,* from Eugenie Dolberg, *Open Shutters Iraq,* 2010. Courtesy of Um Mohammed, *Open Shutters Iraq,* and Eugenie Dolberg.

from the position of the host rather than the guest. She is a tourist in her own ruined city operating from a position of estrangement rather than familiarity: "Now everything we loved about this city has been taken from us; it is not the place it was and I feel the bitterness of this loss" (Dolberg 2010).

For me, *Open Shutters Iraq* is politically important because it demonstrates a clear dispersal of agency that serves to invert the familiar logics of travel, war, distance, and empire. It puts the power of representation in the hands of those most disempowered by military deployment and tells the story of violent cultural encounter from the register of intimate daily life. I agree with Buckley (2011, 83) that this "bottom-up" approach does not make the *Open Shutters Iraq* photographs more authentic, but it does enact a set of politically important disruptions to those who seek to frame Iraq through Western eyes, including the mainstream media, policy officials, art spectators, and, of course, tourists. This is no simple inversion of power in which an "authentic" voice from below speaks effectively back to power. The spirit of *Open Shutters Iraq* is more collaborative not only in its form and content (i.e., using Western photographic techniques to capture the usually hidden lifeworlds of an "exotic" land) but also in its process. The training and editing sessions that took place before and after the photography involved the organizers and participants traveling to Damascus for intense collaborative workshops. Quite centrally, then, the *Open Shutters Iraq* project was constituted by experiences of travel, collectivity, and resistance that stood in opposition to reductive mainstream media accounts of Iraq being either destroyed or saved by Western powers. It is, in the end, an excellent example of what happens when the crossovers between travel and violence create a space in which usually excluded voices can articulate their own stories.

Heterogeneous Futures

This book does not produce a definitive statement about the entanglements of tourism and war, nor does it present a comprehensive history of these relationships. It is a more modest endeavor to begin a conversation about what is at stake when the "serious" world of geopolitics and the "mundane" world of everyday life intersect. By illustrating how dominant architectures of enmity are produced and sustained in places where we least expect it (e.g., in tourist resorts, in the leisurescapes of modern military bases, in well-meaning museum exhibits), the book has sought to critically interrogate dominant intellectual assumptions about what counts as legitimate knowledge in the fields of IR, geography, sociology, and tourism studies. I understand this effort as the start of a conversation rather than the end, because I recognize the obvious limitations of the study. Primarily, my focus on the way British, American, and other Western cultures frame Otherness is undeniably critical, but the critique itself remains enclosed. Though I have sought to foreground the ambivalent and disruptive experiences of encounter, too often, the final word remains with privileged populations of tourists and soldiers. This is, in part, a result of the cultural, visual, and official material to which I have access, but I want to acknowledge the ethical possibilities and limitations of leaving the issue of the return gaze as open as I have. Certainly I could have narrowed the focus of the book to look more specifically at a single encounter so as to better understand the multiple local voices and dispositions that reordered the deployment of privileged tourist and martial sensibilities. I refused this direction for two reasons. First, I think the entanglements of war and tourism are systemic, structural, and global, therefore a single case study—no matter how detailed—would have left the macropolitical architecture of global politics untouched. For me, it is impossible to critically analyze the minute practices of global travel and overseas military deployment without a sense of how different global orders at different times in history seek to order the arrangement and behavior of people on the ground. Second, such a narrow focus would have prompted me to speak for Others in the moment of encounter—always a temptation when speaking from a position of privilege. Though I'm sure I have at times succumbed to this temptation, I want to be clear that this book is intended to clear the ground so that the multiple, heterogeneous, and complex voices that arise in tourism-war connections can either speak for themselves or find other, more competent voices to speak collectively for them. My motivation has been to redistribute agency across different fields of knowledge, disrupt dominant ways of thinking about war and tourism, and create the space in which different voices, dispositions, and behaviors might begin their own conversation.

I see this book, then, as a necessary first step that has performed the service of critique: it has shown how the positions of privilege secured within prevailing architectures of enmity—in this case, tourists and military personnel—seek to restrict and deny the agency of predetermined Others. But it has also shown how those asymmetries are always breaking down because subjects, objects, and ideas always exceed our efforts to contain and arrest them. Of particular interest here are those lifeworlds, experiences, and moments that don't fit within predetermined circuits of tourism and/or war. What is needed now are further studies that extend my critique beyond showing how tourism-war entanglements too often reinforce the asymmetries of prevailing architectures of enmity. One possibility is to produce more detailed studies of particular sites of encounter, and here we need to follow the brilliant work produced by Waleed Hazbun (2008) and Rebecca Stein (2008) on the Middle East, Vernadette Vicuña Gonzalez (2013) on Hawaii and the Philippines, and Margaret Werry (2011) on New Zealand. Moreover, young IR scholars have been detailing the manifestations of global security in specific tourism–war encounters, for example, Elisa Wynne-Hughes's (2012) account of tourism and terrorism in contemporary Egypt; Charlotte Heath-Kelly's (2015) analysis of the current securitization of Bali's commemorative spaces; Elspeth Van Veeran's (2011; 2014) examinations of the unseen and changing lifeworlds of Guantánamo Bay; and Shine Choi's (2015) careful rendering of travel, translation, and resistance in cultural representations of North Korea. A second possibility is to examine more fully how global tourist circuits are adapting to a condition of permanent war. If we are, as many argue, living in a state of exception in which the normal rules governing violence and intervention no longer apply, then how is the tourism industry drawn into pernicious and excessive deployments of sovereign power? A further possibility is to consider the different leisure practices that involve global travel but do not fit within the assumed definition of "tourism." Certainly Wanda Vrasti's (2012) work on volunteer tourism is one example of how the experience of travel is now embedded in the wider production and governance of Western liberal subjects. But this kind of analysis needs to be expanded to look more closely at forms of global travel that are not primarily undertaken for touristic reasons. For example, how do global circuits of sports and fitness (e.g., ultramarathons), health and well-being (e.g., yoga retreats), and professionalization (e.g., industry conferences) reinforce the current modality of liberal rule?

Finally, I want to end with two reflections on the kinds of conversations I hope to inaugurate with this book. First, these conversations will necessarily be interdisciplinary because the scopes of both tourism and war cannot be sequestered within one specific field of knowledge. To be sure, critical IR and critical war studies will feature heavily not only because of what they tell us about war and global violence but also because of the discipline's recent efforts to open up the fields of culture and leisure to scrutiny. What this work shows us is that critical IR is at its best when it engages with insights from geography, sociology, anthropology, literature, and visual culture. Second, my hope is that the ensuing conversations will not be dogmatic or fixed but instead will embrace modes of knowing that acknowledge vulnerability, privilege collaboration, and understand that the most powerful insights most often arrive in unexpected and untimely ways. The only way we can ensure that such critical explorations continue is by constantly tending to the heterogeneity, multiplicity, and complexity of the terrain from which we speak and by ensuring that those who speak back are afforded the same textured ground.

Acknowledgments

In August 2014, I visited the Imperial War Museum (IWM) in London to see the new First World War Gallery that had been completely redesigned in honor of the centenary commemorations. As it had only just reopened to the public, there were huge crowds, and our ticketed entries were carefully and precisely timed. I was initially put off by the chaotic and rambunctious masses lined up to see displays of mass slaughter—so certain was I that my own engagement would be more considered, more ethical, more reverent. That smugness carried me only a little way through the exhibit, until I reached the *Recruitment Wall,* where a group of boys and girls, about six or seven years old, were enthusiastically trying on a range of military uniforms. After reading the wall text covering the requisite height, hearing, and eyesight needed to become a soldier in 1914, one boy plonked a helmet on his head and exclaimed, "Cool! I can go to war!" His friend, already dressed in a full naval uniform, raised his hands and whispered, "This . . . is . . . *awesome!*" Meanwhile, the two girls completely ignored the museum announcement urging them to "Come join us at the new *War in Afghanistan* gallery on the First Floor!" because they were doubled over laughing as they tried (and consistently failed) to button up their heavy wool tunics. Quite apart from the well-curated displays of horrific violence and deprivation, it was this enthusiastic and youthful embrace of war by a group of seven-year-olds that halted my passage through the exhibit. Rather predictably for an academic, my initial response to these kids goofing off was to indulge a well-honed narcissistic fantasy that I am actually an "expert" at something as I hastily marshalled an intellectual response. I immediately began questioning how the museum's tactile and immersive museology (e.g., Try this on! Touch this! Walk through this trench!) attaches the affective responses of audiences to wider discourses of nationalism, victory, and sacrifice. I believe I actually nodded my head slowly and wisely as I constructed this argument in my head and even took notes on the back of the museum map. Rest assured, dear reader, my self-indulgence did not stop there. I went on to consider the ways in which recent military interventions in Afghanistan and Iraq are constitutively shaped by the dominant memories of past wars—in this case how the Great War becomes an ideal commemorative template for subsequent conflicts. My head nodding was really animated now—goodness, I was being clever!

But alas, hubris is most often short-lived, and my smug intellectual posturing was completely undone by the unexpected ways that these children engaged with objects of war (e.g., "How do you undo these trousers for a poo?"; "This helmet is, like, *so* heavy"; "Oh, my God—what if we get *lice*!"). Their easy camaraderie and unconscious irreverence in a space that was *supposed* to be hushed and deferential was a powerful reminder for me. It created a rupture—a fleeting moment in which all those assembled had the opportunity to read the war otherwise. To be sure, these kids were doing exactly what the museum wanted them to do—engaging, enjoying, and, it is hoped, learning—but they were also powerfully disrupting the dominant responses of reverence, commemoration, and piety that are always encouraged by museum exhibits of war. They were also unraveling my own familiar—and rather lazy—efforts to politicize, interrogate, and deconstruct our dominant accounts of war. Of course, I know these interruptions are easily captured by any number of discursive closures, and indeed, those closures are themselves worthy of political interrogation. In this sense, I don't think *all* of my efforts to intellectualize the IWM's *Recruitment Wall* are completely useless and embarrassing—it's just that they are rather limited as a strategy. Quite unexpectedly, a group of seven-year-olds reminded me to *pay attention* to those surprising interruptions, unforeseen connections, and enticing detours precisely because they trouble my usual tendency to squeeze the complexities of war into a rather programmatic critical argument. While a great many visitors tutted and scowled as the seven-year-olds fell about laughing with the World War I uniforms, I found myself grinning like a madwoman and hoping they would intensify their mayhem and drag it through the entire museum. Alas, this brief episode came to an end when a parent enticed them out of the exhibit with the promise of ice cream—the downfall of so many potential revolutions.

I do not want to suggest that this encounter was a kind of epiphany that radically changed my approach or offered me redemption from previously errant ways. Indeed, I actively work against romanticized notions of redemption and catharsis because they are among the most pernicious and difficult closures to resist. What this encounter did was clarify what was making me uncomfortable about my previous work and help me identify how, in Samuel Beckett's words, I might fail better. In this endeavor, I went back to some rather unexpected interlocutors—those figures both known and unknown who have been critical of my work in the past. The charge was that many of my claims were reductive, lacked nuance, and failed to open up spaces of possibility, heterogeneity, and resistance. Or, as one shrewd mentor quietly explained, my arguments had the tendency to be rather... thumping. While these critical assessments were often painful to read and listen to (and I'm sure my responses were often inelegant and defensive), I want to extend my genuine thanks to those who forced me to do some serious thinking: to Shine Choi and Mustapha Pasha for calling attention to the reductive nature of much of my postcolonial analysis; to Paíl Nyíri (2008), whose devastating review of my first book, *The Global Politics of Contemporary Travel Writing* (2006), was generally right and prompted intense and uncomfortable reflections; and to two anonymous reviewers from the University of Minnesota Press, who patiently read through an utterly terrible first draft of this book and, instead of throwing it in the bin—which, trust me, would have been completely justified—made very generous, helpful, and serious suggestions for its improvement. My experience of peer review in this instance has been absolutely ideal, and I have since used their mode of engagement to guide my own critical assessments of fellow scholars. For me, these anonymous reviewers embodied something I have been working toward for a long time: a politics of intellectual generosity.

Much as I love stories of bleakness, shame, and failure, it hasn't all been abject misery. Somewhere along the way, I made an important discovery that the weakest aspect of my work—an undisciplined and totally incontinent curiosity—is also a great refuge and inspiration. I cannot help but be interested in all manner of things that make up the global terrain, from the obvious markers of violence and animosity to the terrifically mundane expressions of leisure and play. Very slowly, I am learning to embrace my haphazard, circuitous, and plural intellectual trajectories rather than lament my inability to stick to a single pathway. As a result, I have become even more stubborn in my pursuit of trans/inter/multidisciplinary research, not just across the social sciences and humanities but also with scientists, engineers, and medics; with practitioners in government, museums, and studios; and with other individuals and collectives that populate the messy realms of everyday life. Though I have not quite worked out what the ideal arrangement of vulnerability, generosity, and collaboration might be, I'm hoping that my increasingly heterogeneous collection of interlocutors will help me discover it. With this in mind, I offer specific thanks to a number of fellow travelers who engaged with this book project in more explicit ways by, for example, listening to draft chapters, critiquing plans and proposals, urging me to develop conceptual hunches, inspiring me with powerful insights, and providing intellectual, emotional, and collegial support: Pete Adey, Louise Amoore, Claudia Aradau, Didier Bigo, Roland Bleiker, Angus Boulton, Antoine Bousquiet, David Campbell, Angharad Closs-Stephens, Costas Constantinou, Martin Coward (especially for epic phone conversations), John Curran, Alex Danchev, Matt Davies, Teresa Degenhardt, Marieke De Goede, James Der Derian, David Dwan, Jenny Edkins, Charlotte Epstein, Phil Frowd, Kyle Grayson, Jairus Grove, Xavier Guillaume, Alex Hall, Lene Hansen, Katy Hayward, Waleed Hazbun, Charlotte Heath-Kelly, Alison Howell, Aida Hozic, Vivienne Jabri, Peter James, Cathal McCall, Maeve McCusker, Michael McKinnie, Susan McManus, Kevin McSorley, James Millen, Laura Mills, Benjamin J. Muller, Can E. Mutlu, Andrew Neal, Peter Nyers, Matthew Patterson, Simon Philpott, Louise Purbrick, Mark B. Salter (especially for his sartorial magnificence), Mike Shapiro, Bal Sokhi-Bulley, Vicki Squire, Margaret Topping, Simon Tormey, Elspeth Van Veeren, Nick Vaughan-Williams, R. B. J. Walker (still!), Lauren Wilcox, Maja Zehfuss, and the many other scholars and friends whom I have not listed here but who supported my research. In my local context, I have benefited enormously from the arrival of young

IR scholars who have radically improved my daily life and provided a focused intellectual community, especially Mike Bourne (who has been valiant and kind in the face of my demagoguery), Dan Bulley (who is the perfect antidote to my monstrous ego), and Heather Johnson (who knows just when to administer a hug or a much-needed slap, sometimes in complex sequences).

Thanks of a more practical nature are due to the School of Politics, International Studies, and Philosophy for granting me the sabbatical needed to complete this book (especially to David Phinnemore, stoic and unwavering in his support); William Blair at the Ulster Museum, who patiently answered my ill-formed questions; Paul Smith at the Thomas Cook Archives; Roger Tolson and the many helpful archivists at the Imperial War Museum in London; the artists, museums, and institutions that granted permission for images to be reproduced in this book; Ivan Ewart, who helped me with the images; Pieter Martin and Kristian Tvedten at the University of Minnesota Press for being so cheerfully professional; and Tarak Barkawi and Shane Brighton for mobilizing such enthusiasm and good will behind the Critical War Studies project. Earlier draft sections of chapter 4 and chapter 5 were previously published as "The Yellow Car," in *Making Things International 2: Catalysts and Reactions,* ed. Mark B. Salter, 181–94 (Minneapolis: University of Minnesota Press, 2016) and "Frontline Leisure: Securitizing Tourism in the War on Terror," *Security Dialogue* 44, no. 2 (2013): 127–46, respectively.

Finally, my immeasurable and unconditional thanks to family, friends, and comrades for all the unseen emotional and physical labor that helped to foster this project from its inception more than a decade ago to its belated birth: to the many exhausted academic parents trying to juggle small children with professional careers—your solidarity and shared stories give me much-needed perspective (especially when I am late for meetings and turn up with porridge in my hair); to Tori Cook for our long and still-evolving narrative arc; to Peppers both near and far for welcoming me (and for entertaining small people while I direct my brain elsewhere); to Lisles very far away whose unqualified loyalty and generosity (coupled with well-timed reminders of my idiocy) have helped me believe that one day I, too, can become a fully functioning human adult; to Marcus and

Sadie for rightly not giving a toss about my struggles over agency, power, and mobility because there are many more important things to be doing, such as playing hide and seek, drawing butterflies, stealing mommy's chocolates, and convening the supreme council of superheroes—thank you, critters, for unravelling me completely (and I apologize for doing Foucauldian readings of *Aliens Love Underpants*); and finally to Andrew, who so gracefully supports my noisy and multiple ambitions while quietly and creatively pursuing his own, who picks up the slack when I am unable to, who gently reminds me to stop working and get playing (and then provides the necessary adventures), and who asks the hard questions when they need to be asked—thank you for supporting me through this book's many diversions and for your bravery, irreverence, and love.

Notes

Introduction

1 Although *Holidays in the Danger Zone* does address how tourism operates within a wider political economy—as the world's largest industry, this kind of analysis is necessary—it does not follow the dominant approach by simply advocating tourism's ability to bolster postwar economic growth. Rather, it builds on Waleed Hazbun's (2008) more comprehensive and critical understanding of political economy, which shows how the tourism industry reproduces wider geopolitical, structural, and institutional inequalities.

2 My insistence that war and tourism are *entangled* practices is a direct reference to this materialist turn—to Hodder's (2012, 89) suggestion that "the social world of humans and the material world of things are entangled together by dependences and dependencies that create potentials, further investments and entrapments" and Pickering's (1995, 22–23) claim that humans and things exist in a "mangle of practice" that operates through a "dialectic of resistance and accommodation."

3 Such an interdisciplinary mixture did not sit well with one critic, who argued that Diller + Scofidio's "unfortunate" tourism-war juxtaposition was too limiting: "in its fixation on the phenomenon of the tourism of war it does indeed play down the much more cogent insight heralded by its contributions—that of the invasion of (military) realism into the symbolism of history" (Ernst 2002). In my view, this critique entirely misses the significance of what Diller + Scofidio were trying to do and their efforts to foreground the practices and materials of everyday life that are shared between war and tourism.

1. The Double Vision of Empire

1 Churchill (1949, 6–9) draws on prevailing anthropological categories to delineate and demonize the different "races" of Sudan, and similar racial categories shaped Gordon's decision to evacuate only Europeans and loyal Egyptians from Khartoum, while leaving the Sudanese allies to their fate at the hands of the Mahdi (*United Service Gazette* 1884, 440).

304　NOTES TO CHAPTER 1

2　Following on from Gregory, Waleed Hazbun (2007) argues that the heterogeneous network Thomas Cook & Son participated in (and helped produce) cannot be understood through traditional disembodied notions of political economy. Rather, "integrated tourism economies are constructed by heterogeneous networks of actors in which the outcome of the process is indeterminate and only stabilized through associations between diverse human and non-human elements and after a process of repeated interactions and adjustment between these actors" (13–14).

3　This *New York Times* (1884, 7) article speaks very frankly about the effect the incoming soldiers had on Cairo: "An Anglo-Egyptian official, who has just returned from Cairo, says the situation in Egypt is deplorable. The city of Cairo especially is becoming debauched by the sudden plethora of money caused by the preparations for the Nile Expedition. Money is pouring into the country not only from England, but also from speculative people from all nationalities, and an enormous bill will have to be footed and paid for by England some day. The officials, both civil and military, are careless and wasteful."

4　From the Contagious Diseases Acts passed in Britain in 1864 to the variety of colonial regulations throughout the Empire that sought to discipline the intimate contacts between soldiers and local sex workers, prostitution in the late nineteenth century was a central practice on which modes of governmentality were exercised. These interventions reaffirmed not only a gendered hierarchy but also hierarchies of race, class, and sexuality. The anxiety caused by prostitution in the colonies was expressed clearly by the European abolitionists, who were not seeking to dismantle regulated prostitution on behalf of colonial women in sexual slavery but instead to eradicate prostitution because it was an abomination against morality and Christianity (Hyam 1990; Levine 2003).

5　More than eighty of the voyageurs elected to stay on to work the Nile, but most chose to return to Canada for the coming logging season. A majority of those left Cairo in March, but while in England, too many of the men were ill, which prevented the Queen from receiving them personally. Lieutenant Colonel Denison followed on from Cairo in May once he had recovered from enteric fever (Stacey 1959, 41–42, 139–40).

6　The Sudan campaign in 1885 was the last time that the British wore their famous red coats, as gray and khaki uniforms became commonplace in subsequent desert battles (Wilkinson-Latham and Roffe 1976).

7　This arrangement in 1896 was much more limited than the previous one in 1884, and Thomas Cook & Son tried (and failed) to charge the British army more for transportation costs for this expedition than it was charging the Egyptian government for regular river traffic (Hunter 2004, 41).

2. Tours of Duty, Tours of Pleasure

1 Other associations providing troop support included the Knights of Columbus, the Jewish Welfare Board, and the Salvation Army. The involvement of the YMCA and other private-sector groups during the First World War gave rise to the much more institutionalized arrangements of the United Service Organizations (USO), created in 1941 to provide recreation and entertainment for American and Allied troops abroad.

2 The pages of Hopps's pencil-written diary are not numbered, and the dates of his entries are sporadic, so it is unclear exactly when he traveled through Ypres. Judging from the dates of the entries, it must have been after he began the diary on July 21, 1915, which would mean anywhere between the third battle of Ypres (Passchendaele, July 31–November 6, 1917) and the final battle (September 28–October 2, 1918).

3 I am not arguing that the nineteenth-century conventions of war photography practiced by Fenton and Brady eschewed moments of leisure and relaxation on the battlefield; indeed, the wet-colloidal process of photography during the Crimean War and the U.S. Civil War meant that action shots were almost impossible. As the Fenton and Brady archives reveal (Fenton, n.d.; Perry, n.d.), a majority of photographs are taken either behind the front lines when soldiers are at rest or after the battle when the corpses lie still on the battlefield. This suggests a much longer genealogy of the juxtaposition of leisure and war and a much clearer visualization of it in the canon of war photography.

4 Thomas Cook & Son was one of the primary British tour operators in the region, but other British companies included Dean and Dawson Ltd., Alpine Sports Ltd., Pickfords Ltd., Polytechnic Touring Association Ltd., Frame's Tours, Lazenby's Tours, Touring Guild, British Touring Club, and American Express (Lloyd 1998, 30).

5 In their first battlefield tour guidebook published in 1920, these personal and physical tourist encounters were portrayed as superior to the cultural, literary, and visual representations of the Great War in circulation at the time: "our ideas of all this can be but vague and incomplete until we have visited the fields of battle and seen trenches and dug-outs, mine craters and wire defences and all the terrible business of warfare" (Thomas Cook & Son 1920a, 3).

6 The collection of the Private Papers of Mrs. L. K. Briggs covers the period from 1919 to 1939, but one of the most detailed accounts of her Ypres journeys was written in 1933 and is organized as an explanatory index to the accompanying photographs covering the previous fourteen years. The initial album details the career of Claude Briggs through letters, pressed flowers,

306   NOTES TO CHAPTER 2

newspaper clippings, poems, and photographs and includes Mrs. Briggs's efforts to find out how her son died and where he was buried. After many letters back and forth, she discovered that he had been killed in the attack on Shrewsbury Wood in September 1917 and initially buried in Hoogecrater Cemetery but was subsequently interred and buried at Bedford Cemetery on June 28, 1921 (Briggs, n.d.).

7 This denigration of home and abroad was also shaped by the ambivalent sexualities of British writers between the wars. The norms of heterosexuality that ruled British culture at the time were legally and morally constricting for these men, and traveling abroad was one way to escape such conventions. Although Fussell's (1980) study of these figures studiously avoids questions of sexuality and masculinity, more recent critics have explored this work more productively from a queer perspective (Carr 2006; Rau 2009).

8 The leisured encounters in Europe were certainly fraught with their own exploitations, for example, Mary Louise Roberts (2013) has shown how prewar representations of French women as "sexually liberated" led to an increase in sexual violence by American soldiers on leave (see also Burds 2009).

9 Steichen initially chose six men who went on to become some of America's most famous photographers: Horace Bristol (photographer for *LIFE* magazine who worked closely with John Steinbeck), Wayne F. Miller (who later became president of Magnum), Charles Fenno Jacobs (*LIFE* magazine and the Farm Security Administration), Charles Kerlee, Victor Jorgensen, and Dwight Long (primarily a cinematographer). They were joined later on by John Swope, Thomas Binford, Charles Steinheimer, and Barrett Gallagher (Bachner 2004, 7; Phillips 1981, 22–27).

10 With that in mind, I disagree that the NAPU images produce a "male odalisque" or a "genre painting with the gender transposed" (Danchev 2005, 25). Traditional odalisques depict a woman looking directly at the painter and the audience and therefore suggest some kind of agency in that gaze. However, in a majority of the NAPU images collected in Bachner's books, the men are *not* looking at the camera but are instead engaged in collective behavior that is being documented by the photographers. A more interesting question in this respect is how agency can be expressed through indifference, for example, by ignoring the camera.

11 Harrison (2006, 824) clarifies how tourism sustained the collection and circulation of skull trophies: "the battlefield conditions cannot explain why servicemen in many cases collected such trophies not for themselves but—as is often the case with souvenirs and holiday mementos purchased by tourists . . . —as gifts for relatives and others back home."

3. Bipolar Travels

1. Kubrick deliberately includes the media apparatus in these shots—cameramen, journalists, sound technicians—so that the privileged place of the heroic, cinematic soldier is automatically displaced. His decision to depict the Vietnam War through the liminal figure of an army photojournalist places Joker in a long line of war correspondents who have translated the Vietnam War through newspapers, television, novels, and film. But Kubrick deliberately resists the easy heroism and popular mythology of the noble, truth-seeking war correspondent and portrays Joker instead as a conflicted, uncomfortable, and morally flawed character—a depiction that owes much to screenwriter Michael Herr, himself a journalist in Vietnam, whose book *Dispatches* (1977) is one of the most fully realized books about the war.
2. A similar individualization occurs at off-site Holocaust museums such as the U.S. Holocaust Memorial Museum, which issues each visitor with an identity card detailing a particular victim or survivor (Edkins 2003, 153–65; Hirsch 2001; Liss 1998, 13–38; Zelizer 1998).
3. These shared struggles were central to the Hiroshima–Auschwitz Peace March in 1962–63, in which four Japanese men of different faiths traveled from Hiroshima to meet museum curators and local officials in Auschwitz (Kossakowski, n.d.; Zwigenberg 2012).
4. This cultivation of American internationalism abroad was simultaneously produced on the home front as a number of important domestic tourist sites (most importantly the Smithsonian's National Air and Space Museum, which was established in Washington, D.C., in 1946) reproduced familiar national myths about the United States's heroic battles against foreign enemies (Luke 2002).
5. Klein (2003) offers a comprehensive example of how the American tourist-diplomat was constructed as an "emblem of America's benign, non-imperial internationalism" through the *Saturday Review*'s World Travel Photographic Awards in 1954 (109–15). In line with the United States's foreign policy agenda, the magazine had long been promoting the cause of the tourist-diplomat, arguing that global travelers could bring back "useful" strategic and visual information about newly colonized and developing nations of the world, including "films, or slides, or snapshots" (114). Tourist-diplomats who were also amateur photographers were encouraged to produce images that would both break down the barriers between East and West and promote U.S. "total immersion" in world affairs. What Klein demonstrates is that these photographs simply reproduced the familiar "othering tropes of

308 NOTES TO CHAPTER 3

Orientalist discourse": those that played host to American tourists became the photographic blank canvas on which tourist-diplomat-photographers, editors, and readers created their exotic fantasies and confirmed their own identity constructions as benign, cosmopolitan internationalists.

6   Salter's (2007) novel *The Hunters* offers a familiar racial and gendered "taxonomic urge" by distinguishing between the prostitutes who worked in bathhouses (which the USAF pilots do visit) and the innocent local girl with whom the main protagonist falls in love. The central R&R sequence takes place in chapters 13–16 of the story, when the main character Cleve Connell and his friend De Leo embark on a standard five-day visit to Tokyo. The interlude has an ethereal quality to it and contrasts well with the grittiness and competition of the flying missions over the Palu River. While Salter does not shy away from writing about the visit to the prostitutes and bathhouses, as well as the plight of women deserted by their GI boyfriends, these women are all portrayed as rather blank slates upon which the protagonist Cleve can project his anxieties. When he meets Eiko, the nineteen-year-old daughter of his father's friend, her obvious signs of innocence and openness allow Cleve to imagine redeeming his life by marrying her. Using women as simple plot devices is not unusual in fiction of the time, especially war fiction, but as a result of this gendered framing, the R&R sections of Salter's book seem weak in comparison to the dramatic tension of the flight sequences that brilliantly explore issues of competition, masculinity, friendship, and purpose.

7   The experience of surfing during the Vietnam War was, of course, crystallized in the infamous scene in *Apocalypse Now* where Colonel Kilgore (Robert Duvall) arranges for a beach to be captured so his American soldiers can go surfing (Studio Canal 2011).

4. Global Interventions

1   The ongoing struggle of militaries to manage the off-duty behavior of their troops was made more difficult after the end of the Cold War because military personnel were not the only "humanitarians" intervening in foreign jurisdictions. UN and NATO support personnel, media companies, charities, religious groups, volunteer organizations, and a variety of NGOs — all with global constituencies — were also active alongside military personnel throughout the ethnic conflicts of the 1990s and 2000s. While each of these groups was there for a particular purpose (e.g., to cover the story, to rescue orphans, to distribute aid, to help refugees), they undoubtedly drew on existing understandings and experiences of tourism — a tourist sensibility — to navigate their foreign surroundings. For example, diplomats

and negotiators may have understood Bosnia as succumbing to "ancient hatreds" (and, indeed, were there to separate the warring parties), but they also understood it as an Eastern European gateway to the exotic Orient. Part of what critical scholars have recently been exploring is the extent to which these nonmilitary populations, under the guise of "helping," actually reinforce the prevailing global asymmetries inherited from colonial rule (Duffield 2001; 2007; Ficher 2007; Li 2007; Sending and Neumann 2006).

2 More scope for critical analysis is evident in heritage studies, which starts from the position that all constructions of dark tourist sites are selective, partial, and ideologically driven and reminds us that any reconstruction of the past—including the reconstruction of war, conflict, and atrocity—is subject to manipulation by those in power (e.g., academics, policy makers, heritage workers, entrepreneurs) (Austin 2002; Ashworth and Hartmann 2005; Hartmann 2014; Turnbridge and Ashworth 1995; Uzzell and Ballantyne 1998; Wight 2006, 122–26). However, while Turnbridge and Ashworth's (1995) concept of "dissonant heritage" is useful, I don't agree with their claim that explicit markers of dissonance in sites of atrocity should be reduced as much as possible by an "inclusivist formula"—what they call a "flexible pragmatic multiculturalism" (272–74). This suggests that the preferred pathway out of dissonance and into peace rests on the same problematic hierarchical geopolitics (i.e., that uncivilized nations remained "mired" in struggle, while civilized nations are peaceful) and a progressive temporality (i.e., that nations climb a predetermined ladder of civilization constructed by liberal rule). In other words, even critical scholars can't help but seek a resolution to the intractable tensions that arise in the juxtaposition of war and tourism.

3 In so-called nonpolitical walking tours such as the Holy Land tours of Bethlehem, Jerusalem, and Galilee, Jerusalem is constructed as "Bible Land" by effacing the history of Arab presence in the region, ignoring contemporary Palestinian communities, and avoiding the familiar flash points of the contemporary Israeli–Palestinian conflict (Feldman 2008). William Miles (2010, 556) argues that "most religious and pilgrimage tours of Jerusalem try to stay clear of the politics of modern-day Palestine/Israel; or rather, they tacitly incorporate a political perspective that is inherently status-quo oriented" (see also Bowman 1992; Brin and Noy 2010).

4 Given this close relationship between tourism and activism, it is possible to frame the many pro-Palestinian activists that arrive in the Middle East as tourists themselves (e.g., members of the International Solidarity Movement). As Koensler and Papa (2011) argue, these activists are members of a global "speed elite" and thus exhibit many problematic orientations such as

ignorance of the political situation, a reductive account of ethnic divisions and political history, and a superficial engagement with local communities (see also Jean-Klein 2002).

5 Around Jerusalem, Bethlehem, and Hebron, there are new opportunities for "justice tourism" aimed not at pro-Palestinian advocates but rather at Israelis and the Jewish Diaspora. As Aviv (2011, 35) explains, new organizations such as *Encounter Programs* and *Zochrot* deliberately ask Jewish tourists to "question and challenge traditional narratives about Jewish collective memory, nationalism, history, justice and the possibilities for peace among Israelis and their neighbours" (see also Brin 2006, 232–33; Isaac 2009; Miles 2010; Noy 2012).

6 I am using the English words for Cypriot places here, for example, Nicosia rather than Lefkoşa.

7 Though I focus on political tourism directed at visitors, there is much research to be done exploring how a tourist sensibility shapes UN and British military forces stationed on Cyprus. Does their transition into off-duty time mobilize a tourist gaze through which they orient themselves toward local people, local landscapes, and visiting tourists? Certainly this disposition is at work in the instances of sexual violence and rape committed by off-duty soldiers making use of the island's many clubbing resorts. For example, British forces were banned from visiting the Ayia Napa resort after a number of drunken incidents culminated in four British soldiers raping and murdering a Danish tour operator there in 1994. After a period of calm, soldiers on R&R rotations from Iraq and Afghanistan were allowed back into the resort, which resulted in further incidents of drunken and violent behavior, including a serious "rampage" in February 2008 in which twenty-five British soldiers attacked each other and local bar owners. Once again, the squaddies have been banned from the resort, and the British military has had to deal with another public relations fiasco as a result of being unable to manage the leisure activities of its soldiers (Gillian and Daugbjerg 2006, 12; Smith 2008, 26; Theodoulou 2008, 15). These incidents have to be contextualized within the complex position of British sovereignty on the island (especially with respect to the two bases) and the everyday relations that are produced between military personnel and local communities (Richmond and Constantinou 2004; Highgate and Henry 2011).

8 As part of a Cultural and Media Studies program Eamonn Hughes and I ran at Queen's University Belfast, I took a group of undergraduate students on the "Living History" bus tour every year from 1999 to 2006. During these events, the students and I spoke at length with the other tourists about

NOTES TO CHAPTER 5   311

their impressions of Belfast and with the tour guides about their own self-presentation and cultivated neutrality (see also Dépret 2006, 153).

9   I want to thank my colleague Vince Geoghegan for this brilliant insight.

10 Alternative approaches to commemoration abound in recent novels, plays, and poetry from Northern Ireland artists. One of the most innovative examples in this vein was *The West Awakes,* a combination of walking tour, taxi tour, and theater production that told the history of West Belfast in four specific sites. Written by four local playwrights (Jimmy McAleavey, former hunger striker Laurence McKeown, Kieron Magee, and Rosemary Walsh), this interactive experience sought to trouble stereotypical accounts of the past and question traditional forms of both theater and commemoration (McAleavey 2010). Another institution that publicly displays alternative accounts of commemoration is the Belfast Exposed gallery of photography, especially its recent exhibitions *Northern Ireland: 30 Years of Photography* (2013), *The Prehistory of the Crisis–2* (2009), *Bonfires* (2008), and *The English in Northern Ireland* (2005) (Belfast Exposed Photography Gallery, n.d.).

5. Connecting Tourism and Terrorism

1   Scholars have documented the specific ways the military is trying to control the official record of war through both traditional forms of censorship (e.g., media blackouts on images of atrocity committed by "our" troops) and more canny forms of assimilation and control (e.g., the entire embed system). For an account of the controversy surrounding the Pentagon's effort to censor images of flag-draped coffins, see Carter, Rutenberg, and Sink (2004); for an account of the initial anxieties over whether soldiers could carry digital cameras, camcorders, and cell phones with cameras, see Agence France Presse (2004) and Dao (2010); for analyses of how the embed system is shaping war reporting, see Haigh et al. (2006), Katovsky and Carlson (2005), Kuypers and Cooper (2005), Paul and Kim (2004), and Pfau et al. (2005); for an account of how the Ministry of Defense in the United Kingdom lifted restrictions on visual and recording devices for "sanctioned" installations in museums, see Scranton (2006) and Smith (2008).

2   The concept of securitization at work here is more attuned to Foucauldian accounts (Aradau and Rens Van Munster 2007; Foucault 1980; 2007; Opitz 2011; Salter 2007) of an apparatus or *dispositif* that assimilates much more of our lifeworlds than simply the speech acts or rhetorical mobilizations favored by constructivist accounts (Buzan, Waever, and De Wilde 1998; Williams 2003).

3   I have argued elsewhere that to fully understand the War on Terror's matrix

of exceptionalism and securitization, it is necessary to acknowledge first the biopolitical register these two forces are now operating within; second, how this matrix has a constitutive material component and cannot be reduced to discourse, rhetoric, or speech acts; third, how these forces operate on the terrain of everyday life; fourth, how exceptionalism and securitization seek to produce and manage the behaviors and dispositions of key subjects; and finally, how these forces have a particular geopolitics with complex antecedents of colonialism and exploitation (Lisle 2013, 128–29).

4 Theorists of touch and movement offer us a radical approach to visual encounters in which the seeing subject is always physically connected to, and in relation with, the objects and technologies she is looking at and the environment within which that looking takes place. Film theorist Laura Marks (2004) argues that haptic visuality is precisely what disrupts modernity's reliance on optical visuality because it changes the emphasis from the symbolic (which distances the observer from the object) to the mimetic (which foregrounds both materiality and embodiment). As Marks explains, "haptic visuality has a strong sense of the material connection between vision and the object. It thus is mimetic: it presses up to the object and takes its shape. Mimesis is a form of representation based on contact, on getting close enough to the other thing to become it" (82) (see also Marks 1999; 2002).

5 This devolution of tourism security to PSCs was evident in the Balinese Hotel Association's employment of private "risk advisor" Andreas Wimmer to author the comprehensive Bali Security Plan implemented by Bali's governor and chief of police. Subsequently, the Australian private security firm SNP Security (which holds the contracts for Sydney Airport and Sydney Opera House) were employed to complete a "comprehensive safety audit" of Bali's tourism industry—an initiative that had the full cooperation of the Indonesian government, local police, and official counterterrorism units (Bali Discovery Tours 2006).

Conclusion

1 A more situated recent effort to develop Diller + Scofidio's project is photographer Rob Hornstra and writer Arnold van Bruggen's (2013) *The Sochi Project*, a comprehensive account of their engagements with leisure, power, travel, memory, and everyday life in the Caucasus during the buildup to the Sochi Winter Olympics in 2014.

Bibliography

Abdallah, Ghassan. 2002. "A Palestinian at Yad Vashem." *Jerusalem Quarterly,* no. 15: 42–45.

Abowd, Thomas. 2007. "Present and Absent: Historical Invention and the Politics of Place in Colonial Jerusalem." In *Reapproaching Borders: New Perspectives on the Study of Israel-Palestine,* edited by Sandra Sufian and Mark Levine, 243–65. Plymouth, U.K.: Rowman and Littlefield.

Acuto, Michele, and Simon Curtis, eds. 2013. *Reassembling International Theory.* London: Palgrave Macmillan.

Adey, Peter. 2004. "Secured and Sorted Mobilities: Examples from the Airport." *Surveillance and Society* 1, no. 4: 500–519.

———. 2009. "Facing Airport Security: Affect, Biopolitics, and the Preemptive Securitization of the Mobile Body." *Environment and Planning D: Society and Space* 27, no. 3: 444–64.

Adey, Peter, Laure Brayer, Damian Masson, Patrick Murphy, Paul Simpson, and Nicolas Tixier. 2013. "Pour Votre Tranquilité: Ambience, Atmosphere and Surveillance." *Geoforum* 49: 299–309.

Advertising Archives. 2014a. "Cuba Tourism." http://www.advertisingarchives.co.uk/index.php?service=search&action=do_quick_search&language=en&q=Cuba+Tourism.

———. 2014b. "Exotic Holiday." http://www.advertisingarchives.co.uk/index.php?service=search&action=do_quick_search&language=en&q=exotic+holiday.

Agence France Presse. 2002. "Seven Australians Identified among 187 Dead." *Sydney Morning Herald,* October 13. http://www.smh.com.au/articles/2002/10/13/1034222664046.html.

———. 2004. "Rumsfeld Bans Camera Phones in Iraq." *Sydney Morning Herald,* May 24. http://www.smh.com.au/articles/2004/05/23/1085250873479.html.

Ahmed, Sara. 2004. *The Cultural Politics of Emotion.* Edinburgh: Edinburgh University Press.

Akbar, Arifa. 2006. "Anger as 'Mob' Forces Muslim Men off Aircraft." *The Independent,* August 21, 12.

Alexander, Bevin. 1991. *Korea: The First War We Lost.* 2nd ed. London: Hippocrene Books.
Allen, James, Hilton Als, John Lewis, and Leon F. Litwack. 2000. *Without Sanctuary: Lynching Photography in America.* Santa Fe, N.M.: Twin Palms.
Allen, James, and John Littlefield. 2005. *Without Sanctuary: Photographs and Postcards of Lynching in America.* http://withoutsanctuary.org/main.html.
Allred, Keith J. 2006. "Peacekeepers and Prostitutes: The Demand for Trafficked Women and New Hope for Stopping It." *Armed Forces and Society* 33, no. 1: 5–23.
Alneng, Victor. 2002. "'What the Fuck Is a Vietnam?' Touristic Phantasms and the Popcolonization of (the) Vietnam (War)." *Critique of Anthropology* 22, no. 4: 461–89.
Alsayyad, Nezar, ed. 2001. *Consuming Tradition, Manufacturing Heritage: Global Norms and Urban Forms in the Age of Tourism.* London: Routledge.
American Hotel and Lodging Educational Institute. 2011a. *Eye on Awareness: Hotel Security and Anti-Terrorism Training.* https://www.ahlei.org/Products/Online-Learning/Eye-on-Awareness_-_Hotel-Security-Training/.
———. 2011b. "New AHLEI Hotel Security and Anti-Terrorism Training Program Focuses on Vital Role of Front-Line Employees." Press Release, April. https://ahlei.org/Press-Releases/New-AHLEI-Hotel-Security-and-Anti-Terrorism-Training-Program-Focuses-on-Vital-Role-of-Front-Line-Employees/.
———. 2013. "Eye on Awareness—Hotel Security Training (Online Program)." http://www.youtube.com/watch?v=S4lCn3synAA.
Amis, Martin. 2007. "No, I Am Not a Racist." *Guardian,* December 1. http://www.guardian.co.uk/books/2007/dec/01/race.islam.
Amoore, Louise. 2006. "Biometric Borders: Governing Mobilities in the War on Terror." *Political Geography* 25, no. 3: 336–51.
———. 2007. "Vigilant Visualities: The Watchful Politics of the War on Terror." *Security Dialogue* 38, no. 2: 215–32.
———. 2009. "Lines of Sight: On the Visualization of Unknown Futures." *Citizenship Studies* 13, no. 1: 17–30.
———. 2014. *The Politics of Possibility: Risk and Security beyond Probability.* Durham, N.C.: Duke University Press.
Amoore, Louise, and Marieke De Goede, eds. 2008. *Risk and the War on Terror.* London: Routledge.
Amoore, Louise, and Alex Hall. 2009. "Taking People Apart: Digitized Dissection and the Body at the Border." *Environment and Planning D: Society and Space* 27, no. 2: 274–95.
Anderegg, Michael, ed. 1991. *Inventing Vietnam: The War in Film and Television.* Philadelphia: Temple University Press.

Anderson, Ben. 2010a. "Preemption, Precaution, Preparedness: Anticipatory Action and Future Geographies." *Progress in Human Geographies* 34, no. 6: 777-98.

——. 2010b. "Morale and the Affective Geographies of the 'War on Terror.'" *Cultural Geographies* 17, no. 2: 219-36.

——. 2014. *Encountering Affect: Capacities, Apparatuses, Conditions*. Farnham, U.K.: Ashgate.

Anderson, John R. 2004. "USAREUR's Reintegration Program Eases Iraq Returns." *Stars and Stripes,* February 1. http://www.stripes.com/news/usareur-s-reintegration-program-eases-iraq-returns-1.16187.

Andrews, Hazel, ed. 2014. *Tourism and Violence*. Farnham, U.K.: Ashgate.

Apel, Dora. 2003. "On Looking: Lynching Photographs and Legacies of Lynching after 9/11." *American Quarterly* 55, no. 3: 457-78.

——. 2005. "Torture Culture: Lynching Photographs and the Images of Abu Ghraib." *Art Journal* 64, no. 2: 92-93.

Aradau, Claudia. 2010. "Security That Matters: Critical Infrastructure and Objects of Protection." *Security Dialogue* 41, no. 5: 491-514.

Aradau, Claudia, and Rens Van Munster. 2007. "Governing Terrorism through Risk: Taking Precautions, (Un)knowing the Future." *European Journal of International Relations* 13, no. 1: 89-115.

——. 2008. "Taming the Future: The Dispositif of Risk in the War on Terror." In *Risk and the War on Terror,* edited by Louise Amoore and Marieke De Goede, 23-40. London: Routledge.

——. 2009. "Exceptionalism and the 'War on Terror': Criminology Meets International Relations." *British Journal of Criminology* 49, no. 5: 686-701.

Ashworth, G. 2002. "Review of *Dark Tourism."* *Tourism Management* 23, no. 2: 190-91.

Ashworth, G., and Rudi Hartmann, eds. 2005. *Horror and Human Tragedy Revisited: The Management of Sites of Atrocity for Tourism*. Putnam Valley, N.Y.: Cognizant Communication Corporation.

Askjellerud, Sashana. 2003. "The Tourist: A Messenger of Peace?" *Annals of Tourism Research* 30, no. 3: 744-47.

Association of Chief Police Officers. 2008. *Counter Terrorism Protective Security Advice for Hotels and Restaurants*. London: National Counter Terrorism Security Office. http://www.scotland.police.uk/assets/pdf/keep_safe/234532/hotels-and-restaurants.

Aufderheide, Pat. 1990. "Vietnam: Good Soldiers." In *Seeing through Movies,* edited by Mark Crispin Miller, 81-111. New York: Pantheon Books.

Auschwitz-Birkenau Memorial Museum. 2014a. "History of the Memorial." http://en.auschwitz.org/m/index.php?option=com_content&task=blogcategory&id=13&Itemid=13.

———. 2014b. "The First Years of the Memorial." http://en.auschwitz.org/m/index.php?option=com_content&task=view&id=228&Itemid=13.
———. 2014c. "Attendance." http://en.auschwitz.org/z/index.php?option=com_content&task=view&id=56&Itemid=24.
———. 2014d. "Rules for Visiting." http://en.auschwitz.org/z/index.php?option=com_content&task=view&id=66&Itemid=31.
Austin, Nathan K. 2002. "Managing Heritage Attractions: Marketing Challenges at Sensitive Historical Sites." *International Journal of Tourism Research* 4, no. 6: 447–57.
Australasian Leisure Management. 2009. "Australians Encouraged to Take Their Leave." April 2. http://www.ausleisure.com.au/news/australians-encouraged-to-take-their-leave/.
Australian Associated Press and Lee-Maree Gallo. 2011. "Australia's Annual Leave Hoard 'a Disgrace': Ferguson." *Sydney Morning Herald*, June 9. http://www.smh.com.au/travel/travel-planning/travel-news/australias-annual-leave-hoard-a-disgrace-ferguson-20110609-1ftsq.html.
Australian Official Photographer. 1918. "The Band of the 21 Australian Battalion Rehearse in the Middle of a Ruined Farmyard, Surrounded by Debris, Cappy, France." Catalog no. E (AUS) 3325. Imperial War Museum Archive, London.
Avella, Amparo E., and Allan S. Mills. 1996. "Tourism in Cuba in the 1990s: Back to the Future?" *Tourism Management* 17, no. 1: 55–60.
Aviv, Caryn. 2011. "The Emergence of Alternative Jewish Tourism." *European Review of History* 18, no. 1: 33–43.
Bachner, Evan. 2004. *At Ease: Navy Men of World War II*. New York: Harry N. Abrams.
———. 2007. *Men of WWII: Fighting Men at Ease*. New York: Harry N. Abrams.
Bailey, Beth, and David Farber. 1992. *The First Strange Place: The Alchemy of Race and Sex in World War II Hawaii*. Baltimore: Johns Hopkins University Press.
Bailey, Paul J. 2011. "'An Army of Workers': Chinese Indentured Labour in First World War France." In *Race, Empire, and First World War Writing*, edited by Santanu Das, 35–52. Cambridge: Cambridge University Press.
Bailey, P. n.d. "Diary of 2nd Lieutenant P. Bailey." Private Papers of 2nd Lieutenant P. Bailey, Documents 13587. Imperial War Museum Archive, London.
Baker, Chuck. 2014a. "The Brownie Camera Page." http://www.brownie-camera.com/index.shtml.
Bal, Mieke. 1993. "His Master's Eye." In *Modernity and the Hegemony of Vision*, edited by David Michael Levin, 379–405. Berkeley: University of California Press.
Bali Discovery Tours. 2006. "Bali Gets High Marks in Australian Safety Audit."

December 16. http://www.balidiscovery.com/messages/printmessage.asp?Id=3553.
Ballantyne, R. 2003. "Interpreting Apartheid: Vistors' Perceptions of the District 6 Museum." *Curator: The Museum Journal* 46, no. 3: 279-92.
Ballard, Jeff. 2005. "My 18th Month Vacation to the Beach." December 25. http://sgtballard.blogspot.co.uk/.
Ballard-Reisch, Deborah. 1991. "*China Beach* and *Tour of Duty*: American Television and Revisionist History of the Vietnam War." *Journal of Popular Culture* 25, no. 3: 135-49.
Baranowski, Shelly. 2004. *Strength through Joy: Consumerism and Mass Tourism in the Third Reich*. Cambridge: Cambridge University Press.
Barkawi, Tarak. 2001. "War inside the Free World: The Democratic Peace and the Cold War in the Third World." In *Democracy, Liberalism, and War: Rethinking the Democratic Peace Debates,* edited by Tarak Barkawi & Mark Laffey, 107-28. Boulder, Colo.: Lynne Rienner.
———. 2004. "People, Homelands, and War? Ethnicity, the Military, and the Battle among British Imperial Forces in the War against Japan." *Comparative Studies in Society and History* 46, no. 1: 134-63.
———. 2006a. "Culture and Combat in the Colonies: The Indian Army and the Second World War." *Journal of Contemporary History* 41, no. 2: 325-55.
———. 2006b. *Globalization and War*. Lanham, Md.: Rowman and Littlefield.
———. 2013. "War, Armed Forces and Society in Postcolonial Perspective." In *Postcolonial Theory and International Relations,* edited by Sanjay Seth, 87-105. London: Routledge.
Barkawi, Tarak, and Shane Brighton. 2011. "Powers of War: Fighting, Knowledge, and Critique." *International Political Sociology* 5, no. 2: 126-43.
Barkawi, Tarak, and Mark Laffey. 1999. "The Imperial Peace: Democracy, Force, and Globalization." *European Journal of International Relations* 5, no. 4: 403-34.
———. 2006. "The Postcolonial Moment in Security Studies." *Review of International Studies* 32, no. 2: 329-52.
Barkawi, Tarak, and Keith Stanski, eds. 2012. *Orientalism and War*. New York: Columbia University Press.
Barry, Kathleen. 1995. *The Prostitution of Sexuality: The Global Exploitation of Women*. New York: New York University Press.
Barthes, Roland. 1993. *Camera Lucida: Reflections on Photography*. London: Vintage Classics.
Basham, Kathryn. 2008. "Homecoming as Safe Haven or the New Front: Attachment and Detachment in Military Couples." *Clinical Social Work Journal* 36, no. 1: 83-96.

Baudrillard, Jean. 2006. "War Porn." *Journal of Visual Culture* 5, no. 1: 86–88.
BBC. 2005a. "Dark Tourism." *Excess Baggage,* Radio 4, March 5. http://www.bbc.co.uk/radio4/excessbaggage/index_20050305.shtml.
———. 2005b. "WW2 People's War: Fact File: Baedeker Raids." http://www.bbc.co.uk/history/ww2peopleswar/timeline/factfiles/nonflash/a1132921.shtml.
Beazley, Olwen. 2002. "A Paradox of Peace: The Hiroshima Peace Museum (Genbaku Dome) as World Heritage." In *A Fearsome Heritage: Diverse Legacies of the Cold War,* edited by John Schofield and Wayne Cocroft, 33–50. Walnut Creek, Calif.: Left Coast Press.
Beech, John. 2000. "The Enigma of Holocaust Sites as Tourist Attractions—The Case of Buchenwald." *Managing Leisure* 5, no. 1: 29–41.
Behdad, Ali. 1994. *Belated Travellers: Orientalism in an Age of Colonial Dissolution.* Durham, N.C.: Duke University Press.
Belfast Exposed Photography Gallery. n.d. "Exhibitions." http://www.belfastexposed.org/belfast_exposed_gallery.
Belfast Newsletter. 2003. "The Maze: Help Find the Key to Prison's Future." December 5, 1, 5.
Belfast Telegraph. 2004. "Maze Can Be Tourist Attraction: SF." August 19.
Bell, Steve. 2002. "War on Turrrism." *Guardian,* November 28. http://www.belltoons.co.uk/bellworks/index.php/leaders/2002/1853-29-11-02_WARONTURRRISM.
Bender, Marylin, and Selig Altschull. 1982. *The Chosen Instrument: Pan Am, Juan Trippe, and the Rise and Fall of an American Entrepreneur.* New York: Simon and Schuster.
Bennett, Ronan. 2007. "Shame on Us." *Guardian,* November 19. http://www.guardian.co.uk/uk/2007/nov/19/race.bookscomment.
Ben-Se'ev, Efrat, and Eyal Ben-Ari. 1999. "War, Heroism, and Public Representations: The Case of a Museum of 'Co-existence' in Jerusalem." In *The Military and Militarism in Israeli Society,* edited by Edna Lomsky-Feder and Eyal Ben-Ari, 117–39. Albany: State University of New York Press.
Benvenisti, Meron. 1998. *City of Stone: The Hidden History of Jerusalem.* Berkeley: University of California Press.
Berman, Mildred. 1994. "D-Day and Geography." *Geographical Review* 84, no. 4: 469–75.
Beurier, Joëlle. 2004. "Death and Material Culture: The Case of Pictures during the First World War." In *Matters of Conflict: Material Culture, Memory, and the First World War,* edited by Nicholas J. Saunders, 109–22. London: Routledge.
Beyers, Christiaan. 2008. "The Cultural Politics of 'Community' and Citizenship in the District 6 Museum, Cape Town." *Anthropologica* 50, no. 2: 359–73.

Biancani, Francesca. 2012. "'Let Down the Curtains around Us': Sex Work in Colonial Cairo 1882-1952." PhD thesis, London School of Economics and Political Science.

Bianchi, Raoul. 2003. "Whose Security? Freedom, Risk, and Dissent in Global Tourism." Paper presented at Managing on the Edge: Shifts in the Relationship between Responsibility, Governance, and Sustainability Conference, University of Nijmegen, September 25-26.

———. 2007. "Tourism and the Globalization of Fear: Analysing the Politics of Risk and (In)security in Global Travel." *Tourism and Hospitality Research* 7, no. 1: 64-74.

Bianchi, Raoul, and Marcus Stephenson. 2014. *Tourism and Citizenship: Rights, Freedoms, and Responsibilities in the Global Order*. London: Routledge.

Bickford, Andrew. 2003. "See the World, Meet Interesting People, Have Sex with Them: Tourism, Sex, and Recruitment in the US Military." *American Sexuality Magazine* 1, no. 5.

Bigo, Didier. 2010. "Delivering Liberty and Security? The Reframing of Freedom When Associated with Security." In *Europe's 21st Century Challenge: Delivering Liberty*, edited by Didier Bigo, S. Carrera, Elspeth Guild, and R. B. J. Walker, 388-420. London: Ashgate.

Bigo, Didier, and A. Tsoukala, eds. 2008. *Terror, Insecurity, and Liberty: Illiberal Practices of Liberal Regimes after 9/11*. London: Routledge.

Black, Jeremy. 2010. *The Age of Total War: 1860-1945*. Lanham, Md.: Rowman and Littlefield.

Blackhouse, Constance. 1999. *Colour-Coded: A Legal History of Racism in Canada, 1900-1950*. Toronto: University of Toronto Press.

Blair, William. 2011. "Engagement and Empathy: 'Post Conflict' Interpretation of the Troubles in Northern Ireland." In *INTERCOM Conference Proceedings*. http://www.intercom.museum/conferences/2011/conference_papers.html.

———. 2012. Interview with the author. April 26.

Blake, A., and M. T. Sinclair. 2003. "Tourism Crisis Management: U.S. Response to September 11." *Annals of Tourism Research* 30, no. 4: 817-20.

Blanchard, Linda-Anne, and Freya Higgins-Desbiolles, eds. 2013. *Peace through Tourism: Promoting Human Security through International Citizenship*. London: Routledge.

Blanchard, Ralph. 1997. "The History of the YMCA in World War I." In *Doughboy Center: The Story of the American Expeditionary Forces*. http://www.worldwar1.com/dbc/ymca.htm.

Bleiker, Roland. 2009. *Aesthetics and World Politics*. London: Palgrave Macmillan.

Blom, T. 2000. "Morbid Tourism: A Postmodern Market Niche with an Example from Althorp." *Norwegian Journal of Geography* 54, no. 1: 29-36.

Boileau, John. 2004. "Voyageurs on the Nile." *Legion Magazine,* January 1.
Bonham, C., C. Edmonds, and J. Mak. 2006. "The Impact of 9/11 and Other Terrible Events on Tourism in the United States and Hawaii." *Journal of Travel Research* 45, no. 1: 99–110.
Booth, Allyson. 1997. *Postcards from the Trenches: Negotiating the Space between Modernism and the First World War.* Oxford: Oxford University Press.
Booth, Janice, and Philip Briggs. 2004. *Rwanda: The Bradt Travel Guide.* 2nd ed. Chalfont St. Peter, U.K.: Bradt Travel Guides.
Bowling, Ursula B., and Michelle D. Sherman. 2008. "Welcoming Them Home: Supporting Service Members and Their Families in Navigating the Tasks of Reintegration." *Professional Psychology: Research and Practice* 39, no. 4: 451–58.
Bowman, Glen. 1992. "The Politics of Tour Guiding: Israeli and Palestinian Guides and the Occupied Territories." In *Tourism and the Less Developed Countries,* edited by D. Harrison, 121–34. London: Belhaven Press.
Bowman, Michael S., and Phaedra C. Pezzullo. 2010. "What's So 'Dark' about 'Dark Tourism'? Death, Tours, and Performance." *Tourism Studies* 9, no. 3: 187–202.
Boyle, Danny, dir. 2000. *The Beach.* United States: Twentieth Century Fox.
Briggs, Mrs. L. K. n.d. "Index and Notes of 500 Lantern Slides, Ypres and District, 1919–1939." Private Papers of Mrs. L. K. Briggs, Documents 21795. Imperial War Museum Archive, London.
Brin, Eldad. 2006. "Politically-Oriented Tourism in Jerusalem." *Tourist Studies* 6, no. 3: 226–30.
Brin, Eldad, and Chaim Noy. 2010. "The Said and the Unsaid: Performative Guiding in a Jerusalem Neighbourhood." *Tourist Studies* 10, no. 1: 19–33.
Brock, D., and D. Walker. 2008. "Hotel Security and the Routine Activities Approach." *The Police Journal* 81, no. 2: 144–53.
Brock, Rita Nakashima, and Susan Brooks Thistlewaite. 1996. *Casting Stones: Prostitution and the Liberation in Asia and the United States.* Minneapolis, Minn.: Augsburg Fortress.
Brooks, Earnest. 1917. "First Army Horse Show, Chateau de la Haie, 25th June 1917. The YMCA Tent on the Ground." Catalogue no. Q 2423. Imperial War Museum Archive, London.
Brooks, Geraldine. 1991. "Please Don't Offend the Saudis." *Esquire,* April, 94–97.
Brough, Graham, and Victoria Bone. 2006. "Malaga Jet Mutiny Pair's Shock at Plane Ejection." *The Mirror,* August 23, 8, 12, 20.
Brown, Frances. 1989. "Is Tourism Really a Peacemaker?" *Tourism Management,* December, 270–71.

Brown, Ian Malcolm. 1998. *British Logistics on the Western Front, 1914–1919.* Westport, Conn.: Greenwood Press.

Brown, Kris. 2008. *Artefacts Audit: A Report of the Material Culture of the Conflict in and about Northern Ireland.* Belfast: Healing through Remembering.

Brown, Michael. 2009. "Public Health as Urban Politics, Urban Geography: Venereal Biopower in Seattle, 1943–1983." *Urban Geography* 30, no. 1: 1–29.

Brown, Michael, and Larry Knopp. 2010. "Between Anatamo- and Bio-politics: Geographies of Sexual Health in Wartime Seattle." *Political Geography* 29, no. 7: 392–403.

Brown, Steven D. 1997. "In the Wake of Disaster: Stress, Hysteria, and the Event." In *Ideas of Difference: Social Spaces and the Labour of Division*, edited by Kevin Hetherington and Rolland Monro, 68–87. Oxford: Blackwell.

Brown, Wendy. 2006. *Regulating Aversion: Tolerance in the Age of Identity and Empire.* Princeton, N.J.: Princeton University Press.

Buckley, Bernadette. 2011. "Eugenie Dolberg: Open Shutters Iraq." *Photoworks*, no. 16: 82–83.

Burds, Jeffrey. 2009. "Sexual Violence in Europe in World War II." *Politics and Society* 37, no. 1: 35–73.

Burchell, Graham, Colin Gordon, and Peter Miller, eds. 1991. *The Foucault Effect: Studies in Governmentality.* Chicago: University of Chicago Press.

Burke, Matthew M. 2012. "Military's New R&R Plan Doesn't Include Leaving Afghanistan." *Stars and Stripes,* June 18. http://www.stripes.com/news/military-s-new-r-r-plan-doesn-t-include-leaving-afghanistan-1.180662.

Burryte, Dovile, and Erica Resende, eds. 2013. *Memory and Trauma in International Relations.* London: Routledge.

Buruma, Ian. 2002. "Loving the Alien: We Mustn't Swallow the East versus West Propaganda over the Bali Bomb." *Guardian,* October 25, 5.

Bush, George W. 2001a. "Address to a Joint Session of Congress and the American People." September 20. http://available at http://georgewbush-whitehouse.archives.gov/news/releases/2001/09/20010920-8.html.

———. 2001b. "My Fellow Americans—Let's Roll: President Discusses War on Terrorism." November 8. http://georgewbush-whitehouse.archives.gov/news/releases/2001/11/20011108-13.html.

———. 2002. "President Delivers State of the Union Address." January 29. http://georgewbush-whitehouse.archives.gov/news/releases/2002/01/20020129-11.html.

Butler, Judith. 2005. "Photography, War, Outrage." *PMLA* 120, no. 3: 822–27.

———. 2007. "Torture and the Ethics of Photography." *Environment and Planning D: Society and Space* 25, no. 6: 951–66.

———. 2009. *Frames of War: When Is Life Grievable?* London: Verso.

Butler, Richard, and Suntikul Wantanee, eds. 2013. *Tourism and War*. London: Routledge.

Buzan, Barry, Ole Waever, and J. De Wilde. 1998. *Security: A New Framework for Analysis*. London: Lynne Rienner.

Calhoun, Craig. 2002. "The Class-Consciousness of Frequent Travellers: Towards a Critique of Actually Existing Cosmopolitanism." *South Atlantic Quarterly* 101, no. 4: 869–97.

Caluya, Gilbert. 2010. "The Post-panoptic Society? Reassessing Foucault in Surveillance Studies." *Social Identities* 16, no. 5: 621–33.

Camon, Alessandro. 2004. "American Torture, American Porn." *Salon*, June 7. http://dir.salon.com/story/opinion/feature/2004/06/07/torture/index.html.

Campbell, David. 2004. "Horrific Blindness: Images of Death in Contemporary Media." *Journal of Cultural Research* 8, no. 1: 55–74.

———. 2007. "Geopolitics and Visuality: Sighting the Darfur Conflict." *Political Geography* 26, no. 4: 357–82.

Campbell-Bannerman, Henry. 1928. "Letter Addressed to Thomas Cook & Son by the Right Honourable Henry Campbell-Bannerman, the Secretary of State for War, 30 July, 1886." Resume of Gordon Relief Expedition, folio 152, February 1928 (6.3.2). Thomas Cook Archives, Peterborough.

Carmichael, Jane. 1989. *First World War Photographers*. London: Routledge.

Carr, Jamie M. 2006. *Queer Times: Christopher Isherwood's Modernity*. London: Routledge.

Carr, Matt. 2012. "Israel's Extreme Tourism: War and Occupation for Fun and Profit." *Ceasefire Magazine*, August 15. http://ceasefiremagazine.co.uk/israels-extreme-tourism-war-occupation-fun-profit/.

Carter, Bill, Jim Rutenberg, and Mindy Sink. 2004. "Pentagon Ban on Pictures of Dead Troops Is Broken." *New York Times*, April 23, A14.

Caruth, Cathy. 1995. *Trauma: Explorations in Memory*. Baltimore: Johns Hopkins University Press.

Causevic, Senija, and Paul Lynch. 2005. "The Significance of Dark Tourism in the Process of Tourism Development after a Long-Term Political Conflict: An Issue of Northern Ireland." http://www.mecon.nomadit.co.uk/pub/conference_epaper_download.php5?PaperID=1355&MIMEType=application/pdf.

———. 2006. "Tourism Development and Contested Communities." http://www.espacestemps.net/articles/tourism-development-and-contested-communities/.

Caute, David. 2003. *A Dancer Defects: The Struggle for Cultural Supremacy during the Cold War*. Oxford: Oxford University Press.

CBC. 2007. "Vietnam War: Bangkok R&R with Bill Cunningham, 1968." http://www.youtube.com/watch?v=JKG_f9_C5-8.
Cecil, Hugh. 1998. "British Correspondents and the Sudan Campaign of 1896–98." In *Sudan: The Reconquest Reappraised,* edited by Edward M. Spiers, 102–27. Abingdon, U.K.: Frank Cass.
Centre for Human Rights, Social Justice, and Democracy. 2002. *Sites of Conscience: A Vision for the Future of the "International Coalition of Historic Site Museums of Conscience."* November 14. New York: Ford Foundation.
Chan, E. S. W., and D. Lam. 2013. "Hotel Safety and Security Systems: Bridging the Gap between Managers and Guests." *International Journal of Hospitality Management* 32: 202–16.
Chang, Emily Nyen. 2001. "Engagement Abroad: Enlisted Men, US Military Policy, and the Sex Industry." *Notre Dame Journal of Ethics and Public Policy* 15, no. 2: 621–53.
Cheah, P., and B. Robbins, eds. 1998. *Cosmopolitics: Thinking and Feeling beyond the Nation.* Minneapolis: University of Minnesota Press.
Chin, Christine B. N. 2008. *Cruising the Global Economy: Profits, Pleasure, and Work at Sea.* Aldershot, U.K.: Ashgate.
Cho, Hyunjung. 2012. "Hiroshima Peace Memorial Park and the Making of Japanese Postwar Architecture." *Journal of Architectural Education* 66, no. 1: 72–83.
Choi, Shine. 2015. *Re-imagining North Korea in International Politics: Problems and Alternatives.* London: Routledge.
Choron-Baix, Catherine. 2009. "Le Vrai Voyage: L'Art de Dinh Q. Lê Entre Exil et Retour." *Revue Européenne des Migrations Internationales* 5, no. 2: 51–68. http://remi.revues.org/4948?lang=en.
Chow, Rey. 2006. *The Age of the World Target: Self-Referentiality in War, Theory, and Comparative Work.* Durham, N.C.: Duke University Press.
Churchill, Winston S. 1949. *The River War: An Account of the Reconquest of the Sudan.* 3rd ed. London: Eyre and Spottiswoode.
———. 1991. "'Up the River with the 21st Lancers': A Dispatch for London's *Morning Post.*" Reprinted in Deborah Manley, *The Nile: A Traveller's Anthology,* 199–200. London: Cassell Illustrated.
Clancey, Michael. 2008. "Cruising to Exclusion: Commodity Chains, the Cruise Industry, and Development in the Caribbean." *Globalizations* 5, no. 3: 405–18.
———. 2009. *Brand New Ireland? Tourism, Development, and National Identity in the Irish Republic.* Aldershot, U.K.: Ashgate.
Clapson, Mark, and Peter J. Larkham. 2013. *The Blitz and Its Legacy: Wartime Destruction to Post-war Reconstruction.* Farnham, U.K.: Ashgate.

Clarke, Richard. 2000. "Self-Presentation in a Contested City: Palestinian and Israeli Political Tourism in Hebron." *Anthropology Today* 16, no. 5: 12–18.

Clayton, Jonathan, and Daniel McGrory. 2002. "Victims of the Terror They Came to Escape." *The Times*, November 29, 1.

Clement, Tracey. 2007. "Blood, Sweat, and Fears: Penny Byrne." *Artlink* 27, no. 2. http://www.artlink.com.au/articles.cfm?id=2980#.

Clements, Kate. 2012. "Podcast 17: Home on Leave." June 19. http://www.1914.org/podcasts.

Clifford, James. 1997. *Routes: Travel and Translation in the Late Twentieth Century*. Cambridge, Mass.: Harvard University Press.

Clifton, Darrell. 2012. *Hospitality Security: Managing Security in Today's Hotel, Lodging, Entertainment, and Tourism Environment*. Boca Raton, Fla.: CRC Press/Taylor and Francis.

Coaffee, John, and David Murikami Wood. 2006. "Security Is Coming Home: Rethinking Scale and Constructing Resilience in the Global Urban Response to Terrorist Risk." *International Relations* 20, no. 4: 503–17.

Coffey, Frank. 1991. *Always Home: 50 Years of the USO—the Official Photographic History*. Dulles, Va.: Potomac Books.

Cohen, Eliot A., ed. 1993. *Logistics and Support*. Vol. 3 of *Gulf War Air Power Survey*. Washington, D.C.: Defense Department and Gulf War Air Power Survey Review Committee.

Cohen, Eric H. 2011. "Educational Dark Tourism at an *In Populo* Site: The Holocaust Museum in Jerusalem." *Annals of Tourism Research* 38, no. 1: 193–209.

Coiste na n-Iarchimí. 2003. *A Museum at Long Kesh or the Maze? A Report on Conference Proceedings*. Belfast: Coiste na n-Iarchimí.

Cole, Lester. 1959a. "Cuban Dictator Fidel Castro." January 10. http://www.corbisimages.com/stock-photo/rights-managed/AAJZ001003/cuban-dictator-fidel-castro?popup=1.

———. 1959b. "Hilton Havana 1959: Lester Cole Photographic Archive." http://www.corbisimages.com/Search#q=Hilton+Havana+1959&p=1.

———. 1959c. "Message on Chalkboard." January 1. http://www.corbisimages.com/stock-photo/rights-managed/AAJZ001062/message-on-chalkboard?popup=1.

Cole, Tim. 2000. *Selling the Holocaust, from Auschwitz to Schindler: How History Is Bought, Packaged, and Sold*. London: Routledge.

———. 2013. "(Re)Visiting Auschwitz: (Re)encountering the Holocaust in its Landscapes." *Cultural History* 2, no. 2: 232–46.

Collet, T. 2009. "Civilization and Civilized in Post-9/11 US Presidential Speeches." *Discourse and Society* 20, no. 4: 455–75.

Commiserat General Au Tourism. 1945. "How to See Paris: For the Soldiers of the Allied Army, Paris." Catalog no. K 00/2221. Imperial War Museum Archive, London.

Commissariat au Tourisme and Franco-Allied Good Will Committee. 1940. "How to See the Côte D'Azur for Soldiers of the Allied Armies, Paris." Catalog no. K 79/1210, Shelf Mark 29(449.4)/5. Imperial War Museum Archive, London.

Conflict Archive on the Internet. n.d. "Memorial Database." http://www.cain.ulst.ac.uk/victims/memorials/search.html.

Conforti, J. 1964. *Conrad N. Hilton, Hotelier.* Minneapolis, Minn.: T. S. Denison.

Connery, Christopher. 2008. "Political Tourism in a Problem Country: Teaching *Moby Dick* in Cyprus." *Postcolonial Studies* 11, no. 4: 401–16.

Connolly, Colm. 2004. "What Will We Do with the Maze?" *Belfast Newsletter,* February 16, 2.

Connolly, William E. 2005. "The Evangelical-Capitalist Resonance Machine." *Political Theory* 33, no. 6: 869–86.

Constantinou, Costas. 2008. "On the Cypriot States of Exception." *International Political Sociology* 2, no. 2: 145–64.

Constantinou, Costas, and Yiannis Papadakis. 2001. "The Cypriot State(s) *In Situ*: Cross-ethnic Contact and the Discourse of Recognition." *Global Society* 15, no. 2: 125–48.

Constitution Hill Museum. 2013. "Programmes and Special Events." http://www.constitutionhill.org.za/site/?page_id=19.

Conway, Maura. 2006. "Terrorism and the Internet: New Media—New Threat?" *Parliamentary Affairs* 59, no. 2: 283–98.

Conway, Maura, and Lisa McInerney. 2008. "Jihadi Video and Auto-radicalization: Evidence from an Exploratory YouTube Study." *Intelligence and Security Informatics,* no. 5376: 108–18.

Cook, John Mason. 1885. *Visit to the Soudan in Connection with the Expedition of 1884–85.* Address delivered at the Royal Normal College for the Blind, Upper Norwood. Peterborough: Thomas Cook Archives, Peterborough.

Cook, Thomas. 1884a. *Cook's Excursionist and Tourist Advertiser, No. XXXIV,* no. 12, December 11.

———. 1884b. *Cook's Excursionist and Tourist Advertiser, No. XXXIV,* no. 11, November 1.

———. 1884c. *Cook's Excursionist and Tourist Advertiser, No. XXXIV,* no. 10, September 8.

———. 1885a. *Cook's Excursionist and Home and Tourist Advertiser, no. XXXV,* no. 12, December 11.

———. 1885b. *Cook's Excursionist and Home and Foreign Tourist Advertiser, No. XXXV,* no. 11, November 2.

———. 1885c. *Cook's Excursionist and Tourist Advertiser,* No. XXXV, no. 1, February 2.

Coon, Charlie. 2006. "Edelweiss: At Garmisch Ski Resort, a Little R&R for the Entire Family." *Stars and Stripes,* April 9. http://www.stripes.com/news/edelweiss-at-garmisch-ski-resort-a-little-r-r-for-the-entire-family-1.47486.

Cornish, Paul. 2004. "'Sacred Relics': Objects in the Imperial War Museum 1917–1939." In *Matters of Conflict: Material Culture, Memory, and the First World War,* edited by Nicholas J. Saunders, 35–50. London: Routledge.

Courtnenay, Ashley. 1941. *Let's Halt awhile in Wartime: Being Some Recommendations from Personal Experience on Where to Spend Your Leave.* London: Ashley Courtenay/Wilding and Son. Catalog no. 82/2355, Shelf Mark 63(41).82/5. Imperial War Museum Archive, London.

Cowan, Deborah. 2010. "A Geography of Logistics: Market Authority and the Security of Supply Chains." *Annals for the Association of American Geographers* 100, no. 3: 1–21.

———. 2014. *The Deadly Life of Logistics: Mapping Violence in Global Trade.* Minneapolis: University of Minnesota Press.

Coward, Martin. 2010. "Between Us in the City: Materiality, Subjectivity, and Community in the Era of Global Urbanization." *Environment and Planning D: Society and Space* 30, no. 3: 468–81.

Crandall, Jordan. 2005. "Envisioning the Homefront: Militarization, Tracking, and Security Culture," in conversation with John Armitage. *Journal of Visual Culture* 4, no. 1: 17–38.

Crang, Mike. 1997. "Picturing Practices: Research through the Tourist Gaze." *Progress in Human Geography* 21, no. 3: 359–73.

Crary, Jonathan. 1992. *Techniques of the Observer: On Vision and Modernity in the Nineteenth Century.* Cambridge, Mass.: MIT Press.

———. 1999. *Suspensions of Perception: Attention, Spectacle, and Modern Culture.* Cambridge, Mass.: MIT Press.

Crawshay, Frost H. 1918. "Two German Prisoners of War Wearing Clown Costumes Made of Sacking for a Theatrical Entertainment at 360 POW Company, France." Catalog no. Q 49578. Imperial War Museum Archive, London.

Crooke, Elizabeth. 2001. "Confronting a Troubled History: Which Past in Northern Ireland's Museums?" *International Journal of Heritage Studies* 7, no. 2: 119–36.

———. 2005. "Dealing with the Past: Museums and Heritage in Northern Ireland and Cape Town, South Africa." *International Journal of Heritage Studies* 11, no. 2: 131–42.

Crownshaw, Richard. 2008. "The German Countermonument: Conceptual

Indeterminacies and the Retheorization of the Arts of Vicarious Memory." *Forum for Modern Language Studies* 44, no. 2: 212-27.

Dale, Crispin, and Neil Robinson. 2011. "Dark Tourism." In *Research Themes for Tourism*, edited by Peter Robinson, Sine Heitmann, and Peter U. C. Dieke, 205-17. Wallingford, U.K.: CABI International.

D'Amore, Louis. 1988a. "Tourism—the World's Peace Industry." *Journal of Travel Research* 27: 35-40.

———. 1988b. "Tourism—a Vital Force for Peace." *Tourism Management* 9, no. 2: 151-54.

Danchev, Alex. 2005. "Bygone Beefcake." Review of Evan Bachner's *At Ease: Navy Men of World War II*. *Times Higher Education Supplement*, February 18, 25.

Dandeker, Christopher, and David Mason. 2009. "Ethnic Diversity in the British Armed Forces." In *Cultural Diversity and the Armed Forces: An International Comparison*, edited by Joseph L. Soeters and Jan Van Der Meulen, 140-53. London: Routledge.

Dann, Graham M. S., and A. V. Seaton. 2001. "Slavery, Contested Heritage, and Thanatourism." *International Journal of Hospitality and Tourism Administration* 2, no. 3-4: 1-29.

Danner, Mark. 2005. *Torture and Truth: Abu Ghraib and American in Iraq*. London: Granta Books.

Dao, James. 2010. "Military Announces New Social Media Policy." *New York Times*, February 26. http://atwar.blogs.nytimes.com/2010/02/26/military-announces-new-social-media-policy/?_r=0.

Deardon, Basil, and Eliot Elisofon, dirs. 1966. *Khartoum*. United States: Julian Blaustein Productions.

De Burlo, Charles. 1989. "Islanders, Soldiers, and Tourists: The War and the Shaping of Tourism in Melanesia." In *The Pacific Theatre: Island Representations of World War II*, Pacific Island Monograph Series 8, edited by Geoffrey M. White and Lamond Lindstrom, 299-325. Honolulu, Hawaii: University of Hawaii Press.

De Goede, Marieke. 2008. "Beyond Risk: Premediation and the Post-9/11 Security Imagination." *Security Dialogue* 39, no. 2-3: 155-76.

De Goede, Marieke, and Samuel Randalls. 2009. "Precaution, Preemption: Arts and Technologies of the Actionable Future." *Environment and Planning D: Society and Space* 27, no. 5: 859-78.

De Holan, Pablo Martin, and Nelson Phillips. 1997. "Sun, Sand, and Hard Currency: Tourism in Cuba." *Annals of Tourism Research* 24, no. 4: 777-95.

Deni, Laura. 2002. "Six Frat Parties and You're the Hooker." *Broadway to Vegas*, August 18. http://www.broadwaytovegas.com/August18,2002.html.

Denison, F. P. 1959a. "Diary of a Canadian Contingent, Nile Expedition." In *Records of the Nile Voyageurs, 1884–1885: The Canadian Voyageur Contingent in the Gordon Relief Expedition,* edited by C. P. Stacey, 93–145. Toronto: Champlain Society.

———. 1959b. "Letter from Captain Egerton Denison to His Brother Clarence." In *Records of the Nile Voyageurs, 1884–1885: The Canadian Voyageur Contingent in the Gordon Relief Expedition,* edited by C. P. Stacey, 201. Toronto: Champlain Society.

De Palma, Brian, dir. 1989. *Casualties of War.* United States: Columbia Pictures.

Department of Homeland Security. 2010. "No Reservations: Suspicious Behaviour in Hotels." December 16. http://www.youtube.com/watch?v=ZLCCvjJJZ4w.

———. 2011. "Safeguarding Hotels from the Threat of Terrorism." February 16. https://share.dhs.gov/p23934518/.

Dépret, Molly Hurley. 2006. "Troubles Tourism: Debating History and Voyeurism in Belfast, Northern Ireland." In *The Business of Tourism: Place, Faith, and History,* edited by Philip Scranton and Janice F. Davidson, 137–62. Philadelphia: University of Pennsylvania Press.

Der Derian, James. 2009. *Virtuous War: Mapping the Military-Industrial-Media-Entertainment-Network.* 2nd ed. London: Routledge.

Derrida, Jacques. 1992. "Response to Daniel Libeskind." *Research in Phenomenology* 22, no. 1: 88–94.

———. 2001. *On Cosmopolitanism and Forgiveness.* London: Routledge.

Desmond, Jane C. 1999. *Staging Tourism: Bodies on Display from Waikiki to Sea World.* Chicago: Chicago University Press.

Dickenson, Greg, Carole Blair, and Brian L. Ott, eds. 2010. *Places of Public Memory: The Rhetoric of Museums and Memorials.* Tuscaloosa: University of Alabama Press.

Diefendorf, Jeffry M. 1993. *In the Wake of War: The Reconstruction of German Cities after World War II.* Oxford: Oxford University Press.

Diller + Scofidio, eds. 1994. *Back to the Front: Tourisms of War.* New York: Princeton Architectural Press/Basse-Normandie FRAC.

Dillon, Michael, and Andrew Neal, eds. 2008. *Foucault on Politics, Security, and War.* Basingstoke, U.K.: Palgrave Macmillan.

Dillon, Mick, and Julian Reid. 2009. *The Liberal Way of War: Killing to Make Life Live.* London: Routledge.

District 6 Museum. n.d.. "Permanent Exhibitions: Digging Deeper." http://www.districtsix.co.za/Content/Exhibitions/Permanent/index.php.

Dittmar, Linda, and Gene Michaud, eds. 1991. *From Hanoi to Hollywood: The Vietnam War in American Film.* Piscataway, N.J.: Rutgers University Press.

Dixon, Paul. 2002. "Political Skills or Lying and Manipulation? The Choreography of the Northern Ireland Peace Process." *Political Studies* 50, no. 4: 725–41.

Dodds, Klaus. 2007. "Steve Bell's Eye: Cartoons, Geopolitics, and the Visualization of the 'War on Terror.'" *Security Dialogue* 38, no. 2: 157–77.

Dolberg, Eugenie. 2010. *Open Shutters Iraq*. London: Trolley Books.

Dornfield, Margaret. 1995. *Turning the Tide: From the Desegregation of the Armed Forces to the Montgomery Bus Boycott*. New York: Chelsea House.

Douglas, Stacy. 2011. "Between Constitutional Mo(Nu)ments: Memorializing Past, Present, and Future at the District 6 Museum and Constitution Hill." *Law and Critique* 22, no. 2: 171–87.

Douzinas, Costas. 2007. *Human Rights and Empire: The Political Philosophy of Cosmopolitanism*. London: Routledge.

Doyle, Michael. 1983a. "Kant, Liberal Legacies, and Foreign Affairs: Part I." *Philosophy and Public Affairs* 12, no. 3: 205–35.

———. 1983b. "Kant, Liberal Legacies, and Foreign Affairs: Part II." *Philosophy and Public Affairs* 12, no. 4: 323–53.

Doyle, Peter. 2010. *British Postcards of the First World War*. Oxford: Shire.

Dubin, M. 2002. *Rough Guide to Cyprus*. 4th ed. London: Rough Guides.

Duffett, Rachel. 2012. *The Stomach for Fighting: Food and the Soldiers of the Great War*. Manchester, U.K.: Manchester University Press.

Duffield, Mark. 2001. *Global Governance and the New Wars: The Merging of Development and Security*. London: Zed Books.

———. 2007. *Development, Security, and Unending War: Governing the World of Peoples*. Cambridge: Polity Press.

Dumper, Michael R. T., and Bruce E. Stanley, eds. 2006. *Cities of the Middle East and North Africa: A Historical Encyclopedia*. Santa Barbara, Calif.: ABC-CLIO.

Dunkley, R., N. Morgan, and S. Westwood. 2011. "Visiting the Trenches: Exploring Meanings and Motivations in Battlefield Tourism." *Tourism Management* 32, no. 4: 860–68.

Dykes, Paul. 2003. "Public Urged to Come Up with Ideas for Maze." *Belfast Telegraph*, December 5.

Eagleton, Terry. 2007. *Ideology: An Introduction*. 2nd ed. London: Verso.

Edensor, Tim. 1998. *Tourist at the Taj: Performance and Meaning at a Symbolic Site*. London: Routledge.

———. 2000. "Staging Tourism: Tourists as Performers." *Annals of Tourism Research* 27, no. 2: 322–44.

———. 2001. "Performing Tourism, Staging Tourism: (Re)producing Tourist Space and Practice." *Tourist Studies* 1, no. 1: 59–81.

Edgar, L. B. 2007. "Soldiers Break from Combat at Freedom Rest." *Army.Mil/News,* April 17. http://www.army.mil/-news/2007/04/17/2706-soldiers-break-from-combat-at-freedom-rest/.

Edkins, Jenny. 2001. "Authenticity and Memory at Dachau." *Cultural Values* 5, no. 4: 405–20.

———. 2003. *Trauma and the Memory of Politics.* Cambridge: Cambridge University Press.

Edwards, Elizabeth. 2003. "Negotiating Spaces: Some Photographic Incidents in the Western Pacific, 1883–84." In *Picturing Place: Photography and the Geographical Imagination,* edited by Joan M. Schwartz and James Ryan, 261–80. London: I. B. Taurus.

Eisenman, Stephen F. 2007. *The Abu Ghraib Effect.* London: Reaktion Books.

Ek, Richard. 2000. "A Revolution in Military Geopolitics?" *Political Geography* 19, no. 7: 841–74.

Eksteins, Modris. 2000. "War, Memory, and the Modern: Pilgrimage and Tourism to the Western Front." In *World War I and the Cultures of Modernity,* edited by Douglas Peter Mackaman and Michael Mays, 151–60. Jackson: University Press of Mississippi.

Elden, Stuart. 2005. "The Place of the Polis: Political Blindness in Judith Butler's Antigone's Claim." *Theory and Event* 8, no. 1. http://muse.jhu.edu/login?auth=0&type=summary&url=/journals/theory_and_event/v008/8.1elden.html.

Elderidge, Eric. 2007. "GIs Frequented Japan's 'Comfort Women.'" *Washington Post,* April 25. http://blog.hoiking.org/pictures/2007/04/AP_Japan_GI_Brothel.pdf.

Elkins, James, ed. 2008. *Visual Literacy.* London: Routledge.

Endy, Christopher. 2004. *Cold War Holidays: American Tourism in France.* Chapel Hill, N.C.: Duke University Press.

Engber, Daniel. 2006. "Why Can't U.S. Soldiers Marry Iraqis?" *Slate,* October 31. http://www.slate.com/articles/news_and_politics/explainer/2006/10/why_cant_us_soldiers_marry_iraqis.html.

Enloe, Cynthia. 1990. *Bananas, Beaches, and Bases: Making Feminist Sense of International Politics.* Berkeley: University of California Press.

———. 1993. *The Morning After: Sexual Politics at the End of the Cold War.* Berkeley: University of California Press.

———. 2000. *Maneuvers: The International Politics of Militarizing Women's Lives.* Berkeley: University of California Press.

Erlanger, Steven. 1991. "Thai Bar Girls Greet Sailors Like Heroes." *New York Times,* March 25, A9.

Ernst, Wolfgang. 2002. "Review, 'Diller, Scofidio, *Visite aux armée/Back to*

the Front' (Trans. Ann Thursfield)." http://www.mediamatic.net/article-9433-en.html.
Essex, S. J., and M. Brayshay. 2007. "Vision, Vested Interest, and Pragmatism: Who Re-made Britain's Blitzed Cities?" *Planning Perspectives* 22, no. 4: 417–41.
Evans, Bradley. 2010. "Foucault's Legacy: Security, War, and Violence in the 21st Century." *Security Dialogue* 41, no. 4: 413–33.
Ewald, François. 2002. "The Return of Descartes Malicious Demon: An Outline of a Philosophy of Precaution." In *Embracing Risk,* edited by Tom Baker and Jonathan Simon, 273–302. Chicago: Chicago University Press.
Ewart, Wilfred. 1920. "After Four Years: The Old Road to Ypres." *Cornhill Magazine,* December.
Eyerman, J. 1998. "Terrorism and Democratic States: Soft Targets or Accessible Systems?" *International Interactions: Empirical and Theoretical Research in IR* 24, no. 2: 151–70.
Fagan, Brian M. 1994. *The Rape of the Nile: Tomb Robbers, Tourists, and Archaeologists in Egypt.* New York: Basic Books.
Fahmy, Khaled. 2002. "Prostitution in Nineteenth Century Egypt." In *Outside In: On the Margins of the Middle East,* edited by Eugene Rogam, 77–104. London: I. B. Taurus.
Fainstein, S. S. 2002. "One Year On: Reflections on September 11th and the 'War on Terrorism': Regulating New York City's Visitors in the Aftermath of September 11th." *International Journal of Urban and Regional Research* 26, no. 3: 591–95.
Fall, L. T., and J. E. Grey. 2005. "The Significance of Crisis Communication in the Aftermath of 9/11: A National Investigation of How Tourism Managers Have Re-tooled Their Promotional Campaigns." *Journal of Travel and Tourism Marketing* 19, no. 2–3: 77–90.
Famagusta Gulf View Point/Garden of Eden. n.d. *Don't Forget.* Pamphlet in English and Greek.
Farish, Matthew. 2005. "Archiving Areas: The Ethnogeographic Board and the Second World War." *Annals of the Association of American Geographers* 95, no. 3: 663–79.
Farmaki, Anna. 2013. "Dark Tourism Revisited: A Supply/Demand Conceptualization." *International Journal of Culture, Tourism, and Hospitality Research* 7, no. 3: 281–92.
Fawcett, Brian C. 2000. "The Chinese Labour Corps in France, 1917–1921." *Journal of the Royal Asiatic Society Hong Kong Branch* 40: 33–111.
Feickert, J., R. Verma, G. Plaschka, and C. S. Dev. 2006. "Safeguarding Your Customers: The Guest's View of Hotel Security." *Cornell Hospitality Quarterly* 47, no. 3: 224–44.

Feldman, J. 2008. "Constructing a Shared Bible Land: Jewish Israeli Guiding Performances for Protestant Pilgrims." *American Ethnologist* 34, no. 2: 351–74.

Fenton, Roger. n.d. "Fenton's Crimean War Photographs." http://www.loc.gov/pictures/collection/ftncnw/.

Ficher, William F. 2007. "Doing Good? The Politics and Antipolitics of NGO Practices." *Annual Review of Anthropology* 26: 439–64.

Finer, Jonathan. 2005. "The New Ernie Pyles: Sgtlizzie and 67cshdocs." *Washington Post,* August 12, A01.

First Battalion, Fiftieth Infantry Association. 2002. "Rest and Recuperation— R&R!" http://ichiban1.org/html/rnr.htm.

Fisher, Ian. 2002. "Terror in Africa: The Grievers; Israelis Return in Trauma from Supposed Haven." *New York Times,* November 30, 1.

Floyd, M. F., H. Gibson, L. Pennington-Gray, and B. Thapa. 2003. "The Effect of Risk Perceptions on Intentions to Travel in the Aftermath of September 11, 2001." *Journal of Travel and Tourism Marketing* 15, no. 2–3: 19–38.

Floyd, M. F., and L. Pennington-Gray. 2004. "Profiling Risk Perceptions of Tourists." *Annals of Tourism Research* 31, no. 4: 1051–54.

Flynn, M. K. 2011. "Decision-Making and Contested Heritage in Northern Ireland: The Former Maze Prison/Long Kesh." *Irish Political Studies* 26, no. 3: 383–401.

Flynn, Thomas R. 1993. "Foucault and the Eclipse of Vision." In *Modernity and the Hegemony of Vision,* edited by David Michael Levin, 273–86. Berkeley: University of California Press.

Foden, Giles. 2002. "Not Again." *Guardian,* November 29, 2.

Fooks, Osmond John Francis. 1914. "Captain Fooks with His Hunting Trophies during a Shoot in Chamba District, Northern India, 1914." Catalogue HU 104040. Imperial War Museum Archive, London.

———. 1917. "British Officer about to Tee-Off at Gulmarg Golf Club in Kashmir, 1917." Catalogue HU 104042. Imperial War Museum Archive, London.

Foucault, Michel. 1980. *Power/Knowledge: Selected Interviews and Other Writings 1972–77.* Translated by Colin Gordon, Leo Marshall, John Mepham, and Kate Soper. New York: Pantheon.

———. 1991. *Discipline and Punish: The Birth of the Prison.* Translated by Alan Sheridan. London: Penguin.

———. 1997. "What Is Critique?" In *The Politics of Truth,* edited by Sylvère Lotringer, translated by Lysa Hochroth and Catherine Porter, 41–81. Los Angeles, Calif.: Semiotext(e).

———. 2001. *Madness and Civilization.* 2nd ed. London: Routledge.

———. 2003a. *Society Must Be Defended: Lectures at the Collège de France, 1975–76.* New York: Picador.

———. 2003b. *The Birth of the Clinic: An Archaeology of Medical Perception.* 3rd ed. London: Routledge.
———. 2007. *Security, Territory, Population: Lectures at the Collège de France, 1977–78.* Houndmills, U.K.: Palgrave Macmillan.
———. 2010a. *The Government of Self and Others: Lectures at the Collège de France 1982–1983.* Translated by Graham Burchell. London: Palgrave Macmillan.
———. 2010b. *The Birth of Biopolitics: Lectures at the Collège de France, 1978–1979.* Translated by Graham Burchell. London: Palgrave Macmillan.
———. 2011. *The Courage of Truth: Lectures at the Collège de France 1983–1984.* Translated by Graham Burchell. London: Palgrave Macmillan.
Freedman, Des, and Daya Kishan Thussu, eds. 2011. *Media and Terrorism: Global Perspectives.* London: Sage.
Freeman, Milo. 2007. "The Ziggurat of Ur." *Calm Before the Sand,* October 14. http://calmbeforethesand.blogspot.co.uk/2007_10_01_archive.html.
Fregonese, Sara. 2012. "Between a Refuge and a Battleground: Beirut's Discrepant Cosmopolitanisms." *Geographical Review* 102, no. 3: 316–36.
Freitag, Tilman G. 1994. "Enclave Tourism Development: For Whom the Benefits Roll?" *Annals of Tourism Research* 21, no. 3: 538–54.
Friedberg, Anne. 2004. "Virilio's Screen: The Work of Metaphor in the Age of Technological Convergence." *Journal of Visual Culture* 3, no. 2: 183–93.
Fukuyama, Francis. 1989. "The End of History?" *National Interest,* no. 16: 1–18.
———. 1993. *The End of History and the Last Man.* London: Penguin Books.
Fuller, Gillian. 2003. "Life in Transit: Between Airport and Camp." *borderlands e-journal* 2, no. 1. http://www.borderlands.net.au/vol2no1_2003/fuller_transit.html.
———. 2008. "Welcome to Windows 2.1: Motion Aesthetics at the Airport." In *Politics at the Airport,* edited by Mark B. Salter, 161–73. Minneapolis: University of Minnesota Press.
Fuller, Gillian, and Ross Harley. 2004. *Aviopolis: A Book about Airports.* London: Black Dog.
Furlough, Ellen. 1998. "Making Mass Vacations: Tourism and Consumer Culture in France, 1930s to 1970s." *Comparative Studies in Society and History* 40: 247–86.
Fussell, Paul. 1975. *The Great War and Modern Memory.* Oxford: Oxford University Press.
———. 1980. *Abroad: British Literary Travelling between the Wars.* Oxford: Oxford University Press.
Fyall, Alan, Bruce Prideaux, and Dallen J. Timothy. 2006. "War and Tourism: An Introduction." *International Journal of Tourism Research* 8: 153–55.

Gaddis, John Lewis. 1986. "The Long Peace: Elements of Stability in the Postwar International System." *International Security* 10, no. 4: 92–142.

———. 1989. *The Long Peace: Inquiries into the History of the Cold War.* Oxford: Oxford University Press.

Garland, Alex. 1996. *The Beach.* New York: Viking.

Giamo, Benedict. 2003. "The Myth of the Vanquished: The Hiroshima Peace Memorial Museum." *American Quarterly* 55, no. 4: 703–28.

Gillem, Mark L. 2007. *America Town: Building the Outposts of Empire.* Minneapolis: University of Minnesota Press.

Gillian, Audrey, and Signe Daugbjerg. 2006. "Parents Vent Fury at Early Release of Daughter's Killers." *Guardian,* August 19, 12.

Glaesser, D. 2003. *Crisis Management in the Tourism Industry.* Oxford: Butterworth-Heinemann and Elsevier.

Gluhovic, Milija. 2013. *Performing European Memories: Trauma, Ethics, Politics.* Basingstoke, U.K.: Palgrave Macmillan.

Goldstone, Patricia. 2001. *Making the World Safe for Tourism.* New Haven, Conn.: Yale University Press.

Goodrich, J. N. 2002. "September 11, 2001 Attack on America: A Record of the Immediate Impacts and Reactions in the USA Travel and Tourism Industry." *Tourism Management* 23, no. 6: 573–80.

Gordon, Bertram M. 1998. "Warfare and Tourism: Paris in World War II." *Annals of Tourism Research* 25, no. 3: 616–38.

Gordon, Charles George. 1928. Letter to Thomas Cook & Son. Resume of the Gordon Relief Expedition, folio 152, February 1928 (6.3.2). Thomas Cook Archives, Peterborough. Reprinted in the *Times,* February 21, 1884, 9.

Gourevitch, Philip. 2008. "Exposure: The Woman behind the Camera." *New Yorker,* March 24. http://www.newyorker.com/reporting/2008/03/24/080324fa_fact_gourevitch?currentPage=all.

Graham, Brian, and Sara McDowell. 2007. "Meaning in the Maze: The Heritage of Long Kesh." *Cultural Geographies* 14, no. 3: 351–53.

Graham, Brian, and Yvonne Whelan. 2007. "The Legacies of the Dead: Commemorating the Troubles in Northern Ireland." *Environment and Planning D: Society and Space* 25, no. 3: 476–95.

Graham, Phil, Thomas Keenan, and Anne-Maree Dowd. 2004. "A Call to Arms at the End of History: A Discourse-Historical Analysis of George W. Bush's Declaration of War on Terror." *Discourse and Society* 15, no. 2–3: 199–221.

Granitsas, Alkman. 2005. "Americans Are Tuning Out the World." *YaleGlobal,* November 24. http://yaleglobal.yale.edu/content/americans-are-tuning-out-world.

Gregory, Alex. 1991. *The Golden Age of Travel, 1880–1939*. London: Cassell Illustrated.

Gregory, Derek. 1999. "Scripting Egypt: Orientalism and the Cultures of Travel." In *Writes of Passage: Reading Travel Writing*, edited by James Duncan and Derek Gregory, 114–50. London: Routledge.

———. 2001. "Colonial Nostalgia and Cultures of Travel: Spaces of Constructed Visibility in Egypt." In *Consuming Tradition, Manufacturing Heritage: Global Norms and Urban Forms in the Age of Tourism*, edited by Nezar Alsayyad, 111–51. London: Routledge.

———. 2003. "Emperors of the Gaze: Photographic Practices and Productions of Space in Egypt, 1839–1914." In *Picturing Place: Photography and the Geographical Imagination*, edited by Joan M. Schwatz and James R. Ryan, 195–225. London: I. B. Tauris.

———. 2004. *The Colonial Present: Afghanistan, Palestine, Iraq*. Malden, Mass.: Wiley-Blackwell.

———. 2005. "Performing Ciaro: Orientalism and the City of the Arabian Nights." In *Making Cairo Medieval*, edited by Nezar Al Sayyad, Irene A. Bierman, and Nasser Rabbat, 69–93. Lanham, Md.: Lexington Books.

———. 2011. "From a View to a Kill: Drones and Late Modern War." *Theory, Culture, and Society* 28, no. 7–8: 188–215.

———. 2012. "Sight-seeing: War and Extreme Tourism." *Geographical Imaginations: War, Space, and Security*, August 31. http://geographicalimaginations.com/2012/08/31/sight-seeing-war-and-extreme-tourism.

Gregory, Derek, and Allen Pred, eds. 2007. *Violent Cartographies: Fear, Terror, and Political Violence*. London: Routledge.

Grey, John. n.d. "Ulster Museum: The Pros and Cons of the New Look Museum after a Three Year Refurbishment." Culture Northern Ireland. http://www.belfastgalleries.com/article.aspx?art_id=2910&cmd=print.

Griffin, Michael. 1995. "Between Art and Industry: Amateur Photography and Middle-Brow Culture." In *On the Margins of Art Worlds*, edited by Marry Gross, 183–205. Boulder, Colo.: Westview Press.

———. 1999. "The Great War Photographs: Constructing Myths of History and Photojournalism." In *Picturing the Past: Media, History, and Photography*, edited by Bonnie Brennan and Hanno Hardt, 122–57. Urbana: University of Illinois Press.

Groenenboom, Karen, and Peter Jones. 2003. "Issues of Security in Hotels." *International Journal of Contemporary Hospitality Management* 15, no. 1: 14–19.

Gronemeyer, Marianne. 1991. "Helping." In *The Development Dictionary: A Guide to Knowledge as Power*, edited by Wolfgang Sachs, 53–69. London: Zed Books.

Grove, Coleridge. 1959. "Report on Canadian Voyageurs, by Lieutenant-Colonel

Coleridge Grove," in *History of the Sudan Campaign,* Part I, Appendix 4, by Colonel H. E. Colvile. Reprinted in C. P. Stacey, *Records of the Nile Voyageurs, 1884–1885: The Canadian Voyageur Contingent in the Gordon Relief Expedition,* 218. Toronto: Champlain Society.

Guardian. 2002. "In the Shadow of Terror: All Are Victims of the Bali Massacre." October 14, 19.

———. 2011. "Banksy at the West Bank Barrier." http://www.theguardian.com/arts/pictures/0,8542,1543331,00.html.

Gunaratna, Rohan. 2008. "The Islamabad Marriot in Flames: The Attack on the World's Most Protected Hotel." *Journal of Policing, Intelligence, and Counter Terrorism* 3, no. 2: 99–116. http://www.pvtr.org/pdf/RegionalAnalysis/SouthAsia/The%20Islamabad%20Marriott%20Hotel%20attack.pdf.

Gurtner, Yetta K. 2007. "Crisis in Bali: Lessons in Tourism Recovery." In *Managing Tourism Crises,* edited by E. Laws, B. Prideaux, and K. Chon, 81–97. Wallingford, U.K.: CABI International.

Gusterson, Hugh. 2004. "Nuclear Tourism." *Journal of Cultural Research* 8, no. 1: 23–32.

Hackforth-Jones, Jocelyn, and Mary Roberts, eds. 2005. *Edges of Empire: Orientalism and Visual Culture.* Oxford: Blackwell.

Hadaway, Nina. 2013. *The Golden Age of Air Travel.* Oxford: Shire Library.

Haessly, J. 2010. "Tourism and a Culture of Peace." In *Tourism, Progress, and Peace,* edited by Omar Moufakkir and Ian Kelly, 1–16. Wallingford, U.K.: CABI International.

Haggerty, Kevin D. 2006. "Tear Down the Walls: On Demolishing the Panopticon." In *Theorizing Surveillance,* edited by David Lyon, 22–45. London: Routledge.

Haigh, Michael M., Michael Pfau, Jamie Danesi, Robert Tallmon, Tracy Bunko, Shannon Nyberg, Bertha Thompson, Chance Babin, Sal Cardella, Michael Mink, and Brian Temple. 2006. "A Comparison of Embedded and Nonembedded Print Coverage of the U.S. Invasion and Occupation of Iraq." *Harvard International Journal of Press/Politics* 11, no. 2: 139–53.

Haldrup, Michael, and Jonas Larsen. 2003. "The Family Gaze." *Tourist Studies* 3, no. 1: 23–46.

Hall, C. M., Dallen J. Timothy, and David T. Duval. 2004. "Security and Tourism: Towards a New Understanding?" *Journal of Travel and Tourism Marketing* 15, no. 2–3: 1–18.

Hamilton, Jill. 2005. *Thomas Cook: The Holiday Maker.* Strand, U.K.: Sutton.

Hariman, Robert, and John Louis Lucaites. 2007. *No Caption Needed: Iconic Photographs, Public Culture, and Liberal Democracy.* Chicago: University of Chicago Press.

Harrington, Peter. 1998. "Images and Perceptions: Visualising the Sudan Campaign." In *Sudan: The Reconquest Reappraised*, edited by Edward M. Spiers, 82–101. Abingdon, U.K.: Frank Cass.

Harrison, Simon. 2006. "Skull Trophies of the Pacific War: Transgressive Objects of Remembrance." *Journal of the Royal Anthropological Institute* 12, no. 4: 817–36.

Hartmann, Rudi. 2014. "Dark Tourism, Thanatourism, and Dissonance in Heritage Tourism Management: New Directions in Contemporary Tourism Research." *Journal of Heritage Tourism* 9, no. 2: 166–82.

Harvey, David. 2000. "Cosmopolitanism and the Banality of Geographical Evils." *Public Culture* 12, no. 2: 529–64.

Hazbun, Waleed. 2007. "The East as an Exhibit: Thomas Cook and Son and the Origins of the International Tourism Industry in Egypt." In *The Business of Tourism: Place, Faith, History*, edited by Phillip Scranton and Janet F. Davidson, 3–33. Philadelphia: University of Pennsylvania Press.

———. 2008. *Beaches, Ruins, Resorts: The Politics of Tourism in the Arab World*. Minneapolis: University of Minnesota Press.

Heath-Kelly, Charlotte. 2015. "Securing through the Failure to Secure: The Ambiguous Resilience of the Bombsite." *Security Dialogue* 46, no. 1: 69–85.

Heidegger, Martin. 1977. "The Age of the World Picture." In *The Question Concerning Technology*, 116–54. Translated by William Lovitt. New York: Harper Torch Books.

Hein, Carole. 2002. "Hiroshima: The Atomic Bomb and Kenzō Tange's Hiroshima Peace Centre." In *Out of Ground Zero: Case Studies in Urban Reinvention*, edited by Joan Ockman, 62–83. New York: Temple Hoyne Buell Centre for the Study of American Architecture.

Henderson, J. C. 2000. "War as a Tourist Attraction: The Case of Vietnam." *International Journal of Tourism Research* 2, no. 4: 269–80.

Henry, Francis, and Carol Tator. 1999. *The Colour of Democracy: Racism in Canadian Society*. Toronto: Harcourt.

Heppenheimer, T. A. 2006. "Steichen's Navy." *Air and Space Magazine*, March 1. http://www.airspacemag.com/military-aviation/steichens-navy-11442318/?no-ist=.

Herr, Michael. 1977. *Dispatches*. New York: Knopf.

Hersh, Seymour M. 2004a. "The Gray Zone: How a Secret Pentagon Program Came to Abu Ghraib." *New Yorker*, May 24. http://www.newyorker.com/magazine/2004/05/24/the-gray-zone.

———. 2004b. "Chain of Command: How the Department of Defense Mishandled the Disaster at Abu Ghraib." *New Yorker*, May 17. http://www.newyorker.com/magazine/2004/05/17/chain-of-command-2.

———. 2004c. "Torture at Abu Ghraib: American Soldiers Brutalized Iraqis. How Far Up Does the Responsibility Go?" *New Yorker,* May 10. http://www.newyorker.com/magazine/2004/05/10/torture-at-abu-ghraib.

———. 2005. *Chain of Command: The Road from 9/11 to Abu Ghraib.* New York: Harper Perennial.

Hicks, George. 2011. *The Comfort Women: Japan's Brutal Regime of Enforced Prostitution in the Second World War.* New York: W. W. Norton.

Higgens-Desboilles, Freya. 2006. "'More Than an 'Industry': The Forgotten Power of Tourism as a Social Force." *Tourism Management* 27, no. 6: 1192–208.

Highgate, Paul, and Marsha Henry. 2011. "Militarizing Spaces: A Geographical Exploration of Cyprus." In *Reconstructing Conflict: Integrating War and Post-war Geographies,* edited by Scott Kirsch and Colin Flint, 133–56. Aldershot, U.K.: Ashgate.

Hill, Geoff. 2004. "Maze of Possibilities for Future of Prison." *Belfast Newsletter,* February 17, 20–21.

Hilliard, Tyra W., and Seyhmus Baloglu. 2008. "Safety and Security as Part of the Hotel Servicescape for Meeting Planners." *Journal of Convention and Event Tourism* 9, no. 1: 15–34.

Hindess, Barry. 2008. "Political Theory and 'Actually Existing Liberalism.'" *Critical Review of International Social and Political Philosophy* 11, no. 3: 347–52.

Hiroshima Peace Site. 2014a. "Museum History." Peace Memorial Park and Peace Memorial Museum. http://www.pcf.city.hiroshima.jp/frame/Virtual_e/tour_e/guide2_4.html.

———. 2014b. "Keloids." Peace Memorial Park and Peace Memorial Museum. http://www.pcf.city.hiroshima.jp/virtual/cgi-bin/museum.cgi?no=4023&l=e.

———. 2014c. "Virtual Tour." Peace Memorial Park and Peace Memorial Museum. http://www.pcf.city.hiroshima.jp/frame/Virtual_e/tour_e/.

———. 2014d. "Shin's Tricycle." Peace Memorial Park and Peace Memorial Museum. http://www.pcf.city.hiroshima.jp/virtual/VirtualMuseum_e/visit_e/vit_ex_e/vit_ex2_e.html.

———. 2014e. "38 A Bomb Dome." Peace Memorial Park and Peace Memorial Museum. http://www.pcf.city.hiroshima.jp/virtual/VirtualMuseum_e/tour_e/ireihi/tour_38_e.html.

———. 2014f. "Walking toward Peace." Peace Memorial Park and Peace Memorial Museum. http://www.pcf.city.hiroshima.jp/frame/Virtual_e/visit_e/west.html.

Hirsch, Marianne. 2001. "Surviving Images: Holocaust Images and the Work of Postmemory." *Yale Journal of Criticism* 14, no. 1: 5–37.

Hitchcock, M., and Putra I. N. Darma. 2007. *Tourism, Development, and Terrorism in Bali*. Aldershot, U.K.: Ashgate.

Hitchens, Christopher. 2005. "Abu Ghraib Isn't Guernica: But Here's Why the Spanish Civil War Analogy Is Worth Exploring." *Slate*, May 9. http://www.slate.com/articles/news_and_politics/fighting_words/2005/05/abu_ghraib_isnt_guernica.html.

———. 2007. "Martin Amis Is No Racist." *Guardian*, November 21. http://www.guardian.co.uk/uk/2007/nov/21/race.religion.

Hixson, Walter L. 1997. *Parting the Iron Curtain: Propaganda, Culture, and the Cold War, 1945–1961*. New York: St. Martin's Press.

Hlongwane, Ali. 2008a. "Inclusive or Exclusive Collections and Displays." Paper presented at Should We Put History Behind Glass?, Queens University of Belfast and Healing through Remembering, April 3–4.

———. 2008b. "Commemoration, Memory, and Monuments in the Contested Language of Black Liberation." *Journal of Pan African Studies* 2, no. 4: 135–70. http://www.jpanafrican.com/docs/vol2no4/2.4_Commemoration.pdf.

Hockenberry, John. 2005. "The Blogs of War." *Wired* 13, no. 8. http://www.wired.com/wired/archive/13.08/milblogs.html.

Hodder, Ian. 2012. *Entangled: An Archaeology of the Relationships between Humans and Things*. Chichester, U.K.: Wiley-Blackwell.

Hogansen, Kristin. 2006. "Stuff It: Domestic Consumption and the Americanization of the World Paradigm." *Diplomatic History* 30, no. 4: 571–94.

Hollier, Robert. 1991. "Conflict in the Gulf: Response of the Tourist Industry." *Tourism Management* 12, no. 1: 2–4.

Hollinshead, Keith. 1999. "Surveillance of the Worlds of Tourism: Foucault and the Eye of Power." *Tourism Management* 20, no. 1: 7–23.

Hollinshead, Keith, and T. B. Jamal. 2001. "Delving into Discourse: Excavating the Inbuilt Power-Logic(s) of Tourism." *Tourism Analysis* 6, no. 1: 61–73.

Hopps, F. W. n.d. "Diary of F. W. Hopps." Private Papers of F. W. Hopps, Catalogue Documents 15027. Imperial War Museum Archives, London.

Hornstra, Rob, and Arnold van Bruggen. 2013. *The Sochi Project: An Atlas of War and Tourism in the Caucasus*. Woking, U.K.: Aperture.

Hotchkiss, Preston. 1955. "Increasing International Travel." *Department of State Bulletin* 2, May.

Hubbard, Phil, Lucy Faire, and Keith Lilley. 2003. "Contesting the Modern City: Reconstruction and Everyday Life in Post-war Coventry." *Planning Perspectives* 18, no. 4: 377–97.

Humphrey, Andrew. 2012. "Shepheard's Hotel: British Base in Cairo." *Grand Hotels in Egypt*, August 11. http://www.grandhotelsegypt.com/?p=576.

Hunt, Nigel Alexander. 2014. "History of the Habana Hilton." http://www.hotelhabanalibre.com/en/history.html.
Hunter, F. Robert. 2004. "Tourism and Empire: The Thomas Cook & Son Enterprise on the Nile, 1868–1914." *Middle Eastern Studies* 40, no. 5: 28–54.
Huntington, Samuel. 1993. "The Clash of Civilizations?" *Foreign Affairs* 72, no. 3: 22–49.
———. 1996. *The Clash of Civilizations and the Remaking of World Order.* New York: Simon and Schuster.
Hüppauf, Bernd. 1993. "Experiences of Modern Warfare and the Crisis of Representation." *New German Critique* 59: 41–76.
Huysmans, Jef. 2006a. "International Politics of Insecurity: Normativity, Inwardness, and the Exception." *Security Dialogue* 37, no. 1: 11–29.
———. 2006b. "International Politics of Exception: Competing Visions of International Order between Law and Politics." *Alternatives: Global, Local, Political* 31, no. 2: 135–65.
Huyssen, Andreas. 1997. "The Voids of Berlin." *Critical Inquiry* 24, no. 1: 57–81.
———. 2000. "Present Pasts: Media, Politics, Amnesia." *Public Culture* 12, no. 1: 21–38.
Hyam, Ronald. 1990. *Empire and Sexuality: The British Experience.* Manchester, U.K.: Manchester University Press.
Hynes, Samuel. 1999. "Personal Narratives and Commemoration." In *War and Remembrance in the Twentieth Century,* edited by Jay Winter & Emmanuel Sivan, 205–20. Cambridge: Cambridge University Press.
Iles, Jennifer. 2008. "Encounters in the Fields: Tourism to the Battlefields of the Western Front." *Journal of Tourism and Cultural Change* 6, no. 2: 138–54.
Imperial War Museum. n.d. "History of IWM." http://www.iwm.org.uk/corporate/about-IWM.
Inayatullah, Naeem, and David Blaney. 2003. *International Relations and the Problem of Difference.* London: Routledge.
Inglis, Fred. 2000. *The Delicious History of the Holiday.* London: Routledge.
Ingram, Alan, and Klaus Dodds, eds. 2009. *Spaces of Security and Insecurity: Geographies of the War on Terror.* Farnham, U.K.: Ashgate.
Inigo, Jessica. 2004. "R&R Crew's Chaplain Tends to Warriors Bogged Down with Stress." *Stars and Stripes,* December 21. http://www.stripes.com/news/r-r-crew-s-chaplain-tends-to-warriors-bogged-down-with-stress-1.27342.
International Centre for Photography. 2004. "Inconvenient Evidence: Iraqi Prison Photographs from Abu Ghraib." http://museum.icp.org/museum/exhibitions/abu_ghraib/.
International Coalition of Historic Sites of Conscience. 2014. Homepage. http://www.sitesofconscience.org/.

International Institute for Peace through Tourism. n.d. "Mission Statement." http://www.iipt.org/AboutUs.html.

Ioannides, Dimitri, and Yiorgos Apostolopoulos. 1999. "Political Instability, War, and Tourism in Cyprus: Effects, Management, and Prospects for Recovery." *Journal of Travel Research* 38, no. 1: 51–56.

Isaac, Rami K. 2009. "Alternative Tourism: Can the Segregation Wall in Bethlehem Be a Tourist Attraction?" *Tourism and Hospitality Planning and Development* 6, no. 3: 247–54.

Isaac, Rami K., and G. Ashworth. 2012. "Moving from Pilgrimage to 'Dark' Tourism: Leveraging Tourism in Palestine." *Tourism, Culture, and Communication* 11, no. 3: 149–64.

Israel Museums. 2011. "Islamic Museum of the Temple Mount." http://www.ilmuseums.com/museum_eng.asp?id=43.

Jaakson, Reiner. 2004. "Beyond the Tourist Bubble? Cruiseship Passengers in Port." *Annals of Tourism Research* 31, no. 1: 44–60.

Jaar, Alfredo. 1994. "Rwanda Project: Signs of Life." http://www.alfredojaar.net/index1.html.

———. 1998. "Let There Be Light: The Rwanda Project, 1994–1998." http://www.imaginarymuseum.org/MHV/PZImhv/JaarRwandaProject.html.

Jabri, Vivienne. 2006. "War, Security, and the Liberal State." *Security Dialogue* 37, no. 1: 47–64.

———. 2007. "Solidarity and Spheres of Culture: The Cosmopolitan and Postcolonial." *Review of International Studies* 33, no. 4: 715–28.

———. 2010. *War and the Transformation of Global Politics*. Basingstoke, U.K.: Palgrave Macmillan.

———. 2012. *The Postcolonial Subject: Claiming Politics/Governing Others in Late Modernity*. London: Routledge.

Jacobson, David, Bernard Musyck, Stelios Orphanides, and Craig Webster. 2010. "The Opening of the Ledra Crossing in Nicosia: Social and Economic Consequences." In *Tourism and Political Change,* edited by Richard Butler and Wantanee Suntikul, 199–207. Oxford: Goodfellow.

Jamieson, Lee. 2010. "Hotel Security: The Changing Face of Hotel Security." *Hotel Industry Magazine,* November 22. http://www.hotel-industry.co.uk/2010/11/hotel-security/.

Janowski, Monica. 2007. "The Airmen and the Headhunters." *Anthropology in Action* 14, no. 2: 80–81.

Jarman, Neil. 1998. "Painting Landscapes: The Place of Murals in the Symbolic Construction of Urban Space." In *Symbols in Northern Ireland,* edited by Anthony Buckley, 81–98. Belfast: Institute for Irish Studies, Queens University Belfast.

Jay, Martin. 1986. "The Empire of the Gaze: Foucault and the Denigration of Vision in Twentieth-Century French Thought." In *Foucault: A Critical Reader*, edited by David Hoy, 175–204. London: Blackwell.

———. 1994. *Downcast Eyes: The Denigration of Vision in Twentieth-Century French Thought.* Berkeley: University of California Press.

Jayawardena, Chandana. 2003. "Revolution to Revolution: Why Is Tourism Booming in Cuba?" *International Journal of Contemporary Hospitality Management* 15, no. 1: 52–58.

Jean-Klein, I. 2002. "Alternative Modernities, or Accountable Modernities? The Palestinian Movement(s) and Political (Audit) Tourism during the First Intifada." *Journal of Mediterranean Studies* 12, no. 1: 43–80.

johnjohn. n.d. "Vintage Travel Destinations/South America—Prints and Posters." *johnjohn* (blog). http://www.johnjohn.co.uk/shop/vintage_art/travel_caribbean01.html.

Jones, Jonathan. 2010. "Belfast's Ulster Museum and the Trouble with the Troubles." *Guardian,* May 19. http://www.theguardian.com/artanddesign/jonathanjonesblog/2010/may/19/museums-northern-ireland-troubles.

Jones, Max. 2008. "Empire, Sexuality, and the Memory of General Gordon." Public lecture, Queens University Belfast, February 27.

Jontz, Sandra. 2004. "Thousands of Troops Who Paid Own R&R Airline Expenses Will Be Reimbursed." *Stars and Stripes,* June 30. http://www.stripes.com/news/thousands-of-troops-who-paid-own-r-r-airline-expenses-will-be-reimbursed-1.21483.

———. 2011. "U.S. Military Ending R&R Program in Qatar due to Lack of Use." *Stars and Stripes,* March 26. http://www.stripes.com/news/u-s-military-ending-r-r-program-in-qatar-due-to-lack-of-use-1.139017.

Judd, Dennis R. 1999. "Constructing the Tourist Bubble." In *The Tourist City,* edited by Dennis R. Judd and Susan S. Fanstein, 35–53. New Haven, Conn.: Yale University Press.

———. 2003. "Visitors and the Spatial Ecology of the City." In *Cities and Visitors: Regulating People, Markets, and City Space,* edited by Lily M. Hoffman, Susan Fanstein and Dennis R. Judd, 23–38. London: Wiley-Blackwell.

Julius, Chrischené. 2008. "'Digging Deeper Than the Eye Approves': Oral Histories and Their Use in the *Digging Deeper* exhibition of District 6." *Kronos* 34, no. 1: 359–73.

Jungsun, K., P. Brewer, and B. Bernhard. 2008. "Hotel Customer Perceptions of Biometric Door Locks: Convenience and Security Factors." *Journal of Hospitality and Leisure Marketing* 17, no. 1–2: 162–83.

Junka, Laura. 2006. "Camping in the Third Space: Agency, Representation, and the Politics of Gaza Beach." *Public Culture* 18, no. 2: 348–60.

Kabir, Nahid. 2006. "Representations of Islam and Muslims in the Australian Media, 2001–2005." *Journal of Muslim Minority Affairs* 26, no. 3: 313–28.

Kahn, Miriam. 2000. "Tahiti Intertwined: Ancestral Land, Tourist Postcard, and Nuclear Test Site." *American Anthropologist* 102, no. 1: 7–26.

Kamin, Debra. 2014. "The Rise of Dark Tourism: When War Zones Become Travel Destinations." *The Atlantic,* July 15. http://www.theatlantic.com/international/archive/2014/07/the-rise-of-dark-tourism/374432/.

Ka Mpumlwana, Khwesi, Gerard Corsane, Juanita Pastor-Makhurane, and Ciraj Rassool. 2002. "Inclusion and the Power of Representation: South African Museums and the Cultural Politics of Social Transformation." In *Museums, Society, Inequality,* edited by Richard Sandell, 244–61. London: Routledge.

Kaplan, Caren. 1996. *Questions of Travel: Postmodern Discourses of Displacement.* Durham, N.C.: Duke University Press.

Kaplan, Robert. 1994. "The Coming Anarchy." *Atlantic Monthly,* February 2, 44–76.

———. 1997. *The Ends of the Earth: A Journey at the Dawn of the Twenty-First Century.* London: Macmillan Papermac.

Kapur, Shekhar, dir. 2002. *The Four Feathers.* United States: Paramount.

Kark, Ruth. 2001. "From Pilgrimage to Budding Tourism: The Role of Thomas Cook in the Rediscovery of the Holy Land in the Nineteenth Century." In *Travellers in the Levant: Voyagers and Visionaries,* edited by Sarah Seawright and Malcolm Wagstaff, 155–74. Oxford: Astene/Oxbow Books.

Katovsky, Bill, and Timothy Carlson. 2005. *Embedded: The Media at War in Iraq.* New York: Lyons Press.

Katriel, Tamar. 2001. "'From Shore to Shore': The Holocaust, Clandestine Immigration, and Israeli Heritage Museums." In *Visual Culture and the Holocaust,* edited by Barbie Zelizer, 188–214. London: Continuum Books.

Kave, Colin. 2005. "Another Day at the Beach." September 14. http://colinjkave.blogspot.co.uk/.

Kavoori, Anandam P., and Todd Fraley, eds. 2006. *Media, Terrorism, and Theory.* New York: Rowman and Littlefield.

Kennedy, Liam. 2008. "Securing Vision: Photography and US Foreign Policy." *Media, Culture, and Society* 30, no. 3: 279–94.

———. 2009. "Soldier Photography: Visualizing the War in Iraq." *Review of International Studies* 35, no. 4: 817–33.

Kennedy, Liam, and Scott Lucas. 2005. "Enduring Freedom: Public Diplomacy and U.S. Foreign Policy." *American Quarterly* 57, no. 2: 310–17.

Kenney, Michael. 2010. "Beyond the Internet: Mētis, Techne, and the Limitations of Online Artefacts for Islamist Terrorists." *Terrorism and Political Violence* 22, no. 2: 177–97.

Khamouna, Mohammed, and Jeffrey B. Zeiger. 1995. "Peace through Tourism." *Parks and Recreation* 30, no. 9: 80–86.

Kim, Samuel S., and Bruce Prideaux. 2003. "Tourism, Peace, Politics, and Ideology: Impacts of the Mt. Gumgang Tour Project in the Korean Peninsula." *Tourism Management* 24, no. 6: 675–85.

Kim, Samuel Seongseop, Bruce Prideaux, and Jillian Prideaux. 2007. "Using Tourism to Promote Peace on the Korean Peninsula." *Annals of Tourism Research* 34, no. 2: 291–309.

Kim, Yong-Kwan, and John L. Crompton. 1990. "Role of Tourism in Unifying the Two Koreas." *Annals of Tourism Research* 17, no. 3: 353–66.

King, Alex. 1998. *Memorials of the Great War in Britain: The Symbolism and Politics of Remembrance*. New York: Berg.

Kirk, Donald. 1991. "Operation Desert Mop-Up—Aftermath of 1991 Persian Gulf War Underscores Rejection of U.S. Military Presence in Saudi Arabia and Other Middle East Countries." *National Review*, August 12, 25.

Klein, Christina. 2003. *Cold War Orientalism: Asia in the Middlebrow Imagination, 1945–1961*. Oakland: University of California Press.

Klein, Daryl. 2009. *With the Chinks*. London: Naval and Military Press.

Koensler, Alexander, and Cristina Papa. 2011. "Political Tourism in the Israeli-Palestinian Space." *Anthropology Today* 27, no. 2: 13–17.

Koikari, Mire. 1999. "Rethinking Gender and Power in the US Occupation of Japan, 1945–1952." *Gender and History* 11, no. 2: 313–35.

Koller, Christian. 2011. "Representing Otherness: African, Indian, and European Soldiers' Letters and Memoirs." In *Race, Empire, and First World War Writing*, edited by Santanu Das, 127–42. Cambridge: Cambridge University Press.

Korda, Zoltan, dir. 1939. *The Four Feathers*. United States: United Artists.

Koshar, Rudy. 2000. *German Travel Cultures*. Oxford: Berg.

Kossakowski, Eustachy. n.d. "Eustachy Kossakowski Archive." Museum of Modern Art Warsaw. http://artmuseum.pl/en/archiwum/archiwum-eustachego-kossakowskiego/934/31174.

Kovner, Sarah. 2009. "Base Cultures: Sex Workers and Servicemen in Occupied Japan." *Journal of Asian Studies* 68, no. 3: 777–804.

———. 2012. *Occupying Power: Sex Workers and Servicemen in Postwar Japan*. Stanford, Calif.: Stanford University Press.

Krakover, Saul. 2002. "The Holocaust Remembrance Site of Yad Vashem Welcomes Visitors." *International Research in Geographical and Environmental Education* 11, no. 4: 359–62.

———. 2005. "Attitudes of Israeli Visitors towards the Holocaust Site of Yad Vashem." In *Horror and Human Tragedy Revisited: The Management of Sites of Atrocity for Tourism,* edited by Ashworth, G. & Hartmann, Rudi, 108–17. Putnam Valley, N.Y.: Cognizant Communication Corp.

Kristof, Nicholas D. 1995. "Fearing GI Occupiers, Japan Urged Women into Brothels." *New York Times,* October 27, A1. http://www.nytimes.com/1995/10/27/world/fearing-gi-occupiers-japan-urgesd-women-into-brothels.html?pagewanted=all&src=pm.

Krohn, Zia, and Joyce Lagerweij. 2010. *Concrete Messages: Street Art on the Israeli-Palestinian Separation Barrier.* Årsta, Sweden: Dokument Press.

Kubrick, Stanley, dir. 1987. *Full Metal Jacket.* United States: Warner Bros.

Kuhnkhe, LaVerne. 1990. *Lives at Risk: Public Health in Nineteenth Century Egypt.* Berkeley: University of California Press.

Kumi, Alex. 2006. "Removal of Men from Holiday Flight Condemned." *Guardian,* August 21, 7.

Kuypers, Jim A., and Stephen D. Cooper. 2005. "A Comparative Framing Analysis of Embedded and Behind-the-Lines Reporting on the 2003 Iraq War." *Qualitative Research Reports in Communication* 6, no. 1: 1–10.

Kwon, Heonik. 2010. *The Other Cold War.* New York: Columbia University Press.

Laderman, Scott. 2009. *Tours of Vietnam: War, Travel Guides, and Memory.* Durham, N.C.: Duke University Press.

Lair, Meredith H. 2011. *Armed with Abundance: Consumerism and Soldiering during the Vietnam War.* Chapel Hill: University of North Carolina Press.

Lancaster, Richard C. 1986. *Serving in the US Armed Forces, 1861–1986: The Story of the YMCA's Ministry to Military Personnel for 125 Years.* Springfield, Va.: Armed Services YMCA.

Lanfant, Marie-François, and Nelson H. H. Graburn. 1992. "International Tourism Reconsidered: the Principle of the Alternative." In *Tourism Alternatives: Potentials and Problems in the Development of Tourism,* edited by W. R. Eadington and Valene Smith, 88–112. Philadelphia: University of Pennsylvania Press.

Larsen, Jonas. 2005. "Families Seen Sightseeing: Performativity of Tourist Photography." *Space and Culture* 8, no. 4: 416–35.

Lasansky, D. Medina. 2004. "Tourist Geographies: Remapping Old Havana." In *Architecture and Tourism: Perception, Performance, and Place,* edited by D. Medina Lasansky and Brian McLaren, 165–86. Oxford: Berg.

Laufer, Robert S., and M. S. Gallops. 1985. "Life-Course Effects of Vietnam Combat and Abusive Violence." *Journal of Marriage and Family* 47, no. 4: 839–53.

Lê, Dinh Q. 2005. "Vietnam: Destination for the New Millenium." Elizabeth Leach Gallery. http://www.elizabethleach.com/Artwork-Detail.cfm?ArtistsID=45&NewID=2144.

Leake, Christopher, and Andrew Chapman. 2006. "Mutiny as Passengers Refuse to Fly until Asians Are Removed." *Daily Mail,* August 20, 1.

Lee, Steven Hugh. 2001. *The Korean War.* Edinburgh: Pearson Education.

Lee, Wendy. 1991. "Prostitution and Tourism in South-East Asia." In *Working Women: International Perspectives on Labour and Gender Ideology,* edited by Nanneke Redclift and M. Thea Sinclair, 79–104. London: Routledge.

Lefever, Michael M., and Cathleen D. Huck. 1990. "The Expropriation of the Habana Hilton: A Timely Reminder." *International Journal of Hospitality Management* 9, no. 1: 14–20.

Leheny, D. 2000. "'By Other Means': Tourism and Leisure as Politics in Prewar Japan." *Social Science Japan Journal* 3, no. 2: 171–86.

Leith, Sam. 2002. "Philip Roth Attacks 'Orgy of Narcissism' Post Sept 11." *Daily Telegraph,* October 5, 21.

Lěncek, Lena, and Gideon Bosker. 1998. *The Beach: The History of Paradise on Earth.* London: Secker and Warburg.

Lennon, J. John, and Mark Foley. 2000. *Dark Tourism: The Attraction of Death and Disaster.* London: Continuum.

Leonard, Jane. 2008. "Towards an Oral History of the Troubles: *Conflict* at the Ulster Museum." In *What Made Now in Northern Ireland,* edited by Maurna Crozier and Richard Froggatt, 125–34. Belfast: Community Relations Council.

Lepp, Andrew, and Heather Gibson. 2003. "Tourist Roles, Perceived Risk, and International Tourism." *Annals of Tourism Research* 30, no. 3: 606–24.

Leslie, David. 1996. "Northern Ireland, Tourism, and Peace." *Tourism Management* 17, no. 1: 51–55.

———. 1999. "Terrorism and Tourism: The Northern Ireland Situation—a Look behind the Veil of Certainty." *Journal of Travel Research* 38, no. 1: 37–40.

Leung, Rebecca. 2004. "Abuse of Iraqi POWs by GIs Probed." *60 Minutes,* April 28. http://www.cbsnews.com/stories/2004/04/27/60II/main614063.shtml.

Levenstein, Harvey. 1998. *Seductive Journey: American Tourists in France from Jefferson to the Jazz Age.* Chicago: Chicago University Press.

Levin, Angela. 2008. "Greetings from Guantanamo Bay . . . and the Sickest Souvenir Shop in the World." *Daily Mail,* May 4. http://www.dailymail.co.uk/news/article-563791/Greetings-Guantanamo-Bay—-sickest-souvenir-shop-world.html.

Levine, Jeremy M. 1999. *The Vietnam War at 24 Frames a Second.* Austin: University of Texas Press.

Levine, Phillipa. 2003. *Prostitution, Race, and Politics: Policing Imperial Disease in the British Empire.* London: Routledge.

Levi Strauss, David. 2005. *Between the Eyes: Essays on Photography and Politics.* New York: Aperture.

Li, Tania Murray. 2007. *The Will to Improve: Governmentality, Development, and the Practice of Politics.* Durham, N.C.: Duke University Press.

Libeskind, Daniel. 1992. "Between the Lines: The Jewish Museum, Berlin." *Research in Phenomenology* 22, no. 1: 82–87.

Lie, John. 1995. "The Transformation of Sexual Work in 20th-Century Korea." *Gender and Society* 9, no. 3: 310–27.

———. 1997. "The State as Pimp: Prostitution and the Patriarchal State in Japan in the 1940s." *Sociological Quarterly* 38, no. 2: 251–63.

Likorish, L. J., and A. G. Kershaw. 1958. *The Travel Trade.* London: Practical Press.

Lippert, R., and D. O'Connor. 2003. "Security Assemblages: Airport Security, Flexible Work, and Liberal Governance." *Alternatives: Global, Local, Political* 28, no. 3: 331–59.

Lisle, Debbie. 2000. "Consuming Danger: Re-imagining the War/Tourism Divide." *Alternatives: Global, Local, Political* 25, no. 1: 91–116.

———. 2003. "Site Specific: Medi(t)ations at the Airport." In *Rituals of Mediation,* edited by Cynthia Weber and Francois Debrix, 3–29. Minneapolis: University of Minnesota Press.

———. 2006a. *The Global Politics of Contemporary Travel Writing.* Cambridge: Cambridge University Press.

———. 2006b. "Defending Voyeurism: Dark Tourism and the Problem of Global Security." In *Tourism and Politics: Global Frameworks and Local Realities,* edited by Peter M. Burns & Marina Novelli, 335–47. Amsterdam: Elsevier.

———. 2006c. "Sublime Lessons: Education and Ambivalence in War Exhibitions." *Millennium: Journal of International Studies* 34, no. 3: 185–206.

———. 2006d. "Local Symbols, Global Networks: Rereading the Murals of Belfast." *Alternatives: Local, Global, Political* 31, no. 1: 27–52.

———. 2007. "Encounters with Partition: Tourism and Reconciliation in Cyprus." In *Contested Spaces: Sites, Representations, and Histories of Conflict,* edited by Louise Purbrick, Jim Aulich, and Graham Dawson, 94–117. Basingstoke, U.K.: Palgrave.

———. 2011. "The Surprising Detritus of Leisure: Encountering the Late Photography of War." *Environment and Planning D: Society and Space* 29, no. 5: 873–90.

———. 2013. "Front-Line Leisure: Securitizing Tourism in the War on Terror." *Security Dialogue* 44, no. 2: 127–46.

———. Forthcoming. "The Yellow Car." In *Making Things International II:*

Assemblages, edited by Mark B. Salter. Minneapolis: University of Minnesota Press.

Liss, Andrea. 1998. *Trespassing through Shadows: Memory, Photography, and the Holocaust.* Minneapolis: University of Minnesota Press.

Litvin, Stephen. 1988. "Tourism: The World's Peace Industry?" *Journal of Travel Research* 37, no. 1: 63–66.

Lloyd, David W. 1998. *Battlefield Tourism: Pilgrimage and the Commemoration of the Great War in Britain, Australia, and Canada, 1919–1939.* Oxford: Berg.

Lloyd, Justine. 2003. "Airport Technology, Travel, and Consumption." *Space and Culture* 6, no. 2: 93–109.

Löfgren, Orvar. 1999. *On Holiday: A History of Vacationing.* Berkeley: University of California Press.

Logan, William. 2008. *Places of Pain and Shame: Dealing with "Difficult Heritage."* London: Routledge.

Loizos, P. 2006. "Bicommunal Initiatives and Their Contribution to Improved Relations between Turkish and Greek Cypriots." *South European Society and Politics* 11, no. 1: 179–94.

Lollis, Edward W. 2013. "Peace Tourism: Peace as a Destination." United Nations World Tourism Organization. http://www.peacepartnersintl.net/tourism.htm.

Lower Manhattan Development Corporation. 2004. "Jury Statement." January 13. http://www.wtcsitememorial.org/about_jury_txt.html.

Luke, Timothy W. 2002. *Museum Politics: Power Plays at the Exhibition.* Minneapolis: University of Minnesota Press.

Lupu, Noam. 2003. "Memory Vanished, Absent, and Confined: The Countermemorial Project in 1980s and 1990s Germany." *History and Memory* 15, no. 2: 130–64.

Lyon, David. 2002. *Surveillance as Social Sorting: Privacy, Risk, and Automated Discrimination.* London: Routledge.

———. 2003. "Airports as Data Filters: Converging Surveillance Systems after September 11." *Information, Communications, and Ethics in Society* 1, no. 1: 13–20.

———, ed. 2006a. *Theorizing Surveillance: Panopticon and Beyond.* Devon, U.K.: Willan.

———. 2006b. "9/11, Synopticon, and Scopophilia: Watching and Being Watched." In *The New Politics of Surveillance and Visibility,* edited by Kevin Haggerty and Richard Ericson, 35–53. Toronto: University of Toronto Press.

———. 2007a. "Surveillance, Security, and Social Sorting: Emerging Research Priorities." *International Criminal Justice Review* 17, no. 3: 161–70.

———. 2007b. *Surveillance Studies: An Overview.* Cambridge: Polity Press.

Mackey, Robert. 2014. "Israelis Watch Bombs Drop on Gaza from Front-Row Seats." *New York Times,* July 14. http://www.nytimes.com/2014/07/15/world/middleeast/israelis-watch-bombs-drop-on-gaza-from-front-row-seats.html?_r=0.

MacLachlan, Angus C. 1983. *Canadian Voyageurs on the Nile, 1884-5.* Ontario: A. C. MacLachlan.

MacLaren, Roy. 1978. *Canadians on the Nile, 1882-1898; Being the Adventures of the Voyageurs on the Khartoum Relief Expedition and Other Exploits.* Vancouver: University of British Columbia Press.

Maclear, Kyo. 1998. *Beclouded Visions: Hiroshima–Nagasaki and the Art of Witness.* New York: SUNY Press.

Maddocks, Nick. 2014. "Hidden Histories: WW1's Forgotten Photographs." BBC4, March 13. http://www.bbc.co.uk/programmes/b03xsrvv.

Madikida, Churchill, Lauren Segal, and Clive Van Den Berg. 2008. "The Reconstruction of Memory at Constitution Hill." *Public Historian* 30, no. 1: 17–25.

Manderson, Lenore, and Margaret Jolly. 1997. *Sites of Desire, Economies of Pleasure.* Chicago: University of Chicago Press.

Manheim, Jarol B. 1994. *Strategic Public Diplomacy and American Foreign Policy: The Evolution of Influence.* Oxford: Oxford University Press.

Mankiewicz, Joseph L., dir. 1955. *Guys and Dolls.* United States: Samuel Goldwyn Company.

Mansfield, Yoel, and Abraham Pizam. 2006. *Tourism, Security, and Safety: From Theory to Practice.* Oxford: Elsevier.

Maoz, D. 2010. "Warming Up Peace: An Encounter between Egyptian Hosts and Israeli Guests in Sinai." In *Tourism, Progress and Peace,* edited by O. Moufakkir & Ian Kelly, 65–82. Wallingford, U.K.: CABI International.

Marcuse, Harold. 2005. "Reshaping Dachau for Visitors, 1933–2000." In *Horror and Human Tragedy Revisited: The Management of Sites of Atrocity for Tourism,* edited by Gregory Ashworth and Rudi Hartmann, 118–49. New York: Cognizant Communication Corporation.

Marcuse, Peter. 2006. "Security or Safety in Cities? The Threat of Terrorism after 9/11." *International Journal of Urban and Regional Research* 30, no. 4: 919–29.

Marks, Laura. 1999. *The Skin of the Film: Intercultural Cinema, Embodiment, and the Senses.* Durham, N.C.: Duke University Press.

———. 2002. *Touch: Sensuous Theory and Multisensory Media.* Minneapolis: University of Minnesota Press.

———. 2004. "Haptic Visuality: Touching with the Eyes." *Finnish Art Review,* no. 2: 79–82.

Marling, Percival. 1936. "The Nile Campaign, 1884–85." *Journal of the Royal Africa Society* 35, no. 139: 143–52.

Marschall, Sabine. 2006. "Visualizing Memories: The Hector Pieterson Memorial in Soweto." *Visual Anthropology* 19, no. 2: 145–69.

Marwick, Arthur. 2001. *Total War and Historical Change: Europe 1914–1955.* Milton Keynes, U.K.: Open University Press.

Masko, David P. 1991. "Alcohol: Gulf Troops Healthy, Successful without It." *Dispatch,* June 28, 6.

Mason, A. E. W. 1902. *The Four Feathers.* London: Macmillan.

Massumi, Brian. 2002. *Parables for the Virtual: Movement, Affect, Sensation.* Durham, N.C.: Duke University Press.

Maze Consultation Panel. 2005. *Final Report: A New Future for the Maze/Long Kesh.* Belfast: OFMDFM.

McAleavey, Jimmy, Laurence McKeown, Kieron Magee, and Rosemary Walsh. 2010. *The West Awakes.* Kabosh Theatre. http://www.kabosh.net/article.php?show=the-west-awakes.

McAtackney, Laura. 2014. *An Archaeology of the Troubles: The Dark Heritage of Long Kesh/Maze Prison.* Oxford: Oxford University Press.

McCarroll, James E., Robert J. Ursano, John H. Newby, Xian Liu, Carol S. Fullerton, Anne E. Norwood, and Elizabeth A. Osuch. 2003. "Domestic Violence and Deployment in US Army Soldiers." *Journal of Nervous and Mental Disease* 191, no. 1: 3–9.

McClelland, Mark. 2012. *Love, Sex, and Democracy in Japan during the American Occupation.* Basingstoke, U.K.: Palgrave Macmillan.

McDonald, Henry. 2003. "Hunger Strike Jail to Be Site of Sports Stadium." *Observer,* May 11, 14.

McDowell, Sara. 2008. "Selling Conflict Heritage through Tourism in Peacetime Northern Ireland: Transforming Conflict or Exacerbating Difference." *International Journal of Heritage Studies* 14, no. 5: 405–21.

McEachern, Charmaine. 1998a. "Mapping the Memories: Politics, Place, and Identity in the District 6 Museum, Cape Town." *Social Identities* 4, no. 3: 499–521.

———. 1998b. "Working with Memory: The District 6 Museum in the New South Africa." *Social Analysis* 42, no. 2: 48–72.

McEnany, Laura. 2008. "Soft Power: American Military Families Abroad." *Diplomatic History* 32, no. 3: 475–79.

McEvoy, Lesley, Kieran McEvoy, and Kirsten McConnachie. 2006. "Reconciliation as a Dirty Word: Conflict, Community Relations, and Education in Northern Ireland." *Journal of International Affairs* 60, no. 1: 81–106.

McHugh, Michael, and David Gordon. 2004. "Land Battle Looms for Maze Jail Site." *Belfast Telegraph,* January 2.

McSorley, Kevin. 2012. "Helmetcams, Militarized Sensation, and 'Somatic War.'" *Journal of War and Cultural Studies* 5, no. 1: 47–58.
Meis, Laura A., Christopher R. Erbes, Melissa A. Polusny, and Jill S. Compton. 2010. "Intimate Relationships among Returning Soldiers: The Mediating and Moderating Roles of Negative Emotionality, PTSD Symptoms, and Alcohol Problems." *Journal of Traumatic Stress* 23, no. 5: 564–72.
Melling, Phil. 1990. "Old History, New History, No History at All? The Vietnam War As Affirmation of American Values." *American Studies International* 28, no. 2: 93–105.
Melville, Stephen. 1996. "Division of the Gaze, or, Remarks on the Colour and Tenor of Contemporary 'Theory.'" In *Vision in Context: Historical and Contemporary Perspectives on Sight,* edited by Teresa Brennan and Martin Jay, 101–16. London: Routledge.
Meredith, Fionola. 2009. "Minimal Troubles at Ulster Museum." *Irish Times,* October 24. http://saoirse32.wordpress.com/2009/10/24/minimal-troubles-at-ulster-museum/.
Merrill, Dennis. 2001. "Negotiating Cold War Paradise: U.S. Tourism, Economic Planning, and Cultural Modernity in Twentieth-Century Puerto Rico." *Diplomatic History* 25, no. 2: 179–214.
Meskell, Lynn, and Colette Scheermeyer. 2008. "Heritage as Therapy: Set Pieces from the New South Africa." *Journal of Material Culture* 13, no. 2: 153–73.
Meudell, W. G. 1918. Letter on January 12, 1918. Private Papers of W. G. Meudell, Catalogue Documents 11177. Imperial War Museum Archive, London.
Michaels, Marguerite. 1994. "Sorry, Wrong Country." *Time,* June 6. http://content.time.com/time/magazine/article/0,9171,980859,00.html.
Michelin. 1920. *Illustrated Michelin Guide to the Battlefields, 1914–1918.* Clermont-Ferrand, France: Michelin.
Middle East Eye. 2014. "Sderot Cinema: Israelis Watch the 'Spectacle' of the Bombardment of Gazans." https://www.youtube.com/watch?v=SnWH4FsC5xI.
Middleton, Victor T. C. 2007. "The Inter-War Years 1919 to 1939 and the Impact of the Second World War (1939–1945)." In *British Tourism: The Remarkable Study of Growth,* 2nd ed., edited by Victor T. C. Middleton and L. J. Likorish, 1–16. Oxford: Butterworth-Heinemann.
Miles, Chris, and Dinh Q. Lê. 2003. *Dinh Q. Lê: From Vietnam to Hollywood.* Seattle, Wash.: Marquand Books.
Miles, William F. S. 2002. "Auschwitz: Museum Interpretation and Darker Tourism." *Annals of Tourism Research* 29, no. 4: 1175–78.
———. 2010. "Dueling Border Tours: Jerusalem." *Annals of Tourism Research* 37, no. 2: 555–59.

Military One Source. 2014. "Military Family Life: What to Expect on an R&R during Times of Deployment." http://www.militaryonesource.mil/health-wellness/deployment?content_id=269180.

Miller, Richard R., dir. 1969. *Where the Girls Are—VD in Southeast Asia*. United States: United States Air Force.

Mills, Juline E., Matthew Meyers, and Sookeun Byun. 2010. "Embracing Broadscale Applications of Biometric Technologies in Hospitality and Tourism: Is the Business Ready?" *Journal of Hospitality and Tourism Technology* 1, no. 3: 245–56.

Min, Pyong Gap. 2003. "Korean 'Comfort Women': The Intersection of Colonial Power, Gender and Class." *Gender and Society* 17, no. 6: 938–57.

Minca, Claudio. 2009. "The Island: Work, Tourism, and the Biopolitical." *Tourist Studies* 9, no. 2: 88–108.

Minca, Claudio, and Tim Oakes, eds. 2006. *Travels in Paradox: Remapping Tourism*. Oxford: Rowman and Littlefield.

Minh-Ha, Trinh T., dir. 1989. *Surname Viet, Given Name Nam*. New York: Jean-Paul Bourdier and Women Make Movies.

Mirzoeff, Nicholas. 2005. "Invisible Again: Rwanda and Representation after Genocide." *African Arts* 38, no. 3: 87. http://www.nicholasmirzoeff.com/Images/Mirzeoff_InvisibleAgain.pdf.

Mitchell, Timothy. 1988. *Colonizing Egypt*. Cambridge: Cambridge University Press.

Mitchell, W. J. T. 1994. *Picture Theory: Essays on Verbal and Visual Representation*. Chicago: University of Chicago Press.

———. 2005a. "There Are No Visual Media." *Journal of Visual Culture* 4, no. 2: 257–66.

———. 2005b. *What Do Pictures Want? The Lives and Loves of Images*. Chicago: University of Chicago Press.

Molasky, Michael S. 2001. *The American Occupation of Japan and Okinawa: Literature and Memory*. London: Routledge.

Möller, Frank. 2009. "The Looking/Not Looking Dilemma." *Review of International Studies* 35, no. 4: 781–94.

———. 2013. *Visual Peace: Images, Spectatorship, and the Politics of Violence*. Houndmills, U.K.: Palgrave Macmillan.

Moon, Katherine H. S. 1997. *Sex among Allies: Military Prostitution in US–Korea Relations*. New York: Columbia University Press.

Moore, Molly. 1990. "For Female Soldiers, Different Rules." *Washington Post*, August 23, D1.

———. 2002. "'Being Abroad Is Also Scary': For Israelis, Kenya Suicide Bombing Represents a Refuge Lost." *Washington Post*, November 30, A01.

Morgan, Joyce. 2007. "Beware, These Pretty Things Bite." *Sydney Morning Herald,* March 6. http://www.smh.com.au/news/arts/beware-these-pretty-things-bite/2007/03/05/1172943354630.html.

Morgan, Nigel, and Annette Pritchard. 1998. *Tourism Promotion and Power: Creating Images, Creating Identities.* Chichester, U.K.: John Wiley.

———. 2005. "Security and 'Social Sorting': Traversing the Surveillance-Tourism Dialectic." *Tourism Studies* 5, no. 2: 115–32.

Morris, Errol. 2008. *Standard Operating Procedure.* United States: Sony Picture Classics/Participant Media. http://www.sonyclassics.com/standardoperatingprocedure/.

Moufakkir, Omar, and Ian Kelly, eds. 2010. *Tourism, Progress, and Peace.* Wallingford, U.K.: CABI International.

Muppidi, Himmadeep. 2012. *The Colonial Signs of International Relations.* New York: Columbia University Press.

Murdoch, Jonathan, and Nkil Ward. 1997. "Governmentality and Territoriality: The Statistical Manufacture of Britain's National Farm." *Political Geography* 16, no. 4: 307–24.

Murikami-Wood, David. 2002. "Foucault and Panopticism Revisited." *Surveillance and Society* 1, no. 3: 234–39.

Museum on the Seam. 2009a. "The Museum." Museum on the Seam. http://www.mots.org.il/Eng/TheMuseum/TheMuseum.asp.

———. 2009b. "The Right to Protest." http://www.mots.org.il/Eng/Exhibitions/TheRightToProtest.asp.

Nahdi, Fuad. 2002. "A Cocktail of Grievances in Paradise." *Guardian,* November 29, 24.

Nanda, Serena. 2004. "South African Museums and the Creation of a New National Identity." *American Anthropologist* 106, no. 2: 379–85.

National Counter Terrorism Security Offices. n.d. "Our Services/Project ARGUS/ARGUS Hotels." http://www.nactso.gov.uk/our-services.

Naval and Military Gazette. 1884. June 11.

Navaro-Yashin, Yael. 2012. *The Make-Believe Space: Affective Geography in a Postwar Polity.* Durham, N.C.: Duke University Press.

Neal, Andrew. 2009. *Exceptionalism and the Politics of Counter-Terrorism: Liberty, Security, and the War on Terror.* London: Routledge.

Neill, William J. V. 2006. "Return to Titanic and Lost in the Maze: The Search for Representation of 'Post-Conflict' Belfast." *Space and Polity* 10, no. 2: 109–20.

Nelson, Elizabeth. 2007. "Victims of War: The First World War, Returned Soldiers, and Understandings of Domestic Violence in Australia." *Journal of Women's History* 19, no. 4: 83–106.

Nelson, L. 1999. "Bodies (and Spaces) Do Matter: The Limits of Performativity." *Gender, Place, and Culture* 6, no. 4: 331–53.
Nelson, Soraya S. 1990. "Cultural Differences a Factor in Saudi Deployment." *Air Force Times*, September 10, 18.
Newbury, Darren. 2005. "'Lest We Forget': Photography and the Presentation of History at the Apartheid Museum, Gold Reef City, and the Hector Pieterson Museum, Soweto." *Visual Communication* 4, no. 3: 259–95.
New York Times. 1884. "Troubles on the Nile." October 26, 7.
Nicholson-Lord, D. 2002. "Against the Western Invaders." *New Statesman*, December 9, 22–24.
Ninkovich, Frank. 1981. *The Diplomacy of Ideas: U.S. Foreign Policy and Cultural Relations, 1938–1950*. Cambridge: Cambridge University Press.
Niven, Penelope. 1998. *Steichen: A Biography*. New York: Clarkson Potter.
Noble, Greg. 2008. "The Face of Evil: Demonising the Arab Other in Contemporary Australia." *Cultural Studies Review* 14, no. 2: 14–33.
Norioki, Ishimaru, M. Li, and Okagawa Mitsugu. 2002. "Research on the Plan of Reconstruction in Hiroshima: A Study on the Activities of the Architect Kenzō Tange (Part I)." *Journal of Architecture, Planning, and Environmental Engineering*, no. 557: 339–45.
Noy, Chaim. 2011. "Articulating Spaces: Inscribing Spaces and (Im)mobilities in an Israeli Commemorative Visitor Book." *Social Semiotics* 21, no. 2: 155–73.
———. 2012. "Narrative and Counter-narratives: Contesting a Tourist Site in Jerusalem." In *Narratives of Travel and Tourism*, edited by Jacqueline Tivers and Tijana Rakić, 135–50. Aldershot, U.K.: Ashgate.
Nye, Joseph S., Jr. 2004. *Soft Power: The Means to Success in World Politics*. New York: Public Affairs.
Nye, Joseph S., Jr. 1990. "Soft Power." *Foreign Policy* 80: 153–71.
Nyíri, Paíl. 2008. "A Self-Invalidating Critique." *Review of Politics* 70, no. 2: 318–20.
Occupy the Buffer Zone. 2014. "Occupy the Buffer Zone." http://www.occupybufferzone.info/.
O'Connor, Mike. 1996. "Bosnia's a Safe and Healthy Place, for the G.I.s Anyway." *New York Times*, July 3, A3.
Oddo, J. 2001. "War Legitimation Discourse: Representing 'Us' and 'Them' in Four US Presidential Addresses." *Discourse and Society* 22, no. 3: 287–314.
O'Dwyer, Carolyn. 2004. "Tropic Knights and Hula Belles: War and Tourism in the South Pacific." *Journal for Cultural Research* 8, no. 1: 33–50.
Odysseos, Louiza, and F. Petito, eds. 2007. *The International Political Thought of Carl Schmitt*. London: Routledge.
Old Blue. n.d. "Afghan Blue III." http://afghanblue.com/.

O'Neill, Martin, and Frank Fitz. 1996. "Northern Ireland Tourism: What Chance Now?" *Tourism Management* 17, no. 3: 161–63.
Opitz, Sven. 2011. "Government Unlimited: The Security Dispositif of Illiberal Governmentality." In *Governmentality: Current Issues and Future Challenges,* edited by U. Brockling, S. Krasman, and T. Lemke, 93–114. London: Routledge.
Oren, Gila, and Amir Shani. 2012. "The Yad Vashem Holocaust Museum: Educational Dark Tourism in a Futuristic Form." *Journal of Heritage Tourism* 7, no. 3: 255–70.
Osman, Colin. 1997. *Egypt: Caught in Time.* Reading, U.K.: Garnet.
Ouyyanont, Porphant. 2001. "The Vietnam War and Tourism in Bangkok's Development." *Southeast Asian Studies* 39, no. 2: 157–87.
Pachachi, Maysoon. 2009. *Our Feelings Took the Pictures: Open Shutters Iraq.* United States: Oxymoron Films. http://www.oxymoronfilms.com/opens hutters.htm.
Page, Stephen. 2009. *Tourism Management: An Introduction.* 3rd ed. Oxford: Butterworth and Heinemann.
Pagonis, William G., and Jeffrey L. Cruikshank. 1992. *Moving Mountains: Lessons in Leadership and Logistics from the Gulf War.* Harvard, Mass.: Harvard Business School Press.
Papadakis, Yiannis. 1994. "The National Struggle Museums of a Divided City." *Ethnic and Racial Studies* 17, no. 3: 407–9.
———. 2005. *Echoes from the Dead Zone: Across the Cyprus Divide.* London: I. B. Tauris.
Parks, Lisa. 2007. "Points of Departure: The Culture of US Airport Screening." *Journal of Visual Culture* 6, no. 2: 183–200.
Parr, Adrian. 2008. *Deleuze and Memorial Culture: Desire, Singular Memory, and the Politics of Trauma.* Edinburgh: Edinburgh University Press.
Parry, Nigel. 2005. "Well-Known UK Graffiti Artist Banksy Hacks the Wall." *Electronic Intifada,* September 5. http://electronicintifada.net/content /well-known-uk-graffiti-artist-banksy-hacks-wall/5733.
Parry, William. 2010. *Against the Wall: The Art of Resistance in Palestine.* London: Pluto Press.
Paterson, Jonathan. 2002. "Guantanamo Bay: Tourist Destination." *BBC News,* June 25. http://news.bbc.co.uk/1/hi/world/americas/2003051.stm.
Paul, Christopher, and James J. Kim. 2004. *Reporters on the Battlefield: The Embedded Press System in Historical Context.* Santa Monica, Calif.: RAND Corporation.
Pearce, Douglas G. 1992. "Alternative Tourism: Concepts, Classifications, and Questions." In *Tourism Alternatives: Potentials and Problems in the*

Development of Tourism, edited by W. R. Eadington and Valene Smith, 15–30. Philadelphia: University of Pennsylvania Press.

Pedlar, Emma. 2002. "Bali: Premiership Win Ends in Disaster for Sturt Football Club." *ABC South Australia,* October 14. http://www.abc.net.au/cgi-bin/common/printfriendly.pl?http://www.abc.net.au/sa/stories/s700999.htm.

People to People International. n.d. "People to People International History." http://www.ptpi.org/about_us/History.aspx.

Percival, Jenny. 2009. "New Strategy Will Train Shop and Hotel Managers to Tackle Terrorist Threats." *Guardian,* March 24. http://www.guardian.co.uk/uk/2009/mar/24/anti-terror-al-qaida-weapons.

Periscope Film LCC Archive. 1967. *A Holiday from Hell.* http://www.youtube.com/watch?v=OwWcPOAL0RY.

Perry, Douglas. n.d. "Teaching with Documents: The Civil War as Photographed by Matthew Brady." http://www.archives.gov/education/lessons/brady-photos/#documents.

Pfau, Michael, et al. 2005. "Embedded Reporting during the Invasion and Occupation of Iraq: How the Embedding of Journalists Affects Television News Reports." *Journal of Broadcasting and Electronic Media* 49, no. 4: 468–87.

Phaswana-Mufaya, Nancy, and Norbert Haydam. 2005. "Tourists' Expectations and Perceptions of the Robben Island Museum—a World Heritage Site." *Museum Management and Curatorship* 20, no. 2: 149–69.

Phillips, Christopher. 1981. *Steichen at War.* New York: Harry N. Abrams.

Philpott, Simon. 2005. "A Controversy of Faces: Images from Bali and Abu Ghraib. *Journal of Cultural Research* 9, no. 3: 227–44.

Phipps, Peter. 1999. "Tourists, Terrorists, Death, and Value." In *Travel Worlds: Journeys in Contemporary Cultural Politics,* edited by Raminder Kaur and John Hutnyk, 74–93. London: Zed Books.

———. 2004. "Tourism and Terrorism: An Intimate Equivalence." In *Tourists and Tourism: A Reader,* edited by Sharon Bohn Gmelch, 71–90. Long Grove, Ill.: Waveland Press.

Pickering, Andrew. 1995. *The Mangle of Practice: Time, Agency, and Science.* Chicago: University of Chicago Press.

Pierkarz, Mark. 2007. "Hot War Tourism: The Live Battlefield and the Ultimate Adventure Holiday?" In *Battlefield Tourism: History, Place, and Interpretation,* edited by Chris Ryan, 153–72. Amsterdam: Elsevier.

Pincus, Simon. 1996. "R&R a Time for Fun, Caution." *The Talon,* April 12, 4. http://www.dtic.mil/bosnia/talon/tal19960412.pdf.

Pizam, Abraham, and Yoel Masfield, eds. 1996. *Tourism, Crime, and International Security Issues.* Amsterdam: Elsevier.

Pollock, Griselda. 2003. "Holocaust Tourism: Being There, Looking Back, and the Ethics of Spatial Memory." In *Visual Culture and Tourism,* edited by David Crouch & Nina Lübbren, 175–90. Oxford: Berg.

Ponder, Ty. 2008. *Between the Lines: The True Story of Surfers during the Vietnam War.* Encinitas, Calif.: Pure Frustrations Productions.

Port. 2005. "My Vacation in Iraq." *Sgt. Port* (milblog), April 29. http://sgtport.blogspot.co.uk/.

Porteous, Katrina. 1988. "History Lessons: Platoon." In *Vietnam Images: War and Representation,* edited by Jeffrey Walsh and James Aulich, 153–59. New York: St. Martin's Press.

Porter, Patrick. 2009. *Military Orientalism: Eastern War through Western Eyes.* London: Hurst.

Postman, Neil. 1990. "Museum as Dialogue." *Museum News,* September/October, 55–58.

Post Wire Services. 2002. "Nabbed Bali Bomber Still Laughing at the Dead." *New York Post,* November 14, 9.

Pratt, Mary Louise. 1992. *Imperial Eyes: Travel Writing and Transculturation.* London: Routledge.

Preston-Whyte, Robert. 2004. "The Beach as a Liminal Space." In *A Companion to Tourism,* edited by Alan A. Lew, Allan M. Williams, and C. M. Hall, 349–59. Oxford: Blackwell.

Prideaux, Bruce. 2003. "The Need to Use Disaster Planning Frameworks to Respond to Major Tourism Disasters: Analysis of Australia's Response to Tourism Disasters in 2001." *Journal of Travel Tourism and Marketing* 15, no. 4: 281–98.

Puar, Jasbir K., and Amit Rai. 2002. "Monster, Terrorist, Fag: The War on Terrorism and the Production of Docile Patriots." *Social Text* 20, no. 3: 117–48.

Purbrick, Louise. 2006. "Long Kesh/Maze, Northern Ireland: Public Debate as Historical Interpretation." In *Re-mapping the Field: New Approaches in Conflict Archaeology,* edited by John Schofield, Axel Klaiemeier, and Louise Purbrick, 72–80. Berlin: Westkreuz.

———. 2007. *Without Walls: Healing through Remembering's Open Call for Ideas for a Living Memorial Museum of the Conflict in and about Northern Ireland.* Belfast: Healing through Remembering.

Rabinow, Paul, ed. 1984. *The Foucault Reader.* New York: Pantheon Books.

Rajchman, John. 1988. "Foucault's Art of Seeing." *October* 44: 89–117.

Rajiva, Lila. 2005. *The Language of Empire: Abu Ghraib and the American Media.* New York: Monthly Review Press.

Rancière, Jacques. 2004. *The Politics of Aesthetics: Distribution of the Sensible.* Translated by Gabriel Rockhill. London: Continuum.

———. 2009. *Aesthetics and Its Discontents*. Translated by Steven Corcoran. Cambridge: Polity Press.

Rankin, Elizabeth, and Leoni Schmidt. 2009. "The Apartheid Museum: Performing a Spatial Dialectics." *Journal of Visual Culture* 8, no. 1: 76–102.

Rasmussen, Karen. 1992. "*China Beach* and American Mythology of War." *Women's Studies in Communication* 15, no. 2: 22–50.

Rassler, Mark. 2010. "Just around the Corner." August 22. http://mrassler.blogspot.co.uk/2010/08/just-around-corner.html.

Rassool, Ciraj. 2000. "The Rise of Heritage and the Reconstitution of History in South Africa." *Kronos: Journal of Cape History* 26: 1–21.

———. 2007. "Memory and the Politics of History in the District 6 Museum." In *Desire Lines: Memory and Identity in the Post-apartheid City*, edited by Noëleen Murray, Nick Shepherd, and Martin Hall, 113–28. London: Routledge.

Rau, Petra. 2009. "The Fascist Body Beautiful and the Imperial Crisis in 1930s British Writing." *Journal of European Studies* 39, no. 1: 5–35.

Reid, Donald M. 2002. *Whose Pharaohs? Archaeology, Museums, and Egyptian National Identity from Napoleon to World War I*. Berkeley: University of California Press.

Reinvestment and Reform Initiative. 2003. *A New Future for the Maze: Proposal for Future Development Form and Guidance Notes*. Belfast: Reinvestment and Reform Initiative.

Reisinger, Yvette, and Felix Mavondo. 2005. "Travel Anxiety and Intentions to Travel Internationally: Implications of Travel Risk Perception." *Journal of Travel Research* 43, no. 3: 212–25.

Reming, Shawn, Jr. 2011. "Sharing the Past in a Divided City: Belfast's Ulster Museum." Unpublished manuscript. http://www.academia.edu/1537849/Sharing_the_Past_in_a_Divided_City_Belfasts_Ulster_Museum.

Remus, Sebastian. 2008. *German Amateur Photographers and the First World War: A View from the Trenches on the Western Front*. Atglen, Pa.: Schiffer.

Rennie, Neil. 1995. *Far-Fetched Facts: The Literature of Travel and the Idea of the South Seas*. Oxford: Clarendon Press.

Richmond, Oliver, and Costas Constantinou. 2004. "The Long Mile of Empire: Power, Legitimation, and the UK Bases in Cyprus." *Mediterranean Politics* 10, no. 1: 65–84.

Riley, Robin, and Naeem Inayatullah, eds. 2006. *Interrogating Imperialism: Conversations on Gender, Race, and War*. London: Palgrave Macmillan.

Risen, James. 2002. "Terror in Africa: Investigation: U.S. Suspects Qaeda Link to Bombing in Mombasa." *New York Times*, November 30, 11.

Ritchie, Brent W. 2004. "Chaos, Crises, and Disaster: A Strategic Approach to Crisis Management in the Tourism Industry." *Tourism Management* 25, no. 6: 669–83.

Robben, Antonius C. G. M. 2011. *Iraq at a Distance: What Anthropologists Can Teach Us about the War in Iraq.* Philadelphia: University of Pennsylvania Press.

Roberts, Andrew. 2008. *Postcards from the Trenches: Images from the First World War.* Oxford: Bodleian Library.

Roberts, Mary Louise. 2013. *What Soldiers Do: Sex and the American GI in World War Two France.* Chicago: University of Chicago Press.

Robertson, D., I. Kean, and S. Moore. 2006. "Tourism Risk Management: An Authoritative Guide to Managing Crises in Tourism." Singapore: Asia-Pacific Economic Cooperation. http://www.sustainabletourismonline.com/awms/Upload/HOMEPAGE/AICST_Risk_management.pdf.

Robin, Ron. 2001. *The Making of the Cold War Enemy: Culture and Politics in the Military-Intellectual Complex.* Princeton, N.J.: Princeton University Press.

Robinson, Peter. 2013. "Full Letter by Peter Robinson on the Maze." *Belfast Telegraph,* August 12. http://www.newsletter.co.uk/news/regional/full-letter-by-peter-robinson-on-the-maze-1-5388583.

Robinson, R. 2002. "Amid the Chaos—Courage, Help—Survivors Recall Their Nightmare." *Courier Mail* (Queensland), October 14, 16.

Rojek, Chris. 1993. *Ways of Escape: Modern Transformations of Leisure and Travel.* Basingstoke, U.K.: Macmillan.

Rolston, Bill. 1995. "Selling Tourism in a Country at War." *Race and Class* 37, no. 1: 1–22.

Ronson, Jon. 2004. "Hotel Auschwitz." *Journal of Cultural Politics* 8, no. 1: 75–90.

Rose, Gillian. 2001. *Visual Methodologies: An Introduction to the Interpretation of Visual Materials.* London: Sage.

Rose, Nikolas. 1989. *Governing the Soul: The Shaping of the Private Self.* London: Routledge.

———. 1996. *Inventing Ourselves: Psychology, Power, and Personhood.* Cambridge: Cambridge University Press.

Rose, Nikolas, and Peter Miller. 2008. *Governing the Present: Administering Economic, Social, and Personal Life.* Cambridge: Polity Press.

Rose, Sonya O. 2010. "Girls and GIs: Race, Sex, and Diplomacy in Second World War Britain." *International History Review* 19, no. 1: 146–60.

Rothnie, Niall. 1992. *The Baedeker Blitz: Hitler's Attack on Britain's Historic Cities.* London: Ian Allen.

RPS Planning and Development. 2003. *Technical Feasibility Study into the Development Potential of the Former Maze Prison and Adjacent Army Base.* Executive summary, Belfast, September.

RTE. 2003. Tom Kelly interviewing David Campbell. *Nationwide,* RTE1, March 10.
Ryan, James. 1997. *Picturing Empire: Photography and the Visualization of the British Empire.* Chicago: University of Chicago Press.
Sackett, Hayley, and David Botteril. 2006. "Perceptions of International Travel Risk: An Exploratory Study of the Influence of Proximity to Terrorist Attack." *e-Review of Tourism Research* 4, no. 2: 44–49. http://ertr.tamu.edu/files/2012/09/194_a-4-2-3.pdf.
Safehotels. n.d. "The Global Hotel Security Standard." http://www.safehotels.se/?page_id=5197&lang=en.
Said, Edward. 1978. *Orientalism.* New York: Vintage.
Salmoni, Barak A. 2006. "Advances in Pre-deployment Culture Training: The U.S. Marine Corps Approach." *Military Review* 86, no. 6: 79–88.
Salon Staff. 2006. "The Abu Ghraib Files." *Salon,* March 14. http://www.salon.com/2006/03/14/introduction_2/.
Salter, James. 2007. *The Hunters.* London: Penguin.
Salter, Mark B. 2007. "Governmentalities of an Airport: Heterotopia and Confession." *International Political Sociology* 1, no. 1: 49–66.
———. 2008a. "Imagining Numbers: Risk, Quantification, and Aviation Security." *Security Dialogue* 39, no. 2–3: 243–66.
———, ed. 2008b. *Politics at the Airport.* Minneapolis: University of Minnesota Press.
———, ed. 2015a. *Making Things International 2: Catalysts and Reactions.* Minneapolis: University of Minnesota Press.
———, ed. 2015b. *Making Things International 1: Circuits and Motion.* Minneapolis: University of Minnesota Press.
Sante, Luc. 2004. "Tourists and Torturers." *New York Times,* May 11, A23. http://www.genocidewatch.org/images/Hate-11-May-04-Tourists_and_Torturers.pdf.
Sather-Wagstaff, Joy. 2011. *Heritage That Hurts: Tourists in the Memoryscapes of September 11.* Walnut Creek, Calif.: Left Coast Press.
Saunders, Nicholas J. 2002. "The Ironic 'Culture of Shells' in the Great War and Beyond." In *Matériel Culture: The Archaeology of Twentieth-Century Conflict,* edited by Colleen M. Beck, William Gray Johnson, and John Schofield, 22–40. London: Routledge.
———. 2004. *Matters of Conflict: Material Culture, Memory, and the First World War.* London: Routledge.
Saunders, Nicholas J., and Paul Cornish, eds. 2009. *Contested Objects: Material Memories of the Great War.* London: Routledge.
Scates, Bruce. 2006. *Return to Gallipoli: Walking the Battlefields of the Great War.* Cambridge: Cambridge University Press.

Schwartz, Rosalie. 1997. *Pleasure Island: Tourism and Temptation in Cuba.* Lincoln: University of Nebraska Press.
Schwarz, Sherry. 2006. "Travel for Peace: An Interview with Louis D'Amore." *Transitions Abroad.* http://www.iipt.org/media/TRANSITIONS%20ABROAD.html.
Scott, Julie. 2012a. "Tourism for Peace? Reflections on a Village Tourism Project in Cyprus." *Anthropology in Action* 19, no. 3: 5-20.
———. 2012b. "Tourism, Civil Society, and Peace in Cyprus." *Annals of Tourism Research* 39, no. 4: 2114-32.
Scott, Julie, and Layik Topcan. 2006. "Cyprus: Building Bridges in the Borderlands of the New Europe." In *Tourism in the New Europe: The Challenges and Opportunities of EU Enlargement,* edited by Derek R. Hall, Melanie K. Smith, and Barbara Marciszewska, 224-40. Wallingford, U.K.: CABI Publishing.
Scott, Stuart. 2008. *Charlie Don't Surf, but Aussies Do: Taking Time Out from the Vietnam War.* Salisbury, Australia: Stuart Scott.
Scranton, Deborah. 2006. *The War Tapes.* Sen Art Films. http://thewartapes.com/trailer/.
Seaton, A. V. 1996. "Guided by the Dark: From Thanatopsis to Thanatourism." *International Journal of Heritage Studies* 2, no. 4: 234-44.
———. 1999. "War and Thanatourism: Waterloo 1815-1914." *Annals of Tourism Research* 26, no. 1: 130-58.
———. 2000. "'Another Weekend Away Looking for Dead Bodies': Battlefield Tourism on the Somme and in Flanders." *Tourism Recreation Research* 25, no. 3: 63-77.
Seenan, Gerard. 2002. "Paradise Turned into a Hellish Reminder of Home for the Israelis." *Guardian,* November 29, 2.
Segal, Lauren. 2004. "The Constitution Hill Museum." Paper presented at the Contested Spaces conference, University of Brighton, November 19-20.
Seib, Philip, and Dana M. Janbek. 2010. *Global Terrorism and New Media: The Post-al-Qaeda Generation.* London: Routledge.
Sekula, Allan. 1975. "The Instrumental Image: Steichen at War." *Artforum* 14, no. 4: 26-35.
Selwyn, Tim. 2011. "Tears on the Border: The Case of Rachel's Tomb, Bethlehem, Palestine." In *Contested Mediterranean Spaces: Essays in Honour of Charles Tilly,* edited by 276-96. New York: Berghahn Books.
Semmens, Kristin. 2005. "'Travel in Merry Germany': Tourism in the Third Reich." In *Histories of Tourism: Representation, Identity, and Conflict,* edited by John K. Walton, 144-61. Bristol: Channel View.
Sending, Ole J., and Iver B. Neumann. 2006. "Governance to Governmentality: Analysing NGOs, States, and Power." *International Studies Quarterly* 50, no. 3: 651-72.

Shachar, Arie, and Noam Shoval. 1999. "Tourism in Jerusalem: A Place to Pray." In *The Tourist City,* edited by Dennis R. Judd and Susan S. Fanstein, 198–214. New Haven, Conn.: Yale University Press.

Shackley, Myra. 2001. "Potential Futures for Robben Island: Shrine, Museum, or Theme Park?" *International Journal of Heritage Studies* 7, no. 4: 355–63.

Shapiro, Gary. 2003. *Archaeologies of Vision: Foucault and Nietzsche on Seeing and Saying.* Chicago: University of Chicago Press.

———. 1997. *Violent Cartographies: Mapping Cultures of War.* Minneapolis: University of Minnesota Press.

———. 2007. "The New Violent Cartography." *Security Dialogue* 38, no. 3: 291–313.

———. 2009. *Cinematic Geopolitics.* London: Routledge.

———. 2013. *Studies in Trans-Disciplinary Method.* London: Routledge.

Sharf, Frederic, and Peter Harrington. 1998. *Omdurman 1898—The Eyewitnesses Speak: The British Conquest of the Sudan as Described by Participants in Letters, Diaries, Photos and Drawings.* Newbury, U.K.: Greenhill Books.

Sharp, Joanne. 2001. *Condensing the Cold War: Reader's Digest and American Identity.* Minneapolis: University of Minnesota Press.

Sharpley, Richard. 2005. "Travels to the Edge of Darkness: Towards a Typology of 'Dark Tourism'." In *Taking Tourism to the Limits: Issues, Concepts, and Managerial Perspectives,* edited by Chris Ryan, Stephen Page, and Michelle Aicken, 215–26. Amsterdam: Elsevier.

Sharpley, Richard, and Philip K. Stone, eds. 2009. *The Darker Side of Travel: The Theory and Practice of Dark Tourism.* Bristol, U.K.: Channel View.

Shearing, Clifford, and Michael Kempa. 2004. "A Museum of Hope: A Story of Robben Island." *Annals of the American Academy of Political and Social Science* 592, no. 1: 62–78.

Shields, Rob. 1992. "Ritual Pleasures of a Seaside Resort: Liminality, Carnivalesque, and Dirty Weekends." In *Places on the Margins: Alternative Geographies of Modernity,* 73–116. London: Routledge.

Shilliam, Robbie, ed. 2010. *International Relations and Non-Western Thoughts: Imperialism, Colonialism, and Investigations of Global Modernity.* London: Routledge.

Shiner, Larry. 1982. "Reading Foucault: Anti-Method and the Genealogy of Power-Knowledge." *History and Theory* 21, no. 3: 382–98.

Siegenthaler, Peter. 2002. "Hiroshima and Nagasaki in Japanese Guidebooks." *Annals of Tourism Research* 29, no. 4: 1111–37.

Signal Corps. n.d. "Signal Corps Photographs of American Military Activity." National Archives. http://research.archives.gov/description/530707.

Silverman, Kaja. 1996. *The Threshold of the Visible World.* London: Routledge.

Sim, Susan, and Jason Jevanathan. 2012. "The 2008 Attack on the Kabul Serena Hotel: Lessons from a Captured Suicide Bomber." In *Defence against Terrorism: Different Dimensions and Trends of an Emerging Threat,* edited by A. Duyan, 49–59. Amsterdam: IOS Press.

Singer, Peter W. 2010. "The Ethics of Killer Applications: Why Is It So Hard to Talk About Morality When It Comes to New Military Technology?" *Journal of Military Ethics* 9, no. 4: 299–312.

Slade, Peter. 2003. "Gallipoli Thanatourism: The Meaning of ANZAC." *Annals of Tourism Research* 30, no. 4: 779–94.

Smith, David. 2008. "All-Clear for Afghan Combat Video Diaries." *Observer,* February 10, 14.

Smith, Elliot Blair. 2003. "Threat of Terrorism Poses Special Challenge to Hotels." *USA Today,* August 6. http://www.usatoday.com/travel/news/2003/08/06-hotels.htm.

Smith, Eric. n.d. "Qatar R&R Site." *afghanchaplain* (blog). http://afghanchaplain.smugmug.com/Travel/Qatar-RR-Site/43914_b9Rnwb#!i=1528284&k=ZjJJDHR.

Smith, Helena. 2008. "Ayia Napa Bans British Soldiers over Bar Brawls." *Guardian,* March, 1, 26.

Smith, Paul. 2007. Interview with the author. November 5–6.

Smith, Valene. 1998. "War and Tourism: An American Ethnography." *Annals of Tourism Research* 25, no. 1: 202–27.

Smith, Wayne William. 2002. "Review of Lennon and Foley's *Dark Tourism.*" *Annals of Tourism Research* 29, no. 4: 1188–89.

Snow, Nancy. 1998. *Propaganda Inc: Selling America's Culture to the World.* New York: Seven Stories Press.

Société des Établissements Gaumont. n.d. "Hello! American and British Soldiers." Poster, Catalogue no. Art.IWM PST 12645. Imperial War Museum Archive, London.

Soh, C. Sarah. 2009. *The Comfort Women: Sexual Violence and Postcolonial Memory in Korea and Japan.* Chicago: University of Chicago Press.

Sönmez, Sevil F. 1998. "Tourism, Terrorism, and Political Instability." *Annals of Tourism Research* 25, no. 2: 416–56.

Sönmez, Sevil F., Yiorgos Apostolopoulos, and Peter Tarlow. 1999. "Tourism in Crisis: Managing the Effects of Terrorism." *Journal of Travel Research* 38, no. 1: 13–18.

Sontag, Susan. 1977. *On Photography.* London: Penguin.

———. 2004a. *Regarding the Pain of Others.* London: Penguin.

———. 2004b. "Regarding the Torture of Others." *New York Times Magazine,* May 23. http://www.nytimes.com/2004/05/23/magazine/23PRISONS

.html?ex=1400644800&en=a2cb6ea6bd297c8f&ei=5007&partner=USE RLAND.
Sorrell, Charlie. 2009. "Bomb-proof Kevlar Wallpaper Stronger Than Wall Itself." *Wired,* November 18. http://www.wired.com/gadgetlab/2009/11/video-bomb-proof-kevlar-wallpaper-stronger-than-wall-itself/.
Soudien, Arthur. 2006. "Memory and Critical Education: Approaches in the District 6 Museum." *Africa Education Review* 3, no. 1–2: 1–12.
Sparrow, James T. 2011. *Warfare State: World War II Americans and the Age of Big Government.* Oxford: Oxford University Press.
Spurr, David. 1993. *The Rhetoric of Empire: Colonial Discourse in Journalism, Travel Writing, and Imperial Administration.* Durham, N.C.: Duke University Press.
Stacey, C. P. 1959. *Records of the Nile Voyageurs, 1884–1885: The Canadian Voyageur Contingent in the Gordon Relief Expedition.* Toronto: Champlain Society.
Stan. n.d. "Doha, Qatar Tour." *javamedic75* (blog). http://www.pbase.com/javamedic75/doha_qatar.
Stanis, Christopher. 2003. "Troops Get 'In-Country' Break at New Baghdad R&R Facility Once Used by Saddam's Republican Guard." *V Corps Release,* October 21. http://www.globalsecurity.org/military/library/news/2003/10/mil-031021-vcorps02.htm#.
Stead, Naomi. 2000. "The Ruins of History: Allegories of Destruction in Daniel Libeskind's Jewish Museum." *Open Museum Journal* 2, no. 5: 1–17.
Steevens, G. W. 1991. "In Praise of Cook Pasha." Reprinted in Deborah Manley, *The Nile: A Traveller's Anthology,* 111. London: Cassell Illustrated.
Steichen, Edward J., ed. 1946. *U.S. Navy War Photographs: Pearl Harbour to Tokyo Harbour.* New York: U.S. Camera.
Stein, Rebecca L. 2008. *Itineraries in Conflict: Israelis, Palestinians, and the Political Lives of Tourism.* Durham, N.C.: Duke University Press.
Stinson, Liz. 2014. "All the Stuff Soldiers Hev Carried in Battle, from the 11th Century to Today." *Wired,* August 19. http://www.wired.com/2014/08/all-the-stuff-soldiers-have-carried-in-battle-from-the-11th-century-to-today/.
Stone, Oliver, dir. 1986. *Platoon.* United States: Metro-Goldwyn-Mayer.
Stone, Philip R. 2005. "Dark Tourism Consumption—a Call for Research." *e-Review of Tourism Research* 3, no. 5: 109–17. http://ertr.tamu.edu/files/2012/09/224_a-3-5-2.pdf.
———. 2006. "A Dark Tourism Spectrum: Towards a Typology of Death and Macabre Related Tourist Sites, Attractions, and Exhibitions." *Tourism: An Interdisciplinary International Journal* 54, no. 2: 145–60.
Stone, Philip R., and Richard Sharpley. 2008. "Consuming Dark Tourism: A Thanatological Perspective." *Annals of Tourism Research* 35, no. 2: 574–95.

Stott, Rory. 2013. "Future Uncertain for Daniel Libeskind's Maze Peace Centre." *ArchDaily,* August 19. http://www.archdaily.com/417398.

Strange, Carolyn, and Michael Kempa. 2003. "Shades of Dark Tourism: Alcatraz and Robben Island." *Annals of Tourism Research* 30, no. 2: 386–405.

STRATFOR Global Intelligence. 2009. "Special Security Report: The Militant Threat to Hotels." http://www.stratfor.com/sample/analysis/special-security-report-militant-threat-hotels.

Struk, Joanna. 2011. *Private Pictures: Soldiers' Inside View of War.* London: I. B. Taurus.

Stubblefield, Thomas. 2011. "Do Disappearing Monuments Simply Disappear? The Counter-Monument in Revision." *Future Anterior* 8, no. 2: xii–11.

Studio Canal. 2011. "*Apocalypse Now*—Kilgore Talks Surfing and Napalm." http://www.youtube.com/watch?v=Jts9suWIDlU.

Sullivan, Kathleen. 2004. "Atomica World: The Place of Nuclear Tourism." In *Tourism Mobilities: Places to Stay, Places in Play,* edited by Mimi Sheller and John Urry, 192–204. London: Routledge.

Sun, Sue. 2004. "*Where the Girls Are*: The Management of Venereal Disease by United States Military Forces in Vietnam." *Literature and Medicine* 23, no. 1: 66–87.

Suntikul, Wantanee. 2012. "Thai Tourism and the Legacy of the Vietnam War." In *Tourism and War,* edited by Richard Butler and Wantanee Suntikul, 92–105. London: Routledge.

Surveillance Studies Centre. 2014. Homepage. http://www.sscqueens.org/.

Sylvester, Christine. 2008. *Art/Museums: International Relations Where We Least Expect It.* Boulder, Colo.: Paradigm Books.

———. 2010. *Experiencing War (War, Politics, and Experience).* London: Routledge.

———. 2012. *War as Experience: Contributions from International Relations and Feminist Analysis.* London: Routledge.

Syson, Neil, and Martin Philips. 2009. "The Two Sides of Guantanamo Bay." *The Sun,* January 23. http://www.thesun.co.uk/sol/homepage/news/article2162553.ece.

Taglit, Birthright Israel. 1999. Homepage. http://www.birthrightisrael.com/Pages/Default.aspx.

Tanaka, Yuki. 2002. *Japan's Comfort Women: Sexual Slavery and Prostitution during World War II and the US Occupation.* London: Routledge.

Tanner, Captain. n.d. "The British Army on Leave in Italy, June 1944." War Office Official Photographer. Catalogue nos. TR 1955; 1956; 1958; 1959; 1960; 1965; 1966; 1971; 1980; and 1981. Imperial War Museum Photographic Archive, London.

Tarlow, Peter E. 2005. "Dark Tourism: The Appealing 'Dark' Side of Tourism and More." In *Niche Tourism: Contemporary Issues, Trends, and Cases,* edited by Marina Novelli, 47–57. Amsterdam: Elsevier.

———. 2006a. "Terrorism and Tourism." In *Tourism in Turbulent Times: Towards Safe Experiences for Visitors,* edited by J. Wilks, D. Pendergast, and P. Leggat, 80–92. Amsterdam: Elsevier Press.

———. 2006b. "A Social Theory of Terrorism and Tourism." In *Tourism, Safety, and Security: From Theory to Practice,* edited by Y. Mansfield and A. Pizam, 33–48. Oxford: Elsevier.

Tarplee, Susan. 2008. "After the Bomb in a Balinese Village." In *Tourism at the Grassroots: Villagers and Visitors in the Asia-Pacific,* edited by J. Connell and B. Rugendyke, 148–63. London: Routledge.

Taylor, John. 1991. *War Photography: British Realism and the Press.* London: Routledge.

———. 1998. *Body Horror: Photojournalism, Catastrophe, and War.* Manchester, U.K.: Manchester University Press.

Teaiwa, Teresa. 1994. "Bikinis and Other (S)pacific N/otions." *Contemporary Pacific* 6, no. 1: 87–109.

Teeger, Chana, and Vered Vinitzky-Seroussi. 2007. "Controlling for Consensus: Commemorating Apartheid in South Africa." *Symbolic Interaction* 30, no. 1: 57–78.

Tétreault, Mary-Ann. 2006. "The Sexual Politics of Abu Ghraib: Hegemony, Spectacle, and the Global War on Terror." *NWSA Journal* 18, no. 3: 33–50.

Tharp, Mike. 1991. "The Desert Warriors Are Straight, Sober, and Focused." *U.S. News and World Report,* February 18, 30–31.

Theodoulou, Michael. 2008. "Nine Soldiers Charged over 'Smashing Up' Ayia Napa Bar." *Times,* February 4, 15.

Thomas Cook & Son. 1884. *The Soudan Campaign 1884.* Guardbook no. 16, "Introduction: National Army Museum" (n.p.). Thomas Cook Archive, Peterborough.

———. 1885. "Background of Gordon Relief Expedition, 1884/5: General Gordon in the Sudan (6.3.3)." Thomas Cook Archives, Peterborough.

———. 1919. *The Traveller's Gazette: An Illustrated Journal Devoted to Travel,* LXIX, no. 8 (August).

———. 1920a. *How to See Paris and the Battlefields.* Paris: Thomas Cook & Son. Catalogue no. K 74771, Shelf Mark 29 (44)/3. Imperial War Museum Archive, London.

———. 1920b. *The Traveller's Gazette: An Illustrated Journal Devoted to Travel,* LXX, no. 7 (July).

———. 1920c. *The Traveller's Gazette: An Illustrated Journal Devoted to Travel,* LXX, no. 6 (June).

———. 1920d. *The Traveller's Gazette: An Illustrated Journal Devoted to Travel,* LXX, no. 4 (April).

———. 1920e. *The Traveller's Gazette: An Illustrated Journal Devoted to Travel,* LXX, no. 3 (March).

———. 1924. *How to See Paris and the Battlefields: Motor Tours.* Paris: Thomas Cook & Son. Catalogue no. K.40498, Shelf Mark 184.4 (44). Imperial War Museum Archive, London.

———. 1926. *Cook's Automobile Tours.* London: Thomas Cook & Son. Thomas Cook Archives, Peterborough.

Thompson, Jenny, ed. 2006. *My Hut: A Memoir of a YMCA Volunteer in World War One.* Bloomington, Ind.: iUniverse.

Tilson, Bettina E. 1996. "R&R Policy Officially Begins April 15th." *The Talon,* April 12, 4. http://www.dtic.mil/bosnia/talon/tal19960412.pdf.

Time. 1945. "The New Pictures." January 22. http://content.time.com/time/magazine/article/0,9171,791953,00.html.

———. 1967. "Recreation: Five-Day Bonanza." December 22, 40–45. http://content.time.com/time/magazine/article/0,9171,899932,00.html.

———. n.d. "R&R at Kandahar Air Field." http://content.time.com/time/photogallery/0,29307,2026304_2201165,00.html.

Times, The. 1895. "The Nile Waterway." April 20, 14, col. B.

Times, The. 2002. "Tourists as Targets: Al-Qaeda Returns to the Scene of Earlier Atrocities." November 29, 25.

Timothy, Dallen J., Bruce Prideaux, and Samuel S. Kim. 2004. "Tourism at Borders of Conflict and (De) militarized Zones." In *New Horizons in Tourism: Strange Experiences and Stranger Practices,* edited by T. V. Singh, 83–94. Wallingford, U.K.: CABI International.

Tomczyszyn, Pat. 2004. "A Material Link between War and Peace: First World War Silk Postcards." In *Matters of Conflict: Material Culture, Memory, and the First World War,* edited by Nicholas J. Saunders, 123–33. London: Routledge.

Tomljenović, R. 2010. "Tourism and Intercultural Understanding or Contact Hypothesis Revisited." In *Tourism, Progress, and Peace,* edited by Omar Moufakkir and Ian Kelly, 17–34. Wallingford, U.K.: CABI International.

Toolis, Kevin. 2002. "Bin Laden's Men Have Discovered Another Target in Their Bloody War with the West...Innocent Tourists." *The Mirror,* October 14, 6.

Torrie, Julia S. 2011. "'Our Rear Area Probably Lived Too Well': Tourism and the German Occupation of France, 1940–1944." *Journal of Tourism History* 3, no. 3: 309–30.

Tourism Australia. 2009a. "No Leave, No Life: Research." http://www.tourism.australia.com/campaigns/no-leave-no-life/8299.aspx.

———. 2009b. "No Leave, No Life: Program Benefits." http://www.tourism.australia.com/campaigns/no-leave-no-life/benefits.aspx.

———. 2009c. "No Leave, No Life: Tools and Templates." http://www.tourism.australia.com/campaigns/no-leave-no-life/tools-and-templates.aspx.

Truong, Thanh-dam Truong. 1990. *Sex, Money, and Morality: Prostitution and Tourism in Southeast Asia*. Atlantic Highlands, N.J.: Zed Books.

Tsfati, Yariv, and Gabriel Weimann. 2002. "www.terrorist.net: Terror on the Internet." *Studies in Conflict and Terrorism* 25, no. 5: 317–32.

Turnbridge, J. E., and G. J. Ashworth. 1995. *Dissonant Heritage: The Management of the Past as a Resource in Conflict*. London: John Wiley.

Turner, Bryan S. 2007. "The Enclave Society: Towards a Sociology of Immobility." *European Journal of Social Theory* 10, no. 2: 287–304.

———. 2010. "Enclosures, Enclaves, and Entrapment." *Sociological Inquiry* 80, no. 2: 41–60.

Turn Off Your Television. 2011. "Zionist 'War Tourists' Picnic with Views of Gaza Massacre." http://www.youtube.com/watch?v=0eqAmWvuKLU.

Ugowar. 2007. "The Joker Giving an Interview." March 20, 0:18. http://www.youtube.com/watch?v=u_6UIGXajEA.

Ungerleider, John. 2001. "Bicommunal Youth Camps for Peace in Cyprus." *Peace Review* 13, no. 4: 583–89.

United Nations Peacekeeping Force in Cyprus. 2010. "The Story of the Maple House." *The Blue Beret*, June/July, 10. http://www.unficyp.org/media/Blue%20Beret%20-%20pdf%20files/2010/BB%20June-July%202010.pdf.

———. 2014. "Around Cyprus." http://www.unficyp.org/nqcontent.cfm?a_id=1586.

United Service Gazette. 1884. no. 2684, June 14.

United Service Organizations. n.d. "History." http://www.uso.org/history.aspx.

Urry, John. 1990. *The Tourist Gaze: Leisure and Travel in Contemporary Societies*. London: Sage.

U.S. Army. 1969. *Personal Hygiene in a Hot Climate*, 52:14–1:06:54, http://militaryvideo.com/index.cfm?film=detail&titleID=BOOM&do=detail&search=Boom.

———. 2010. "Rest and Recuperation (R&R)." http://www.armyg1.army.mil/randr/default.asp.

———. 2011. "Equal Opportunity Branch." http://www.armyg1.army.mil/eo/.

U.S. Army Family and Morale, Welfare, and Recreation Programs. 2014a. "Family and MWR Vision and Mission." http://www.armymwr.com/commander/mission.aspx.

———. 2014b. "Armed Forces Recreation Center Resorts." http://www.armymwr.com/travel/recreationcenters/.

U.S. Army in Europe. n.d. "A Soldier's Guide to Dealing with Media Interest in the R&R Program." http://www.eur.army.mil/g1/content/Programs/RR/docs/mediaInterest.html.

U.S. Central Command. 2007. *Rest and Recuperation (R&R) Leave Program: Information Paper,* March 6. http://www.armyg1.army.mil/randr/docs/About%20the%20Program.pdf.

USS *Midway.* n.d. "Liberty Port Souvenirs." http://www.midwaysailor.com/midwaymemorabilia/libertysouvenirs.html.

Utaka, Yushi. 2009. "The Hiroshima 'Peace Memorial': Transforming Legacy, Memories, and Landscapes." In *Places of Pain and Shame: Dealing with Difficult Heritage,* edited by William Logan and Keir Reeves, 34–39. London: Routledge.

Uzzell, David. 1992. "The Hot Interpretation of War and Conflict." In *Heritage Interpretation: The Natural and Built Environment,* vol. 1, 33–47. London: Bellhaven Press.

Uzzell, David, and Roy Ballantyne. 1998. "Heritage That Hurts: Interpretation in a Post-modern World." In *Contemporary Issues in Heritage and Environmental Management,* 152–71. London: Stationary Office.

Valiunas, Algis. 2002. *Churchill's Military Histories: A Rhetorical Study.* Oxford: Rowman and Littlefield.

Van Crevald, Martin. 1979. *Supplying War: Logistics from Wallenstein to Patton.* Cambridge: Cambridge University Press.

Van Doren, Carlton S. 1993. "Pan Am's Legacy to World Tourism." *Journal of Travel Research* 32, no. 1: 3–12.

Van Munster, Rens. 2004. "The War on Terrorism: When the Exception Becomes the Rule." *International Journal for the Semiotics of Law* 17, no. 2: 141–53.

Van Veeran, Elspeth. 2011. "Captured by the Camera's Eye: Guantanamo and the Shifting Frame of the Global War on Terror." *Review of International Studies* 37, no. 4: 1721–49.

———. 2014. "Materializing US Security: Guantanamo's Object Lessons and Concrete Messages." *International Political Sociology* 8, no. 1: 20–42.

Van Vleck, Jenifer L. 2007. "The 'Logic of the Air': Aviation and the Globalism of the 'American Century'." *New Global Studies* 1, no. 1: 1–37.

Var, Turgut, Russ Brayley, and Meral Korsay. 1989. "Tourism and World Peace: Case of Turkey." *Annals of Tourism Research* 16, no. 2: 282–86.

Var, Turgut, Regina Schlüter, Paul Ankomah, and Tae-Hee Lee. 1989. "Tourism and World Peace: The Case of Argentina." *Annals of Tourism Research* 16, no. 3: 431–34.

Vicuña Gonzalez, Vernadette. 2013. *Securing Paradise: Tourism and Militarism in Hawaii and the Philippines.* Durham, N.C.: Duke University Press.

Vinegar, Aron, and Jorge Otero-Pailos. 2012. "On Preserving the Openness of the Monument." *Future Anterior* 9, no. 2: iii–vi.
Virilio, Paul. 1989. *War and Cinema: The Logistics of Perception.* Translated by Patrick Camillier. London: Verso.
Visscher, Marco. 2007. "Tourism Can Bring Peace: An Interview with Louis D'Amore." *Ode Magazine,* November, 80. http://www.iipt.org/pdf/1107%20ONE%20LAST%20D%27Amour%20Mockup.pdf.
Vrasti, Wanda. 2012. *Volunteer Tourism in the Global South: Giving Back in Neoliberal Times.* London: Routledge.
Walker, R. B. J. 2006. "Lines of Insecurity: International, Imperial, Exceptional." *Security Dialogue* 37, no. 1: 65–82.
Wall, Geoffrey. 1996. "Terrorism and Tourism: An Overview and an Irish Example." In *Tourism, Crime, and International Security Issues,* edited by Abraham Pizam and Yeol Mansfield, 143–58. Chichester, U.K.: John Wiley.
Wall, Melissa. 2010. "In the Battlefield: The US Military, Blogging and the Struggle for Authority." *Media, Culture, and Society* 32, no. 5: 863–72.
Walters, William. 2010. *Governmentality: Critical Encounters.* London: Routledge.
Walther, Daniel J. 2013. "Sex, Public Health, and Colonial Control: The Campaign against Venereal Diseases in Germany's Overseas Possessions, 1884–1914." *Social History of Medicine* 26, no. 2: 182–203.
Warner, Jonathan. 1999. "North Cyprus: Tourism and the Challenge of Non-recognition." *Journal of Sustainable Tourism* 7, no. 2: 128–45.
Warshaw, Matt. 2005. *The Encyclopedia of Surfing.* Fort Washington, Pa.: Harvest Books.
Waters, Somerset R. 1955. "Importance of International Travel to the Foreign Trade of the United States." *Department of State Bulletin,* October 17. http://www.mocavo.com/Department-of-State-Bulletin-Oct-Dec-1955-Volume-33/298915/102.
Weaver, David Bruce. 2000. "The Exploratory War-Distorted Destination Life Cycle." *International Journal of Tourism Research* 2, no. 3: 151–61.
Weber, Cynthia. 2005. *Imagining America at War: Morality, Politics, and Film.* London: Routledge.
Webster, Craig, and Dallen J. Timothy. 2006. "Travelling to the 'Other Side': The Occupied Zone and Greek Cypriot Views of Crossing the Green Line." *Tourism Geographies* 8, no. 2: 162–81.
Weingartner, James J. 1992. "Trophies of War: U.S. Troops and the Mutilation of Japanese War Dead." *Pacific Historical Review* 61: 53–67.
Wendle, John. 2011. "US Men at War: BlackBerrys and iPads on the Afghan Front." *Time,* August 30. http://content.time.com/time/world/article/0,8599,2089184,00.html.

Werry, Margaret. 2011. *The Tourist State: Performing Leisure, Liberalism, and Race in New Zealand*. Minneapolis: University of Minnesota Press.

Wharton, Annabel Jane. 2001. *Building the Cold War: Hilton International Hotels and Modern Architecture*. Chicago: University of Chicago Press.

White, Geoffrey M. 1995. "Memory Wars: The Politics of Remembering the Asia-Pacific War." *Asia Pacific Issues*, no. 21: 1–8.

White, Leanne, and Elizabeth Frew. 2013. *Dark Tourism and Place Identity: Managing and Interpreting Dark Places*. London: Routledge.

Whiting, Charles. 1987. *Three Star Blitz: Baedeker Raids and the Start of Total War, 1942–45*. Glasgow: First Impression.

Wiener, Jon. 1997. "Cold War Tourism, Western Style: Visiting the Nevada Test Site, the Most Poisoned Place on the Planet." *The Nation*, October 6, 33–35.

Wight, A. Craig. 2006. "Philosophical and Methodological Praxes in Dark Tourism: Controversy, Contention, and the Evolving Paradigm." *Journal of Vacation Marketing* 12, no. 2: 119–29.

Wilcox, Lauren. 2015. *Bodies of Violence: Theorizing Embodied Subjects in International Relations*. Oxford: Oxford University Press.

Wilkinson, Tracy. 1991. "In Alcohol Free Gulf, GIs Stayed Out of Hot Water." *Los Angeles Times*, March 29, 15.

Wilkinson-Latham, Robert, and Michael Roffe. 1976. *The Sudan Campaigns 1881–98 (Men-at-Arms)*. Oxford: Osprey.

Wilks, Jeff. 2006. "Current Issues in Tourist Health, Safety, and Security." In *Tourism in Turbulent Times: Towards Safe Experiences for Visitors*, edited by Jeff Wilks, Donna Pendergast and Petter Leggat, 3–18. Amsterdam: Elsevier.

Williams, Michael. 2003. "Words, Images, Enemies: Securitization and International Politics." *International Studies Quarterly* 47, no. 4: 511–31.

Williams, Paul. 2000. *Memorial Museums: The Global Rush to Commemorate Atrocities*. London: Bloomsbury.

Wilson, Rob. 2000. *Reimagining the American Pacific: From South Pacific to Bamboo Ridge and Beyond*. Durham, N.C.: Duke University Press.

Wines, Michael. 1990. "Standoff in the Gulf: U.S. to Rent Cruise Ship for Gulf G.I. Furloughs." *New York Times*, December 15, 9.

Winter, Caroline. 2010. "First World War Cemeteries: Insights from Visitor Books." *Tourism Geographies* 13, no. 3: 462–79.

Winter, Jay. 1995. *Sites of Memory, Sites of Mourning: The Great War in European Cultural History*. Cambridge: Cambridge University Press.

Withey, Lynne. 1997. *Grand Tours and Cook's Tours: A History of Leisure Travel 1750–1915*. London: Aurum Press.

Withnall, Adam. 2014. "Israel-Gaza Conflict: 'Sderot Cinema' Image Shows Israelis with Popcorn and Chairs 'Cheering as Missiles Strike Palestinian Targets.'" *Independent*, July 13. http://www.independent.co.uk

/news/world/middle-east/israelgaza-conflict-sderot-cinema-image-shows-israelis-with-popcorn-and-chairs-cheering-as-missiles-strike-palestinian-targets-9602704.html.

Wollaston, Sam. 2002. "Tears and Anger as Kenyan Village Mourns Dancers." *Guardian*, November 30, 1.

World Tourism Organization. 2001. *Tourism after 11 September 2001: Analysis, Remedial Actions, and Prospects*. Madrid: World Tourism Organization.

Wright, Edgar. 1917. "Posters for the YMCA." Catalogue Art.IWM PST 13227/ PST 13229/PST 13222. Imperial War Museum Archive, London.

Wynne-Hughes, Elisa. 2012. "'Who Would Go to Egypt?' How Tourism Accounts for 'Terrorism'." *Review of International Studies* 38, no. 3: 615–40.

Yamazaki, Takashi. 2011. "The U.S. Militarization of a 'Host' Civilian Society: The Case of Postwar Okinawa, Japan." In *Restructuring Conflict: Integrating War and Post-War Geographies*, edited by Scott Kirsch and Colin Flint, 253–72. Aldershot, U.K.: Ashgate.

Yde, Robert. 2007. "Soldiers Focus Inward at Freedom Rest." *Defend America*, April 2. http://www.defendamerica.mil/articles/apr2007/a040207pc1.html.

Yea, Sallie. 2003. "Former Comfort Women as Touristic Objects in South Korea." In *Sex and Tourism: Journeys of Romance, Love, and Lust*, edited by Thomas G. Bauer and Bob McKercher, 139–54. London: Haworth Press.

Yoneyama, Lisa. 1999. *Hiroshima Traces: Time, Space, and the Dialectics of Memory*. Berkeley: University of California Press.

Yoshiaki, Yoshimi. 2001. *Comfort Women: Sexual Slavery in the Japanese Military during World War II*. New York: Columbia University Press.

Young, James. 1992. "The Counter-monument: Memory against Itself in Germany Today." *Critical Inquiry* 18, no. 2: 267–96.

——. 1993. *The Texture of Memory: Holocaust Memorials and Meaning*. New Haven, Conn.: Yale University Press.

——. 1997. "Germany's Problem with Its Holocaust Memorial: A Way out of the Quagmire." *Chronicle of Higher Education*, October 31, B14.

——. 1999. "Memory and Counter-memory: The End of the Monument in Germany." *Harvard Design Magazine*, Fall, 3–10. http://partizaning.org/wp-content/uploads/2014/01/Memory-and-Counter-Memory.pdf.

——. 2000a. "Daniel Libeskind's Jewish Museum in Berlin: The Uncanny Arts of Memorial Architecture." *Jewish Social Studies* 6, no. 2: 1–23.

——. 2000b. *At Memory's Edge: After Images of the Holocaust in Contemporary Art and Architecture*. New Haven, Conn.: Yale University Press.

——. 2002. "Germany's Holocaust Memorial Problem—and Mine." *Public Historian* 24, no. 4: 65–80.

Yu, Larry, and Moo Hyung Chung. 2001. "Tourism as a Catalytic Force for

Low-Politics Activities between Political Divided Countries: The Cases of North/South Korea and Taiwan/China." *New Political Science* 23, no. 4: 537–45.

Zehfuss, Maja. 2003. "Forget September 11." *Third World Quarterly* 24, no. 3: 513–28.

———. 2006. "Remembering to Forget/Forgetting to Remember." In *Memory, Trauma, and World Politics: Reflections on the Relationship between Past and Present*, edited by Duncan S. A. Bell, 213–30. Basingstoke, U.K.: Palgrave Macmillan.

———. 2007. *Wounds of Memory: The Politics of War in Germany*. Cambridge: Cambridge University Press.

Zelizer, Barbie. 1998. *Remembering to Forget: Holocaust Memory through the Camera's Eye*. Chicago: University of Chicago Press.

Zimmerman, Fred. 2004. "Close to Combat, Yet Far Away." *Stars and Stripes*, June 20. http://www.stripes.com/news/close-to-combat-yet-far-away-1.21160.

Zwigenberg, Ran. 2012. "The Hiroshima–Auschwitz Peace March and the Globalization of Victimhood." Paper presented at the International Graduate Students' Conference on the Holocaust and Genocide. http://commons.clarku.edu/chgs_papers/10/.

Index

abjection, 41, 77, 83, 118, 120, 122, 123, 164, 175, 177, 253
Abu Ghraib, 251–54, 271, 283; familiarity and, 252; and hunting frame, 252; and lynching frame, 251–52; and pornography, 251–52; and tourist frame, 252–54
Abu Klea, Battle of, 36, 53
aesthetics, 24, 78, 112, 270. *See also* emptiness
affect, 4, 21, 129, 130, 134, 140, 236, 263–64, 268–70, 271, 278–79, 297
Afghanistan, 142, 239, 241, 242, 246–47, 254, 271
Africa, 12, 13, 14, 19, 29–68, 69, 70, 97, 127, 142, 144, 148, 287, 290
African National Congress (ANC), 218, 222
agency, 83, 121–22, 129, 135, 147, 198, 206–7, 218, 221, 261, 272, 287, 292, 294, 306n10
aircraft carriers, 22, 99, 103–4,
airports, 14, 22, 254, 263–71, 274; anticipatory frame, 266, 274; and architecture, 269–70; and biometrics, 15, 265, 268, 283; and mobility, 270; Moi International (Kenya), 257–58; networked, 270; norm/deviant logic, 266–67; passenger profiling, 265; and relationality, 270–71; screening process, 265–66, 269, 271; and security technologies, 15, 265; and sorting, 265
Allied Occupation (of Japan), 159–64; and "comfort facilities," 159; tourist framing of, 160–63
al-Qaeda, 15, 239, 257, 272
ambivalence, 55–56, 91, 113, 115–16, 125, 138, 147, 212, 285, 293
America, 12, 13, 56, 114, 124, 145
American: audiences, 104, 110, 140; citizens, 100, 142, 177; culture, 23, 244–45, 251; diplomacy with Cuba, 152; Expeditionary Forces (WWI), 102; as focus of Vietnam War films, 176–77; forces/troops, 99, 101, 104, 108, 110–14, 124, 126, 142; hegemony, 126, 143, 148; ideas, 17; internationalism, 144, 148–50, 307n4, 307–08n5; Legion, 84; military, 103, 109–11, 112; nurses serving in Vietnam, 176; occupation of Hawaii, 100; occupation of Japan, 159–63; occupation of Pacific, 112, 139; propaganda, 113; protectorates, 71; prudishness, 151; public, 103, 120; Red Cross, 97; sailors, 108, 111, 118; soldiers, 2, 17, 18, 74, 99, 100, 101, 113, 117, 158–78, 186–92, 248–54, 262–63; sphere of influence, 13, 125–26, 141, 144,

148; tourist industry, 142–43; tourists, 40, 96–97, 101, 125, 139, 143–45, 148, 150–52, 182; victory, 110; women, 100. *See also* military bases
"Americanization of the world," 111, 141, 143–44, 147
Anselles-La-Plage, 94–95
architectures of enmity, 11–12, 14, 16, 22, 24, 71, 178, 204, 212, 215, 239–40, 283, 285–86, 293–94; and agonism, 207–8. *See also* geopolitical imaginaries; geopolitics
Armed Forces Recreation Center Resorts (AFRCs), 191
Ashworth, G. J., 196, 198
Asia, 12, 47, 70, 97, 127, 142, 148, 158–78
assemblage, 10, 81, 271
asymmetry, 4, 9, 11, 13, 16, 25, 37, 41, 46, 50, 68, 81, 97, 112, 115, 141, 147, 150, 164, 175, 177–78, 184, 201, 217, 228, 232, 237, 253–55, 263, 271, 284–285, 294
atrocity, 8, 28, 118, 127, 128, 129, 192, 195–96, 198, 212, 236–38; sanitation of, 128, 196–98, 287, 309n2
Auschwitz, 13, 125, 127–35, 140, 152, 158, 196, 307n3; crematoria, 131–32; "Death Wall," 130; mediation of, 131; moralization of, 133–34; opening of permanent exhibit, 130; pilgrims vs. tourists, 133; strategies of identification, 132; as template of commemoration, 140–41; transformation into tourist site, 130–35; universal mode of address, 132; visitor logistics, 131, 133. *See also* authenticity; commemoration
authenticity, 78, 84, 86–87, 155, 192–93, 194, 219–20, 222, 226, 246, 250, 292; and Auschwitz, 130–31, 133–34; escape from modern life, 93; as hardship, 219–20; and inauthenticity of tourism, 181–82

Baedeker Raids, 94
Baghdad, 79, 245, 248
Bahrain, 187–88, 244
Bailey, Second Lieutenant P., 76–77
Bali, 242, 278; bombing of 2002, 257–63, 272; Paddy's Pub, 257; relations with Australia, 258–59; Sari Nightclub, 257, 262
Bangkok, 126, 168–70, 176. *See also* Thailand
Barkawi, Tarak, 70, 301
Batista, President Fulgencio, 151–52
battlefields, 10, 13, 23, 27, 59, 64, 66, 70–74, 76, 78, 81, 84–88, 97, 122, 285; transformation of, 127–28
battlefield tours, 83, 196; commercialization of, 85; denigration of mass tourism, 83–85, 87; and disrespect, 85, 88; and duty, 86; and objects, 87; sacred vs. profane, 84–85, 88; in Sudan, 59, 63–65, to the Western Front, 71, 83–91, 305n5. *See also* Briggs, Mrs. L. K.; commemoration: of Great War; Thomas Cook & Son: WWI battlefields
Beach, The (film and novel), 177
beaches, 23, 104–6, 107, 108, 110–11,

150, 165–66; China Beach (Bac My An), 166, 172; Eagle Beach, 166; Gaza Beach, 206–8; Kuta Beach, 257; as liminal spaces, 104–6; Logman's Beach, 166; for military landings, 104–5; preparing for future tourism, 106; Vung Tau Beach, 166–67, 172
Behdad, Ali, 12, 31, 93
Belfast. *See* Northern Ireland
Bell, Steve, 260
Between Iraq and a Hard Place (performance), 187
binaries, 5, 12, 17
biopolitics, 51–52, 159–60, 163, 263, 270, 311–12n3
bipolarity, 125, 141, 147, 158, 178, 185, 240
Birkenau. *See* Auschwitz
bodies, 15–16, 20–21, 22, 24, 26, 39, 41, 46, 50, 51, 105, 115–16, 137, 219, 241, 268; dead bodies, 117, 120; deviant bodies, 264–67; and embodiment, 21, 237, 263; and hygiene, 174–75; sexualized, 170–75; of women, 118, 159–63, 170–73
borders, 182, 209–11, 215, 240, 263–64. *See also* Cyprus (Buffer Zone)
boredom, 85, 119, 127, 134, 156, 243, 248–49
Bosnia, 181, 185, 189, 192, 228, 308–9n1
Bowman, Michael S. and Pezzullo, Phaedra C., 198–99
Briggs, Claude, 89, 305–6n6
Briggs, Mrs. L. K., 89–92, 305–6n6
British rule in Egypt, 30–32, 37; dissolution of, 46; envelope of security, 45; imperial taxonomy, 39; and sovereignty, 37, 63; and superiority, 40
brothels, 50, 73, 76, 98, 100, 114, 159, 160, 162, 165, 169, 188; no-brothels policy, 186–87. *See also* massage parlors
Brown, Wendy, 16, 218
Building the Cold War (Wharton), 148–50
Bush, George W., 239, 255–57, 259–60
Butler, Judith, 19
Byrne, Penny, 282–83

Cairo, 32, 34, 36–37, 47, 49, 50–52, 64, 75, 79, 97–98, 148–49, 304n3, 304n5
camel corps, 36, 43–44, 47
camels, 43–44, 66
camera: cine-camera, 89; at the front, 12; in the Pacific, 101, 117; personal, 12, 71, 165–66, 252; Rolleiflex, 103; in Vietnam, 165–66
Campbell, David, 19
Canada, 12, 35, 54–55, 57, 69, 157, 304n5
Caribbean, 149–50
carnivalesque, 104, 156, 170
Castro, Fidel, 126, 151, 153, 156–57
Casualties of War (film), 176–77
causality, 10, 285
China Beach (television program), 176–77
"Chinaman," 89–92
Chinese Labor Corps, 70, 89–90
Chow, Rey, 164
Churchill, Winston, 29, 33, 40, 63–64, 303n1

civilized/uncivilized binary, 12, 14, 16, 39, 76, 174, 255; and barbarity, 38, 41, 256; civilizing mission in Egypt, 37–38, 41; discourse of civilization, 240; and ideological struggle, 194; ladder of civilization, 40–41, 77; and "natives," 108; as territorialization, 39; and terrorists, 255–56. *See also* visuality: imperial gaze
class, 12, 46, 52, 56, 69, 77, 93, 101, 112, 148, 160, 304n4
Cold War, 13, 124–80, 181–82, 185, 284; end of, 125, 237; ideology, 150; Japan–US relations, 139; mode of exhibition, 125, 147–48; and spheres of influence, 13, 125, 141–42; superpower rivalry, 141–42
Cole, Lester, 152–56, 158
Cole, Tim, 131, 133
colonial encounters, 12–13, 48, 52, 89–91, 109–10, 114, 147, 250, 286; and global sensibility, 13, 70–71; as performance, 41. *See also* asymmetry; colonial logics; colonizer/colonized framework
colonialism, 13, 15–16, 25, 98–99, 108–9, 118, 163, 176, 183, 284; history, 145, 147, 287, 289, 311–12n3; as lingering force, 123, 308–9n1
colonial logics, 98–100, 112, 145–47, 290; reordering of, 123, 292. *See also* colonizer/colonized framework
colonial nostalgia, 65–66, 99, 106, 210
colonizer/colonized framework, 4, 30, 37, limitations of, 41, 57, 68, 250–51
comfort women, 114, 159
commemoration, 27, 28, 71, 125, 193, 195, 199, 216, 221, 225, 238; of Auschwitz, 127–35; and authenticity, 84, 134; critical forms of, 223, 234–36, 311n10; in Cyprus, 208–9, 212, 213–14; and denigration of mass tourism, 129; discourse of, 128–31, 134, 140, 196; vs. entertainment, 195–96; as escape, 83; of Great War, 12, 83, 86–88; in the Middle East, 203–4; in Northern Ireland, 225–36; remembering and forgetting, 128–29, 140, 196, 212, 215, 226; and reverence, 88, 128–29, 134–35, 141, 198, 219; singular narrative of, 128, 220–21; and WWII, 125. *See also* museums
commodification, 69, 93, 129, 161, 182, 197; of the Other, 4, 90, 147
Communism, 126, 144, 147, 157, 173, 175, 178–79; and anti-Communism, 148, 151
comparative politics, 217, 232
conflict. *See* war
Conflict: The Irish at War (exhibition), 227
consumerism, 4, 69, 88, 93, 104, 125, 143–45, 149–50, 159, 161, 168–69, 242, 244–45
contingency, 5–6, 147, 240, 284, 287
Connolly, William, 10
Cook, Albert, 36, 60
Cook, John Mason, 32, 33–34, 36–37, 39, 45, 47, 59–63
Cook, Thomas, 32, 47

INDEX 379

cosmopolitanism, 69–70, 181–82, 184, 255–59, 273, 290, 307–8n5; as fantasy, 260–261. *See also* diversity
counterterrorism. *See* hotels: counterterrorist training; War on Terror: counterterrorism
Crandall, Jordan, 264, 268
critical thinking, 10, 129, 184, 294, 298–300
Cuba, 126, 142, 150–58, 282; American boycott of, 157; cultural dissemination in America, 151; Fidelistas (revolutionaries), 151–53, 158; laissez-faire tourism policy, 150–51; revolution, 152. *See also* Havana
cultural sensitivity, 185–87
cultural sources, 24, 28
Cyprus, 185, 199, 200, 208–15, 217, 228, 282, 310n7; British sovereign bases (Akrotiri and Dhekelia), 208, 310n7; Buffer Zone (Green Line), 208–15; Cyprus Tour Guides Association, 210; Famagusta Gulf View Point, 212; Greek Cypriots vs. Turkish Cypriots, 208–15; Green Line Tour, 210, 214; Holy Cross Catholic Church, 211; Maple House UN Post, 213; substitution of oppressors, 210; and tourism of ruins, 212–15; and unification, 212; and Yellow Morris Minor, 213–14. *See also* Nicosia, Varosha

dahabeah (sailing vessel), 32, 34–36, 43, 59, 65

D'Amore, Louis, 183
Danchev, Alex, 104, 116, 306n10
dark tourism, 14, 27, 127, 181, 184–85, 192, 193–99; of Buffer Zone (Cyprus), 213; critique of, 195–99, 238, 309n2; denigration of tourism, 196; and ethical reflection, 197–98; geopolitics of, 193–94, 197–98, 237; and modernity, 196–97; normative framework of, 197–99; Positivism and, 197, 199; reproduction of liberal norms, 193–95, 197–99; serendipitous tourists, 195; taxonomy of, 194; voyeurism, 27, 194, 197. *See also* political tourism
Dark Tourism (Lennon and Foley), 194, 196–97
D-Day, 94–95, 105
decolonization, 13, 93, 98–99
dehumanization, 26, 112, 117, 126, 161, 242, 246, 250, 252–54, 283
Denison, Lieutenant Colonel F. C., 52, 57, 304n5
Diamond Head, 110–11
difference: and deviance, 266–67; and display, 147–48; and domination, 4, 5, 11, 16, 25, 26, 100, 102, 117, 121, 250, 282, 284; logic of, 26, 102, 283; multiplicity of, 8; production of, 4, 10, 92; reordering of, 122; within empire, 39–41. *See also* identity; Otherness
digital technologies, 241–42, 246–48; privacy and, 242–43. *See also* Internet; milblogs; social media
Diller + Scofidio, 22–24, 284, 303n3, 312n1
diplomacy. *See* tourist-diplomats

dispositif, 20, 263, 311n2
dispositions, 311–12n3; alternative, 6, 23: critical, 6, 294; solipsistic, 243; tourist, 144, 156, 293; watching/watched, 264, 268
Dissonant Heritage (Turnbridge and Ashworth), 127–28, 309n2
dissonant heritage, 203, 229, 309n2; "history that hurts," 128, 199
distance, 55, 117, 125–26, 145, 148–49, 241, 246, 248, 250, 284
diversity, 176, 182–84, 205, 221, 255; and recognition, 183, 185; workshops, 186
Dolberg, Eugenie, 291–93
domination. *See* difference: and domination
Dongola, 36, 46, 60, 62

egalitarianism, 185–92
Egypt. *See* British rule in Egypt: Thomas Cook & Son
emotion, 4, 190, 220, 222, 289; as response, 119, 129, 237. *See also* affect; empathy
empathy, 132, 222
empire, 12, 17; anxiety over, 65; British Empire, 30, 74, 76, 283; military geography of, 70; as overdetermined, 41; as polyvocal, 54, 68; slippages in, 66, 68. *See also* British rule in Egypt
emptiness, 233–34; 236–38, 291; and contemplation, 236–37; and minimalism, 236
enclave. *See* tourism: enclave
Endy, Christopher, 148
enemy, 4, 5, 15, 26, 75, 81, 94, 122, 161, 174, 209, 240–41, 246, 250, 285, 307n4; territory, 71–72;

visualization of, 109, 113, 117
Enloe, Cynthia, 27, 114, 160, 169–70, 188
entanglement, 10, 303n2; of war and tourism, 5–6, 10, 12, 15–17, 23–25, 28, 34, 44–45, 69–70, 83, 123, 125, 152–53, 158–59, 176, 179, 208, 248, 254, 278, 283–85, 287, 293–94. *See also* relationality
ethics, 10, 120, 139, 196, 197–99, 229, 281, 284, 286–87, 289, 293, 297
ethnic conflict, 14, 181, 188, 192, 239, 308–9n1
Europe, 12, 13, 30, 69–70, 92, 96–97, 120, 142, 145, 148, 149, 157, 182
European, 39, 40, 49, 303n1; battlefields, 13, 70–71, 73, 96–97, 102, 127, 142, cities, 79, 83; citizens and subjects, 33, 39; civilization, 37, 41; concentration camps, 127; culture, 30; funding, 225, 233; interests, 37; as occupiers, 40, 42, 68; tourists, 29–32, 38, 42–43, 50–51, 56, 58, 63–64, 66, 83, 86, 94, 97, 135; vision, 30, 43
everyday life, 6, 9, 22, 71, 95, 126, 190, 207, 210, 240, 255, 264, 272, 278–79, 285–86, 291, 293, 300, 311–12n3; in colonial Egypt, 30; as military propaganda, 103; of modern soldiers, 243; and objects, 137; as subversion of order, 46; and Vietnam War, 126, 173
exception. *See* terrorism
exercise. *See* fitness
exotic, 4, 70, 77, 79, 93, 100, 106, 110–11, 125, 144–45, 147, 149,

161, 166, 168, 172, 175–79, 241, 253, 259, 293, 307–8n5, 308–9n1
Eye on Awareness: Hotel Security and Anti-Terrorism Training Program, 276–77

fear, culture of, 264–66, 271, 278
feminine gaze, 56–57
feminism, 25, 114, 161, 175
Fighting Lady, The (film), 103
film, 23–24, 29, 65, 74, 89, 106, 124, 151, 163–64, 172–77, 187, 246, 251, 291, 307n1, 307–8n5
First World War, 12, 69–92; 196, 297, 305n1; battlefields, 13, 70–78, 81, 83–92; cosmopolitan troops, 69–70; diaries, 74–75, 81; frontiers, 13, 70. *See also* battlefields; battlefield tours; commemoration; R&R
fitness, 104, 115, 160, 187, 189, 244–45, 295
foliated agency (Gregory), 43–44, 46, 54, 206
Fooks, Lieutenant Colonel Osmond, 79, 81, 88, 91
Foucault, Michel, 9, 28, 262; power, 20; visuality, 20–21; war, 9, 263
Four Feathers (novel and films), 29, 65
front line, 25–26
Full Metal Jacket (film), 124–25, 178–80
Fussell, Paul, 93, 306n7
futures, 6, 11, 128, 135, 194, 196, 204, 215, 217, 274–75

Gallipoli, 13, 76, 77
Gaumont Palace Cinema, Paris, 74
gaze. *See also* return gaze; tourist gaze; visuality

gender, 4, 6, 51, 56, 88, 97, 100, 101, 102, 104, 112, 114, 116–17, 160, 163, 173–75, 265–66, 304n4, 308n6; and feminization, 118; Madonna/whore logic, 173; and misogyny, 163, 177, 186, 192, 251, 306n8, 310n7; and patriarchy, 118, 163, 176, 198; and sexism, 185. *See also* bodies; masculinity; militarized prostitution; sexuality
geopolitical imaginaries, 11–12, 19, 24–25, 184, 260–61, 279; of Empire, 29–31, 37, 39, 41, 46, 63
geopolitics: antagonistic structure of, 10, 3092; assumptions of, 28, 178, 242, 311–12n3; of danger, 193, 237–38; and global order, 4–6, 142, 181, 239, 261, 283–84, 286, 293–94; and political economy, 303n1
Germany, 127, 142, 191
Gladstone, William, 33, 36
global consciousness, 13, 69, 70–71, 122
globalization, 14, 69, 182, 184, 192–94, 237, 240, 272–73
global politics, 286, 294. *See also* International Relations
Global South, 13, 15, 93, 125, 141, 147, 233, 290
Gordon, General George, 29, 33, 36, 54
Gordon Relief Campaign, 29–30, 33, 36–39, 45, 52, 58–61, 66, 68; cultural framing of, 46, 66; leisure practices in, 46–47
governance, 9, 31, 51, 97, 159–60, 198, 220, 221, 224, 242, 254–55, 263–64, 277–78, 295; and counterconduct in museums,

134–35, 224; and docile subjects, 269; as intervention, 51–52; of intimate relations, 159–63, 171–73; of leisure time, 1–2; in museums, 220–24; and Nikolas Rose, 182; of public health, 50–52, 159–63, 171–75; and reconciliation, 217; and securitization, 278–79; through sex education, 188; of soldiers' lives, 184, 189–90; of tourist behavior, 134–35, 147, 219. *See also* biopolitics; governmentality; intimacy; museums
governmentality, 50, 56, 71, 171, 304n4; willingly embraced, 20, 190; of soldiers returning home, 189; of tourism, 144; through Pocket Guides, 171. *See also* governance
Great War. *See* First World War
Gregory, Derek, 42–43; colonial nostalgia, 65; critique of Orientalism, 43. *See also* foliated agency; heterogeneous networks
Grove, Lieutenant Colonel Coleridge, 54–55
Guantánamo Bay, 271, 281, 295
Guantánamo Bay Souvenirs (installation), 282–83
guidebooks, 23, 95, 96–97, 101, 290, 305n5; Pocket Guides to Vietnam, 171, 175
Gulf War, first, 21, 184, 185, 186–89, 190, 246

Habana Hilton, 126, 150–58; labor relations, 152, 157; modernist design, 153–54, 156, 158; nationalization of, 157; opening of, 152; rebels relaxing in, 153–56; as revolution's headquarters, 152–53, 156–57
Harat el Wasser, 50, 51
Havana, 126; New Year's Eve (1958), 150–58
Hawaii, 99–101, 106, 110, 114, 145, 191
Hazbun, Waleed, 43, 294, 303n1, 304n2
hedonism, 151, 170, 175, 186
heritage, 94, 127, 150, 194, 203, 219–20, 229, 309n2. *See also* dissonant heritage
heterogeneity, 5, 9, 130, 131, 135, 207–8, 212, 227, 259–60, 263, 284–87, 294–96, 300; of colonial encounter, 54–55, 68, 83 and empire, 41, 57, 68. *See also* multiplicity
heterogeneous networks (Gregory), 41, 44–46, 55, 66, 304n2
Hilton, Conrad, 148, 157
Hilton Hotels, 126, 147–58; resistance to, 149–50. *See also* Habana Hilton; hotels
Himalayas, 98–99
Hiroshima, 120, 125, 127–29, 135–41, 152, 158, 196, 307n3; A-Bomb dome, 136, 137–39; absence of perpetrator, 139–40; debate over lights, 139; disappointment at, 141; effacing Japanese war crimes, 138–39; effacing U.S. decision to drop the bomb, 139–40; goals of peace, 136–39; *hibakusha* (bomb victims), 146–37, 139, 217; objects within museum, 137; Peace Park, 137, 209; as template

for commemoration, 140–41; transformation into tourist site, 136; universal mode of address, 138
Hitler, Adolph, 94, 143
HMS *Speaker,* 121–23
holidays. *See* tourism
Holocaust, 201, 203, 236. *See also* Auschwitz
home front, 11, 71, 104, 114, 116, 165, 240, 307n4; soldiers returning for R&R, 189–90
Hong Kong, 97, 98, 126, 168
Honolulu, 99, 110, 121, 168
hope, 86, 148, 219, 221, 236
Hopps, F. W., 75, 305n2
host/guest relations, 6, 8, 15, 26, 40, 81, 102, 110, 122, 150, 161, 163, 186, 187, 198, 205, 206, 243, 245–46, 285, 292, 310n7
hotels, 14, 22, 32, 64, 73, 76, 79, 96, 158, 187, 257, 264, 273–74; American Hotel and Lodging Educational Institute (AHLEI), 276–77; Caribe Hilton Hotel, 150; and counterterrorist training, 275–79, 312n5; as enclaves, 187; Global Hotel Security Standard, 277; Hotel California (Riyadh), 187; Hyatt Hotels, 276; Oasis (Riyadh), 187; Paradise Hotel Resort (Mombasa), 257–58, 262; pre-emptive surveillance in, 274; securitization of, 273–77; security apparatus of, 273–74, 277; Sinai Hilton Hotel, 206. *See also* Eye on Awareness; Habana Hilton; Hilton Hotels; No Reservations; Shepherd's Hotel
humanitarian intervention, 14, 65, 181, 184, 194, 239, 290; benign account of, 184; and peacekeeping, 181, 184
humanitarianism, 185–92; and helping, 290, 308–9n1
human rights, 65, 185, 205, 219, 224, 228, 230, 281–82
Hunters, The (Salter), 164, 308n6

identity, 4, 8, 11, 51, 101, 112, 128, 177, 203, 237, 266
ideological incarceration, 199–215
ideology, 15, 150
improvisation, 33, 101, 134, 153
inclusion, 41, 132, 140, 184–85, 199, 221, 226, 231, 259, 263, 278
India, 13, 47, 71, 79, 98, 145
"Indians" (Canadian), 55. *See also* voyageurs
indigenous populations, 111, 115
intensification, 12, 14, 16, 63–65, 70–72, 74, 85, 97, 100, 132, 145, 151, 168, 170, 176, 237, 254, 258, 263–64, 284, 298
interdisciplinarity, 24, 293, 295, 300, 303n3
international relations, 6, 24, 293, 295. *See also* global politics
Internet, 183, 241, 243–47, 250, 252. *See also* digital technologies; milblogs
interwar years, 70, 71, 81–93, 161, 306n7
intimacy, 115–16, 118, 190, 292, 304n4
Iraq, 239, 241, 242, 245, 247, 250–51, 254, 271, 291–93. *See also* Baghdad
Islam, 178, culture tours, 187–88; leaders, 187; in museums, 201
Istanbul, 148–49

Jaar, Alfredo, 287–91
Japan, 21, 157, Allied Occupation of, 126, 135–36; complicity in nuclear politics, 139–40; rehabilitation of, 164. *See also* Allied Occupation; Tokyo
Japanese empire (WWII), 100, 110
Japanese soldiers. *See* POWs
Jerusalem, 200, 202–3, 205, 310n5
Junka, Laura, 206–8

Khartoum, 33, 35–36, 47, 62, 64, 66, 303n1
Khartoum (film), 29, 65–66
Kitchener, Lord, 63–64
Klein, Christina, 144, 307–8n5
Korean War, 163–64, 168
Kosovo, 181, 185, 233
Kubrick, Stanley, 124–25, 307n1
Kuwait, 192, 244

Laderman, Scott, 171
Lair, Meredith, 165–70, 245–46, 248–49
Latin America, 142, 151, 157
Lê, Dinh Q., 178–80
leisure, 1–2, 4, 6, 8, 9–10, 15, 17, 25–28, 37, 46, 71–73, 75, 104, 106, 110, 148, 165, 168, 173, 186–87, 207, 242, 245, 248. *See also* tourism
"lessons of history," 132, 194, 197, 209
liberal rule, 181, 184, 259–60, 263–64, 277–78, 295; vs. illiberal states, 260–61, 278, 264; liberal democratic order, 185; and liberal subjectivity, 182, 255; orthodoxies of, 260–61; teleology of, 193. *See also* dark tourism: reproduction of liberal norms

Libeskind, Daniel, 233–34
LIFE magazine, 98, 306n9
Lloyd, David W., 84–86
London, 57, 73–74, 96, 127, 273, 297
Luxor, 32, 52, 64, 254, 272

Mahdi, 29, 33, 41, 54, 64
Malta, 76–77
Mandela, Nelson, 219, 222
Manila, 168, 176
masculinity, 57, 115–17, 173, 186, 192, 308n6; on display, 115–16, 306n10; hypermasculinity, 26, 102; male desire, 160; and vulnerability, 173
M*A*S*H (film and television program), 164
massage parlors, 169–70, 174, 188. *See also* brothels
materiality, 9, 21–22, 43–44, 263, 270–73, 284, 303n2, 311–12n3; and architecture, 149, 156, 207, 270, 291; and critical infrastructure, 272, 279; and infrastructures, 22, 264, 271–72; and object-world, 270; as remnants of war, 88–89. *See also* objects
Maze/Long Kesh. *See* Northern Ireland
media: culture, 64, 124, 181, 292–93; dissemination, 243, 247, 308–9n1, 311n1; and journalism, 246–47, 307n1, 311n1; mainstream, 247, 258; saturation, 246; sources, 24; spectacle, 192
memorials, 27, 88, 128, 138, 194, 211, 215; and countermemorials, 236; Ground Zero memorial, 233, 236; Holocaust memorials, 236; memorial museums (Williams),

216, 236; Monument to the Unknown Soldier (Baghdad), 248; Newfoundland Memorial Park, 88; and reflection, 236; Sehitlik Maryrs Memorial, 209
memory. *See* commemoration
mental health, 184, 190. *See also* well-being
Merrill, Dennis, 149–51
Middle East, 12, 19, 47, 70, 77, 79, 97, 142, 149, 185, 199–208, 215, 217, 228, 233, 309–10n4; Bethlehem, 203, 309n3, 310n5; graffiti, 203; Israeli occupation of Palestinian areas, 201, 204; Israeli-Palestinian struggle, 200–201, 203, 205–6, 262, 309n3; Jewish settlements, 202–3; militarization, 201; mobilities, 206; Mosque of Ibrahim, 202; Second Intifada, 205–6; separation barrier, 200, 202–4; Sinai resorts, 205–6; West Bank, 202
middlemen, 30, 39, 48, 126
migrants, 14–15
milblogs, 239, 242, 247–50
militaries: alcohol in, 187, 189, 192, 244, 263; apparatus of, 56; culture, 184, 186; demobilization, 158; Department of Defense (DOD), 247; and discrimination, 185–86; and families, 189–91, 281; and host cultures, 186; as humanitarian, 185; judicial system in, 177; and morale, 189–90; multilateral forces, 183; no-fraternization policy, 242, 244, 246, 249–50; professionalization of, 184, 186; public/private distinction, 189; recruitment practices, 21, 102–3, 190, 243; and sexism, 185; and training techniques, 186; uniform, 60, 118, 304n6. *See also* humanitarian intervention: peacekeeping; humanitarianism; militarism; militarized prostitution; soldier-tourists

militarism, 72, 100, 101, 106, 110, 114, 116, 159, 163, 173
militarized prostitution, 26–27, 50, 114, 186, 263, 306n8; bodies of prostitutes, 51, 159–61; in colonial Cairo, 50–52, 304n4; constituted by tourist sensibility, 171, 175–76; deregulation of, 162; efforts to ban, 186, 189, 192; in Hawaii, 114–15; institutional collusion over, 51, 114, 161–62, 169–71, 188; logistics shared with tourism industry, 161; normalization of, 161, 170; and pleasure belts, 169–70; in Seoul, 163–64; and sex education, 188; taxonomy of prostitutes, 171–72, 308n6; in Tokyo, 159–63; during Vietnam War, 169–76, 188. *See also* brothels
military bases, 99, 126, 163, 165, 242–46, 248, 281, 293; Camp Alpha, 168; Camp as Sayliyah, 244; Camp Delta, 281; as enclaves, 241–45; isolation in, 245–46, 248–49; Long Binh Post, 165; Tan Son Nhut Airbase, 168
military logistics, 25, 27, 69; in colonial Egypt, 33–35, 38, 60, 62–63; in WWII, 96
militourism, 72, 96, 100, 247. *See also* O'Dwyer; soldier-tourists; Teaiwa

mobilities, 5–7, 15, 23, 41, 206, 240, 265, 270, 285–86
Mohammed, Um, 291–93
Mombasa, 189, 242, 257, 259–63, 272, 278
monarch-of-all-I-survey. *See* Pratt, Mary Louise
morale. *See* militaries: and morale
multiplicity, 4–6, 8, 10, 129, 181, 240, 250–51, 263, 286–87, 293, 296; effaced by propaganda, 113; of Egyptian subjects, 40, 48, 54; of meaning, 18; of Vietnamese, 175–76
museology, 125, 128, 134, 140, 193, 209–10, 221, 227–28, 297
museums, 24, 127–28, 194, 284, 293, 297–99; Apartheid Museum (Gold Reef City, South Africa), 219, 222; as challenging, 223; Constitution Hill Museum (Johannesburg), 219, 223; curators, 214, 220, 222, 224, 235, 238; didactic pedagogy, 129, 134–35, 141, 232–33; District 6 Museum (Cape Town), 223–24, 230; Enola Gay exhibit, 140; exhibitionary rhetoric, 137; Gulag Museum (Perm), 230; Hector Pieterson Museum (Soweto), 219, 222; Imperial War Museum, 83, 297–99; interpellation of visitors, 138; Islamic Museum on Temple Mount (Jerusalem), 201; Israel museum (Jerusalem), 200; Jewish Museum (Berlin), 233; as "living museums," 223–24; Maison des Esclaves (Dakar), 230; Maple House Museum (Nicosia), 213–14; Museum of Barbarism (North Nicosia), 209; Museum of Struggle (South Nicosia), 209–10; Museum of Tolerance (Jerusalem), 205; Museum on the Seam (Jerusalem), 205; sanitizing war, 128, 140, 222, 234; shaping consciousness, 221; Tower of David (History of the History of Jerusalem), 200; Turjeman Post Museum (Jerusalem), 204–5; Ulster Museum, 225, 227–29; U.S. Holocaust Memorial Museum (USHMM), 130, 307n2; visitor logistics, 128, 131, 162; war displays and museums, 129, 140, 200. *See also* curators; governance
Muslim populations, 242, 262–63

Nagasaki, 120, 121–23, 127, 140
nationalism, 98, 100, 137, 163, 196, 198, 208, 297, 310n5
Naval Aviation Photography Unit (NAPU), 102–21, 306n9, 306n10; propaganda framing, 109–21
neoliberalism, 6, 182, 198, 240, 278–79
"Never Again" narrative, 128–30, 132, 135, 141
Nicosia, 208–14, 310n6; opening of Lidhra Street, 210–11
Nile: British army on, 29, 33–35, 43, 52–53; cataracts, 32, 34–36, 38, 54, 59, 62; as Cook's Canal, 32; tourism on, 32, 36, 38, 45, 53, 58–60, 63–64. *See also* Thomas Cook & Son
No Reservations: Suspicious Behavior in Hotels, 276–77

INDEX 387

Normandy, 66, 94–95; beaches, 95, 105
norms, 8, 16–17, 183–84, 190, 218, 221
Northern Ireland, 185, 215, 217, 225–36, 282; ambiguity, 231; An Coiste, 230; Black Taxi Tours, 225, 226, 234; and "cacophony of voices," 226; conflict transformation, 231–32; Crumlin Road Gaol, 225; and didactic pedagogy, 231–33; and expertise, 232; Good Friday Agreement, 225; Healing Through Remembering (HTR), 235; hunger strikers, 229–31; International Centre for Conflict Transformation (ICCT), 230–33; "living history" tour, 225–27, 310–11n8; Maze/Long Kesh, 227, 229–31; murals, 225, 234; and neutrality, 226–29, 231, 234, 310–11n8; Northern Ireland Tourist Board (NITB), 225; Peace-Building and Conflict Resolution Centre (PbCRC), 233–34; Republican vs. Loyalist narratives, 230–31; and sectarian politics, 225–27, 232, 235–36; as template for others, 228–29; Troubles, 224, 226–29, 232–34; Troubles Gallery, 227–29; and "two communities" narrative, 216; Ulster Museum, 225, 227–29; universal mode of address, 226–27

O'Dwyer, Carolyn, 17–18, 24, 72, 100–101, 117–18
objects, 22–23, 44, 79–81, 87, 294, 298; absence of, 228; decaying, 212–15, 291; as detritus of war, 89, 108, 120, 121–23, 142; displacing bodies, 137; foregrounded in tourism, 201; of foreign policy, 192; phallic machinery, 115; preserved in museums, 132, 209, 227; and ruins, 213, 291; shells, 87–88. *See also* materialities; objectification; souvenirs
objectification, 90, 117, 120–21, 161–62, 169–76, 252. *See also* bodies; commodification; militarized prostitution; objects
Office of Morale, Welfare and Recreation (MWR), 189–90, 244–45
Open Shutters: Iraq (installation), 291–93
Orientalism, 30, 37, 43, 76, 77, 145, 178, 241
Otherness: 4, 11, 22, 29, 39–40, 48, 65, 81, 92, 122, 126, 145, 147, 175–76, 183, 186, 195, 199, 203, 209, 213, 252–54, 256–57, 284–85, 293–94; and foreign landscapes, 5, 77, 107, 122; taxonomy of, 76, 81, 102, 174–75, 177; as toxic, 174. *See also* difference

Pacific, 22, 72, 97, 99–100, 113, 142; as paradise, 18, 19, 100–101, 106–7, 168; as primitive, 106–7
palm trees, 79, 106, 111, 248
Pan American Airlines, 92, 143, 145–46, 168; Clipper, 145–46
panopticon, 20, 50, 264, 268
passport, 143, 257, 271
Pattaya, 168, 188

388   INDEX

peace. *See* tourism–peace model
perpetrators, 128, 132–33, 138–40, 199, 203, 212, 216, 251, 258
photography: albums, 89; amateur, in Egypt, 64–65; amateur, in WWI, 17–18, 77–79; in Baghdad, 248–49; "buddy" images, 249; classical conventions of, 153–55, 206; and collaboration, 292–93; conventions of tourist photography, 108, 110, 117, 156, 248–50; documentary and evidentiary frames, 78, 89, 155; of Gaza Beach, 206–8; Kodak Brownie, 77, 89; Orientalist tradition, 78–81, 307–8n5; as military strategy on D-Day, 94–95; misreading of, 113; as museology, 221, 227–28, 311n1; and objectification, 90, 118; and production, 18; role of photographer, 116, 306n9; as source material, 24; tourist photographs, 48, 285, 307–8n5; as visual stories, 291–93; war photography, 18, 78, 117, 120, 305n3, 311n10; of war remnants, 78. *See also* Abu Ghraib; Cole, Lester; Naval Aviation Photography Unit (NAPU)
photojournalism, 103, 117
Platoon (film), 176–77
political tourism, 199–238; antagonistic structure, 200, 203, 215; and co-existence, 204–5; confusing narratives, 210; and contemplation, 236–38; "extreme tours," 201; Israeli occupation within, 201–2; as justice tourism, 202, 310n5; and neutral narratives, 204; official/community distinction, 225; as partisan, 199, 208–9, 211–12, 226; pro-Israeli narrative, 200–201, 203; pro-Palestinian narrative, 201–2, 204, 309–10n4; soldiers and, 208–9; vs. traditional tourism, 199–200. *See also* dark tourism; Middle East
postcards, 64, 73, 81, 94–95, 106, 149, 156, 178–79, 287–91
post–Cold War: and interventions, 185; tourist imaginary, 182
postcolonialism, 25, 44, 299
postconflict spaces, 184–85
power, 5, 9, 44, 309n2; as apparatus of forces; 20; shift from disciplinary to biopower, 20
practices: as action, 21; as encounter, 20; of tourism and war, 4, 6, 13, 22, 31; and ways of seeing, 17
Price, Captain Conrad T., 79–81, 91
Prisoners of War (POWs), 117–21
private security companies, 277, 312n5
prostitution. *See* militarized prostitution
Pratt, Mary Louise: and contact zones, 5, 125, 147; monarch-of-all-I-survey, 39, 44, 49, 77, 91
Princess Cunard (cruise ship), 187–88
public health. *See* governance: of public health
Puerto Rico, 150–51
pyramids, 47, 56, 76

race and racism, 4, 6, 41, 50, 55–56, 89–90, 101, 112, 114, 118, 145,

148, 160, 163, 174, 175, 176–77, 185–86, 192, 251, 265–67, 303n1, 304n4, 308n6
R&R (rest and relaxation): 2, 8, 25–26, 72, 243, 263, 310n7; as A&A (ass & alcohol), 164; in Baghdad, 245, 248–49; benign account of, 101, 164, 168–69, 176; Cold War, 126–27, 158–78; "comfort-for-morale" equation, 245–46; in country leave, 165–66, 243–45; and cultural difference, 97–98; and domestic violence, 192, 310n7; and exploitation, 26, 100–102, 158–64, 169–78, 186; and families, 190–91, 281; First World War, 73–83; fifteen-day leave, 186; five-day passes, 164, 165, 168; Germans in occupied Paris, 96; in Hawaii, 99–101; as I&I (intercourse & inebriation), 164, 170; in Korea, 163–64; media reports of, 164, 168–69; negative stereotype, 190–91, 244, 310n5; Onward Travel Program, 243; Pass Program, 244; as precursor to postwar tourism, 97, 100–101, 168; professionalization of, 185–92; proximal sites, 26; as "rape and run," 170, 310n7; rest homes, 110; rest-in-place policy, 244; returning home (fourteen day scheduled leave), 189–92, 243; Second World War, 96–112, 114–23; stand-down centers, 166; in Tokyo, 158–64, 308n6; supervised day-trips, 187–88, 244; support structures for, 190; three-day passes, 73, 96, 166, 187, 243–44; United States Riviera Rest Area, 96; Vietnam War, 126, 165–78. *See also* beaches; military bases; soldier-tourists
rear echelon mother fuckers (REMF), 165
reconciliation, 15, 28, 197, 208, 210, 212, 215, 219, 226; benign account of, 217–18; as depoliticizing, 217–18, 226, 234; developmental teleology of, 217; as dirty word, 217; discourse of, 164, 215–17, 234–36; and forgiveness, 216, 220; as governance, 217, 234; as inevitable, 216; overstated, 222; pedagogy of, 232–33; as political imperative, 217; remembering and forgetting, 216–17
Recreation and Amusement Association (RAA), 159–62
redemption, 177, 299; and catharsis, 219
relationality, 270–71, 285
remembering. *See* commemoration: remembering and forgetting
resilience, 182, 190, 219, 272–73, 279
resistance, 25, 28, 44, 65, 101, 125, 126, 135, 147, 151, 262, 286–87, 293; and local negotiation, 149–50, 262
return gaze, 81, 101, 116, 121–23, 147, 150, 213, 291–93. *See also* visuality
reverence. *See* commemoration: and reverence
risk, 1, 15, 263, 274–77, 312n5; applied to travellers, 15; bodies, 16; risk assessment, 275; risk management, 274, 277; and

security apparatus, 274
Robben Island, 219–22; and
   Mandela's cell, 219, 222; political
   prisoners as guides, 219–21;
   singular narrative at, 220–21;
   transformation of, 219
Rwanda, 181, 185, 192, 287–91

Saigon, 165, 173
satire, 124–25
Saturday Review (magazine), 144, 307–8n5
Saudi Arabia, 186–87
Second World War, 13, 70–72, 93–123, 150, 158, 164, 256
security. *See* tourism industry: securitization of
self-management, 190. *See also* governance; governmentality
Seoul, 126, 163
September 11 terrorist attacks (9/11), 15, 241, 254, 256–58, 265
sexuality, 4, 6, 51, 56, 113, 114–17, 265–66, 304n4; and heteronormativity, 115–17, 306n7; and homoeroticism, 115; and homophobia, 185, 224
sexually transmitted diseases (STDs). *See* venereal disease
Shapiro, Michael, 10–11
Sharm el-Sheikh, 206, 278
Shepherd's Hotel (Cairo), 47, 48–50, 52, 76, 98
Sierra Leone, 181, 192
signification, 4, 79, 81, 106, 108, 113, 119, 177
Signs of Life (installation), 287–91
skull trophies, 79, 117, 306n11
Smith, Valene, 143, 195
social media, 241–42, 247, 252. *See also* milblogs

soft power, 183, 256–57
soft targets, 239, 242, 254, 272–73. *See also* tourism: targeting of
soldier-tourists: in Asia during Cold War, 158–78; in Baghdad, 248–49; becoming tourists, 25; as clients of Thomas Cook & Son, 45, 47, 305n5; in Cuba, 154–56; and exploitation, 114–23; in Guantánamo Bay, 281; in first Gulf War, 186–88; in Middle East during WWI, 78–81; in the Pacific during WWII, 96–123; transition from battlefield into tourism, 26, 53, 57, 74, 102, 121–23, 127, 158, 161, 168, 285
solidarity, 122, 138, 150, 162, 178, 183, 240, 255, 259, 261–62, 278, 285. *See also* inclusion
Somalia, 181, 185, 192. *See also* Mombasa
Somme, 86, 88
Sontag, Susan, 118–19, 251–52, 286–89
South Africa, 185, 215, 217–24, 230, 282; anti-apartheid liberation narrative, 216, 220–22; centrality of Mandela's story, 221–22; and consensus building, 218, 221–22; as "rainbow nation," 218, 219, 221–22; troubling anti-apartheid consensus, 223–24; and Truth and Reconciliation Commission (TRC), 217, 219, 222, 224. *See also* Robben Island
souvenirs, 12, 23, 24, 37, 63, 79, 87–88, 117, 159, 163, 245, 281–83, 306n11
sovereignty, 37, 111, 202–4, 208, 240, 258, 286, 295;

Israeli statehood, 203–4, 207; Palestinian claims to, 204, 207
Soviet Union, 13, 125, 130, 141, 148, 157
Sphinx, 47–48, 56–57, 76
Sri Lanka, 108, 192, 233, 282
Standard Operating Procedure (film), 251–52
steamers (sailing vessel), 32, 34–35, 38, 52, 58–59, 63, 65, 66
Steichen, Edward J., 102–21; classical style, 103–4, 110, 112, 119; commercial work, 102–3, 106, 110; editorial control of NAPU, 103, 108, 112, 120; propaganda framework, 112–13; sanitation of military practice, 113, 115–16, 120; visibility and invisibility, 112–13, 116; in WWI, 102. *See also* Naval Aviation Photography Unit
Stein, Rebecca, 205–6, 294
stereotype, 144–45, 150, 172, 190, 206, 287, 289–90, 311n10
Struk, Johanna, 78–79, 248, 250
subaltern, 69, 70, 115
sublime, 85, 86, 138
Sudan, 33, 38, 65
sunbathing, 104, 106, 108, 115, 187, 206
surfing. *See* Vietnam War: surfing
surveillance, 15, 20, 50, 52, 100, 160, 189, 202, 240, 242, 254–55, 263–77; and algorithms, 266; anticipatory, 266–67; comforting gaze of, 268–69; and data, 274; pleasures of, 268–69, 271; and torture, 271
Sydney, 97, 168, 262
symbolism, 37, 38, 65, 88, 94, 137–38, 143–45, 148, 241, 312n4

Taipei, 126, 168, 171
Teaiwa, Teresia, 72
technoscience approach, 39; subverted by local knowledge, 44
temporality, 7, 11, 16, 128, 139, 195, 309n2. *See also* futures
terrorism, 15, 239–80; and counterterrorism training, 275–77; as exceptional threat, 240, 254–58, 272, 278, 295; National Counter Terrorism Security Apparatus (NaCTSO), 275–76; and suicide bombers, 272; and vulnerability, 258, 273, 275. *See also* Eye on Awareness; No Reservations; War on Terror
Thailand, 165, 168–69, 188
Thomas Cook & Son, 12, 29, 31, 304n1, 305n4; as benevolent employers, 40–41, 60; commercial ethos of, 45; contract with British Government, 34, 36–37, 59, 63, 304n7; in Egypt, 32, 34–35, 36, 39–41, 43, 45–47, 58; and Egyptian labor, 40; engaging in diplomacy, 62; extending Nile exploration into Sudan, 60–64; patriotism, 58; targeting British soldiers as customers, 47, 59; and WWI battlefields, 86–87
Tokyo, 126, 127, 159–64, 168, 176; Metropolitan Police, 159; as "pleasure playground," 161
tolerance, 16–17, 184, 205, 218, 221, 228, 257, 278; exclusions of, 218
tourism: advertising campaigns, 1, 3, 58, 66, 81, 143, 145, 151; and backstage, 50; battlefield, 12; beaten path/established itineraries, 47, 52, 151, 192; brochures, 143; and

contemplation, 215, 236–37; and cultural capital, 182, 273; democratization of, 92; and depoliticization, 212, 238; disciplining of, 95; enclave, 26, 187, 242, 262–63; as exploitation, 5, 8, 26, 100, 113; independent travel, 182; and inequality, 8–9, 97, 150–51, 183, 206, 260–61, 278, 284, 303n1; intersections with war, 4–6, 9–10, 16–17, 22, 23, 66, 70, 282, 305n3; as lifestyle, 144, 148; and luxury, 92, 126, 163; and mass tourism, 12–13, 65, 83, 93; package tourism, 182; post-conflict contexts, 7, 14–15, 177; rights to, 92; vs. strategy, 250–51; targeting of, 151, 241, 254–63; and U.S. foreign policy, 142, 144–45, 148. *See also* leisure; political tourism; soldier-tourists; tourist sensibility

Tourism Australia: "No Leave, No Life" campaign, 1–4, 25, 28

tourism industry, 6–8, 14, 125, 140, 142–43, 149–50, 178, 182–83, 188, 196, 208, 242, 262; 295; and best practice, 275; colonial Egypt, 30–31, 32, 37, 40, 63; Cuba (post-1958), 157–58; growth of, 92, 142–43; in Hawaii, 101, 114; infrastructure, 84, 150, 242, 255; and labor force, 242, 255, 259, 264, 273, 277–79; and policy, 256; in Puerto Rico, 150; recovery from 9/11, 256–58; and risk, 275; securitization of, 15, 111, 239, 277, 242, 254–79, 311n2; in Thailand, 168–69. *See also* risk; Thomas Cook & Son

tourism–peace model, 6–9, 27, 195, 199, 283–84, 286; consensus over, 6–7, 9, 16, 226; and cross-cultural understanding, 183; and economic lens, 8; as engine for peace, 183; International Institute for Peace through Tourism (IIPT), 183; masking domination, 183–84, 218; and mobility, 7–8; and peace industry, 8, 70; and reconciliation, 8, 226

tourism studies, 6–7, 293; complicity in War on Terror, 255–56, 272, 275, 283–84

tourist-diplomats, 4, 125, 127, 141, 143–48, 182–83, 255, 259; as aspirational subjects, 148; and cultural diplomacy, 256–57, 307–8n5; and track-two diplomacy, 183

tourist gaze, 42, 54, 71, 122, 179, 289–90, 310n7; folded into militourist gaze, 100–101. *See also* return gaze; visuality: imperial gaze

tourists: confidence, 59; as cultural ambassadors, 144; desire for sightseeing, 58; framed in advance, 231–32; Imperial Travelers, 93, 99; and inappropriate behavior, 134–35; inequality and, 261; and innocence, 256, 266–67; middle-class, 12, 262; pacification of, 218; "playing soldier," 60–63, 285; posing, 253; vs. travelers, 93, 133, 182, 192; as vigilantes, 267–68; visiting war zones, 25, 27, 57, 63–65, 70, 192, 194–208, 225. *See also* American: tourists;

European: tourists
tourist sensibility, 71–72, 73–4, 77,
  81, 93, 106, 116, 120, 121, 127,
  161, 163, 165–66, 171, 175–76, 178,
  188, 241, 192, 243, 248, 250, 282,
  286, 293–94, 308–9n1, 310n7
transgression, 115–16, 125
trauma, 125, 127–29, 224
travel. *See* tourism
travel writing, 24, 52, 60, 75, 77
truth, 17, 113, 128, 129, 155, 226

UN (United Nations), 164, 207,
  308–9n1
UNESCO, 130, 219
UNFICYP (United Nations Forces
  in Cyprus), 208, 213–14
United States. *See* America;
  American
*Untitled from Vietnam: Destination
  for the New Millennium*
  (installation), 178–80
U.S. Air Force, 99, 103, 110, 172,
  308n6
U.S. Marine Corps, 2, 21–22, 171
U.S. Navy, 22, 102–3, 110, 117–19,
  188
USO (United Service
  Organizations), 165, 305n1

Varosha, 208, 213
venereal disease: and AIDS, 188;
  and biopower, 51; in colonial
  Cairo, 51–52; gonorrhea, 160,
  172; syphilis, 160, 173; as threat,
  172; in Tokyo, 160, 162; in
  Vietnam, 171–76
Versailles, Treaty of, 70, 87
veterans: as tourists, 143, 177
victims, 128, 131–33, 196, 197–98,
  203–4, 212, 216, 219, 251;
  democratization of, 259;
  displays of, 136, 209, 259, 261;
  identification with, 128, 132, 137,
  140; individualization of, 131–32,
  140, 307n2; and innocence,
  137, 173, 175, 177, 198, 216,
  259, 261–63; statistics, 132;
  victim consciousness, 136–37;
  victim culture, 133, 203–4;
  victimization, 199, 208
victory culture, 2, 110, 199, 297
Vicuña Gonzalez, Vernadette, 100,
  255, 294
Vietnam War, 124–26, 142, 165–78,
  188; administrative roles in,
  165; cinematic consensus over,
  176–78, 307n1, 308n6; critical
  accounts of, 176, 178–80; cultural
  representations of, 176–78;
  hygiene during, 174–75; as a
  "mistake," 185; surfing in, 167,
  170, 308n7; Vietcong, 173. *See
  also* R&R: Vietnam War
visuality, 17–21; and aesthetics, 24;
  anticipatory, 266; and complicity,
  287–89; contradictory ways of
  seeing, 53; and display, 49–50;
  and distance, 117; dominant ways
  of seeing, 17–19, 21; embodied
  mode of perception, 21;
  envisioning, 17, 178; everyday, 19;
  haptic, 269–70, 312n4; imperial
  gaze, 39–41, 60, 107–8, 118, 250,
  289; intersecting gazes, 50, 56,
  118, 149; looking/not-looking,
  289–90; mediated, 64; militourist
  gaze, 100, 247; ocularcentrism,
  21, 270; ontology, 17, 19; parallel
  structure of gazing, 17, 19, 24,

100–101; perspectival mode, 264; and pleasure, 268–70; political understanding of, 18, 24; and power, 264–65; reordering, 101; representational violence, 118, 292; scopophilia, 100, 268; of soldiers' lives, 247–48; spectatorship, 43, 116, 118–19, 289; technologies, 264–68; and transparency, 149; truth claims, 17; viewing subjects, 20; vigilance, 267; visual field, 19; world-as-picture, 11. *See also* enemy: visualization of; photography; return gaze; surveillance; tourist gaze; voyeurism
voyageurs (Canadian), 35–36, 54–57, 304n5; as tourists, 56–57. *See also* "Indians" (Canadian)
voyeurism, 85, 112, 116, 133, 136, 148. *See also* dark tourism: voyeurism

Wadi Halfa, 34, 36, 54, 60
Wagh-al Birkah, 50
walking tours, 200, 311n10; of Jerusalem, 201–2, 309n3; of Gaza Strip, 202; of Hebron, 201–2; of Nicosia, 208; of the West Bank, 202–3
war: addressed in tourism studies, 6; agonistic framing of, 9; asymmetric, 246; hierarchy over tourism, 6, 17, 95; permanent/total war, 71, 242, 295; spectacle of, 27, 124; technologized, 240, 246, 248. *See also* ethnic conflict; terrorism; War on Terror
war effort, 13, 71, 95, 100, 102, 115
war museums. *See* museums
War on Terror, 17, 178, 239–42, 251, 254–80; "coalition of the willing," 241–42; and counterterrorism, 15, 254, 275–76; as deterritorialized, 240–41, 260–80; exceptionality and securitization matrix, 255, 311–12n3; front line of, 272; as networked, 240; and privacy, 265; security apparatus of, 254, 265, 271, 274–78; us vs. them architecture, 239–40, 265. *See also* airports; risk; terrorism
well-being, 2–3, 184, 189–90, 295
whaling boats (Royal Navy), 35, 38, 54
Wharton, Annabel Jane, 48, 148–50
Where the Girls Are—VD in Southeast Asia (film), 172–73
Wolseley, General, 54, 58
Wooley, Edgar, 75–76
world order, 6, 8
World War I. *See* First World War
World War II. *See* Second World War

Yeagar, Henry "Rip," 101, 117, 118
YMCA, 72–73, 79, 97, 305n1
Yoneyama, Lisa, 136–37
Ypres, 75, 86, 89–91, 305n2

zoos, 121, 165, 191

Debbie Lisle is a reader in international relations in the School of Politics, International Studies, and Philosophy at Queen's University Belfast. She is the author of *The Global Politics of Contemporary Travel Writing*.